Masters of the Victory Garden

Masters of the Victory Garden

Specialty Gardeners Share Their Expert Techniques

Jim Wilson

Little, Brown and Company
Boston Toronto London

Library of Congress Cataloging-in-Publication Data

Wilson, James W. (James Wesley), 1925–
Masters of the Victory garden: specialty gardeners share their expert techniques / by Jim Wilson. — 1st ed.
p. cm.
Includes bibliographical references.
ISBN 0-316-94501-3 (hc) — ISBN 0-316-94500-5 (pb)
1. Gardening. 2. Gardeners—Interviews. I. Victory garden (Television program) II. Title.
SB453.W5624 1990
635—dc20 89-49071
CIP

Designed by Dianne Schaefer

RAI-WI

Published simultaneously in Canada by
Little, Brown & Company (Canada) Limited
PRINTED IN THE UNITED STATES OF AMERICA

To my friends on the Victory Garden *staff, WGBH-TV, and especially executive producer Russ Morash, who suggested that I write this book from our experiences on location*

Contents

Preface

Often, when we are on location taping segments for *The Victory Garden*, the Executive Producer, Russell Morash, will say to me, "There's a lesson here, Jim: tell home gardeners what it means to them."

That's how this book came about. Over the years, as we visited gardens large and small, a "big picture" emerged, much more significant than the thousands of lessons we created for viewers. The revelation slowly unfolded that gardening is a two-way street. The accepted concept is that gardeners shape gardens. We believe that, even more important, gardens shape gardeners; it changes their personalities and their lifestyles, and all to the good.

We call such committed gardeners "Masters of Gardening," for, indeed, they have mastered so many of the elements that day-to-day duties are completed almost automatically. They are left with more time to enjoy their hobby, and it shows in their good nature, self-confidence, and feeling of oneness with Nature.

At some time in their gardening careers, Masters of Gardening take up a specialty plant as a hobby, and come to know it so well that they become enthusiasts, missionaries for their hobby. Their enthusiasm is infectious; they willingly share information and plants with novices and bring them into their circle of friends, usually within a specialty plant society.

Over the years, *The Victory Garden* has introduced its audience to many Masters of Gardening. We not only admire what these gardeners have accomplished, but we also like them as warm and sharing human beings. Russell Morash felt that other gardeners could benefit by reading about how they got into their hobby plant; their challenges, triumphs, and disappointments; and how plants changed their lives.

Russell asked me to write this book, and I jumped at the chance. Garden writing isn't new to me (I sold my first garden magazine article in 1956), nor is interviewing home gardeners and commercial growers. But, I can tell you that I never before learned so much about gardening and gardeners in such a short time. It was a tremendously exciting and inspiring time in my life. I have written the names and addresses of these Masters of Gardening in my address book because there is not a one of them I would not want as a close friend.

My job of interviewing these gardeners and accumulating and validating much information about their specialty plants went easily because of the affection and loyalty accorded *The Victory Garden*. It all started with James Underwood Crockett, the original host of the show. His depth of information, natural enthusiasm, and warm ways helped many a first-time gardener feel the delight of biting into a home-grown, vine-ripened tomato. A tragic illness claimed Jim's life in 1979, and it is a tribute to this remarkable man that his memory is still strong among gardeners across this great country.

Jim tended a made-for-television garden in a corner of the parking lot behind the WGBH-TV studios in Boston. It was built around large existing crabapple trees and expanded to include vegetable and flower gardens, landscaped seating areas, and a small greenhouse. Viewing these shows was a personal experience, like coming right into Jim's own home and garden. But, Jim's death meant a change for the show.

A new host was brought in, a well-established nurseryman and keen home gardener, Bob Thomson. Bob was given the almost impossible task of taking over for someone who had won the hearts of viewers. In time he, too, became a trusted friend and adviser, through his honest and unpretentious ways and mastery of gardening. Bob brought to the show a passion for tasteful landscaping; it came at a time when gardeners seemed ready to extend their horizons beyond the vegetable patch.

At that time, the program was being broadcast nationally on Public Television but had a distinctly northeastern focus. This was due partly to Jim and Bob's down east and Boston accents and partly to the timing of gardening projects, set by New England weather. And, even though good garden culture travels well to most parts of the country, the time seemed right to develop regional gardens. Utilizing local hosts and regional plants, and timed for the seasons of each region, such gardens could add credibility and enhance loyalty.

I came on board at that time. *The Victory Garden* knew me from a guest spot I had done with Bob. So, when a regional garden was projected for Callaway Gardens in Pine Mountain, Georgia, I was asked to serve as host. I had been in home and commercial horticulture for nearly forty years, grew up in the South, and still talked "southern." My wife, Jane, and I operated an herb farm just over the border in South Carolina.

My first appearance in March of 1984 must have been painful for the crew because I knew nothing about being in front of a camera. What saved me, I think, was years of experience in public speaking and exposure to all sorts of plants around the world. With the help of the crew, good gardeners all, I began to give southern flower and vegetable gardens their due. When this old Mississippi boy praises turnip greens, okra, and purple hull peas, he has been there!

Since then, we've expanded the show's outreach to include Victory Garden West at Rogers' Garden Center near Newport Beach, California. Bob Smaus, Garden Editor for the *Los Angeles Times*, does a great job of introducing to western gardeners the amazing variety of plants that will thrive in their mild climates. Rogers' is open year round and is nationally known for its creative uses of unusual plants and planters.

Two changes were made in Massachusetts. The parking-lot garden was moved to the grounds of a marvelous retail nursery and garden center, Lexington Gardens, in the historic town of Lexington. Bob Thomson introduces all programs from the quarter-acre garden, open to the public spring through fall. Also, a new "Suburban Garden" was begun on the outskirts of Boston, where enough open space exists to demonstrate major garden construction projects from start to finish. Roger Swain, Science Editor for *Horticulture* magazine, joined the team in 1986 and serves there as host.

Often, Roger will end a show by delivering fresh vegetables from the garden to Marian Morash, a bona fide chef. She never fails to come up with wonderful ways to prepare them.

In addition to taping segments at regional Victory Gardens, the show travels extensively throughout North America, giving each of us a chance to see what other gardeners are up to. And in recent years, we've roamed the world with British plantsman Peter Seabrook. Peter does a masterful job of presenting some of the great gardens of the world, sending reports from Europe, Asia, New Zealand, and Australia. How times have changed on *The Victory Garden* since our parking-lot days of 1976!

The one constant throughout this long history of service to gardeners has been Russell Morash. *The Victory Garden* was his vision and, to this day, he continues to impart his creative genius, keen eye, and talent for gardening to the show. John Pelrine, who began as the manager of the greenhouse in Crockett's days, has advanced to Producer. Another veteran is the Director of Photography, Dick Holden, the only person I know who can back uphill while taping, following a twisting, rutted path, and never bobble his hand-held camera. He translates Russell's ideas into vivid images.

We've been blessed with a great crew that you never see on camera: Chip Adams, Derek Diggins, Nina Sing, Sally Cook, and the technical staff at the studio who, within forty-eight hours of receiving our raw tape, can uplink a finished program to a satellite and transmit it to nearly three hundred PBS stations nationwide.

If I look good on TV, credit it more to the WGBH-TV staff than to my talent, and especially to my associates at Callaway Gardens, Bob Hovey and David Chambers. They work in Victory Garden South every day of the year and keep all 9,500 square feet neat and shining for visitors. It is a major attraction at this great horticultural center and 2,500-acre resort.

I am blessed to be in a position to work with gardeners all over the country and to record for you the stories of some of the best. When I think of these newfound but fast friends, a line from a hymn I learned in Epworth League these many years ago comes to mind . . . "Blest be the tie that binds."

Acknowledgments

If this book entertains and enlightens you, it will be due more to the gardeners I interviewed and horticulturists I asked to help, than to what I know about gardening. If it fails, it will be because I was unable to absorb the huge amount of information involved, or to translate it into the working language of gardeners.

Most gardeners are generalists, and that includes me. In my years of gardening, I rubbed up against all sorts of hobby plant specialists, both amateur and professional, but never absorbed a great deal of information about any given plant. I don't mind telling you that I had to hit the reference books, the telephone, and the U.S. mail to write in depth about the eleven hobby plants featured in this book. I queried skilled amateurs, commercial producers, public garden curators, and plant societies in many states.

I am indebted to Christina Ward, my editor at Little, Brown, who would not let me stop short of delivering the best that was in me, and to my associates at *The Victory Garden*, who have unselfishly shared their rich experiences.

It is a marvel that the featured gardeners didn't run me off, or chase away the photographers—we took up so much of their time with interviews, correspondence, and phone calls. They gave us what we call in the South "a gracious plenty" of cooperation. Bless every one of them!

So many people helped on daylilies: Roy Klehm of Klehm Nursery, Van Sellers of Iron Gate Gardens, and John Elsley of Wayside Gardens, to name a few.

Susan P. Martin, Curator of Conifers of the U.S. National Arboretum, sent a list, compiled by Tom Dilatush, of conifer collections open to the public. Gwen Fawthrop, a fellow garden writer, advised me on collections in Ontario. Jeanette Windham of Greensboro, North Carolina, checked my hardiness data on dwarf conifers.

I would be remiss in not thanking my wife, Jane, for double-checking my memory on how herbs grow in the South, and our friend Tom DiBaggio of Earthworks, Arlington, Virginia, for information on rosemary, oregano, and lavender. The Executive Director of The Herb Society, Julie McSoud, and Bob Hovey, the Resident Gardener at Victory Garden South, kindly helped me.

Roy Klehm, Van Sellers, and John Elsley also helped me with hostas, as did Peter Ruh of the Homestead Division of Sunnybrook Farms. Gene Ellis of Tallahassee Nurseries and Ken Chatham of Crabapple Nurseries, Roswell, Georgia, helped me pinpoint the southern adaptation of hostas.

Dorothy B. Schaefer of the American Lily Society put her twenty-five years of experience at my disposal.

Elsley and Klehm read my copy on peonies. My information on peppers came partly from Dr. Jean Andrews Smith's book, partly from David Chambers of Callaway Gardens, and partly from my special interest in them.

Adele Jones, of the American Rhododendron Society, started me off on the right foot, and Fred Galle, "Mr. Azalea" himself, read my copy.

A fellow garden writer, Maggie Oster, led me to the Jeremiases, where I did the rose story. Anne Reilly counseled me on miniature roses and my friend of many years, Bill Fike of Jackson & Perkins, on rose hardiness.

Nell Lewis of Greensboro, North Carolina, let me shoot photos in her superb woodland wildflower garden and introduced me to Dr. Elwood Fisher, who is every bit as knowledgeable about wildflowers as he is about antique fruit trees.

Photo Credits

Half title: John Pelrine
Title page: Russell Morash
Preface: Stephen Butera
Introduction: Stephen Butera
Rhodedendrons: photos by Don Normark, except p. 21, by Erin Smith
Hostas: photos by Kim Kauffman, except pp. 33, 35 (both), 41 (top), by John Pelrine; p. 47 (all), by Jim Wilkins
Daylilies: photos by Roy Klehm
Roses: photos by Chuck Armour, except pp. 70, 76, 81 (left), by Russell Morash; p. 81 (right), by Stephen Butera
Antique Fruit Trees: photos by Robert C. Simpson, except pp. 93, 97, by Jim Wilson; p. 95, by Elwood Fisher
Herbal Arts: photos by Stephen Butera
Dwarf Conifers: photos by Ann Reilley, except p. 147 (all), by Jim Wilson
Peonies: photos by Roy Klehm
Wildflowers: photos by Beth Maynor, except p. 189 (bottom row), by Jim Wilson
Lilies: photos by John Croft
Peppers: photos by Larry Albee, except p. 229, by John Pelrine; p. 230 (top left and bottom left), by John Swan

Masters of the Victory Garden

Masters of Gardening

It was my happy privilege, for the better part of a year, to travel across the U.S.A., interviewing some of the best gardeners I have ever met. By design, these were all hobby growers of specialty plants. Most were noncommercial and involved only in gardening. Others had taken up plant breeding in addition to gardening. A few sold enough plants to help support their hobbies. I chose to interview mostly noncommercial growers because a person's attitude toward plants can alter when he or she begins to sell them. Evaluation of plants can change from favoring the traits the gardener likes to those he or she feels the general public will like enough to cause them to purchase the plant. Some had been featured on *The Victory Garden* program; others are scheduled for future productions. For lack of a better name, we call them "Masters of the Victory Garden." None has the hubris to proclaim, "I am the best!" They flinch at the term "expert," and even grumble at being called an "authority."

You see, what these seasoned gardeners have discovered is that no individual ever completely masters gardening. Much of the fascination in one of this country's most popular hobbies is that one revelation leads to another, and another. Gardening is a lifelong voyage of discovery.

Early on, these Garden Masters confronted the fact that an enormous amount of information had to be absorbed before they could become knowledgeable about gardening. I think they reached that conclusion at about the time they became pretty good general gardeners, capable of raising vegetables and herbs, annual and perennial flowers, bulbs, roses, and a few basic trees and shrubs. They became frustrated, I believe, at the difficulty of advancing their knowledge of gardening on such a broad front.

The Garden Masters I interviewed enjoyed learning about one plant at a time, through reference books, discussions with fellow hobbyists, lectures by authorities, and actual experience in the garden. They felt "in control" of the situation, instead of vaguely uneasy about the impossibility of absorbing the vast amount of information on general gardening. They felt, and I agree, that it makes good sense to narrow the amount of data you need to absorb to succeed at growing.

I expect you know what they are talking about. Just the process of learning where to find gardening information and how to winnow relevant and reliable guidance from the mass of often specious "facts" on general gardening is bewildering. Translating all that information into action is enough to intimidate anyone and to paralyze a few.

Some of the Garden Masters worked their way, at least superficially, through one or more hobby plants on their way to their present specialty. Others, having reached a high degree of competence with one specialty plant, retained it but took on one or two others as well.

It seems to me that most gardeners sort of drift into a specialty plant. It often starts with an affinity with a plant they have bought or received as a gift. The plant "grows on them," and they begin looking for more cultivars in the same genus or species, building little families of related plants. They buy garden books about their specialty and usually join a plant society. Some grow mostly for the enjoyment of friends and family, others not only for the challenge of growing new plants but of doing it better than anyone else in their area. Some work all season long at growing, mostly for the thrill of entering their handiwork in shows.

One commonality in backgrounds of these Garden Masters fascinated me. I encountered it in the first of the interviews, and my initial impression was reinforced with each succeeding gardener I came to know. It seems that every good gardener has a role model, a "mentor." With some, it was a parent or a grandparent. With others, particularly those who took up a specialty plant in later years, it was an advanced specialty grower, one who cared and shared.

That revelation speaks to every specialty plant society, every garden club, every horticultural society. It says, "Make a real effort to be friendly and sharing with newcomers." There is much more to this than merely perpetuating the organization. If you are the advanced gardener who reaches out to educate and inspire a newcomer, you may be amazed at the impact of your sharing. Without intending it, you may become a mentor. Just read the experiences of these Garden Masters and you'll get an idea of the place role models play in gardening.

I found all of our Masters of the Victory Garden to be decent, likable, intelligent individuals, sometimes eccentric, but always fun-loving. None sees himself or herself as a "Creator" but as a willing apprentice in the natural order of things. Some are aware that they have become role models to other gardeners and are humbled by that realization.

Another commonality among these Garden Masters is the need to control their garden. Gone are the days when, faced with weather or other environmental problems, gardeners would capitulate. Now, they seek out and use many means and devices to moderate the impact of weather, plant diseases and insects, soil deficiencies, and even space restrictions. Certain of these Garden Masters have realized that, in order to progress in gardening, understanding the environment is vital. They have become "Stewards of the Earth" or, at least, of that small part upon which they pay taxes. Two or three have become effective environmentalists.

Let me share with you one more observation about these Garden Masters, which is admittedly subjective and colored by my own approach to gardening. I realize the subject of the motives behind gardening is sensitive, so let me assure you that this observation is meant to compliment anyone who recognizes his own leanings. . . .

Some gardeners, I believe, use gardening as outdoor theater, with themselves as directors. Some prefer the security of repeating a similar production year after year; they thrive on the praise heaped on their efforts. Others prefer the challenge of new tableaux each year; the thrill of learning about new plants and how to fit them into the gardening environment is what gives them satisfaction. Some, in order to understand the plants who are players, imbue them with human characteristics. They talk to them, praise them, interact with them, move them around the stage, change the lighting . . . but, ultimately, if they fail to perform, they reach for the stage hook.

My new friends would be the first to admit that I would not have gone wrong had I chosen some other Garden Master in their specialties. The woods are full of good hobby gardeners growing specialty plants. I chose to feature these particular Garden Masters to present a cross section of backgrounds, ages, lifestyles, aspirations, and climates. I believe you will agree that they are the kind of gardeners you would enjoy meeting and learning from, even emulating.

I know I will get letters from advocates of other specialty plants. They are no less important than the few that could be featured in depth within these covers. If fortune smiles on this small beginning, perhaps we can cover other specialties in future books.

It is my hope that, in reading about these diverse plants and skilled gardeners, you may find intriguing possibilities and even role models. You may think of yourself as a generalist or "plain dirt gardener," and be happy in your situation. Well and good; you are among the majority of gardeners. But, should the day come when you feel flat and burned out with gardening, pick up this book and read how these Garden Masters rise above disappointments to wring more out of every day in their gardens.

Rhododendrons

Jeanine and Rex Smith's passion for rhododendrons transforms a dense northwestern forest into a landscaped showplace.

(Left) Jeanine's artistic talent shows in this landscape arrangement of R. *'Ken Janek' with sweet woodruff,* Galium odoratum, *and London pride,* Saxifraga umbrosa, *around a weathered log.*

Few other flowering plants have the visual impact of rhododendrons, not just in bloom, but in flower bud and new growth stages, summer foliage, and winter form. The flower buds remind me of a coiled spring, winding tighter and tighter, swelling and swelling until, on one happy day, they burst through their restraining bud scales to dazzle the eye and nourish the spirit. The flowers are anything but ephemeral; in cool climates they remain fresh and unfaded for many days. Through careful selection of cultivars, gardeners can enjoy rhododendrons in bloom over many months. After the flowers drop, and the plants have summoned a new burst of energy, colorful new shoots branch from vegetative buds to grow a new canopy of leathery, evergreen leaves. During the summer, rhododendron plants are like a corps de ballet . . . beautiful, but subordinate to the principal dancers of the season. During the winter, in forest underplantings, the persistent foliage, dark green, often glossy, shines against the background of bare trunks, branches, and fallen leaves.

The history of rhododendrons is replete with stories of great sacrifices by plant explorers who braved harsh winters, nearly impassable terrain, hostile villagers, and venal officials to bring back species to enrich our gardens. In the early days of plant exploration, all members of the genus were called "rhododendrons." Later, certain species, some deciduous, some evergreen, came to be known collectively as "azaleas." Thus, all azaleas are rhododendrons, but only a few rhododendrons are azaleas.

Any attempt at a concise, precise distinction between the plants we call rhododendrons and the ones we call azaleas is doomed to failure. Yet, most experienced gardeners can tell garden cultivars of azaleas from rhododendrons at a glance. Most garden azaleas are hybrids between species, and come under such classes as Indian hybrids, Glen Dale hybrids, Kurume hybrids, Ghent hybrids, Robin Hill hybrids, and Shammarello evergreen hybrids. Many azaleas are deciduous, particularly the native American species and hybrids between them. Individual azalea flowers are shaped like funnels, sometimes fragrant, and are relatively slender, as compared to the more bell-like individual flowers of rhododendrons. A typical cluster or "truss" of rhododendron flowers is larger and denser than one of azaleas, and typical rhododendron leaves are much larger, evergreen, and usually glossy.

Generally, the species and hybrids we call rhododendrons, and the evergreen azaleas, occur in mountain ranges where cooler temperatures and higher moisture levels are kind to broad-leaved evergreens. By far the greatest number of rhododendron species are native to Asia, where they are most numerous on mountains and foothills that receive abundant rainfall and, often, snow cover. However, the tropical species of rhododendrons grow as understory plants in jungles. The deciduous azalea species generally occur at lower elevations and can thrive on drier soil. The species rhododendrons are more demanding in their soil and climatic requirements than the hybrids, yet are the favorites of many rhododendron enthusiasts because of their simplicity and grace.

Only in recent years have rhododendrons emerged as a major landscaping plant in the United States. Forty years ago, rhododendrons had established a foothold in three regions that were ideally suited to their culture, with relatively cool summers, mild winters, abundant rainfall, and acid soils. On the West Coast, the fog-shrouded or rain-washed coastal plain from Santa Cruz north into British Columbia provided the ideal site for growing the spectacular semihardy hybrids. On the East Coast, the temperate bays, estuaries, or islands from Boston south to the DelMarVa peninsula pampered a then-new generation of rhododendron hybrids hardy to 5 degrees F. Further inland, along the uplands of the Appalachian chain, the old Ironclad hybrids, based partly on hardy American native

R. *'Bow Bells' has rather small leaves and pendant flowers (left). The pale yellow blossoms of* R. hanceanum *contrast beautifully with its smooth, dark green foliage.*

rhododendrons, endured great extremes in temperature and fluctuations in soil moisture and humidity. Wild stands of species rhododendrons could be found in roughly the same areas.

Rhododendrons held unimaginable potential for American gardeners, but it could not be realized without more adaptable hybrids, efficient production and marketing methods, and greater publicity. Around the country were immensely talented geneticists, taxonomists, nurserymen, and amateur specialists in rhododendrons, all working more or less independently. Largely, theirs was a work of love; no one made much money out of new cultivars and some producers went broke. No one knew much about propagating rhododendrons on a commercial scale, and plants could not be patented. It all began to come together with the formation of the American Rhododendron Society after World War II.

The early rhododendron hybridizers wanted significant improvements in cold tolerance and resistance to dry soil conditions. They wanted fuller plants, and greater variety in foliage and plant habit. Above all, they wanted new and clearer colors. Cherry and magenta reds abounded in hybrids, along with muddy pastels. Desirable colors were available in species rhododendrons, but thousands of crosses were necessary to develop desirable

Landscaping for a succession of bloom: the white R. *'Alf Bowman' will be followed by the coral* R. *'Paprika Spiced' and* R. *'Lem's Cameo', right. The yellow is* R. *'Golden Witt'.*

hybrids from them. Progress was slow because of confusion in nomenclature, duplication in naming, inadequate pedigrees on existing hybrids, and the need for a broader genetic base.

World War II had an unexpected and positive effect on rhododendron breeding. Servicemen sent back seeds of rhododendron species from the far corners of the earth, and these deepened the genetic pool. The Europeans, with their generally "softer" climate, had been ahead of us in rhododendron improvement for some time, but their hybrids weren't tough enough for our more variable climate. After the war, using new Asian blood and native American species, our breeders rapidly began developing hybrids that were hardy as a rock, and as beautiful as any of the temperamental hybrids from Europe. The hardy eastern *Rhododendron catawbiense* and *R. maximum* were their mainstays and the more tender western *R. macrophyllum*.

During the first flush of enthusiasm over improved rhododendrons, new hybrids flooded arboreta, parks, and estates. Years passed before the plants matured sufficiently that their form, endurance under stressful weather, and resistance to insects and diseases could be evaluated fully. Today, although some of the better old hybrids linger on, vastly improved cultivars are taking over the market, some from other parts of the world. Plants are being bred for attractive foliage and neat form as well. Leaves may be blue-green or silvery, or dusted with velvety tomentum, the undersides purple, rust-colored, or white. New growth can be bronzy red, or as pale and fuzzy as a bunny's ears.

Even before *glasnost,* the cultivar *R. luteum* 'Batumi Gold' reached the U.S. National Arboretum from Russia's Batumi Botanical Garden. Two outstanding breeders, David Leach and the late Ed Mezitt, took the obvious route of developing and evaluating new hybrids in severe winter areas and introduced new lines of compact hybrids for today's smaller gardens. The Leach Hybrids provide extended bloom along with more attractive foliage and crisp, clean colors.

The improvements in rhododendrons have greatly increased their adaptability to other regions of the country. Still, in all of North America, no area can match the Pacific Northwest, from southwestern British Columbia through western Oregon and Washington, for growing a wide range of rhododendron hybrids and species. A few rhododendrons are native to the mountains in this area. Particularly near water level, the climate is temperate, the air and soil are moist for several months of the year, and the soil is porous and acidic, due to the abundance of decomposing organic matter and the leaching action of winter rains.

At their hillside home in Woodinville, Washington, Rex and Jeanine Smith have capitalized on all these advantages to amass a spectacular collection of rhododendrons, not lined up like an ill-assorted guard, but tastefully blended into a stunning landscape.

Under the high canopy of shade, rhododendrons line the winding lane to the Smiths' home.

When I turned into the driveway of the Smiths' secluded home, I was struck by the abundance of color and variety of choice rhododendrons. Pastel colors predominated, with an occasional accent mark of dark or bright, or a highlight of cream, yellow, or white like a shaft of sunlight. Plants ranged in height from groundcovers to taller than my head. Although basically a rhododendron garden, the landscape included azaleas, groundcovers, and choice perennials. I parked some distance from the Smiths' house and walked in, so I could get an idea of the number of rhododendrons in their collection. There must have been a hundred rhododendrons or more in the front yard alone! Rex and Jeanine are still working on the back yard of their three-acre lot. Only a few months ago, loggers dropped and hauled away the last of the hundred-foot-high Douglas firs tagged for removal. The lot hasn't been stripped of trees; far from it—more than a hundred firs, western red cedars, and hemlocks were left standing both to provide the high canopy of shade that rhododendrons like and to block the view of homes beyond their back and side fences.

Along the back fence stand several head-high rhododendrons. Jeanine, the hybridizer and propagator in the Smith family, told me that these big plants date back to her earliest experiments in growing rhododendrons from seeds. She grew them from hybrid seeds brought to a Seattle Rhododendron Society meeting in 1971 by Dr. Ned Brockenbrough, an amateur hybridizer. Little did she dream that, out of the thirty-five plants which she grew to maturity, would come an award-winning cultivar, 'Apricot Fantasy'.

In 1987–1989, Jeanine served as president of the nearly 450-member Seattle chapter of the American Rhododendron Society. She has good reasons for feeling strongly that one of the most important obligations of experienced plant society members is to introduce novices to the joys of growing specialty plants. "It was at one of those first meetings," she related, "that I received the seeds from Dr. Brockenbrough and, following the instructions in David Leach's book *Rhododendrons of the World,* I filled a covered plastic shoebox with moist milled sphagnum moss, planted the seeds, and grew dozens of tiny rhododendron seedlings on the bright end of our kitchen counter, out of the direct sun.

"Succeeding at my first attempt at germinating rhododendron seeds was so exciting!" she said. "It started me collecting and propagating rhododendrons from cuttings and, over the next three years, hundreds of small plants filled our city lot. Rex and I began thinking about having a piece of property large enough to grow and display our collection of rhododendrons."

Then she laughed and said, "I didn't know it, but I was already a 'Rhodoholic.'" She passed me a short essay by Heidi Shelton, a member of the Seattle chapter of the ARS, entitled *"The Five Stages of Rhodoholism."*

1. Patient buys commonly available hybrids ('Elizabeth', 'Hon. Jean Marie de Montague', 'Scintillation', 'Gomer Waterer', 'Pink Pearl', etc.). Notices the pretty flowers and relatively easy care, goes on to stage 2.

2. Begins to comb more prestigious and out-of-the-way nurseries for more unusual varieties and smaller plants (keeping in mind that he/she will run out of garden space in the near future as this acquisitive habit continues unfettered). Throws out or gives away perfectly healthy plants (especially non-rhodies) to make room for more of his favorites. Buys every book on rhododendrons available. Plants trees whose sole purpose it is to provide just the right amount of dappled shade for rhodies. Begins to collect plants for showy foliage alone. Tries rooting some cuttings. Joins the Rhododendron Society. *The disease can be halted at this stage but not reversed.*

3. Starts to look at "real estates" (minimum three acres) in outlying areas because garden is at capacity. Builds a greenhouse and makes some crosses, "just to see what happens." Dreams about owning a rhododendron nursery. If financial and physical resources are adequate for realizing this dream, patient may live out his/her life growing, hybridizing, exhibiting and selling rhodies and sharing experiences with like-minded people. All the while he/she harbors the secret hope to be the hybridizer of the next 'Lem's Cameo', i.e., a plant that will take the rhody world by storm and bring if not fortune, at least fame to its creator. *Recovery at this stage is difficult if not impossible, due to the fact that the patient sees the disease as entirely benign, even pleasurable.*

4. Admiration for rhododendron species, which began late in stage 2 or early in stage 3, begins to take over now. Patients will travel long distances to seek out unusual plants. Beauty of flowers or even acquisition of plants matters less and less; rarity is what patient is after. May sell house and car to finance a trek to the Himalayas. *Patient's family, if still intact at this point, gives up on his/her sanity.*

5. Patient shaves his head, dons a yellow robe, and becomes a Tibetan monk to live among his beloved species. It is not known how females cope with this stage; possibly they disguise themselves as mountaineers, naturalists, or missionaries. *As no case of recovery from stage 5 is known in the literature, it is generally considered terminal.*

At this point, Rex was smiling broadly. He likes rhododendrons, too, but the malady has not progressed as far in his case.

Jeanine continued her story. "Rex was gone from home a great deal as a pilot with Northwest Airlines and, in the evenings, I would pore over the rhododendron literature, which always filled my nightstand. The breaks between Rex's flights give us the time to pursue our projects.

"In 1973 we purchased three acres of land, in what was then a rural area northwest of Seattle. In 1976 we completed our present home and moved in with our daughter, Erin, then eighteen months old, and our sons, Greg, nine, and Kirk, seven years old. Building and moving at that time was difficult and it derailed my rhododendron hobby. Nevertheless, when we moved to our new home, we brought along several favorite large plants and countless small 'rhodies' including, of course, my treasured seedlings. We planted these in nursery beds. After the house was made livable, we began to tackle the vast project of clearing trees and brush, burning stump piles, designing gardens, building decks, and preparing soil.

"Actually, before I caught the rhododendron bug," Jeanine said, "I was interested in gardening and in landscape design. I have a background in art, and would have liked to have spent more time painting, but found that, while raising three children, the uninterrupted blocks of time weren't available. However, I could garden with children around me, and arranging plants in pleasing landscape designs fulfilled my creative instincts. Rex trusts my judgment about landscaping and never complains if a rhody has to be moved. I couldn't ask for a more supportive partner, in all things. Rex worked long and hard to clear this land of salal, brambles, brush, and tree trimmings after the loggers left. He built the service building, greenhouses, and cold frames and is now installing a sprinkler system."

Rex looked a little embarrassed when she told the following story about his willingness to help. "When we were about to move into our first home in 1968, I wanted to take a course in landscape design but was very pregnant with our second son. I knew I wouldn't be able to finish the class before delivery. Rex went instead, took notes, and reviewed them with me after each session."

Asked if he does any hybridizing, Rex smiled and answered, "No. I know how to hybridize but Jeanine knows why. I get my kicks out of helping her succeed, but I also enjoy building and heavy gardening. I guess that growing up around farms in Montana accustomed me to it. I'll tell you one thing: when I get out of that cockpit and rest up a little to get over jet lag, I enjoy the relaxation I get from building and gardening. Jeanine and I like working together on my days at home."

I like the way the Smiths defer to each other's strengths. When Rex finished talking about his involvement, Jeanine took over to show me

Rex and Jeanine mulch around a choice rhododendron hybrid that was grown from seed. This one has survived the evaluation process.

the steps of propagating rhododendrons. She began by demonstrating how to take, root, and "grow-on" cuttings to a size that can safely be transplanted to a nursery bed or border.

Jeanine showed me that, with the aid of rooting hormones, potting soils, bottom heat, and cold frames, increasing rhododendrons by taking cuttings is easy and almost foolproof. Now that their space is filling up rapidly, she has little room for plants other than her own seedlings, and has virtually discontinued growing from cuttings. It is quite a sacrifice because, as Jeanine puts it, she "likes to put roots on things." Nevertheless, she won't turn down a cutting from a rare rhododendron, and she will clone her own hybrids by cuttings when required.

Space limitations are also forcing Jeanine to be very selective about hybridizing. Long past the learning stage of making random crosses, she directs each cross toward what she sees as attainable goals, mostly new colors and improved growth habits. Through her ARS connections, Jeanine can receive pollen from species and hybrids not in her collection, even from foreign countries. In return, she sends pollen from her plants on request. Records of crosses and pollen donations are kept in what she calls her "stud book."

Jeanine is particularly fond of the plant habit and foliage of hybrids based on *R. yakusimanum* and, along with other hybridizers, is incorporating this species into her breeding program. The species is low growing and its rather slender leaves with truncated ends clothe the plants densely. New growth is colorful. The undersides of leaves are felty and give a bicolor effect when they blow in the breeze. The lack of a wide range of natural colors doesn't bother Jeanine, because she can cross *R. yakusimanum* with other species to get the colors she wants. She is aiming for full yellow, apricot, or orange trusses on compact, low-growing plants with attractive foliage.

I was struck by Jeanine's confident approach to difficult hybridizing goals. She explained how she got started: "I was inspired to try hybridizing by a dear lady, Elsie Watson, who taught me the techniques of crossing and encouraged me to join the hybridizers group of the Seattle chapter. She was my role model and her lovely hybrids gave me the assurance that, with a little luck and a lot of hard work, I might do the same. Elsie has several of her creations in the commercial trade, but is still searching for the elusive 'true blue' rhododendron, with no trace of purple color in the flower."

She showed me her pollen bank. Nestled in dozens of neatly tagged gelatin capsules were anthers and pollen grains, not only from her garden but also mailed from elsewhere. Pollen must be gathered from unopened or freshly opened blossoms. Wind and insects can vector in foreign pollen soon after blossoms open and contaminate hybrids.

Jeanine prefers gelatin capsules because moisture can escape through them and be absorbed by the layer of calcium chloride desiccant in the bottom of the sealed storage jar. She cools fresh pollen for two or three weeks at 40 degrees F. before transferring it to the freezer. Rhododendron pollen can keep for about three years when frozen.

(Right) On the deck behind their home, Jeanine and Rex enjoy the fruits of their labors, surrounded by the variegated Japanese maple, Acer palmatum *'Ukigomo', the pale yellow* R. *'Butterfly', a pink rhododendron the Smiths hope to identify, and the large coral* R. 'Fabia x bureauvii'.

I learned that rhododendrons set prodigious numbers of seeds as fine as petunias. Jeanine germinates hybrid seeds in one-pint plastic freezer containers filled to within one inch of the top with moist milled sphagnum moss. She showed me her bank of three fluorescent light fixtures that illuminate a table with a surface area of sixteen square feet.

In this restricted space, she could grow plants in one hundred containers, without sunlight. Each container could hold fifty to one hundred seedlings, but there is no way her outside production and display area could absorb so many. So, Jeanine uses 75 percent of the lighted area for growing on transplanted seedlings of choice hybrids which she wishes to accelerate.

When the seedlings are ready to transplant, she transfers them to plastic flats filled with a mixture of peat, perlite, and finely ground fir bark. These are kept under fluorescent lights until time to transplant again, at which stage they are moved to their lean-to greenhouse. There, they are

acclimated and transplanted to six-inch pots. The seedlings are fed periodically with a weak solution of water-soluble fertilizer.

Under such forcing, the seedlings can put on several flushes of growth and reach a height of six to eight inches the first year.

The first winter, the potted seedlings are protected in the greenhouse or cold frame. Root growth continues during the winter, and new top growth will begin the following spring. If a branched plant is desired, Jeanine will pinch or snap out the center bud to force side buds to develop. At each transplanting, Jeanine culls out the seedlings that show poor foliage.

"I can hardly wait to see the first blooms appear on my seedlings," Jeanine said. "By that time, at least two years will have passed since I started seeds of the hybrid under lights. Some seedlings will keep me waiting for as long as five years before they will bloom!

"First bloom is the moment of truth for hybrid seedlings. I have to be ruthless about eliminating those which are deficient in color or form: only about one out of one hundred seedlings makes it past this stage of evaluation. Even so, Rex has to condense the few survivors of trial rows to make room for new seedlings. As soon as they grow enough to take shape, I evaluate them for landscape potential. Perhaps one out of fifty may survive the second screening."

From the plants grown to this stage, Jeanine will choose the most promising for moving into a landscaped border for growing on to the next "go or no-go" stage. Each seedling is tagged with its heritage. Within a year or two, any shortcomings of the few surviving seedlings will be evident. It is painful to have to dig these up and give them to friends after a gestation period of up to ten years, but that's what happens to all but the crème de la crème. Jeanine asks her friends to grow her discards as "unnamed seedlings" and occasionally revisits them to double-check her judgment.

Jeanine's goal is to produce hybrid seedlings that are not just good, but distinct from and superior to both parents. That may qualify the seedling for registration with the ARS, provided no one else has beat her to the punch with a similar cross. Qualifying for registration is difficult; technically you could win a red, white, or blue ribbon in a prestigious show and still not have a cultivar worthy of introduction.

After this relentless scourging, only one out of one thousand hybrid seedlings may remain in the landscape border. At this stage comes the moment that Jeanine and Rex have been working toward; judgment of their work by their peers in rhododendron growing and hybridizing. They cut a large truss of blossoms, stick the stem in a bottle of water, and take it to the annual show of the Seattle chapter of the ARS. Every hybridizer's dream is to win a "Best New Hybrid" ribbon, for it can catch the attention of commercial growers. It is gratifying to develop a new

1) 2) 3) 4) 5) 6)

Hybridizing Rhododendrons

Here, Jeanine takes me through the steps involved in hybridizing rhododendrons. To prevent self-pollination, the blossom of the female parent is (1) emasculated by removing the anthers. Anthers and pollen are stored in gelatin capsules (2) tagged with the name of the donor cultivar and the date of collection. The pollen is transferred (3) by inserting the receptive stigma into a gelatin capsule containing pollen from the male parent. Jeanine uses fluorescent light fixtures for germinating and growing rhododendron crosses and species from seeds (4). In the greenhouse (5), potted-up seedlings and cuttings are grown to sufficient size for transplanting. Rex covers overwintering young plants (6) with a poly "tunnel," which is removed when the weather warms in the spring. Root growth continues over the winter, with new top growth appearing in the spring. At least two full years will have passed before the seedlings' first bloom.

Jeanine gathers rhododendron trusses for a show. Rear, left to right: R. augustinii, R. luteum, R. oreotrephes. *Front, left to right:* R. *'Hotei' x 'Tropicana' seedling,* R. *'May Day',* R. *'Hotei',* R. *'Paprika Spiced'.*

seedling that tops all others in shows, but even more fulfilling to see it increased for many home gardeners to enjoy.

Jeanine is not discouraged that, after so many years of educating herself in hybridizing and showing, she has only one seedling that has been registered and has commercial potential. 'Apricot Fantasy' won the "Best New Hybrid" award in a Seattle chapter show and was increased for introduction on a limited basis for spring of 1989 planting. I understood the reason for her optimism when I saw some of the beautiful seedlings in her landscape borders. She has the touch!

While we toured the evaluation trials and borders in the back and side yards, Rex told me some of their secrets for growing rhododendrons in the landscape. "In our climate," he said, "proper soil conditioning and mulching can influence a rhododendron's ability to perform in full sun. I've tried several kinds of soil amendments and prefer to add pulverized fir bark when preparing the soil. I'm lucky to have a small diesel tractor with five chisel points on a drawbar. I can gear down and loosen the soil to a depth of twelve inches. Chiseling breaks up soil compacted by the log trucks, and drags out tree roots. I spread a three- to four-inch layer of bark and about four pounds of ammonium sulfate per one hundred square feet, and mix it into the soil with a tiller. The nitrogen speeds the conversion of the raw bark into humus.

"I work three other organic materials into the soil when I can get them: wood shavings, stable manure, and chipped wood from the power company and road maintenance crews. We supplement sawdust with nitrogen to avoid nitrogen drawdown. Sawdust breaks down quickly, but I think it is worth the effort of application. We have purchased topsoil occasionally, but it always seems to bring in weeds. Consequently, we prefer to amend the existing sandy soil with organic matter. Cheaper to do it that way, too!"

I like the setup Rex has for lining out hybrid seedlings in rows for first and second evaluations. He has installed a solid-set sprinkler irrigation system with 36-inch risers pinned against posts to hold them erect. Looking ahead to possible water conservation restrictions, he used water-conserving micro-sprinkler heads. Combined with organic mulches, the efficient sprinklers should minimize water use.

Rex feels that they are blessed with not having many insect or disease problems. Root weevils can become a nuisance but are controllable. Mildew sometimes appears on susceptible types, but he controls it quickly with mild fungicidal sprays.

I spent three days with Rex, Jeanine, their daughter, Erin, and the photographer, dodging in and out between rain showers. It was a

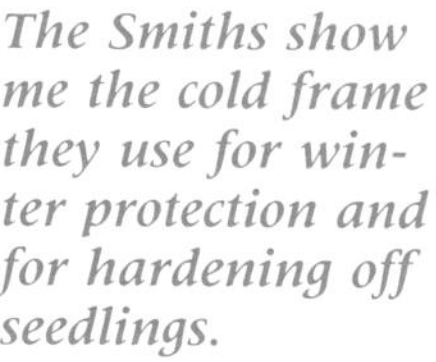

The Smiths show me the cold frame they use for winter protection and for hardening off seedlings.

Jeanine's prized creation, 'Apricot Fantasy', won the "Best New Hybrid" of the ARS.

delightful time because, with their cool spring weather, the rhododendron buds seemed to take forever to open. It gave me an opportunity to appreciate the great show that rhododendron buds can put on, and to enjoy the changing moods created by sun, shade, and showers.

Rex and Jeanine garden on a scale that would intimidate most gardeners. I asked how many hours Jeanine spent in the garden per week, on the average. "Oh, ten to fifteen hours a week," she answered; "more in the spring, less during the rainy winter season. Actually, I spend a lot of time in the garden just looking. I appreciate the principles of good garden design and have tried to express them in the front and side yards, and around the deck in the back. But, I believe the main purpose for a garden is to provide enjoyment for the owner, and should reflect his or her special interests. Good design can suffer when a person grows large numbers of a specialty plant. We've solved the old 'design versus plant collection' dilemma for now by locating our breeding and production grounds on the back of the property.

"I still have time," she said, "for my duties with the Seattle chapter of ARS. I feel I have benefited from the organization and should give something in return. We in the chapter are especially proud of our contribution to Meerkerk Rhododendron Gardens on Whidbey Island, near Seattle. It was given to the chapter a few years ago by Anne Meerkerk so that her large collection of rhododendrons and companion plants could be preserved. A hybrid test garden has been established for rating the performance of new hybrids in our climate. There are acres of woodland gardens for strolling and enjoying mature rhododendrons and towering forests. This large garden is open to the public during the spring and summer and should continue to improve with the work of the chapter."

Rex was less definite about how much time he spends in the garden. It was as if I had asked him which leg of his pants he pulls up first. He thought for a while and said, "I really can't say for sure. I'm usually home four days between trips and put most of my spare time to building and gardening. We have the opportunity to travel but, at this stage in our lives, most of our leisure time is spent gardening. We like it here. We've put a lot of ourselves into this home and garden."

He looked off into the distance and mused, "Then, again, Jeanine and I have talked about visiting the rhododendron gardens in Great Britain and perhaps New Zealand. . . ."

Something tells me that, in a few years, when Erin has flown the nest, Rex and Jeanine will be looking for a larger piece of property, nearer the water for frost protection. If only one of each one thousand hybrid seedlings she now has under way makes it to the landscape border, they will soon run out of space. It appears that Stage 4 of Rhodoholism is about to set in!

More about Rhododendrons

To grow rhododendrons that remain beautiful and flower-filled from youth to old age requires more attention than growing, say, vegetables or herbs. Climate is the principal success factor, for without a hospitable balance of humidity, protection from intense sun and temperature extremes, and acid soil, even the hardy new cultivars will not flourish.

Purchasing Rhododendrons

To determine how rhododendrons will do in your area, make a few excursions to large home gardens in the vicinity, gardens with a few years behind them. Rhododendrons increase in beauty and stateliness with age. The garden owner can tell you if your climate is so fickle that it will damage or destroy rhododendrons periodically. Take note, especially, of his siting of rhododendrons in respect to shade, drainage, wind flow, and adjacent trees or shrubs.

If you are persuaded to go on, check out the better retail nurseries in your area at peak rhododendron time . . . early through late spring. Members of local ARS chapters can steer you to them. If the nursery offers only a few plants of rhododendrons and other acid-loving species such as pieris, leucothoe, and mountain laurel, it is a safe bet that rhododendrons are only marginally adapted to your area. At that point, you may decide either to find a mail-order source of hardy modern hybrids, or transfer your attention to the more ubiquitous azaleas.

Next, write to a few of the commercial rhododendron growers for catalogs. Most are located in prime rhododendron-growing areas and have retail stores as well. At first, patronize only those in your part of the country because they can offer you sound advice on adapted cultivars and species of rhododendrons and azaleas. They can tell you how to prepare the soil, using locally available materials. They will tell you how to control the few insect and disease problems of rhododendrons and will usually offer you a broader selection of cultivars than most general retail nurserymen.

On the other hand, if you live in an area where rhododendrons are popular, by all means start with your local nurseryman. Certain retail nurseries offer extraordinary assortments of rhododendrons.

I love to read rhododendron catalogs. As with most horticultural catalogs, they describe cultivars so compellingly that you find yourself condensing your wildly optimistic "want list" to a "need list" and finally to an "absolutely can't do without" list. But, at the core of descriptions is rock-solid information such as the relative hardiness of the cultivar, its average height and spread at ten years of age, foliage characteristics, and preference for protection or exposure in your climate zone. It is hard to fit all that on a plant tag in a retail nursery.

Adaptability

Before you invest in the cultivars on your "absolutely must have" list, you might consider contacting the ARS to determine if a chapter is based anywhere near you. If not, the next best alternative is to visit the nearest botanical garden or arboretum. At the reception desk ask if they have plantings of rhododendrons, or literature on their culture. Another good information source is your local association of Master Gardeners, accessible through your County Extension Office.

Site Selection

Next, consider the sites you have for planting rhododendrons. Here's what they like:

- High humidity to balance evaporation from their broad leaves. If summers are dry or hot in your area, plan on installing sprinklers.
- Protection from intense sun, either by fog or high, filtered shade. Only in favored areas can rhododendrons thrive in full sun. Hybrids vary in their tolerance for sun; as a rule, the smaller the leaf, the more sun the plant can tolerate. The small-leaved alpine types are exceptions; they are native to misty mountain ridges and can't tolerate hot, drying sun.
- Protection from rapid, drastic fluctuations in temperature, either by proximity to bodies of water or provision of a favorable microclimate, where drying winds are blocked off.
- Porous, well-drained, highly organic soil, pH 4.5 to 5.5.

Soil and Planting

How you plant rhododendrons depends on whether you have sandy or clay soil. With clay or clay loam soils, till the soil and spread a 3-inch layer of coarse sphagnum peat moss, pulverized pine bark, or, in the West, composted sawmill waste. Work it into the soil.

Do not dig deep planting holes. Instead, make up a pile of planting mixture composed of equal parts of organic matter, sand, and garden soil pulverized by tilling. Set the new plant on top of the tilled soil. Tap it out of the container or, if the root ball is wrapped in burlap, remove the pins or ties and let it fall flat.

- Carefully scratch away the outer ½ to 1 inch of the root ball to expose root tips. This will help them grow into the surrounding planting mix rather than retreat into the old restricted root ball.

- Shovel the prepared planting mix around the root ball. Firm it down by hand. Be generous. Build up the soil level even with the top of the root ball, extending out at least 2 feet from the trunk. A skinny little cone of planter mixture will dry out quickly or wash away.

- Plant as described above if your soil is a shallow layer of sandy or loamy soil overlying clay. But, on deep sandy or gravelly, fast-draining soils a different approach is called for.

- Spread a 3- to 4-inch layer of organic matter over the soil and turn it under as deep as you can with a spade or tiller. Thoroughly mix it with the soil. Dig generous planting holes. Set the plant in place so that the top of the root ball stands 1 to 2 inches above the surrounding soil. Gently scarify all sides of the root ball to encourage rooting. Fill around the plant with the excavated soil and firm it down with your hands.

Watering and Mulching

Before mulching, set a sprinkler near the transplanted rhododendron and let it run at low pressure for an hour. Then, spread a 3-inch-deep mulch around the plant, extending out 2 or 3 feet. Finally, pull the mulch away from the trunk of the plant to eliminate the possibility of rotting.

You can select from many materials for mulching: pinestraw, shredded hardwood leaves, composted sawdust, woodchips, hardwood bark mulch, or forest floor leaf mold. Be sure to pile sawdust with a little manure or a sprinkling of ammonium sulfate and garden soil for a month or so before use. Wet the pile and cover loosely with plastic to hasten heating. Raw sawdust can cause recurring problems with nitrogen drawdown if not composted before mulching. Chipped green wood, pinestraw, shredded leaves, and bark mulches rarely induce nitrogen shortages.

Jeanine Smith advises, "Take care the first year that the newly transplanted rhododendron does not dry out. Until roots have spread out into the surrounding soil, the root ball is especially susceptible to drying out. When this happens, overhead watering can fail not only because the canopy of leaves tends to shed water but also because bone-dry soil can be difficult to rewet. You may need to lay a hose or a sprinkler directly on the root ball and allow it to run slowly until the dry soil is thoroughly moist."

Fertilizing

It is in feeding rhododendrons that many gardeners get into trouble; they apply too little or too much, too early or too late. Just remember that, in nature, rhododendrons get by with a low level of plant nutrients, mostly derived from rotting vegetation and ozone nitrogen from thunderstorms. Micronutrients are usually in good supply, due partly to the low soil pH in natural populations of rhododendrons. When the soil pH level begins to creep up, iron deficiency chlorosis can show up.

In most areas, two light applications of fertilizer per year are sufficient, but in coastal California, where there is little danger of cold-weather damage, three light applications may be made. Organic fertilizers such as cottonseed meal, soybean meal, or blood meal release nitrogen in the ammoniacal form preferred for rhododendrons. Or, you can use specially compounded azalea/rhododendron food. Application rates are one-third those for organic fertilizers: ⅛ cup for 18-inch plants; ¼ cup for 24-inch plants; and ½ cup for 36-inch rhododendrons. Top-dress around plants in early spring and again at blossom drop. In coastal California feed again just after fall rains begin.

The danger in feeding after midsummer comes from "tenderizing" the plants. They should go into the winter "hard," not growing rapidly.

The principal danger in overfeeding is the stimulation of overly long internodes, which results in lanky, sparsely leaved plants or, in extreme cases, failure to bloom. This can happen if organic fertilizers are applied in the spring when the soil is too cool for them to break down. The gardener sees no response to the fertilizer and applies more. Warm weather increases the soil temperature and the activity of organisms that decompose organic fertilizers. Suddenly, the plant is given a strong push into vegetative growth instead of a gentle, steady pull.

One of the most efficient feeding programs combines late fall mulching with an application of a slow-release plant food such as Osmocote 14-14-14 Controlled Release Fertilizer. Since Osmocote ceases releasing nutrients at soil temperatures below 40 degrees F., there is no danger of stimulating winter growth.

Spread Osmocote at the recommended rate and cover with 2 to 3 inches of organic mulch. Little or no nutrient release will take place until spring weather warms the mulch to the depth of the Osmocote. All the nutrients will be metered out within 90 to 120 days. The noted azalea enthusiast Fred Galle cautions that, because of the high percentage of nitrogen in the Osmocote formulation, application rates should be those recommended on the package for fertilizer-sensitive species.

You can opt to apply Osmocote at half the recommended rate and supplement with a top-dressing of organic fertilizer at half rate when the blossoms drop. The organic fertilizer should supply most of the micronutrients needed by rhododendrons except where the soil and water are limy or basic. There, chelated iron may be needed as well.

When it comes to mulching, you could do worse than to follow Rex Smith's example, but it is possible to overdo it. The idea is to simulate the layer of litter that carpets forest floors. If you lose plants to root rot, poor drainage and mulching may have to share the blame . . . for if you plant a rhododendron too deep, mulching will compound the problem.

Housekeeping

Ideally, you should aim for two flushes of new vegetative growth of moderate length followed by the formation of flower buds in late summer and fall.

When rhododendrons are small, and a dense, well-rounded form is preferred, the terminal buds can be pinched or snipped off to force more lateral buds to grow into shoots. Do this when new growth appears, or soon after blooming.

Cutting back forces more compact, less leggy growth. New growth will come from the buds below the shears.

Housekeeping should not be neglected; spent rhododendron blossoms should be picked up and composted and seed pods should be snapped off as they begin to form. With a little practice, you will learn to prune rhododendrons to produce more flushes of growth per season, thus shorter internodes and bushier, leafier plants.

Pests and Diseases

Rhododendrons have few serious insect and disease problems, but those need to be dealt with promptly and firmly. As with any broad-leaved evergreen, you don't want to risk allowing insects to disfigure leaves, because they are not replaced every year.

The rhododendron lace bug is probably the worst pest; the tiny nymphs suck plant juices and mottle the leaves, depositing unsightly black excreta on the undersides. You can't confuse their damage with that of the rhododendron bud moth; their grubs tunnel inside leaves, twigs, and the buds of flowers and new growth.

If you see sawdust around stems and breakage from the weakening, suspect the rhododendron borer; it is most troublesome in the East. Your State Cooperative Extension Service can suggest a spray program to control these and other local pests.

Diseases are relatively few; mildew on leaves is easily identifiable and dealt with. Root rots and the resulting wilting are symptomatic of poor drainage. Taking up and repositioning the plant may work, but usually comes too late to save the plants.

Once you have braved the mainstream of rhododendron growing, you may find yourself digging out, containerizing, and selling or giving away some of the more ornate rhododendron hybrids you acquired early in your hobby, to make room for less-formal species. A home garden can accommodate just so many prima donnas, each trying to upstage the other. But however your collection may evolve, the rewards will be gratifying.

Hostas

Jim and Jill Wilkins: a Michigan physician's dexterity and his wife's artistic eye team up to create new vistas for hostas.

Dainty, low-growing, edging-type hostas act as a foil for tall iris. H. *'Gold Drop' lines the path; at lower left is* H. *'Princess Karafuto', backed by* Hosta longissima; *at right is* H. ventricosa *'Aureo-Marginata'.*

How can it be possible? A foliage plant with only four basic leaf colors and unremarkable flowers has become the leading shade plant for American gardens. For the answer, all you have to do is see a well-grown collection of hostas. Plant breeders have achieved outstanding foliage color combinations in shades of green, gold, white, and blue-green, and fascinating leaf shapes. They have perfected plant sizes and growth habits for every garden situation.

Plant breeders understand that the true glory of the several species of the genus *Hosta* is in the size, shape, color, texture, and stance of the leaves, not necessarily in the flowers. You hardly notice that the basic foliage colors are rather ordinary because the variations are as endless as cloud formations on a June afternoon. The flower spikes of most hostas lack the visual impact of sun-loving flowers but are valuable because so few flower species will bloom in moderate shade.

Plant breeders are now working to increase the size and longevity of hosta flower spikes, and the range of colors. As they stand, today's simple hosta flowers, in shades of purple, lavender, or white, combine well with the strong foliage colors without clashing or competing for attention. Some hosta cultivars have a mild, pleasant fragrance, especially the hybrids derived from the white flowered *H. plantaginea*. When mature, hosta seed heads can be dried for use in winter bouquets and wreaths. Hostas begin flowering as early as June with some varieties, and flowering continues for several weeks.

One characteristic of hostas that varies dramatically is the "stance" of the plants . . . the angle at which stems and leaves are held. Some mature plants are tall, open, and airy. Others have huge, overlapping leaves that look like shingles on a roof and shed rain accordingly. Other leaves are like cupped hands; they hold enough water to attract birds for a sip. The visual density of plants is just as important as color and mature height and the little "added attractions" such as fancy leaf formations of certain cultivars.

Visitors to hosta collections are awed by the huge variation in plant sizes between cultivars. Some are man-high, with leaves as large as tobacco plants; others grow to a height of only two or three inches. The wee hostas such as *H. venusta* were so valued and jealously guarded in their Japanese homeland that introduction to the United States was delayed by many years.

We need only to look at the place of hostas in Japanese gardens today to predict a new use for them in this country. With little or no open garden space around homes, the Japanese long ago turned to growing hostas in containers. On the northern islands they move hostas indoors before cold weather comes, so that growth is not checked by a period of dormancy. The Japanese also chop and steam the petioles as we do asparagus, or sauté them. American gardeners may not be ready for hosta omelettes, however.

In this country, the popularity of hostas is greatest in the Midwest and lower New England, and decreases as you go south and west. Although they are valued for performance under conditions that would either kill or discourage most flowering species, they don't like hot, dry weather. They grow pretty well in the central and upper South and Northwest, but only a few rugged cultivars will survive in the deep South and dry, warm Southwest. Where adapted, hostas have the happy habit of quickly settling in and rounding into a colorful mound. A little plant in a four-inch pot can increase in size and beauty a dozen times over during the frost-free growing season. They look good from late spring into early fall; some cultivars are attractive when yellowed by fall cold but in hot, dry climates

Stair-stepping hostas up a slope displays the shape and substance of each variety. The hostas are set off splendidly by companion plantings of Hemerocallis *'Eenie Weenie,' in the lower right corner;* Chamaecyparis obtusa nana, *and* Picea pungens *'Montgomery'.*

merely look weatherbeaten. Hostas have few diseases and pests, except for slugs and snails. Hostas are very cold tolerant, yet can endure short periods of high heat and humidity such as occur during midwestern summers. They shade out weeds and require little maintenance. They give much but ask little from the gardener in return.

The dramatic increase in the popularity of hostas came late, in comparison with other perennials, and is largely due to enthusiastic promotion by the American Hosta Society. The United States boom actually began before the founding of the society in 1969. It may have been sparked by the need for more and better shade-tolerant plants. The many homes built during the decades following World War II are rapidly becoming shaded by trees planted by the new owners. As these trees grow, they complicate gardening with sun-loving shrubs, flowers, and food plants. Consequently, homeowners are looking for colorful, shade-tolerant plants. Potted hosta plants displayed in the shade plant sections of nurseries sell themselves.

The world of hostas is big, and can be bewildering to beginners. Hundreds of cultivars appear in catalogs of specialists, so many that commercial growers must drop obsolete varieties in order to add new ones. Still, the number of cultivars offered in catalogs is bound to increase substantially. It is rather sad that so many beginners plant their gardens with the limited selection of old varieties available from mass marketers because some are decades behind the times in plant density, color impact, and leaf elaboration.

To assist gardeners in learning about hostas, the American Hosta Society has divided the genus *Hosta* into four rather loose categories: "edgers": compact, rather upright; "groundcovers": low-growing, spreading mostly by rhizomes; "background": tall and rather massive; and "specimens": any size plant, but it must look exceptionally good when displayed alone.

No such categories existed when hostas first appeared in this country, probably in the early 1800s. No one knows for sure who had the honor of planting the first hosta garden in the United States. Plants and seeds came through Europe on their way here, but the genus is native to Japan, Korea, and China. Hosta plants are very long-lived and some eastern U.S.A. gardens could still be populated with descendants of the original imports. A second group arrived when the Japanese began trading with the occidental world.

Dormant hosta plants and seeds could be transported easily by settlers and, once established in their new homes on the frontier, could be divided and passed around. It is a testimony to the goodness of the human spirit that, amidst the confusion and apprehension of moving by wagon or riverboat to a hostile frontier, someone thought to bring starts of flowers.

A more significant avenue of entry for hostas opened during the nineteenth century, when advanced plant hobbyists brought improved selections here from England. "Hostamania" was epidemic there in Victorian days, not just among the wealthy, but among the inhabitants of cottages and row houses.

Today, hostas are second only to *Hemerocallis* (daylilies) in popularity among herbaceous perennials. Their fascinating diversity in the home landscape is abundantly demonstrated in the garden of Dr. James and Jill Wilkins.

The Wilkinses gave me a tour of their elegantly landscaped hosta collection during taping for The Victory Garden. *The Japanese painted fern,* Athyrium goeringanum, *right foreground, combines well with* Hosta 'Northern Halo,' *left front.*

Jim and Jill Wilkins's large and lovely garden is the display area for their hobby of breeding and growing hostas, and for Jill's growing collection of dwarf conifers. The garden provides a serene setting for showing about twenty-five hundred plants of seven hundred hosta cultivars. It is one of five large private hosta gardens in the Jackson, Michigan, area that drew the twentieth annual convention of the American Hosta Society to their city in June 1988. About two hundred hosta enthusiasts trooped through the gardens to see their favorite plant in imaginative settings.

Visitors to the Wilkinses' garden enter through a path that meanders around hillocks, peninsulas, and islands, and offers new vistas at every turn. Large conifers, remnants of the forest that once clothed their property, have been thinned and limbed up to provide light shade for hostas. All the free-form display beds are of generous size to accommodate many groups of the smaller cultivars, individual specimen plants of massive hostas, and edgings of miniature cultivars. While all the hostas are stairstepped by height, groups of taller plants are occasionally brought forward to interrupt the regularity. Colors and variegations are placed for greatest total effect. The cultivars with more white or light yellow in the foliage variegations stand farther back in the shade of trees and the green or blue varieties are brought out toward stronger sunlight.

It must take great self-control to restrain a hosta enthusiast from planting display beds solidly with hostas. The Wilkinses leave enough room between groups of hostas to plant complementary perennials and groundcovers. These make the hostas stand out from the background, and separate the groups visually. Jill has taken a special interest in astilbes, epimediums, and primroses, shade-tolerant perennials that look good interplanted among hostas. Some of these bloom before and after the peak season for hostas. Jill has a good eye for color and avoids the jarring hues that would conflict with hosta foliage.

The garden slopes down from the house to a large grassy clearing in the back, then upward to meet a looming wall of dark, tall pine trees. Considerable forethought and work capitalized on the site and broke it into a number of intimate vistas, while maintaining flow and integrity.

Jim and Jill started by identifying the major "overlook" points into their garden. While one stood at an overlook, the other moved around the yard with a flag atop a tall pole for visibility. In this way, they identified the trees that had to be removed; the stand was so dense that nothing but moss would grow in the gloom. Once they completed thinning and limbing up the survivors to let more sun in, and to open up views, they used the flagpoles again to locate planting sites for choice trees or shrubs.

With the foundation of the garden established, they laid out a garden hose to outline "islands" beneath the shade of the large pine trees. They sprayed the area with a nonselective herbicide to kill broad-leaved perennial weeds and the invasive perennial quack grass. They had the soil tested, and spaded in the recommended nutrient sources and lots of organic matter. The islands became raised beds, 6 to 8 inches in height, which is just high enough to avoid their being flooded during thunderstorms.

To add interest, they sighted-in and laid out curving "berms," built-up hillocks that look perfectly natural. The berms serve to guide the numerous visitors into and through the back yard, and out the other side. They were major constructions and required severals loads of hauled-in topsoil to build them up to the desired height.

On the berms, they first applied a layer of chipped wood mulch to reduce soil erosion, then planted Jill's expanding collection of choice dwarf conifers. She placed the all-green types in full sun and the variegated, golden, and silver types where shade from afternoon sun would prevent browning and fading. Dwarf conifers are so appealing that you want to reach out and touch them; elevating them well above ground level lets you appreciate them fully. In sunny areas between islands and berms, a thick turf of bluegrass and fine-leaved fescue sets off the scene as would a pretty frame around a picture. Jim and Jill edge the turf with hoes, to keep it from encroaching on their ornamentals. Somehow, the natural line between turf and flower beds looks better than an artificial edging.

The Wilkinses have most of the heavy labor of garden construction behind them. After twelve years of work, their garden has expanded (to three acres), as has their enjoyment of it. They have added a service area well off from the side of the house, a large barn with an attached greenhouse, a new lath house for propagation, a food garden with numerous fruit trees, and a pen full of noisy "watch geese." Although each addition is functional, each is attractive, blends into the landscape, and agrees with the architecture of the home.

Both Jim and Jill came by gardening naturally. Born during World War II when money was scarce, Jim's birth was "paid for with gladiolus and Shasta daisies." In their Victory Garden, Jim's parents grew not only food for the war effort, but also flowers to cut and sell for extra income.

(Above) A tricolor beech fills the space between the low hostas and the leggy pines. 'Gayfeather' and 'Curly Top' in the left foreground are backed by 'Golden Cascades'.

(Right) The highly popular and adaptable H. *'Frances Williams' is set off by the yellow-flowered perennial* Corydalis lutea.

Jill's parents were good gardeners. At their home in Ann Arbor, they followed the traditional division of food gardening for men and flower growing for women. Her mother's specialty is roses.

During Jim's long years in pre-med and med school, Jill completed two degrees, in zoology and education. While both were putting in long hours at school and living in a low-income housing development, they found time to beautify their little home with flowers and shrubs. Neighbors saw what they had accomplished and began to plant surrounding yards. Now, after more than twenty years and countless occupants, that little cluster of houses still boasts remarkably beautiful plantings. Their gardening had to be curtailed while Jim served his residency and completed a tour of duty in medicine with the U.S. army, but resumed in earnest upon his return to civilian life. Three daughters blessed the family; all are interested in gardening and environmental preservation.

Jim and Jill recall fondly the day they became interested in hostas. They were already good gardeners but their efforts lacked focus. Then, they visited the garden of a man who was to become their friend and mentor, Herb Benedict. He grows and breeds hostas at nearby Hillsdale, Michigan. "Herb gave us a start with numerous cultivars of hostas, convinced us to join the American Hosta Society, and showed me the elements of hybridization," said Jim.

"Hostas got us so fired up that we have persuaded a number of friends to take up gardening as a hobby and, in particular, with hostas. We are involved in several community projects, but bringing others into gardening may prove to be our most important contribution."

At Hosta Society meetings Jim listened closely to experienced hybridizers to learn their techniques and to get ideas on areas of hosta improvement that are within the reach of amateur plant breeders. Hosta breeding isn't a simple "A + B = C" proposition; the parentage of modern cultivars is so complex that it is impossible to predict what will come out of crosses. Success has a lot to do with the number of seedlings a breeder can grow and evaluate.

In selecting parent plants, breeders look for unusual color combinations and patterns, and graceful plants with an attractive ratio of leaf size to plant size. They lean toward hostas that emerge later in the spring and so avoid frost damage.

I asked Jim for some of the goals of hosta breeders. He said, "I think that more attention will be paid to hosta flowers and fragrance, which are now considered distinctly secondary to the colorful foliage. And, with the gardeners in the upper South using more hostas, I expect to see more sun-resistant cultivars. Not all cultivars are genetically stable and tend to revert to solid colors or throw color variations in the perimeter divisions taken from clumps. I think we will find ways to keep cultivars true to type. Now that we have learned from the Japanese how to keep hostas

Jill grooms a dwarf Alberta spruce planted among the hostas. The variegated border plantings are H. *'Louisa' and* H. *'Bold Ribbons'. At lower right is 'Gold Regal'; at far left,* H. *'Krossa Regal'.*

from going dormant, I think we will find ways to use them indoors during the winter as foliage plants. That is bound to have an effect on breeding programs. Certainly, we will see more hostas grown in containers, which will open up new applications for the small-framed cultivars."

Jim is by nature methodical and thorough; here's how he organized his hosta breeding program:

"First, I set up a system for record-keeping: good notes and labeling are essential. I use 4×6 cards to record crosses—one card for each plant. I also plan ahead which crosses I want to make, with a specific goal in mind.

"The night before I make the cross, I remove the petals from the pod parent's flower, that is, the flower that would be opening the next day. This prevents bees from being attracted to the flower and pollinating it instead of my doing it.

"The next morning, I remove stamens from the pollen parent and carry them to the pod parent. I hold the filament of the stamen like a paintbrush and literally paint the pollen from the anther onto the stigma, which is at the tip of the pistil. If the pistil is receptive, I can see the pollen stick to it and coat the tip.

"I use color-coded wire from telephone cable to mark the cross. When I have completed transferring the pollen, I loop a two-inch piece of colored wire around the stem (pedicel) below the flower. Then, I record the

Starting Hostas from Seed

Jim Wilkins explains how he starts hostas from seeds. Seedlings are started in cell-packs (1) like the one shown here next to dried seed pods. Later, the tiny seedlings are transferred to book planters like this one (2), where their roots grow long and strong. The book planters allow Jim to transplant the young hostas with little or no root disturbance. Three stages of seedlings are shown here (3): just after sprouting, about one month old, and seven months old, ready for transplanting. After a winter under lights (4), the seedlings are transplanted to the lath house, where Jim can give them concentrated attention for the first year. Optimum fertilizer, moisture, and drainage maintain vigorous growth until the plants are large enough to be evaluated.

1)

2)

3)

4)

color of the wire on the index card identifying the cross by pod parent and pollen parent.

"When the seed pods are ripe, the seeds will turn black. I harvest the hybridized pods then, put them into small paper bags, and label them with the parentage of the cross. The seed pods will split open in a few weeks. I clean them by rubbing gently and carefully blowing away the chaff.

"The seeds can be handled in three ways: if I have room under the fluorescent lights, I will plant them immediately. Or, if the soil is in condition for planting, I will plant them in short, labeled rows in the garden. If not, I will store them in a sealed jar with a desiccant until spring. I have heard that hosta seed is difficult to carry from season to season, but this has not been my experience."

Normally, a time span of two years from harvesting hybrid seeds is required to produce plants large enough for evaluation of foliage characteristics and plant habit. After a few years' experience with the slow process of growing new hybrid hostas from seeds, Jim decided to see what he could do to speed it up. He installed a battery of fluorescent light fixtures in the basement and experimented with burning the lights for various time spans. "Actually, I stumbled onto the answer," he said. "I forgot and left the lights burning day and night over my flats of hosta seedlings, instead of the usual fifteen to eighteen hours. To my surprise, I learned that, in the seedling stage, hostas grow faster under lights that burn twenty-four hours a day.

"The fixtures are on chains and can be lowered to no more than two inches above the tops of seed flats. The gentle warmth and intense radiant energy from the tubes keeps the surface of the potting medium at 70 to 75 degrees F., the preferred range for germinating hosta seeds. The twenty-four-hour lighting not only causes seedlings to grow faster but also to form superior root systems."

Jim uses a standard seed flat mixture of peat moss and vermiculite to start hosta seeds and covers them to about three times their diameter with potting medium. Seeds come up within ten to fourteen days with the fluorescent lights lowered to where they nearly touch the tops of the seed flats. "The intensity of the lights falls off drastically as the fixtures are raised," he explained. "As the seedlings grow, I raise the light fixtures a link or two at a time on the supporting chains, but never higher than two to three inches above the tops of plants."

Jim also experimented with various sizes and types of pots for growing on the seedlings he sprouted and grew in flats of soil. He settled on a plastic "book" planter that opens into mirror-image halves, hinged on one side. The book has long concavities that are filled with moist potting medium. The small, rooted seedlings from under the lights are pricked out from flats and positioned so that their tops protrude from the book when it is closed and snapped shut. The planted book is tipped up and stood on edge in holding trays, plants up, of course.

I asked Jim why he chose the book planters instead of standard pots. "The secret of the book planters," he replied, "is that the long, cylindrical root balls hold more soil than small pots of the same diameter, and give roots room to grow long and strong. When spring frost danger is past and hostas can be planted outside, the books can be popped open and the plants tipped out with little or no root disturbance. I feel that the long, strong root systems get my seedlings off to a faster start.

"I move the trays of plants in books out to the solar greenhouse in March, where I have black-painted drums of water against a reflecting wall. Even at that early date, the drums will have absorbed enough heat from the sun to protect plants from freezing at night. Ours is a south-facing, lean-to greenhouse with a slanted glass front. Nothing would be gained by moving plants there earlier because winter days are short and dark at our latitude. By April, hostas in the greenhouse begin responding to the increasing heat and longer, brighter days. I want them to grow rapidly and to be ready for transfer to the lath house or garden spots by late May. I wouldn't dare put hostas into an unheated greenhouse in March were it not for the tempering effect provided by five 55-gallon drums. They absorb daytime heat and radiate it at night to hold temperatures at 45 degrees Fahrenheit or higher. I have a backup gas heating system but have never had to use it."

As the last stage in accelerated propagation, Jim takes the now-sizable seedlings from the greenhouse and sets them in deep binlike planting beds of potting soil under shade in his lath house. He has one hundred square feet of these waist-high planting bins, space enough to plant three hundred hosta seedlings.

"The lath house is much more than a garden decoration," says Jim. "Beneath 50 percent shade from the lath, and protected on one side from wind, many seedlings will flower the first year. Controlled-release fertilizer, excellent drainage, and abundant moisure push the seedlings into optimum growth rates. I couldn't give my seedlings that kind of attention if they were scattered around the garden or lined out in nursery rows."

The end result of the accelerated propagation is a time span of only ten to twelve months from harvesting and planting hybrid seeds to producing plants large enough for evaluation of foliage characteristics and plant habit. The old method of propagation required two full years. Through the American Hosta Society, Jim published a technical paper on the subject: "Accelerated Growth of Hosta" in *The Hosta Journal* (No. 55).

The few seedlings that survive Jim's rigorous process of selection for color, variegation, vigor, and uniqueness are grown in the garden for

(Above) Raised beds in the lath house are at a good height for evaluating hybrid seedlings.

(Below) Handsome hostas: the gold in the foreground is H. 'Ultraviolet Light', at the right edge is H. 'Fort Knox'. The green hostas are hybrid seedlings bred by Jim Wilkins and registered in 1989.

(Left) A variety of unnamed seedlings put on a fine display with gold hostas 'Fort Knox', at right, and 'Ultraviolet Light' to its left.

another year to note their flower color, size, and fragrance, and to measure the height and spread of the mature plant. If any are felt to be sufficiently good, and distinct from existing cultivars, they will be named and their parentage registered with the American Hosta Society.

"Out of every thousand seedlings I grow from crosses," said Jim, "perhaps one plant will be sufficiently novel to justify introduction. But, I don't throw the others away; I plant the other 999 in the vegetable garden. Jill and I grow them to use as gifts for visitors, family, and friends. Every now and then, we'll get sentimental, dig up an unregistered hybrid seedling, and plant it in the hosta garden. It may not be unique, but it is one I just can't bear to part with."

I asked Jim what he feels lies ahead for hostas. "Bigeneric hybrids could be possible," he said, "and who knows what can be achieved with gene splicing? My hope would be the addition of the red/orange spectrum to foliage colors. Now, we are limited to shades of green and blue-green, plus gold, yellow, cream white, and silver.

"Above all," he continued, "I expect to see the Hosta Society institute tighter controls on registration to discourage the introduction of cultivars that are similar in many respects to existing hostas. There must be two thousand named cultivars, but even the experts have difficulty identifying hostas when they venture beyond the five hundred or so most popular cultivars."

Jim and Jill are concerned that beginners might be put off by the sheer numbers of hosta cultivars. They suggested this "starter list" to fit a cross-section of hostas into a small garden. In their list, the initial "H" indicates the genus *Hosta*, "Aureo-marginata" means simply "gold-edged," and "nebulosa" means "cloudlike."

- *H.* 'Hadspen Blue': Groundcover type; blue foliage.
- *H.* 'Wide Brim': Specimen type; blue-green leaves, irregularly margined with cream.
- *H.* 'Gayfeather': White-centered green.
- *H.* 'Aspen Gold': Medium height; gold, highly seersucked plant; lots of substance.
- *H. ventricosa* 'Aureo-marginata': Groundcover type; large green leaves with irregular margins of yellow to white.
- *H. tokudama* 'Aureo-nebulosa': Rare; textured green leaves with blue streaks; short stems.
- *H.* 'Blue Umbrellas': Large-leaved, blue, background type.
- *H.* 'Tot-Tot': Dwarf, with distinctive wedge-shaped dark green to blue-green leaves.
- *H. montana* 'Aureo-marginata': Large background type; huge glossy-green leaves with irregular margins; award winner.

- *H.* 'Gold Standard': Groundcover type; pale yellow-geen with green margins.
- *H.* 'Krossa Regal': A popular background type; blue-gray leaves and very tall flower spikes.

The Wilkinses caution beginners that only a few of these select cultivars will be available in retail garden centers, which tend to offer the old favorites.

As for Jill's striking combinations of dwarf conifers that set off the hostas in the Wilkinses' landscape, she recommends the following cultivars in her garden:

Chamaecyparis (false cypress)
- *C. obtusa* 'Filicoides'
- *C. obtusa* 'Corraliformis'
- *C. pisifera* 'Little Jamie'
- *C. pisifera* 'Snow'
- *C. pisifera* 'Filifera Nana'

Microbiota decussata (Siberian carpet cypress)

Picea (spruce)
- *P. abies* 'Little Gem'
- *P. abies* 'Pygmaea'
- *P. abies* 'Conica'
- *P. abies* 'Nidiformis'
- *P. abies* 'Gregoryiana Parsoni'

Tsuga (hemlock)
- *T. canadensis* 'Bennett'
- *T. canadensis* 'Gentsch White'
- *T. canadensis* 'Jacqueline Verkade'
- *T. canadensis* 'Lewisi'
- *T. canadensis* 'Sargenti'

She also added, "Hostas look good, as well, with *Buxus, Ilex, Kalmia, Rhododendron, Azalaea,* and, I suspect, *Pieris*."

"Given no more hostas than we have today," says Jim, "a home gardener just beginning to collect hostas for landscaping will find a lifetime of fun and challenge. As for me, I can come home from a frustrating day at the office, feeling out of sorts with the world, and just ten minutes in my hosta garden will straighten me out. During the winter, I can unwind by inspecting the seedlings in the basement to see if that one-in-a-million breakthrough has finally occurred. It's a good life, and I recommend it to everyone!"

More about Hostas

Climate has so much bearing on success with hostas that I called on friends who are commercial growers for advice, and asked the Wilkinses to put me through a short course on hosta growing.

Sources

Hosta plants lend themselves to both mail-order and retail sales. They can be shipped while dormant or grown in pots in greenhouses and sold as young plants. Local plant farms can dig up the hostas of your choice and sell them to you at any time during the growing season. Mail-order companies offer the newest cultivars, while retailers tend to offer mostly the old favorites, some of which are still highly rated.

Some producers grow plants in the field, others in greenhouses, still others by tissue culture. The advantages of tissue culture are that plants can be mass produced, thereby increasing availability and (eventually) lowering cost; systemic plant diseases such as virus can be eliminated, allowing healthy plants to reach their full potential. Someday, micropropagation may solve the problem of the color changes that come with age on some hosta cultivars: some take years to develop typical patterns, others tend to revert to the all-green color, especially in new growth coming from the margins of crowns. Tissue-culturing of hostas is now done mostly in the early increase stages of valuable new hybrids.

When ordering hostas, it is always a good idea to inquire if the varieties in which you are interested will perform well in your climate. While most cultivars are widely adapted, some, for reasons not clearly understood, have a distinct preference for certain areas of the country. One condition is universally liked by hostas, regardless of region: protection from wind. Windswept areas dry out rapidly and plants are subject to breakage of petioles.

Plant Performance

Experienced hosta growers know that catalogs should be used only as guides and that there is no such thing as a hard-and-fast description. For example:

Plant height and spread can vary considerably, due to the latitude of your area affecting day length, the amount and distribution of moisture, drainage, and the prevailing level of plant nutrients.

Flowering and foliage color can be affected by the degree and hours of shade. Beds in full sun and watered sparsely will flower more heavily and foliage colors will be richer, but there is always the chance of marginal scorch during extremely hot, dry, windy weather, especially on the lighter-colored cultivars.

The hostas with blue foliage prefer locations near a pool or on a streambank, where the high humidity keeps the air cooler. Some growers achieve this effect by modifying their soil highly with organic matter so that it can evaporate lots of moisture while retaining enough to meet the needs of plants' metabolism. In the South, growers employ sprinklers to keep the humidity high during hot, dry weather.

Shade Quality

The quality of sunlight and shade can differ from area to area. In some gardens, high humidity and or smog can cause refraction. Plants will perform differently in such locations than where the atmosphere is usually clear. The slope of the land can affect solar absorption. Fully exposed south- or west-facing slopes can stress hostas. Shade quality is determined largely by whether the shade comes in the morning or afternoon. In most climates, afternoon shade is preferred or, even better, high, filtered, daylong shade.

Considering the decided preference of many hosta species for high shade, you may want to limb up trees with low-hanging branches. You'll be surprised at not only the better growth of your hostas but also the brighter display provided by the stronger light.

Fragrance

Fragrance may depend not only on the species (*H. plantaginea* and its crosses are the most fragrant) but also on dryness, wind, and the time of day.

Soil Preparation

Take note of the advice in catalogs, or on packages, of the preferred site for the cultivar or cultivars you will be planting. Prepare the soil by mixing in a 1- to 2-inch layer of moist peat moss, pulverized pine bark, rotted sawdust or compost, and, if your soil is heavy clay, a similar amount of sharp sand as well. This will raise the level of the bed somewhat above the surrounding terrain. Hostas are not notably particular as to soil pH, but extremely acid soils should be limed to bring them up to about pH 6.0.

Planting

Planting should be delayed until about ten days after the average frost-free date. Watch out for low-lying frost pockets; if you have an option, plant hostas where they can get good air drainage. In such favored locations, hostas push up tender growth from their strong crowns in mid-spring, after frost danger is past. However, where cold air collects, new growth can be hurt by late frost. The plants are rarely killed but development can be delayed a month or two.

When setting-in hostas, leave room between plants for them to spread out to full size. (Some of the large background hostas can spread to 3 to 5 feet across.) Hostas display better if the outer leaves of mature clumps just touch adjacent plants. Groundcover types can be planted closer together.

Before setting your plants in the garden, the Wilkinses advise, soak dormant plants for a few hours in warm water, and trim off dead roots. Loosen the root system and spread it out when planting. Position the "crown" or top of the rhizome level with the surface of the soil, or about 1 inch below it if your soil drains well. In very dry soil, fill the planting hole with water and let it soak in. Then, pull loose soil in around the plant and trickle water around it to settle the soil and eliminate air pockets. Careful planting and watering-in can make a critical difference to the plants' survival.

Plant Care

Weeding is a problem only when hostas are young. As they mature, they crowd out, or shade out most weeds. Grass encroaching from turf pathways, or stoloniferus grass such as quack or Bermuda, can be controlled with edgings or spot treatment with a nonselective herbicide.

Water the new plants once or twice weekly until they are well established. After the plants have emerged, mulch around them. Once well rooted, hostas can go for two or three weeks without rain unless they are in soil that is invaded by tree roots. Experienced growers are careful about watering hostas.

1)

Dividing Hostas

2)

Hostas benefit from occasional division. Unlike many other perennials, hostas can, with care, be moved at any time the ground is not frozen, though the optimum time varies according to region. Here, a crowded clump is taken up with a spading fork (1). The soil is rinsed from the roots in a bucket of water to make division easier (2). Then the clump is cut or pulled apart (3). The divisions are ready for transplanting in soil modified with organic matter and fertilizer. Complete the process with a thorough watering. If you divide in the fall, after the foliage has been killed by frost, mulch the new plants so that they will root well before the ground freezes.

3)

They follow the "occasional deep drink" principle. They try to water before noon, which gives the plants time to dry off before nightfall. Sun-baked beds of hostas, especially those with a southern or western exposure, may need weekly waterings.

Give hostas light applications of fertilizer. For example, each year, just after shoots emerge, the Wilkinses work a phosphate and magnesium source, "MagAmp," into their soil and add greensand to provide potassium. The decay of organic mulches provides sufficient nitrogen. Farther south and west, or on lighter soils, two or three applications of dry granular fertilizer per season may be needed.

Maintain tight control of slugs and snails: the Wilkinses' garden is surrounded by forest, and is infested with 2-inch long gray slugs. They use bran cereal or wheat bran from a feed store, sprinkled lightly with liquid metaldehyde, to control them. By making their own bait, slug-control cost is kept at only fifteen dollars per year. If they relax the slug-control program for even a short while, damage quickly gets out of hand, especially in years with average or above-average rainfall.

Inspect occasionally for bug damage. Hostas have very few insect or disease pests in the North. Black vine weevils may periodically notch hosta leaves, but they can be controlled with one spray application of Carbaryl.

Division

Divide established hostas occasionally. While it is true that hosta plants can live for decades without being divided, certain clumps can grow too large for their sites. They can be taken up, divided, and replanted in soil modified with organic matter and fertilizer. In areas with severe winters, divide in late summer so that a strong root system can be established before the ground freezes. Hosta clumps are easy to pull or cut apart after soil has been rinsed off in a bucket of water. Unlike many other perennials, hostas can (with care) be moved at about any time the ground is not frozen. Therefore, they are not "set in concrete" and can be shifted around the garden to make just the right combinations of cultivars. Be sure to water divisions thoroughly after transplanting and to work rapidly to avoid their drying out during the process.

The admirable Graham Stuart Thomas in his book *Perennial Garden Plants* suggests a beautifully simple way for dividing large clumps of hostas. Quite correctly, he brings out the mixed feelings one has when approaching beautiful old specimens, with spade in hand. Rather than dig the entire plant up, cut out pie-shaped segments and use them as new starts. Fill in the hole with compost.

It has been my experience that you can take about half of a hosta crown in a single season without harming the established clump. I prefer to divide dormant plants in early spring. The growing season is so long in the Southeast where I live that hostas have plenty of time to establish themselves before hot weather. Up north, it seems that the new shoots begin popping up right after the soil has thawed and dried out. I hesitate to touch hostas then because the tender shoots can break so easily. If you divide in the fall, after the foliage has been killed by frost, you will need to mulch new plants to make sure they root strongly before the ground freezes.

In cold-winter areas where perennials are often damaged by heaving of soil, mulch established hostas after the soil has frozen and you have twisted off the dead tops. If you mulch too early, mice may invade the hosta beds and damage crowns.

Hybridizing

Jim Wilkins encourages hobby gardeners, and they don't have to be experts, to try their hand at hybridizing hostas. The individual flower parts are large and visible enough to be easily reached. He offers the following advice about selecting hosta parents for hybridizing, based on his own experience:

"In general, hostas which have solid central or marginal color variegation will produce only solid-colored offspring. However, a plant that is 'streaked' or 'splashed' with contrasting colors will often produce variegated offspring when it is used as the female or 'pod' parent." (The trait for variegation is carried in the chloroplast of maternal cells.)

"The offspring from crosses using streaked or splashed cultivars as the pod parent may eventually form stable central or marginally variegated plants. They need to be watched for a few years to detect solid color reversions.

"The pod parents I have found most reliable for producing variegated offspring are *H.* 'Dorothy Benedict', *H.* 'Northern Mist', and *H.* 'Color Fantasy'. Pod parents that give good solid gold-colored offspring are *H.* 'Aspen Gold' and *H.* 'Gold Regal'. Pod parents that produce blue offspring are *H.* 'Dorset Blue' and *H.* 'Blue Moon'. For breeding toward beautiful blooms I use as pod parents *H. kikutii* (a species hosta) and *H.* 'Maruba Iwa'. And, to produce beautiful leaf shapes I use *H.* 'Holly's Honey' and *H.* 'Donahue Piecrust'.

"If the beginning hybridist stays with these cultivars, he or she will avoid the hostas that are sterile, such as *H.* 'Krossa Regal' and *H.* 'Birchwood Parky's Gold'. If any fertile hostas are incompatible in crosses, I am not aware of them. One hosta species, *H. ventricosa*, is 'apomictic,' and produces offspring almost always identical to itself, without genetic input by the pollen parent."

Daylilies

In nearly seventy years of service to humanity, Brother Charles Reckamp lets his light shine through his love for daylilies.

In all its glory: Brother Charles Reckamp's unnamed hybrid seedling 86-123 shows the multiple branching and high bud count desired by daylily enthusiasts. Note the prominent ruffling.

Daylilies can be cast as the stars or the spear carriers of your garden grand opera. Massed in phalanxes or marshaled into small squads, they can back up or flank the stars on center stage. Like good troops, sturdy, adaptable daylilies can be moved about or dug in for a long occupation. Yet, among their ranks are individuals of such brilliance that they are destined to command attention. Daylilies are fast becoming the most popular herbaceous perennial in North America. Bright and bold, they require little care, can be planted at any time during the growing season, offer a broad variety of plant sizes, blossom colors, and conformations, can be tucked into niches in landscapes rather than requiring special beds, and thrive in containers.

Daylilies have long been beloved for their cheerful, sunny colors: yellow, gold, and orange. Plant breeders, however, were not content with such a limited palette and have added colors that, only a decade or two ago, would have seemed beyond the realm of possibility. Neither were the hybridists content with the rather brief shows of colors of the older cultivars, and they have significantly lengthened the duration of bloom. They have also stretched the season of bloom by developing early cultivars that bloom right after peonies, and late cultivars that bloom during the shortening days of late summer. They are introducing cultivars with remontant (repeat) blooming. They have increased the bud count to more than a hundred on well-established plants and have selected plants for precocious flowering. They have added peachy-coral pastels and somber dark hues, crystalline petal textures, broad petals, ruffled and waved.

If, when you hear the word "daylilies," you still think of the humble tawny daylilies that have naturalized along country roads over much of America, shake off this outdated stereotype. Today's cultivars are light-years removed from their country cousins. Entirely new colors and color patterns have been developed, entirely new classes of plants such as the miniatures and triploids have been introduced, the size and substance of blossoms have been improved, and the plants have been made more resistant to windstorms. If you have not recently visited a collection of modern daylilies at a public garden, you would hardly believe your eyes. You would recognize the new cultivars as daylilies—they still have the family resemblance—but what gorgeous creations they are. It would be hard to find another genus of plants so transformed in such a short time!

In no other plant specialty have amateur plant breeders contributed so much to the improvement of a hobby plant. (I'm counting as amateurs all who are not geneticists or who lack advanced education in the field of botany.) Back-yard plant breeders have contributed many of the twenty-five thousand or more cultivars developed during the past half century. The exciting part of daylily breeding is that much remains to be accomplished and that any reasonably intelligent, meticulous person might just be the one to make the next breakthrough.

Much of the potential for improvement lies in the deep genetic pool available to plant breeders. *Hortus III* lists about fifteen species within the genus *Hemerocallis*, all resembling typical daylilies enough to be easily identifiable. Even though there are differences in flower-head arrangement, foliage, and roots, the resemblance is strong between the species. Crosses between species, while difficult, are made with increasing frequency.

Long ago, civilized countries began planting daylilies for food rather than flowers. In their native China, gathered from the wild and eaten fresh or dried, daylilies were a staple in good times and a survival food during famines. Even now, dried daylily blossoms are exported in large quantities to be added to soups as thickeners or reconstituted to use as garnish. Curiously, it appears we are coming full circle: fine chefs in the U.S.A. are now using fresh daylily buds as an edible flower.

The bicolored Reckamp hybrid seedling 84-42 shows the broad, ruffled petals and striping favored by Brother Charles.

Daylilies deliver a lot of color for the small space they occupy and, during medieval days, were "naturals" to be taken from the wild and cultivated in the compact gardens of wealthy Chinese and Japanese. Early on, good plantsmen began making selections from the wild species. This caused considerable confusion among early plant explorers, who tended to assign a new name to every new acquisition if it differed from the norm for the species. Further confusing the issue was the tendency of daylily species to sport new forms in response to different environmental conditions.

It is believed that the first daylilies reached Europe in the middle of the sixteenth century. By the late sixteenth century, Dutch and English botanists were growing daylilies, but some of their early herbals posted confusing descriptions and inaccurate artwork. Little did the Europeans know that, because they were neither trusted nor respected in the Orient, the wealthy Chinese and Japanese held back their best developments and did not allow them out of their gardens.

The Western world didn't see the best daylilies from the Orient until Albert N. Steward, a botanist, and his wife, Celia B., taught there for many years and gained respect and trust. They sent to their friend, Dr. A. B. Stout, around fifty excellent cultivars and previously unknown species from private gardens on their travels in China. Their shipments set the stage for a quantum leap in daylily breeding. Perhaps the most important find of the Stewards was a seed-bearing plant of *Hemerocallis fulva:* previous introductions of this species were sterile and of little use in hybridizing.

Dr. A. B. Stout was one of the "greats" in horticulture, disciplined, insightful, and afire with a zeal for improving *Hemerocallis* and bringing order out of the chaos of daylily nomenclature. As director of the laboratories at the New York Botanical Garden and a colleague of many of the leading horticulturists between the two world wars, he was in the right place at the right time for his crusade. More than any other person, Dr. Stout set the course for daylilies and gave them a flying start to their present place as a bright star in the firmament of plants.

The very best cultivars developed by Stout were named and farmed out for increase. Some of his creations have stood the test of time and are still listed. He incorporated into new hybrids all but one of the traits he set up in his list of priorities: earliness, hardiness, higher bud count, showier (but not necessarily fancier) blossoms, new colors and variegations, greater extension of flower scapes above the foliage, and sturdy, blue-green leaves, not given to breakage or early yellowing. The one elusive dream? A pure white daylily: it remains to be found.

Since Dr. Stout's day, many hobby breeders of daylilies have upscaled to commercial production as they have developed an inventory of their own hybrid seedlings. They, along with less-advanced fanciers, keep track of the latest developments by visiting performance trials and by attending regional and national conferences of the American Hemerocallis Society. Just learning to recognize the thousands of cultivars by sight, and under different climate and soil conditions, requires several years of study. Fortunately, it is fun, and the advent of camcorders and videotape is accelerating the rate of recording and retaining information.

With most amateur daylily breeders, profit is a distinctly secondary consideration. Recognition from their peers in the daylily world is important, and a sense of contributing to the advancement of a plant they genuinely love. Brother Charles Reckamp is one of the world's foremost amateur breeders of daylilies, and is certainly not in it for profit. To see him at work evaluating his seedlings is to understand the satisfaction a person can realize from working to improve his chosen specialty plant.

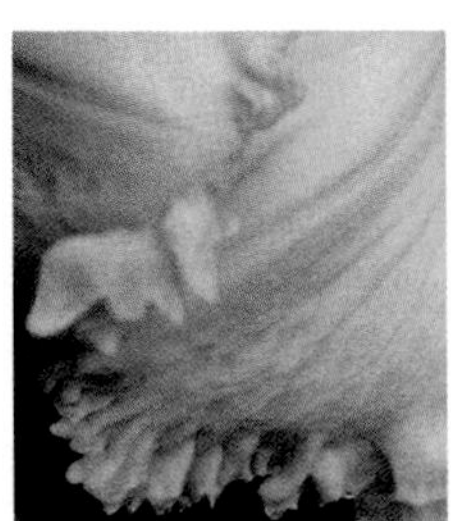

Many of Brother Charles's seedlings don't make the "first cut," his evaluation in first-year seedling rows.

You may never be tempted to pick up a camel's-hair brush and transfer pollen from one flower to another. For some people, however, attempting to improve a species by hybridization is a natural step in learning about their chosen specialty plant. Some dabble in hybridization while maintaining large and beautiful gardens. Some become so wrapped up in plant improvement that they subordinate gardening to hybridizing and evaluating seedlings of their specialty plant.

If he chose to, Brother Charles Reckamp could grow the plants for a magnificent landscape. He has spent more days on the business end of a hoe than some of us enjoy on earth. But, more than fifty years ago, he made the choice to minimize gardening and maximize his efforts to improve daylilies through hybridization and selection. Long before I met Brother Charles, I had heard of his plant-breeding work. He, Dr. Robert A. Griesbach, and Nathan Rudolph are about the only survivors of the daylily specialists in the Chicago area who began revolutionizing the genus in the 1940s. Figuring that he had to be in his eighties, I expected to meet a frail, elderly man. When I arrived at the Society of the Divine Word U.S.A. headquarters in Techny, Illinois, I found how wrong preconceptions can be.

A brother at the residence pointed to a group of three men wrestling with transplanting a ten-foot-tall serviceberry tree. It had a root ball that must have weighed six hundred pounds. He said, "That's him over there, the one on the left." I went over and introduced myself to a bright-eyed, vigorous man who, while small in stature, was doing his share of the grunt work. Come to find out, he and an employee named Wally and a lay volunteer had transplanted several such trees in the heavy clay land around the campus. Wally and the layman appeared to be in their seventies. They courteously declined my offer to help, possibly because they considered me too old!

To understand Brother Charles's involvement in daylilies as a hobby plant, you need to know a little about his background. He came from a poor farm family who lived north of St. Louis, Missouri, near a town called Ethlyn. Times were hard and he never had a chance to attend high school, not unusual in those days. In 1927, as a young man, he was accepted as a working brother by the society, and, since then, has not ventured far from northern Illinois.

The Society of the Divine Word exists for educational and missionary work in some of the poorest districts of the poorest countries, as well as in the United States. Priests and brothers periodically rotate back to the headquarters for rest and medical treatment. Finally, when they grow too old to shoulder the load, they retire to the residence of the society at Techny.

Since its founding, the society has depended on working brothers to grow grain, livestock, vegetables, fruit, and bees to help feed the staff, visitors, and retirees. That was Brother Charles's first job but, soon, he became involved in growing nursery stock, garden plants, and flowers to cut and sell to the burgeoning suburban Chicago market. The society needed the income to augment that which they received from donations.

Among the flowers grown for cutting were gladiolus, peonies, and iris. At the time, Brother Charles was kept busy growing and harvesting and, during the winter, helping operate a large greenhouse for growing bedding plants. When I say "busy," you must understand that working brothers rise before dawn for devotions, labor hard through long days, and retire at dusk.

Two local men who went on to become legends in daylily breeding, Orville Fay and David Hall, took a liking to Brother Charles and showed him how to cross-pollinate and propagate iris from seed. At the time, Brother Charles had no idea that this newfound skill would lead to the second great love of his life. The mentor-friend relationship between him and established plant breeders opened the door to new opportunities and convinced this modest man that he, too, could make a success of plant breeding.

The good fortune then enjoyed by Brother Charles seemed almost inconceivable to him, but got even better. In the 1940s, Dr. Robert A. Griesbach began breeding "tetraploid" daylilies by treating seeds and seedlings with colchicine to double their chromosome number. He lived in the area and shared his techniques with Brother Charles. Also, James Marsh, a leading amateur plant breeder from Chicago, often came up to Techny. Concurrently, the developer of the famous 'Stella d'Oro' daylily, Walter Jablonski of Merrivale, Illinois, was making great strides in hybridization but was not part of Brother Charles's group.

Reckamp, Hall, Fay, Griesbach, and Marsh held long discussions on the improvements needed in daylilies, and how to go about achieving them. Even though Dr. A. B. Stout had made tremendous progress in improving the genus, he had only scratched the surface. The range of plant sizes, blossom colors and patterns, petal and sepal width and texture were still limited. Cultivars tended to hide their blossoms amidst the foliage, were rather shy bloomers, basically midsummer flowers.

It happens that daylilies are one of the easiest plants to hybridize; the reproductive parts are large and readily accessible. Anthers can be quickly removed from yet-to-open buds, and pollen transferred to the receptive stigma from a desirable pollen parent. Pollen from early bloomers can be dried and stored for crossing on later cultivars.

Brother Charles was still young and had the energy to keep up his food- and flower-growing duties while learning plant breeding. However, he decided to put iris breeding on the back burner because of his conviction that daylilies held greater potential for improvement, and greater possibilities as a landscape plant. He explained to me how daylilies came to be improved so greatly in a relatively short time span.

"It was the vast improvement in iris created by the introduction of tetraploids that convinced our little band of plant breeders to try the same approach on daylilies. When you double the number of chromosomes in a plant, a number of things can happen: its progeny can be dwarfed, with thicker stems, more massive flowers, and thicker petals. Hybrids between species are sometimes possible, when you work with tetraploid male and female parents.

"Dr. Griesbach had the scientific mind and equipment for the demanding task of experimenting with the powerful gene-altering drug, colchicine. He spent many hours in the lab at DePaul University, treating

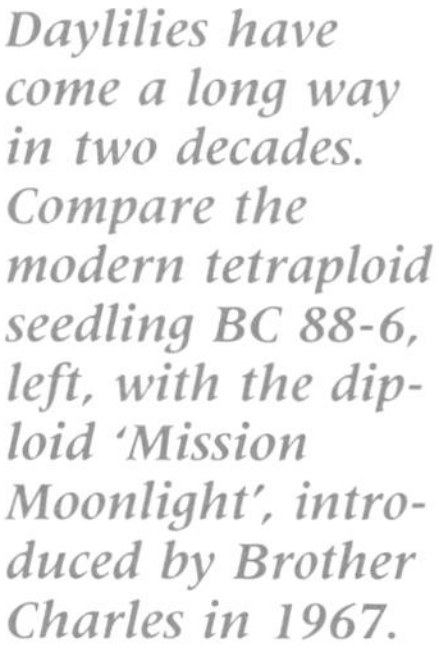

Daylilies have come a long way in two decades. Compare the modern tetraploid seedling BC 88-6, left, with the diploid 'Mission Moonlight', introduced by Brother Charles in 1967.

newly germinated daylily seeds with various concentrations of colchicine to double the number of chromosomes within cells. The treatment is traumatic, very few seedlings survive, and those are slow to regain their natural fertility. All seedlings have to be grown to maturity in trials because many survivors will have the normal chromosome count but some will be crippled or deformed.

"Orville Fay worked closely with Dr. Griesbach, and they soon had a few tetraploid mutations that set marginally fertile seeds. It took several generations for the plants to regain full fertility. These tetraploids were hybridized to begin their daylily breeding program. It was like starting all over again; their tetraploid hybrids were like nothing we had ever seen before in daylilies.

"The price tag on the first tetraploid daylily introduced by Orville Fay was two hundred dollars per plant. It was the cultivar 'Crestwood Ann'. My superiors had confidence in me and purchased one plant as the start for a tetraploid gene pool of my own.

"I was fortunate to have working with me the young Brother Daniel Yunk. He had a good feel for daylilies and tried his luck with colchicine treatments. He succeeded in producing several nice tetraploids, which we restored to fertility and used in crosses with 'Crestwood Ann'. The resulting seedlings became the foundation stock for my future hybridizing. At this time, I also had access to valuable pollen from Orville Fay's collection, which included daylily cultivars I could not afford.

"During the 1950s, the five of us, while still friends, developed different goals in daylily breeding and began working independently. For example, Orville Fay was centering on wider petals and open-faced blossoms with ruffled edges. Griesbach was all wrapped up in creating new tetraploids, in which he did very well. One of his top achievements was a line of improved red daylilies with larger flowers, wider petals, and brighter, sunfast hues.

"I began finding extraordinary pastel shades amongst my hybrids and transferred the traits for ruffling and wider petals to them. My hybrids looked good and began to sell. I returned all the income to the society and they let me have a plot of farmland to evaluate my experimental seedlings.

"Gradually, my hybrids began to show a common 'signature'—a combination of wide petals and highly visible sepals. My latest hybrids show a tinge of gold around the ruffled edges. Most of my work has been with the creamy pastels, which, to me, seem richer than the straight pastels.

"For years I had searched for exceptional ruffling and found it in the hybrid I named 'Amen'. As a pollen parent, it passed on the ruffling to succeeding generations. Another turning point was the development of 'Milepost', a pastel pink. It became the source for an intensified pink blush color in my later hybrids.

Brother Charles's "signature" of huge flowers, soft but clean colors, and broad, ruffled petals all show in his tetraploid seeding BC 86-42.

"I've tried the red colors, but haven't produced anything to brag about. I haven't tried breeding miniature daylilies. Crosses between species are beyond my expertise in genetics. I haven't tried to pick up breeding lines from the evergreen *Hemerocallis*. I've stuck pretty close to the plants in the 20- to 36-inch class. Yet, there's still so much to be done in this category that I haven't felt at all limited."

In 1975, young Roy Klehm came over from nearby Barrington and offered to market all future Reckamp hybrids through the Klehm Nursery mail-order catalog. Brother Charles accepted; now, when you see the credit line of Reckamp-Klehm behind a cultivar name, you know it was introduced in or after 1975. Roy comes over to Brother Charles's plots, digs out most of the plants, and moves them to his own nursery for further evaluation and increase of promising lines. The only plants remaining are those Brother Charles tags to keep for use in his breeding work.

"At first," Brother Charles said, "Roy and I always saw eye-to-eye on the experimental hybrids. But now, thirteen years later, Roy has become more knowledgeable and a lot more critical. I like it because he makes

me defend my judgments. One thing we did agree on was to continue my practice of giving my introductions 'heavenly' names such as 'Amen' or 'Angel's Delight'. I don't consider myself any closer to the angels than anyone else, except perhaps due to my age, but 'heavenly' names come easily to me and I think they are memorable."

Brother Charles was experiencing long and dangerous delays in crossing busy Waukegan Road to reach the old daylily plots, so he moved his garden to a new location near the residence building. He showed me the new 85×125-foot trial garden. Klehm brought in a crew and large machines, and laid 900 feet of drain tile for it in a single day. After removing the sod from the garden plot, he hauled in an eight-inch layer of rotted leaves plus several loads of manure and turned them under with a chisel plow.

I think that Brother Charles has for so long given himself to serving others, that much of his life's pleasure comes from his ability to create beauty for others to enjoy. When asked what advice he could give to aspiring daylily growers, he said, "Visit demonstration gardens first, to find out which cultivars do well in your area, and which ones you like. Go on an early summer morning to catch most cultivars at their best. The hot, humid weather of late summer fades the colors quickly. The cultivars called 'rebloomers' offer a special advantage. When the first 'scapes,' or blossom sprays, have finished blooming, additional scapes develop to prolong the production of flowers.

"Unless you are making solid plantings of dwarf daylilies for groundcovers, plant them in groups of three or five of the same cultivar for best effect. Don't jumble up a bunch of different cultivars in the same bed; they will look like a hodgepodge. If you want to show several different cultivars in one bed, intersperse low-growing perennials between them, especially those with silvery leaves or blue flowers. Daylilies will take a half day of shade but the blossoms will face the sun. Keep that in mind when choosing a site for daylilies.

"Realize that individual daylily blossoms remain open only one day but are replaced by new flowers the following day. This is why planting a cultivar with a high bud count is so important. You may not be able to be home at ten A.M.; that is the best hour for freshness and color. Yet, some of the harsher colors look better to me when the afternoon sun has subdued them. Conversely, some of the dark colors lose a lot of character when faded by the sun. When evening comes, you will be glad for planting light-colored cultivars such as the creams and light yellows because they will show up better at dusk.

(Left) Brother Charles spaces his evaluation rows for easy cultivation with a small power tiller.

"If you can, plant daylilies in front of evergreens or deciduous shrubs. They display better with a green background. But, avoid planting them too near greedy, aggressive shrubs that will rob them of nutrients and water. Work organic matter deeply into the area to be used for planting, and don't set crowns any deeper than they grew in the container or nursery bed.

"If you have a choice, plant daylilies in September. They will bloom the next year. Spring-planted daylilies often are shy about blooming the first season. Large, containerized plants get off to a fast start but, often, only the old standard varieties are offered in containers. Some mail-order sources offer young plants grown in pots.

"Your plants may occasionally have problems with spider mites and various leaf spots. Neither is terminal, but both will disfigure plants. I have a thirty-gallon power sprayer and use captan, Benlate and malathion, but only when I see outbreaks.

"In my rich soil modified with leaf mold, I feed only once a season, in spring with 5-10-5, worked in. Our deep soil seldom requires watering, except for newly transplanted seedlings, but I did have to turn on the sprinklers during the 1988 drought. I get color from late June through September, counting the rebloomers. Few other flowers can match that. Home gardeners can get color over such a long season, also, by choosing cultivars for season of bloom as well as for color and height.

"I like to divide daylilies more often than other specialists because the young plants are so vigorous, and because I need to grow several plants for proper evaluation of a new seedling. Every second year, I dig up old crowns with a spading fork, wash them off with a sharp spray of water, and use a sharp, stiff butcher knife to cut the crowns into four pie-shaped segments. I don't separate crowns into individual plants or 'fans' because some would not bloom until the second year. If I miss a crown and it grows large and dense, I do the first dividing with a sharp spade, and then pick up the knife.

"On the deciduous daylilies, which make up most of my collection, the tops shrivel to practically nothing after a hard winter. I leave them in place and twist them off during spring cleanup."

I asked Brother Charles for a starter list of daylilies for beginners—cultivars he really likes. After much hemming and hawing, which is typical for anyone who has seen thousands of cultivars, he offered this list:

- 'Priceless Pearl': A pale yellow tetraploid with a pink blush. The petals are edged with a golden yellow band, and have lacy, ruffled margins. Individual blossoms can reach 6 inches in diameter on 36-inch plants. *A late bloomer.*
- 'My Sunshine': These tetraploid plants are somewhat shorter than 'Priceless Pearl', with yellow blossoms up to 7 inches in diameter, suffused with pink and cream. Ivory midribs and deep golden, heavily ruffled petal margins add character to the large flowers. The recurved sepals that back up the three petals are blushed pink toward the centers. *Midseason.*

A subtle overlay of yellow on a cream base lights up a garden. This is BC 88-14, still under evaluation.

- 'Heavenly Treasure': A most unusual tetraploid with a yellow-to-olive-green throat that sets off the apricot-melon petal color. The 36-inch-high plants sport blossoms of 6½-inch diameter. A thin yellow edge and tight, lacy ruffles dress up the petals. *Midseason.*

Brother Charles is a cheerful man who delights in recalling the many pleasant and humorous experiences he has enjoyed in daylily breeding. One of his favorite stories is the reaction of a fellow daylily breeder when he first saw the Reckamp cultivar 'Heavenly Treasure'. "Brother Charles," he said, "if this is what I can expect to see in heaven, I'm going to start leading a better life!"

If there is any connection between a hobby plant and one's reaching a serene, productive old age, I believe that Brother Charles has found it . . . in daylilies.

More about Daylilies

My first recollection of daylilies was of a clump thrown on a pile of coal ashes and clinkers in an alley in Paducah, Kentucky. I was only five years old, but can recall how impressed I was at how that plant took root, grew, and bloomed in that impossible situation! I wouldn't recommend such severe treatment for any plant, but daylilies are one tough flower. They will thrive in all but the most severe climates and on a wide range of soil types. You need to pay attention to one of their peculiarities. Daylilies are separated into two major categories: deciduous and evergreen. The deciduous types are adapted all across the North, New England, and the upper South. The evergreen types are preferred for the Deep South and warm West. The two types look and are grown much alike but the evergreen types die back only partially or not at all during the winter, depending on minimum temperatures.

Treat daylilies as a sun-loving flower. In the South and West, light afternoon shade won't hurt but, up north, shade can cause plants to stretch and to flower sparsely. You can tell when plants are receiving more shade than they like; flowering will be delayed and sparse.

Planting and Division

You can plant new daylilies or divide old crowns at any time after flowering. Containerized plants can be set in the ground in full bloom. Observe one precaution . . . up north, plant them by late summer. The crowns need several weeks to send out the anchor roots that keep them from being heaved out of the ground by frost. That complicates the dividing of late bloomers because some of them are still showing color in September. Wait out the blooming, and mulch the divided plants heavily to keep the ground warm enough for root formation well into the fall season.

Daylilies require dividing about every five years. First, cut off the top growth about 6 to 8 inches above the ground. Use two spading forks for dividing. Shove them deep into the middle of the crown, back to back and touching. Lever the handles to split the crowns, pull the spading forks out, and repeat the process crosswise to make four divisions. Uproot the crown with the spading forks, invert the segments, and blast off the soil with a sharp spray of water to expose the roots. You can strip individual plants, called "fans," from the segments but most gardeners prefer to plant the entire segment to get abundant color, and faster.

You can transplant crown segments or fans, water them in, and do nothing else . . . they will eventually get over the shock and regrow. The cut-back plants will bleach from the sun and suffer in silence. You can ease the adjustment and hasten recovery by mulching transplants with a light scattering of straw to cast shade and reduce evaporation. Common sense will tell you to water transplants well and frequently for several days.

I try to rotate daylily planting every four or five years when I divide the crowns. I plant the new crowns in soil that has been fortified with organic matter by tilling in green manure crops such as winter rye. Mulches of compost, rotted sawdust, or chopped straw help to maintain a high level of organic matter, which encourages beneficial predatory nematodes and predatory bacteria. I

Note the strong root system on these year-old hybrid daylily seedlings grown from seeds started indoors in late winter.

use organic fertilizers or concentrated manures to replace all but liquid fertilizers. This approach is too new to claim complete control, but it looks promising.

Rotating daylily beds in small gardens is, of course, impractical. There, the best approach, when daylilies begin to decline, is to dig up the crowns, divide them, and incorporate generous amounts of organic matter and organic fertilizers before replanting. Organic fertilizers are safer to use at planting time than dry granular chemical fertilizers.

Soil and Fertilizer

Despite the tolerance of daylilies for a wide range of soils, you need to add organic matter to the soil to get new plants or divisions off to a fast start and to get an acceptable show of color the first season after planting.

Add and mix in enough organic matter to build the beds up for good drainage in heavy soil, and to improve water-holding capacity in sandy soil: a layer of organic matter about 2 inches deep should be sufficient. Add and work in pelleted dolomitic limestone, if needed, to bring the soil pH into the 6.0 to 7.5 range. When planting, dig generous holes and make a mound of loose soil in the bottom of each. Spread out the roots of fans or segments and add or remove soil from the mound to position the crown level with the surrounding soil.

Don't add any fertilizer at planting time, except for a phosphate source. Young plants need to generate a new feeder-root system before they can take plant nutrients. Usually, two applications of balanced granular fertilizer per year will suffice for established plants: one in late spring and another just after blooming. You be the judge; if the foliage color begins to lighten (and it well might on poor, sandy soil), make a third application. Southern and western growers often make one or two applications of liquid fertilizer in addition to the granular feedings because of the length of their growing seasons. Be careful not to feed in the fall where winters are severe. Late fertilization can force plants to continue to grow later than they should, and delay the onset of dormancy. This makes plants vulnerable to injury from winter cold.

Hybridizing

Should you wish to cross daylilies to get a new seedling you can call your own, have at it. The odds of your finding a distinctive, different, and deserving seedling in the progeny of random crosses are about 1,000 to 1, but you wouldn't be ashamed to give any of the remaining 999 to your mother.

Start with valuable modern hybrids or tetraploids that differ considerably in color, blossom conformation, but that bloom at the same time. You can minimize seed sterility problems by crossing diploids with diploids and tetraploids with tetraploids. The flower parts are easy to reach and work with. I watched Brother Charles do it; here's how:

1. Select a female parent. Slit a flower bud that is about a day away from opening and trim off the petals so you can see the reproductive parts. Remove the pollen-bearing anthers. They are on long, translucent filaments that can be pinched off or tweaked off with tweezers. Tear off a square of aluminum foil and fold it to about half the size of your hand. Crimp it over the entire emasculated flower to exclude foreign pollen.
2. Within twelve to twenty-four hours, inspect the stigma of the covered blossom. If it feels sticky to the touch, it is receptive to pollen, ready for hybridization.
3. Select a male parent that is shedding pollen. Tap it into a small container such as a pillbox and transfer the pollen to the sticky stigma with a camel's-hair brush or a frayed toothpick. Pollen is large enough to be seen clearly; it should cling to the stigma.
4. Carefully cover the pollinated stigma to keep out insects, which could carry pollen from other daylily blossoms. If your timing was right, fertilization should take place and seeds should form. The first sign of success is a swelling of the ovary, behind the stigma. Label the cross in permanent ink with the names of the male and female parents and the date of the cross.
5. Watch the ripening seed pods. When they begin to turn brown, but before they split, gather them and put them in a warm, dry place to ripen. When the seeds are dry, shell them out and store them in a sealed bottle in the refrigerator until early the following spring.
6. Sow the seeds in vermiculite or in a special seed flat mixture and sprout and grow them under fluorescent lights. When the seedlings have four to six true leaves, transplant them to individual 2½-inch pots and grow them to a size large enough to move into the garden.
7. In late spring, harden off the seedlings and transplant them into a garden row, about 6 inches apart. Label the row with the parentage of the cross, date made, and date transplanted.
8. Although a few vigorous seedlings might form late-season blooms the same year, you won't be able to evaluate them properly until the second or third year. Discard or give away inferior seedlings or those which closely resemble either of the parents. Transplant any promising-looking seedlings to a flower border and invite a knowledgeable *Hemerocallis* specialist to see them in full bloom. They will probably tell you, "Close, but no cigar!" Don't be disappointed; beauty is in the eye of the beholder.

1) 2) 3) 4) 5)

Hybridizing Daylilies

Brother Charles's hybridizing process begins with these simple tools of the trade: cotton swabs, aluminum foil, scissors, scalpels, tags and marking pens, and envelopes for collecting pollen (1). The female parent is selected and tagged (2). Pollen-laden anthers and stigma of the female parent are visible in this photo of tetraploid seedling BC 87-15 (3). The anthers are removed and the flower protected from foreign pollen with a square of aluminum foil. When the stigma of the covered blossom feels sticky to the touch — within twelve to twenty-four hours — it is ready for hybridization. Pollen is applied from the male parent, and the cross is indicated on the tags (4), shown with these developing seed pods. The ripe seed pods of this tetraploid *Hemerocallis* (5) are at the prime stage for picking.

Weeding

Put away your chopping hoe when it comes time to weed around daylily plants. Daylily roots are shallow and deep cultivation can injure them. I prefer to use a push-pull scuffle hoe for weeding between plants and to hand-pull the weeds growing close to daylily clumps. Scuffle hoes slide just beneath the surface to stir the soil and uproot weeds without disturbing the roots of adjacent ornamentals. Mulching with pinestraw, composted pine bark, wood chips, or saltmarsh hay can greatly reduce the frequency of weeding.

Pests and Diseases

I haven't seen many insects on daylilies at the regional Victory Gardens. Occasionally, thrips or aphids will jump on weak cultivars as they begin to set blooms, but they are easy to control with botanical insecticides such as pyrethrum, or with insecticidal soap. Southern and western gardens occasionally suffer outbreaks of spider mites during hot, dry weather. Sharp sprays of water directed at the undersides of leaves will blast off many insects and mites, and a program of spraying with insecticidal soap should get rid of the rest. The important thing is to prevent small outbreaks of spider mites from spreading throughout your garden.

A serious problem with daylilies in the South and Southwest is with nematodes, especially on dry, sandy soils. The usual method of control is periodic fumigation of the soil with a chemical such as methyl bromide. I find that such drastic measures are self-defeating. A better approach seems to be using organic amendments and natural fertilizers to keep nematode populations at levels that create little or no injury to plants. Nematodes have always been present in warm-climate soils. They always will be and, in order to eliminate them, you have to kill every living thing in the soil.

Other than a few leaf spots, I have seen few diseases on daylilies. Good sanitation every spring, gathering and composting old leaves from deciduous species, seems to keep diseases in check.

Landscaping with Daylilies

Arranging daylilies in landscapes is not complicated. Heights range from about 12 to 48 inches at maturity; catalog listings are usually reliable. Your first consideration should be to place daylilies where they won't tower over plants growing behind them. Your second consideration should be toward selecting a range of blooming dates in cultivars to extend the season of color. Finally, look at colors, patterns, and fancy frills; lean toward the yellows and pastels, with just enough dark colors for a bit of variety. Too many dark hues can deaden a color scheme.

If you buy plants from a local grower or a mail-order source in your geographical region, you can count on getting adapted cultivars. Northern and midwestern growers will sell only hardy deciduous cultivars; southern and western growers will specialize in evergreen types.

A single, well-grown, mature plant of a tall daylily cultivar can make an impressive specimen. However, most daylily specialists prefer to plant individual cultivars in groups. If you have a large garden, you can plant three to five fans of the same cultivar in a circle about three feet across. In a small garden, where the impulse is to cram more variety into a given area, you can make up the group from different cultivars having related colors. Plants within groups should bloom together for impact; make up other groups from earlier or later cultivars to extend the season of color.

There must be more to this landscaping approach than the numerological significance of threes and fives. I see variations of such groupings used in many gardens. Grouping the same or related colors in threes or fives looks so much better than jumbling colors in a pastiche that gives the eye no rest and the stress-ridden mind no solace.

Miniatures and Dwarfs

You may want to try your hand at hybridizing "miniature" daylilies. They have been the center of the latest flurry of activity in daylily breeding, and interest is continuing to grow. Miniatures are distinct from dwarf daylilies. Surprisingly, the term "miniature," as applied to daylilies, doesn't necessarily pertain to the size of the plant. The American Hemerocallis Society classifies a miniature daylily as one having a flower of 3-inch diameter or less, with no mention of plant height.

If short daylily plants with flowers larger than 3 inches are not miniatures, what are they? They are dwarfs. You can buy dwarf species daylilies, dwarf diploid (normal) hybrids, and dwarf tetraploids.

The increase in interest in container growing has helped to further advances in miniature and dwarf daylilies. Full-size clumps, with crowns a foot or more across, can be grown in 5- to 7-gallon tubs. Plants a year or two old can be accommodated in a 3-gallon can. The dwarf miniatures can also serve as edgings, giving a welcome change from liriope as an edging in the South. The most rugged miniatures are in the 12- to 18-inch height range, which makes them practical for edging taller daylilies or perennials.

As with all gardeners, I have my own set of preferences and biases. In daylilies, I like the bright or light colors that can be seen from a distance, rather than the darker hues that seem to disappear when the sun is low in the sky. I like a little frilling and waving on the petals but not so much doubling that the blossoms look clunky. Nothing pleases me so much, however, as a high flower bud count, which tells me I can expect fresh flowers to open every day for weeks. My great expectations for daylilies are seldom disappointed.

Roses

Charles and Lee Jeremias's life is filled with roses: growing, showing, and sharing them with others.

(Left) A view of the Jeremiases' front verandah evokes the timeless appeal of roses. The polyantha roses in the foreground are, left to right: the red-orange 'Golden Salmon', the white 'Clotilde Soupert', and the pink 'La Marne'.

Deep within the subconscious of every man or woman is a rose. What else could trigger instantaneous comparisons between freighted stimuli: fragrances, textures, forms—and roses. Where would we be without the simile "like a rose"?

Man never was good at leaving well enough alone. Despite the beauty, fragrance, and ruggedness of wild roses, man began domesticating and improving them long before the dawn of systematic botany. Rose culture had to be the province of the wealthy or educated because common man was busy dawn to dusk, wresting a living from the soil or the sea. But we can believe that he, too, responded to the beauty of the roses of the field. Perhaps it was this common experience that planted an archetypal rose in the soul of each of us.

Long ago, rose culture expanded beyond the great gardens of the wealthy and the few public gardens, into the gardens of less-favored people. Along the way, roses collected champions: military, clerical, scholarly, and purely commercial. Collectively, these friends of the rose raised the level of awareness of their favorite and improved the genus *Rosa* tremendously. The name "rosarian" became attached to one who knew enough about roses to be regarded as an "authority" by his or her peers.

Over the centuries, rosarians have developed arbitrary divisions for the huge genus *Rosa*, dividing it more by form and function than by species. Without being divided into categories, the genus would be incomprehensible. Novices would be so bewildered by the thousands of cultivars in commerce that they would not know where or how to begin learning about roses.

Since the turn of the century, rosarians have evolved tight standards for naming, recording, showing, and judging roses. Gradually, they are resolving differences in international standards and are attempting to coordinate research to make rose growing easier and more gratifying for everyone. Progress has been rapid since World War II. Prior to that time, when German was the accepted scientific language, international communications were mostly limited to scientists and the few multilingual European nurserymen. With the coming of English as the major language of commerce, scientists, nurserymen, and amateur rose enthusiasts worldwide can work together more readily at international rose conferences.

Generally, the United States rose trade is a bit looser about divisions than the European. You will doubtless recognize some of the standard divisions that appear in American catalogs: hybrid teas, floribundas, grandifloras, climbers, miniatures, shrub roses, old garden roses, and polyanthas. (These are discussed in greater depth in the section "More about Roses" at the end of this chapter.) Of these divisions, "old garden roses" is the most heterogeneous. Any rose introduced before 1867 is automatically in this category.

Botanical historians have exhaustively studied geological and archaeological findings to trace when roses first appeared in fossils and artifacts. Fossils can validate origins that might otherwise be obscured by introduced plant material. Botanical artifacts—paintings, sculptures, medallions, carvings—can augment written records of man's wanderings, systematic exploration, war- or famine-induced migrations, or territorial expansion.

(Right) An artful arrangement of old roses by Lee Jeremias: (clockwise from bottom) 'Sombreuil', 'Belle de Crecy', R. rugosa *'Alba'. Top: 'Salet', 'Shailer's Provence'; center, 'Paquerette'.*

Asia is believed to be the home of the greatest number of rose species of proven value. Reverence for roses was evident in early Chinese writings and, not much later, in poetry from India, Persia, and Southeast Asia. Always, roses were the stuff of romance, redemption, spirituality, grace, and surpassing beauty.

Rose species and "sports" (natural mutations) were collected, traded, bestowed as gifts, and transported over increasingly long distances as early centers of civilization expanded and coalesced. Long-distance transfers of plants were rare before the Crusades. Until that time, rose gardens were

filled with improved wild roses collected within the short range of trading ships, caravans, and limited military expeditions. Thus, each major center of civilization had its own set of rose species.

Roses, like tulips at a later date in Holland, were at times revered, exalted, and pursued to the point of irrationality. Blossoms, petals, oils, attars, and extracts were used prodigiously in festivals, anointments, funerals, and bacchanals. The numerous nurseries needed to produce fresh and dried rose blossoms for imperial Rome, at the expense of food production, were typical of the excesses and indulgences that toppled the empire.

The poignant effects of poverty, not only of the pocketbook but also of the mind, were typified in the decline and metamorphosis of rose culture during the Dark Ages. Cultivation persisted mostly around monasteries, where roses were grown more for medicinal uses than for landscaping or cut flowers. Commercial nurseries and royal gardens disappeared.

But, it would be a mistake to see the rose as a product of Christian endeavor. Islamic incursions into Europe—the Moors into North Africa and Spain, the sultans through the Balkans all the way to Austria—introduced Eastern species and highly refined landscape applications.

It was the spice trade that gave Renaissance scholars and gardeners access to the vast range of rose species from China, Southeast Asia, and, later, Japan. But it was not until the time of Josef Gottlieb Koelreuter in the mid-1700s that much progress was made in rose breeding. Well before Mendel, while working in the royal park at Karlsruhe, Germany, Koelreuter described the flower parts of roses and their functions.

Leadership in rose breeding moved around from France, Holland, and Germany to England and back, depending on the fortunes of royal or commercial underwriters of great gardens, and on freedom from the ravages of war. Competent and ethical nurseries developed to supply the demand for improved roses, including those from the Colonies.

The nineteenth century was the heyday of plant explorers from Europe and the United States. They descended on Afghanistan, China, Japan, India, Korea, and Burma. They were not always welcome and sometimes had to work through trusted, English-speaking native entrepreneurs. Some of the species roses in these areas are now threatened by agricultural expansion; these collectors may have saved certain wild roses from extinction.

North America is the home of several species of wild roses, but not until later years were these incorporated into the bloodlines used by plant breeders. For example, the first rose cultivar developed in the U.S.A. was produced from parental lines from Europe. This was 'Noisette', bred by John Champney of Charleston, South Carolina, in 1815.

Appreciation of roses in the United States is just as strong as in Europe. Roses are a bit more difficult to grow in many sections of the country, but easier in favored climates such as the West Coast. Some cultivars perform well in certain areas, but not in others. The trying winters across the North, and the heat and humidity of the South have necessitated the creation of American Rose Society Rose Testing Panels to evaluate the regional performance of new hybrids. Rose enthusiasts innovate new ways to grow, feed, water, prune, and spray roses to maximize performance under their particular conditions. While some cultural practices are common across the country, others vary widely.

The garden I visited is in South Carolina, on the northern edge of climate zone 7. It is large by any standard, with an old-fashioned, informal look. The dozens of beds are separated by broad turf paths. Neatly pruned modern and miniature roses are placed up front, with the huge, mounded plants of old-fashioned and shrub roses to the back and side of the property. Roses run up fences and over arches, mark boundary lines, and guide you from one section of the garden to another.

Mother's Day attracts visitors from all over the upstate of South Carolina to the rose garden of Charles and Lephon Jeremias in the historic town of Newberry. Families bring their mothers to see and smell the roses: some wear white roses to honor a mother who has passed on. Everybody calls Charles "Doctor" because he headed the chemistry department at Newberry College and holds a Ph.D. Lephon is known as "Lee," and hosts a local radio program, "Coffee with Lee," over station WKDK, Newberry.

The Jeremiases often grow old roses for identification. This tea rose grew from a cutting taken in an old cemetery; they are still trying to identify it.

One look at the rose garden of Charles and Lee Jeremias and you know it is a full-time activity. A closer look will reveal a few sensible concessions. When you learn the extent of the Jeremiases' involvement in the American Rose Society, rose shows, and community activities, you have to marvel at how they manage to keep their roses weeded, pruned, fed, and trained. Somehow they find time to care for nearly a thousand bushes, perhaps because they have sectioned off their garden and have planted each section with roses that require similar culture. Special areas are provided for old roses, miniatures, shrub roses, and modern hybrids such as grandifloras, multifloras, and hybrid teas. More than six hundred visitors showed up on Mother's Day the year the Jeremiases' garden was featured on *The Victory Garden*. Another six hundred or so trickle through the garden throughout the balance of the major bloom season, which, in an average year, can last into June. Every visitor is made welcome and headed out on a self-guided tour. Many visitors come especially to see the Jeremiases' collection of about six hundred old roses. Gradually, the Jeremiases are focusing on old roses because of their nostalgic charm and because the state of South Carolina has proved a good hunting ground for roses planted prior to the War Between the States.

It is obvious to visitors that Charles and Lee Jeremias are excellent rose growers and that they have an outstanding collection of old, modern, and miniature roses on their one-acre lot. What isn't obvious, and the Jeremiases aren't given to boasting, is the national standing of these two modest people. Charles was elected President of the 25,000-member American Rose Society in 1988, having worked up through ARS district and regional offices and a national vice-presidency. He is an ARS Life Judge of Long Standing and a Consulting Rosarian, often called on for advice in rose-growing.

Lee is a North Carolina farm girl by birth, an ARS Life Judge, and so knowledgeable about old roses that she took the first national trophy awarded to old garden roses in 1973.

The Jeremiases operate a small business, Bynum Manor Roses, chiefly as a vehicle for identifying, propagating, and preserving old roses that are adapted to the Southeast. The business was named for the Victorian home on the property, the townhouse of the original owners, the Bynum family. Charles and Lee do no plant breeding, other than watching for mutations that appear to have horticultural value. They sell a few old roses, which are difficult to obtain elsewhere, but the business is strictly secondary to their first love: growing and showing roses competitively. Their huge rose garden unquestionably helps them in exhibiting roses because of the choice it offers in varieties and blooms at various stages of maturity.

No quick answer comes when the Jeremiases are asked why roses mean so much to them. The answers may be rooted in their distinct personalities. Charles is a methodical man, analytical and precise, as one might expect in a chemist who holds important patents from his work in industry. His approach to taking up roses as a hobby in 1959 was typically objective. He cut out color pictures and descriptions of roses he liked, taped them on a board, studied them and rose gardening for a year, and finally bought seventeen plants for his first rose garden.

Lee is a natural gardener, strongly influenced by a dear and knowledgeable grandmother. She loves to recount how, as a wee girl, she grew curious about the progress of a rose cutting. Her grandmother was rooting it under a half-gallon Mason jar (which used to be the way most folks started rose bushes). Lee pulled up the plant to see if it was growing roots. Grandmother watched the tableau from the kitchen window, replanted the rose, and delivered a stern but loving lecture that cemented Lee's developing bond with gardening. Years later, when she was established as an authority on old roses, Lee returned to the old home place to help her grandmother identify an old rose that had been growing there for more than a hundred years. It turned out to be 'The Bishop', of the centifolia division.

Following a traditional education at Wake Forest, Lee worked in public relations for several years, then did something she really wanted to do. She took a two-year course in horticulture at Forsyth Tech. Along the way she began specializing in roses and winning top awards as an exhibitor. Judging followed, and she soon became respected for her fairness and helpfulness to exhibitors.

Both Charles and Lee were established rosarians when they married in 1981. They soon settled in at Bynum Manor, a rambling Victorian home surrounded by enormous sweet gum trees. They faced a full acre of neglected lawn, part of which had for years been under horse barns and corrals. Gradually, the side and back yards filled up with roses.

Even veteran rosarians such as Charles and Lee will, after some soul-searching, admit to having a favorite rose . . . or several. Lee likes 'Sombreuil', a fragrant white climbing tea. She calls it a "crowd pleaser." Then, 'Casino', a yellow pillar climber, and 'Dortmund' of the Kordesii class, red with a white eye. From the miniatures, she picks 'Jennie La-Joie', a climbing pink with tiny, exhibition-quality tea rose blooms.

Charles's first choice, "just for its marvelous fragrance," is the old 'American Beauty'. But to show his evenhandedness, he names a newer rose next, the yellow hybrid tea 'Sunbright'. For its historical significance he likes the first-ever polyantha rose, 'Paquerette', with clustered white blossoms brushed with pink. The colors of the tea rose 'Catherine Mermet' endear it to him . . . pink with overtones of lavender and white. From the miniatures he favors 'Rainbow's End', opening pure yellow and turning red.

Fragrance is high on the Jeremiases' reasons for preferring old roses. They recall with satisfaction the reaction of a blind and wheelchair-bound lady brought to the garden with a tour from the Council on Aging. Her attendant was fussing around wheeling her from place to place in the garden, when the blind lady stopped her. With her face wreathed in smiles she cried out, "Just leave me here, honey, I can smell every rose in the garden!" Such memorable experiences more than compensate Charles and Lee for the time they spend with visitors.

Charles has plenty of time for the garden, now that he is retired. Other than the period leading up to and during "Show Time!" at Mother's Day, he spends about sixteen hours weekly with the roses. Lee's job at the radio station leaves her only about half as much time. Visitors are amazed at the amount of work they do, and well, in such a few hours. Both are energetic and organized. Having done every task many times before, they whip through them quickly in order to have more time just to walk among and enjoy their roses.

It is frustrating to have the time and energy but not the space to grow more roses. The few trees on their property cast high afternoon shade, a desirable consideration for roses in the South (but not where summers are cooler). A deep edging each spring, with a sharp spade, cuts tree roots that would compete with the roses. All the incidental space is filled with containerized roses. Generous walkways have been provided to accommodate visitors, so they have no more lawn to convert to rose beds.

Charles and Lee are choosy about the roses they acquire, but they never discard any. A few plants were lost to the bitterly cold Christmas Eve freeze of 1985 when, following unseasonal weather in the 60s, the temperature plummeted to minus 3 degrees Fahrenheit. (Unaccountably, the old teas and hybrid perpetuals withstood the cold better than hybrid teas and floribundas.) A few more were lost to intensely hot and dry summers. The rugosa hybrids suffered most from the heat and dryness.

Chores around the rose garden are shared. "She does the buying, I do the planting," Charles jests. He does the weekly spraying, a necessary but tedious chore. Lee's legs are a bit younger, so she takes care of the miniatures to spare Charles the stooping. These two strong personalities do everything so well in rose-growing that they have found it works better if they labor separately in the garden rather than shoulder to shoulder. Yet, all the planning and preparation for shows is done together.

The Jeremiases have had to adapt traditional rose culture to their southeastern climate, soil, and unusual rose cultivars. Before planting a new acquisition, they research its origin for clues on how to grow and prune it.

New acquisitions usually arrive as small own-rooted or budded plants. Budding on a vigorous rootstock can mean better performance from a weak or disease-susceptible cultivar. However, many old roses are grown "own-rooted," which means not grafted. With the relatively mild winters at Newberry, own-rooted roses survive reliably.

New plants are potted up and grown on for a year, or until a place in the garden opens up. This gives the Jeremiases an opportunity to inspect the new plant for any sign of mosaic virus disease, and promptly pitch it if this transmittable systemic disease shows up.

Some of their roses are grown from cuttings given to them on visits to other growers of old roses, or from branches sent to them for identifica-

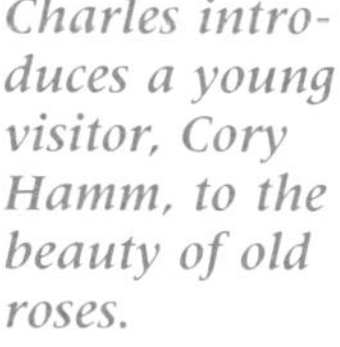

Charles introduces a young visitor, Cory Hamm, to the beauty of old roses.

tion. The cuttings are treated with Rootone rooting hormone and "stuck" in a propagating bed resembling a cold frame. The bed is filled with a mixture of equal parts of moistened peat moss, perlite, and white quartz sand. Softwood cuttings "take" quickly and form a good root system prior to winter.

The soil at Bynum Manor varies from heavy clay to sandy loam. Only the sandy spots dry out enough to require regular watering. Charles scrapes up basins around plants with a hoe and waters deeply, usually fertilizing at the same time.

The heavier soil has a high water table, and planting holes dug in the spring tend to fill with water. If they do, Charles dumps in a deep layer of gravel with a topping of soil, then positions the plant and backfills around it with native soil. He is careful to settle in the plant by flowing water around it to eliminate air pockets. Tramping down the heavy soil would compact it unnecessarily.

Own-rooted plants are set to a depth where the soil line in the container lines up with the surface of the garden soil. Grafted plants are set in with the bud union an inch or two below the soil line, to discourage sprouting by the understock. By northern standards, their roses, even the miniatures, are set far apart, because of the size to which rose plants develop in the Jeremiases' garden.

Upright rosebushes are grown without support. Climbers and large shrub roses are positioned around perimeter fences or at the back of the yard where wire trellises, resembling grape arbors, help in tying up plants and keeping them under control. The Jeremiases keep roses well away from walls because solid surfaces trap humidity and increase the incidence of foliar diseases.

Over the years, the Jeremiases have brought in so many leaves from neighboring yards that their soil is in excellent tilth. They compost the leaves in a pile so large that it would turn most gardeners green with envy. As the pile builds up, they scatter fertilizer and lime to speed the breakdown and to counteract the natural acidity. After the soil has warmed up in the spring, Charles and Lee dress the decomposing leaves around established rose plants. The mulch discourages weeds, conserves moisture, and prevents soil from splashing on the foliage. The continuing replenishment of organic matter in the soil also partly explains why their roses have never been damaged by nematodes, troublesome in some southern soils.

Charles's training as a chemist helps him select and use rose insecticides and fungicides efficiently. Summers in South Carolina are hot and humid. Without a regular preventative program, red spider mites, mildew, and blackspot would take over. For some time, Charles has alternated weekly sprayings with Orthene and Diazanon for insect and mite control. To prevent fungus diseases he uses Daconil 2787 and Triforene.

(Left) The old rose 'May Wallace', run up and over an arch of rebar steel, is an attention-getter.

(Right) 'Sweet Surrender' is one of the Jeremiases' favorites.

Sometimes, Actidione PM or Baleton is used, depending on the problem. All these are brand names for proprietary products.

Charles feels that waiting to spray until a problem is evident won't work in the South. "I don't believe in waiting until I see the whites of their eyes," he says. Yet, Charles and Lee are concerned about the amount of spray used, both from the standpoint of environmental responsibility and cost. They put away pump sprayers when they found that an electric Atomist unit did the job with only one-third as much active ingredient. Its only drawback is the long and heavy cord required to maintain the electric current while reaching all corners of the garden.

Recently, Charles began evaluating Safer Insecticidal Soap products for controlling insects, mites, and fungi. He hopes that these will reduce the amount of chemicals required to keep his roses clean, and the preliminary findings look good.

Their rose-feeding program is based on eight- to nine-month Osmocote Controlled Release Fertilizer and a potassium-magnesium source,

'Dortmund', a shrub rose of the Kordesii *class, flowers heavily.*

"K-Mag." Four ounces of each are top-dressed around established plants in the spring and covered with mulch. If growth appears to slow or if the foliage color goes off during the summer, Peters Plant Food, Schultz Instant Plant Food, or Ra-Pid-Gro is applied as a foliar spray and drench. Dolomitic limestone is worked into the soil as indicated by the soil tests, which Charles does himself.

The date and severity of pruning depends mostly on the habit of growth of the bush and whether the flower buds are formed on new or second-year growth. The Jeremiases handle the hybrid teas, floribundas, grandifloras, polyanthas, and hybrid perpetuals pretty much alike, pruning to four or five strong canes and shortening these to about two feet in length, somewhat longer than other rose specialists. They wait until January to begin, because such late (for zone 7) pruning causes new growth to come in in February and March, after the coldest weather is past. The new growth usually escapes frost damage because it has had time to harden off before late frosts come. January pruning is, of course, far too early for more northerly gardens.

The rather deep pruning of the exhibition roses concentrates the vigor of the bush into a few strong stems and generates larger blossoms for cutting and show. However, many of the old roses are grown more for landscape value than for exhibition. More often than not they are large, vigorous plants that can't be reduced to the size of modern roses without loss of color and plant vigor. And, some of them, mainly the climbers, bloom chiefly on second-year wood: deep spring pruning would reduce the number of blooms severely. Other old roses grow into shrub forms, some stiffly upright, and others arching and spreading.

The beautiful hybrid tea, 'Christopher Stone', circa 1935, is still found in some gardens.

Charles minimizes pruning on shrubby old rose varieties. Pruning of shrubby varieties consists mostly of tipping back unruly canes and removing weak or dead canes at the base. On those which are one-time bloomers, he delays pruning until after blossom drop. At that time he also removes weak canes flush with the crown. The plants bleed little because he paints the cut stems with a black material called "Tree-Cote," to prevent the cane borer fly from laying eggs.

On climbers, Charles first notes the stronger canes formed the previous year. They will be tipped back and saved because most of the blossoms will be formed on them. Then, he uses loppers to remove canes which are two years old, plus the weak year-old canes, by cutting them flush with the crown. Older stems are recognizable by their heavier bark and more knobby appearance.

Lee has found that little pruning is necessary on her miniature roses, other than occasional shaping and training, and removal of weak canes or those which are causing congestion in the center of the plant. Some of her miniatures grow three feet tall by the end of the season but are immediately recognizable from standard cultivars by their smaller blossoms.

For those interested in growing old roses, there are not many sources. Some of the best known have gone out of business, victims of catastrophic weather or of the difficulty of keeping the skilled labor required for propagation. Few people are qualified to operate old rose nurseries because of the encyclopedic knowledge of cultivars required and the extreme accuracy demanded to insure correct identification at every step in propagation and marketing.

Only one class of roses gives the Jeremiases difficulty in growing—the hybrid rugosas. They suffer more than other roses from hot weather and dry soil. Oddly, just one hundred miles north at Winston-Salem, the rugosas do pretty well. It may be that the slightly hotter, longer summers in South Carolina push the rugosas past their stress threshold.

Charles and Lee have some advice for beginners who are considering going into roses as a hobby. First, they advise, don't bite off more than you can chew. Start with no more than a dozen plants. Then, spend a few seasons gaining confidence in growing and in pest control. Before you get serious about showing, attend a few rose shows. Ask for copies of the schedules and read up on the various classes. Buttonhole one of the "helpers," the judges who are at shows to assist exhibitors. Ask them about points to look for or to avoid in showing. Generally, it isn't a good idea to bother exhibitors with questions when they are busy setting up or grooming. Some are so competitive and intent on what they are doing that they don't welcome questions.

Join your local Rose Society, they add, or, if you don't live in a city, sign up as a Member at Large. At Society meetings, rosarians are much more relaxed than at shows. They will cheerfully answer questions about stem length, cleaning foliage, grooming, and potential disqualifications. They can tell you how and when to disbud so that fresh scars won't disqualify your entry.

Most of all, keep a positive mental attitude. Be at shows when the doors open. Take one or two backup stems for each cultivar you intend to enter. Have your entry tags made out in advance. Enter the "Novice" class; some of the advanced exhibitors are so skilled that they could qualify as professionals. And, by all means, bring only as many roses as you have time to groom and set up; be selective in your entries.

On mental attitude, Lee Jeremias advises, "Don't take the decisions of judges personally. You may not win a ribbon your first time out. If you don't, ask a helper what specific shortcoming or disqualification you need to fix in your next rose show. Maybe it was nothing more serious than cutting your stems at the wrong time. We cut our old roses the evening prior to shows, and don't refrigerate them. Many exhibitors of modern roses do refrigerate them overnight. You have to know your cultivars to anticipate how far ahead of prime condition to cut, and how to transport them to shows."

You may not be as fortunate as Charles in his first garden and his first show. He grouped the first seventeen rosebushes he bought into a large raised bed. A lady saw them, stopped and identified herself as a local nursery owner, and complimented Charles's garden as the prettiest rose garden she'd ever seen. And, in his first show, he entered just one rose, a long-stemmed deep red 'Mr. Lincoln'. It took "King of the Show," second best among all entries. ("Queen of the Show" is tops.)

Lee grooms miniature rose blossoms for a show. She is brushing 'Pierrine'; 'Break O'Dawn' is in the white cup.

Your experience with roses will be more rewarding, the Jeremiases believe, if you collect a basic library of rose books. There is no single great American reference book on roses. Charles is a tireless researcher and has a large library, including many out-of-print books. Whenever he publishes papers or articles on old roses, he bibliographs to a depth and accuracy seldom encountered outside of universities.

Both Charles and Lee have a strong sense of public service. Their hobby gives them a means of serving others with garden tours while enjoying themselves. Yet it leaves time for Lee to work at a local radio station and for Charles to teach Sunday School and to lecture on roses. They haven't taken a conventional vacation since their marriage. Instead, they travel to ARS district and regional rose shows and to the two yearly meetings of the national.

Lee laughed when asked "What next?" in her career. She quipped, "I want to write a book entitled *Is There Life after Roses?*" Then she admitted she wants to exercise her gift for artistic arrangements—abstract and advanced compositions. Both she and Charles have enrolled as Apprentices in Artistic Arrangements with the ARS but Charles freely acknowledges Lee's advantage. She has an instinctive feel for it but his lifetime of disciplined effort may work against the spontaneity that inspires abstracts.

More about Roses

The best place to learn about roses is a rose garden, not a book. But it will help if you will take with you on your first visit to a rose garden, a list of the eight major rose divisions generally accepted by the American rose trade:

Hybrid Teas At one time the best known of the divisions, the hybrid teas were created by crossing the old tea rose of China with selections from other species. The original tea roses were marginally winter hardy and lacked the colors deep yellow and dark red. For many decades, rose breeders concentrated on hybridizing to improve this division through greater winter hardiness, broader range of colors and bicolors, repeat blooming, and increased vigor. Unfortunately, the majority of hybrid teas produced in the first hundred years of modern rose breeding lacked strong fragrance; some lacked scent entirely.

Exquisite blossom form is probably the best-known attribute of hybrid teas—high-centered, tightly wrapped, symmetrical in the bud stage, long-stemmed, with few distracting leaves on the upper extension of the stem. Breeders look for other features as well: vigorous plants of medium height, blossoms with strong necks and good holding ability before and after cutting, resistance to major diseases, brilliant color, and a strong, pleasant fragrance, preferably fruity or spicy.

By the year 1940, more than six thousand hybrid tea cultivars had been introduced. Many did not last long in the marketplace and were displaced by superior cultivars. Unfortunately, short-sighted hybridization had introduced or overlooked some undesirable characteristics into hybrid teas: susceptibility to certain major rose diseases, or lack of fragrance. Breeders abandoned the trouble-making lines and have restored the image of hybrid teas to its former glory. However, in the interim, breeding emphasis began to shift to other divisions. If you like to display long-stemmed roses in vases, individually or in arrangements, you should have some hybrid teas in your garden. There are better landscape roses, but none can match the elegance of hybrid teas for cut roses.

Floribundas A floribunda can be recognized at a glance from its medium- to large-sized blossoms borne in clusters. A quick guess can often be validated by a sniff: most floribundas are scentless.

Rose breeders listened to the buying public when they developed floribunda roses. All cultivars are in the short to medium height range preferred for landscaping. The plants are rugged, dark green, and vigorous, except for the yellow colors, which tend to look less robust.

Most floribundas are winter hardy except in the northern Great Plains and upper Great Lakes area, where winter protection is advised. Nearly every color known to the rose world has been incorporated into this division.

Some time ago, rose breeders began infusing more hybrid tea blood into the floribundas to produce larger blossoms with the depth of tea roses. That trend continues and is already blurring the distinction between floribundas and the newer grandifloras. Certain of the newer floribundas have loose clusters of medium-sized blossoms, with tight, high-centered, vase-shaped buds, much like down-scaled hybrid tea blooms.

Grandifloras If you are just starting to buy roses, the place for the grandifloras is in ranks behind lower-growing floribundas and hybrid teas, or in tall flowering hedges.

This greater height, up to six or seven feet in warm climates, is only one of the hallmarks of the grandifloras. Additionally, they have large blossoms of the classic double tea rose conformation, borne in small clusters. Some of the first cultivars in this recently created division were not quite as hardy as contemporary floribundas, but the newer ones are. Some grandifloras lack scent and only a few have strong fragrance.

The distinctions between grandiflora, floribunda, and hybrid tea roses are wavering as breeders strive for repeat blooming, larger and better-formed blossoms, somewhat shorter plants, and intensified winter hardiness. Breeders are also working on strengthening disease resistance and incorporating fragrance in new releases.

Climbing Roses "Climbing" roses are tall bushes with very long canes that can be espaliered, tied to trellises, or run over arbors. Some were developed from tall mutations from bush cultivars and bear names such as 'Climbing Peace'. Others have no bush rose counterparts. You may think of climbers as old-fashioned, more appropriate for the Victorian era when the tall vines could be trained up porch pillars and high walls. But, gardeners are discovering that contemporary landscapes can benefit from the addition of arbors, trellises, and pillars for training climbers. These vertical accents can add considerable interest to otherwise flat landscapes. The Rose Garden at the National Arboretum is an excellent example.

When you buy climbers you may find them divided into three groups:

Ramblers Perfect for draping over fences, the late-blooming, nonrepeating ramblers have long, limber stems and numerous clusters of small flowers. Most are winter hardy but, when espaliered against a wall, tend to get mildew disease from the still, moist air.

Some of the famous old ramblers such as 'Dorothy Perkins' have no scent; their appeal was in the tremendous show of color they put on at peak bloom season in early summer. They have largely been superseded by the large-flowered climbers that have heavier, less pliable canes, bloom over a longer span, and which are fragrant. Some of the ramblers can escape in mild climates and infest pastures. Their low, spreading growth and habit of rooting wherever they touch the ground make them extremely difficult to eradicate. (Except for kudzu, 'Dorothy Perkins' is the worst weed on my farm.)

Large-Flowered Climbers This group includes not only the popular climbing hybrid teas, but also the half-hardy *Bracteata* and *Gigantea* cultivars known mostly in California. The stems are longer and stiffer than the ramblers and tend to grow more erect.

Most cultivars are fragrant and the newer ones are repeat bloomers. Before you buy, ask about winter hardiness. Severe dieback or pruning can reduce bloom on marginally hardy climbers.

Some old roses go way back. 'Austrian Copper', an R. Foetida *bicolor, left, was introduced in 1590, 'Old Blush', center, in 1752. The Eglantine or Sweetbriar rose, right, was first mentioned in writings dated 1551.*

Pillar Roses These plants have shorter, sturdier canes that can be pulled together and tied up to a pillar, or trained up a tall cage. The flowers and foliage are altogether beautiful and the plants are hardier as a group than the large-flowered climbers.

Modern Shrub Roses You will be seeing more of these roses as tolerance to extreme cold, disease resistance, and repeat-blooming traits are strengthened. Four distinct types are currently in the forefront of shrub roses: they are hybrids incorporating the species *Rosa rugosa, R. rubiginosa, R. spinosissima,* and *R. moschata.*

Of these four, much of the recent North American work has centered on *R. rugosa* hybrids. The Canadian Department of Agriculture has recently released new *R. rugosa* hybrids with great cold tolerance, extended bloom, disease resistance, and large, colorful hips. These were developed for low-maintenance landscaping and as a source of winter food for birds.

While shrub roses vary considerably in appearance, you can, with a little practice, recognize them. As compared to the grandifloras, for example, *rugosa* hybrids usually have lower, denser, more solid looking bushes, some with rough-surfaced, ribbed leaves.

Rosa rubiginosa hybrids have dense, upright bushes, loads of medium-sized, fragrant, single blossoms, and apple-scented foliage. Traditionally, the *rubiginosa* hybrids have been more important in Europe than in the United States.

Rosa spinosissima is a name given to hardy cultivars developed from the wild species *R. pimpinellifolia.* Selections from the species were used as parents in *spinosissima* hybrids. Gardeners use these hybrids as background plants where their tall, open, lanky bushes can arch out to their heart's content. One of the first roses to bloom, the *spinosissima* hybrids are covered with large, fragrant, single or double blossoms.

One of the parents of modern hybrid musk shrub roses is *R. moschata*, the musk rose. It contributed a heavy but pleasant fragrance that characterizes the class, regardless of the modern rose used as the other parent. The vigorous plants grow five feet tall in most areas and up to eight feet high in the South and West. The clustered flowers are short-stemmed, medium in size, semidouble, and numerous, and come in red, pink, or creamy white and yellow shades. The plants bloom over a long period and bear attractive hips in the fall and winter.

Old Garden Roses The name evokes images of quaint, charming rose gardens, but will your dream characters be dressed in medieval or Victorian costumes? Any date before 1867 will do. The American Rose Society chose this cutoff date; any garden rose introduced prior to 1867 will be entered in the Old Garden Rose division. This division is the largest, if not the most popular among all roses.

Most old garden roses are selections from wild species, but some are old natural or manmade hybrids, or mutations. The cultivars you are most likely to see in the gardens of old rose specialists are derived from:

Rosa alba, the white rose
R. burboniana, the Bourbon rose
R. centifolia, the cabbage or Provence rose
R. chinensis, the Chinese rose
R. damascena, the damask rose
R. gallica, the French rose
Hybrid perpetual or remontant rose
Portland rose
Tea rose

Miniature Roses Tiny blossoms, but not necessarily tiny plants, distinguish miniature roses. Miniature roses, however, are not toys; they are sturdy, cold-hardy, reblooming garden and container flowers that are beginning to win high marks in the "Award of Excellence" competition established by the American Rose Society as well as All-America Rose Selections awards.

Some miniature roses grow only fourteen to eighteen inches high and spread out twice as wide; this type makes good container or hanging-basket roses. Others, under long-summer conditions, can reach thirty inches in height. However, if you look at the tiny individual blossoms or blossom clusters, you can immediately tell that they are miniatures, not low-growing, large-flowered standard roses.

It is significant that miniature roses boomed in popularity at about the time that soilless growing media became widely available, when fluorescent lights became the norm for indoor growing, and when controlled-release fertilizers proved their value for rose culture. All these advances made the growing of miniature roses in pots, larger containers, and hanging baskets easier and more reliable.

By the way, "minis" are not just for containers: they do well in outdoor plantings, excelling as edgings, bedding, or low background plants in well-drained soil and full sun. They combine beautifully with perennials, annual flowers, and seasonal bulbs.

Rose breeders have been able to transfer almost all desirable rose traits to miniatures, while retaining a height range of three to eighteen inches (under northern climates)—all colors, winter hardiness, disease resistance, and repeat blooming. Some of the cultivars are scentless. A few climbing miniatures have been introduced but are regarded by most rose enthusiasts as curiosities.

Polyantha Roses You won't find many polyanthas in general nurseries in the U.S.A.; the division has been largely supplanted by the floribundas. This old division is not sufficiently venerable to fall under the Old Garden Rose division. It dates back to the bringing of a pink, semidouble form of *Rosa multiflora* to England. As a parent in crosses, it produced plants with numerous clusters of small flowers. Some polyantha cultivars are single-flowered; others are double.

Note: not to confuse you, but the American Rose Society recognizes many more categories of roses than these few divisions. They do it mostly so judges can compare "apples with apples" and "oranges with oranges" at rose shows. The additional categories include climbing cultivars of standard rose classes, greatly changed selections from species roses, and hybrids between species that don't fall into any of the major divisions. You can find these categories listed in the fine booklet updated annually by the American Rose Society, entitled *Handbook for Selecting Roses.*

Planting Bare-Root Roses

You can buy rosebushes as "dormant" or "containerized." Dormant bushes are dug from the growing fields after the leaves have dropped (or have been removed by a defoliant) and are cut back severely, graded, and often waxed to reduce evaporation from the stems. They are usually sold in illustrated bags enclosing shavings around the roots to keep them moist. Containerized roses are grown by potting up dormant roses in containers of 2- to 3-gallon size.

Dormant roses are usually planted in the fall in zone 5 and farther south, and in late spring where winters are extremely severe. In zones 5 and 6, fall-planted roses should be mulched after the surface of the soil freezes, to minimize heaving from freezing and thawing. Spring-planted roses bloom little the first season and should be watered faithfully during the early summer, when they are putting down roots.

Soak the roots of dormant roses in tepid water for a day before planting. Trim off frayed or broken roots and dig planting holes before bringing the plants out in the drying wind. Pour the holes full of water and let it soak in, but don't wet the soil to be used for backfilling. If your plants arrive during very cold weather, pot them up in containers of planter mix and let them develop a root system for a month before tapping them out and setting them in the ground.

Make planting holes for rose bushes 18 to 24 inches across and 12 inches deep. Allow 3 feet space on all sides of the bush, and 4 or 5 feet for climbers or large shrub roses. Mix moistened sphagnum peat moss or pulverized pine bark with the excavated soil, one part to three parts soil, and, if your soil is poor, mix in a cupful of superphosphate to encourage rooting. Shovel a cone-shaped pile of amended soil into the center of the hole, then spread out the roots and fit them over the cone. Lay a shovel handle across the hole and raise or lower the plant until the soil line on the central stem of the plant is about 1 inch below the shovel handle. This places the "bud union," the point where the desirable rose wood was grafted to the rootstock, about 1 inch beneath the surface of the soil.

Depth of planting is extremely important. Too-deep planting can cause roses to refuse to bloom properly or can bring on root rot in heavy soil. Yet, if you expose the bud union fully or partially by shallow planting, the understock may try to shoot up sprouts.

Some authorities recommend filling in 2 or 3 inches of soil around the roots, treading on it to firm it down, shoveling in another layer and treading on it, and so on until the hole is filled level with the surface of the soil around it. This works fine if you amend your soil with organic matter or if it is naturally sandy. However, if you are working with moist, heavy clay, treading on it will squeeze out the air spaces and make it so dense that it won't drain. It would work better if you trickled water in slowly as you shovel in layers, to make the clay flow among and around the roots. The idea is to firm the soil just enough to eliminate big pockets of air, which could dry out the roots.

On poorly drained, heavy clay soils in high rainfall areas, rose beds should be built up 3 or 4 inches above the surrounding soil. That guarantees that the bud union won't be submerged under standing water.

Containerized roses can be transplanted to the garden at almost any time, even when they are in bloom. Northern growers know to get their containerized roses in by late summer so they will have plenty of time to send down roots before the soil grows too cold for root proliferation. Some nurseries rush the sale of containerized roses, before a good root system has formed. You may want to slide a root ball out of a container and check it before purchasing; the root ball should not fall apart and it should not be matted and girdled with roots.

Planting Containerized Roses

When setting containerized roses in the garden, be aware that they are usually grown in artificial mixes containing principally organic matter and little or no soil. Roots may find it difficult to grow beyond the confines of the root ball if the texture of the surrounding soil is too different. Therefore, you should amend the backfilling soil with moist peat moss or pulverized pine or fir bark to raise its level of organic matter.

Gently clean the planter mix away from the central stem of the bush and check the depth of the bud union below the surface. It should be about 1 inch deep. If it is deeper, shave off the top of the planter mix until the union is at the right depth. Before setting the root ball in the hole, brush off any roots that are girdling the sides or the bottom. Firm the soil in the bottom of the hole so that it won't settle and position the plant so that the top surface of the root ball is level with the surrounding soil. Settle backfill soil around it layer by layer, by either treading on it or trickling water over the backfill.

Newly planted roses, dormant or containerized, should be watered every three or four days when the weather is dry. A square of the recently introduced spun-bonded synthetic landscape cloth, 2 feet on the side, can be laid over the soil around the plant. Weeds won't come through it. Cover the landscape cloth with hardwood mulch, pulverized pine or fir bark, freshly chipped wood or bark nuggets to keep the soil cool and to conserve moisture.

Antique Fruit Trees

Elwood Fisher, Virginia Renaissance man, "rescues the perishing" by finding and saving ancient fruit tree varieties for posterity.

The apricot cultivar HW 407 escaped spring frosts to fruit heavily at Harrisonburg, Virginia.

The "tree fruits" include all the species and cultivars of fruit borne on trees or large shrubs, but not the "small fruits" borne on bushes, canes, vines, or small herbaceous plants. The tree fruits predate most of man's other food plants because man did not have to cultivate them: he simply had to beat the animals to the ripening fruits, and reach or climb up and pick them. Later, man learned how to preserve fruit by drying, and it became one of his principal foods.

By the time the first "permanent" settlers sailed for North America, a huge pool of improved selections from fruit tree species had been developed in Europe. Previously, traders and warriors as far back as Alexander the Great had brought seeds and cuttings to Europe from all over the known world. Significantly, one of the most important items brought to North

America with colonists were fruit tree seeds and cuttings. Parts of the New World proved very favorable to tree fruit culture, but some areas were disappointing. Colonists discovered a number of new fruits in North America, including native plums and beach plums, papaws, persimmons, and the red mulberry, *Morus rubra*. They were also mystified to find peach trees, not realizing that Indian tribes, on their journeys to Florida, had brought back and planted peach pits from old Spanish settlements.

The few colonists who were farmers understood how particular tree fruits can be about site, soil, exposure, and length and dependability of season. It was difficult to transpose European experience to this vast continent, with its wild swings in temperature, extremes of weather, and hungry wildlife. Yet, within a few years, colonists had begun to stake out sloping land near bodies of water or hilly table land shielded by mountains.

Later, as successful home growers expanded and began to sell their fruits and fruit products, locations near navigable waterways became a consideration. Fresh fruit and cider were too fragile or heavy for oxcart transportation over rough roads. Dried fruit and cider became important export items in the colonial economy and, when faster sailing ships were developed, fresh fruit joined the list. Settlements in the West Indies were especially good markets because pome and stone fruits grow poorly in the tropics.

Looking back on the statistics for fruit production in colonial days, it is unbelievable how much fruit and cider were produced by small farmers for home consumption and sale. Fruit was prepared in so many ways: it was dried, made into fruit leathers, boiled down into syrups to use as a sugar substitute, preserved as fruit butters in crocks, but, above all, expressed for fermentation into cider. Colonial cider was strong stuff, running 12 to 15 percent alcohol, yet was the most popular beverage excepting (arguably) water. Northern farmers soon learned how to concentrate cider even further by letting barrels of cider freeze and drawing off the concentrated hard cider liquid.

One reason cider was so important was that European varieties of grapes could not be grown successfully in our climates, despite many attempts. Wine had to be imported. Stills for making liquor from grains were yet to come.

A wide selection of fruits was grown by the home gardeners and farmers for the next three centuries. Apples were the shoo-in favorite, followed by pears, peaches, plums, cherries, apricots, nectarines, quince, figs, and medlars. The old trees planted around settlers' homes languished as towns grew up around them and city people began buying rather than growing fruits and vegetables. A few trees, however, lived to great ages, two hundred years for apple trees in favorable climates.

The concentration of people in cities led to the development of commercial tree fruit orchards in favorable climates, near rail transportation or

Elwood propagated this ancient pear by grafting a cutting to a seedling pear understock.

navigable rivers. Apples, pears, and cherries, which are not notably resistant to summer heat or extremely cold winters, were grown in cool, upland areas. Early-blooming peach and cherry orchards were located where bodies of water and sloping land protected them against loss of blossoms or young fruit to late freezes. The mid-Atlantic and southern colonies offered many good peach and fig sites. Among the peach sites were a few especially favored locations where the more demanding apricots and nectarines could be successfully grown. Plums are very adaptable, especially the native species, but have never been as popular as the leading tree fruits.

Until this era, tree fruit cultivars were selected for flavor, juice content for cider making, season of maturity, winter hardiness of the rootstock and scion, season of bloom, self-fertility, and production. Farmers had long since mastered the principles of grafting: in fact, they were as good or better at it than we are now. They had little or no means of insect or disease control, but their tolerance for blemishes on fruit was greater, and they could always consign wormy apples or bruised pears to the cider press or vinegar vats.

Then, as shippers began to control the fruit market, and the equipment and chemicals for pest control became available, specialists in fruit trees emerged. They began to tinker with the dwarfing rootstocks from Europe, to give farmers smaller trees, handier for picking, pruning, and pest control. The thickness of skin, color, size, and holding quality in cold storage became important considerations. Many fine-tasting old fruit cultivars brought from Europe were discarded because of the small or soft fruits of indifferent color, too-dry or too-juicy flesh. Even some of the selections made in North America, early in the life of the Colonies, such as 'Rhode Island Greening', became obsolete.

Tree fruit nurseries geared up to meet the demand for the new cultivars, customized for commercial production. This marketing shift decided the cultivars which would be principally available to home gardeners until a revival of interest in the delicious old varieties occurred. Brief but significant booms in fruit tree growing occurred during the Liberty or War Garden days of World War I and the Victory Garden days of World War II.

All the while, with every passing year, antique tree fruit cultivars were disappearing. Once gone, fruit tree cultivars cannot be retrieved. For a long time, virtually no one seemed to care that this irreplaceable genetic treasure was being allowed to slip away. We are all beneficiaries of the foresight of the few people who did care, and did what they could to save what was still left. Their concern has grown into a worldwide movement with networking and exchanges to lessen the chance of losing rare cultivars, some of which were literally down to only one tree in all the world.

Elwood shows me that fruit size decreases when the trees are not thinned.

At his home in Harrisonburg, Virginia, Elwood Fisher maintains one of the finest collections of antique varieties of fruit trees, grapevines, and berry bushes in North America. His orchard and vineyard cover more than half an acre of his back yard and adjacent property leased from a neighbor. And while other fruit tree hobbyists might grow trees for fun or profit, Elwood grows principally because he is concerned about the loss of germ plasm when antique cultivars of fruits and berries die out. His hobby has gained him international notice.

Friends marvel at how much Elwood accomplishes in the time remaining from his teaching position at James Madison University. He leads wildflower tours deep into the mountains of his native West Virginia, teaches courses on identifying and using wild foods, including mushrooms, leads birding expeditions, and is a consulting parasitologist. That's just what he does away from home!

Inside and all around the Fishers' home are signs of his skill as a craftsman. Beginning twenty-one years ago, he and his wife, Madge, took a roughed-in house and gradually converted it into a beautiful home. Outside, hundreds of feet of precisely laid stone walls, more than head-high in places, are his handiwork. Each chunk of broken limestone is fitted with a flat surface out, and the mortar joints are raked and brushed out to a uniform 1-inch depth. The walls break his steeply sloping lot into terraces; they required heavy poured footings and extensive drainage to prevent buckling under hydraulic pressure.

Before we toured their beautiful home and gardens, Madge served us a generous piece of marvelous apple pie. We talked about what led up to Elwood's strong sense of commitment and his well-developed skills as a plantsman, artist, and craftsman.

Fortified with apple pie, Elwood and I meandered around the house and adjacent gardens, with many stops to admire unusual plant material and constructs. The front entrance and heavily used areas inside the home are floored with serpentine, but the construction that really catches your eye is a wall-to-wall fireplace made of strips of serpentine.

Stonework is Elwood's thing; for several years, dynamic Madge busied herself hanging the wall and roof insulation and doing much of the fine finishing inside the house while Elwood was wheelbarrowing seventeen tons of stone through their front door.

More stonework lies outside. All around the house are sculptures made from the stone excavated from the home site and, in the back lawn, you can see the flat tops of huge limestone boulders left in place rather than blasted out. Madge and Elwood chipped out cavities to use as bird feeders and they work beautifully. Inside the home are several of Elwood's whimsical wood or stone sculptures, sleek and functional or slyly amusing.

Alongside the house is an exquisite Japanese garden, actually a deep grotto with walls made of water-worn limestone. Some of the pieces are of awesome size. Elwood described, with understandable pride, how he singlehandedly maneuvered each piece into place using a simple iron pipe tripod to lift, and the power of his International Harvester Scout to skid stones into place. Then, he used hydraulic jacks to tilt and rotate rocks so that they fitted the design in his mind's eye. You can walk across the grotto on thick cylinders of limestone standing on end. (They are actually 16-inch-thick cores from holes drilled on a nearby building site, to accommodate the hydraulic equipment of an elevator.)

Elwood realizes that the time has come to begin winding down some of his more physical projects. Although still in good condition, he is of World War II vintage and has to pace himself on heavy jobs. Reminders of the long hours he works around the house and yard are everywhere but none more telling than the tall poles for streetlights that enable him to work in the yard at night.

Searching out and saving ancient fruit trees, berry and grape varieties, south to Georgia and the Carolinas and north through New York State, has taken much of Elwood's spare time and energy for twenty-odd years. The expense in time and travel has been considerable. He continues his crusade largely because he is uniquely qualified to find and preserve old fruit tree cultivars.

The area of West Virginia where he was raised was settled in the 1700s largely by German immigrants. These good farmers brought cuttings (scions) of fruit trees, berry bushes, and grapevines over with them, often keeping cuttings alive by sticking the cut ends in potatoes. Over the mountains to the east, major landholders of English stock, including Thomas Jefferson, imported starts of apple trees of varieties they or their forebears knew and grew in the old country.

Early on, Elwood was marked for growing fruit trees. His grandfather Shuman, on his farm near Clarksburg, had eighty-four varieties of apples, pears, peaches, plums, gooseberries, and currants. By the time Elwood was seven years of age, his grandfather had him grafting fruit trees. As the two of them traveled around the coves and ridgeland, his grandfather would point out old trees and have Elwood memorize their

A bird's-eye view of Elwood's orchard shows the density of planting and the size of the trees, all of which have multiple grafts.

variety names. Elwood told me, with mixed pride and regret, "I have found every apple cultivar that Grandfather Shuman grew except the one named 'Seedless' (without pips). It was developed in Vermont in 1869."

His grandmother Fisher figured equally in teaching mountain skills to Elwood. While Grandfather Fisher ran a country store, Grandmother served as the local folk authority on herbal medicine; she diagnosed by looking at patients . . . the color of their eyes, skin, and nails, condition of their hair, and other signs that old-time general practitioners knew to watch for. Customers got "doctored" while they were shopping for supplies and clothing.

Elwood tagged along behind his grandmother while she collected native plants, and cultivated vegetables and herbs for poultices, potions, antiseptics, emetics, and expectorants. She knew not only where to find the plants she wanted, but when to harvest them and how to store them for maximum potency. Twenty years later, when Elwood went on his first field trip with a botany class, he amazed the professor by identifying every plant and giving its medicinal use.

Elwood remembers his grandmother collecting yellow root, ginseng, black cohosh, golden ragwort, may apple roots, and dozens of other species for medicine, and how his grandfather sold smokeless sumac wood to moonshiners. At night, his grandmother practiced the traditional German "fractur" art of embellishing marriage licenses, certificates, and homilies with traditional German art.

Elwood was only seventeen when, late in World War II, he volunteered for the U.S. Navy. Seeing the world convinced Elwood that he didn't wish to follow the strict Dunkard upbringing of his childhood, but a driving curiosity about other religions and cultures led him into divinity school, and later into studies of art and history and, finally, botany. School followed a hiatus of several years after he came home, during which he worked as a lineman for a power company and as a welder on a pipeline.

Elwood and Madge met when she was teaching home economics in Ohio and he was teaching high-school biology, history, and art. Later, he completed work on his masters in zoology at Miami University. Madge also helped while he went on to get his doctorate in biology at Virginia Polytechnic Institute in Blacksburg. Since he "owed her one," Elwood helped her become certified in library sciences, once he joined the staff at James Madison University. Madge is now a librarian at an elementary school in Rockingham County.

Elwood wasn't thinking about fruit trees during their first years in Harrisonburg; he was busy teaching medical entomology, parasitology, ornithology (Grandma taught him birds, too), zoology, and history of botany. Then, three developments conspired to shape his future for him. First, he watched with concern as southern corn blight disease threatened to decimate the corn crop because geneticists had allowed the gene pool of maize to shrink. Next, the Seed Savers' Exchange asked him to collect seeds of old varieties to assist them in preserving germ plasm. But the turning point came when someone asked him if he knew where to find the old apple variety 'Winter Banana' that had originated in Indiana. Yes, he knew just where to find 'Winter Banana' . . . on Grandfather Shuman's farm, where he had seen it as a lad. But, when he got there, he found that a landslide had hit the orchard, burying two trees. Those two were the only 'Winter Banana' trees on the place and they were dead as a doornail!

That incident started Elwood thinking, and he realized that he was one of the few people in the entire country who knew many old fruit varieties on sight, and where to find them. Coincidentally, he and Madge had moved to their present home and had a large lot for planting trees, berries, and vines.

So began Elwood's quest to find and save old varieties, and he admits that he had no idea, then, how involved and all-consuming it was to become. He used many ingenious methods to find old trees. "I would come into a little town," he recalls, "and ask who around those parts grafts trees for home orchards. Usually, I would start at the town filling station, and would get my answer right there. Professional fruit tree grafters were always local men and were always willing to cooperate when I explained what I was after. Of course, it helped that I grew up in the mountains and could still talk like one of them!

"Circuit-riding ministers are getting hard to find now," he said, "but there were quite a few around when I first began searching for old trees. They rode horseback in the roughest parts of the mountains and, since they were put up and fed by local families, they knew who served the best apple pies. I've had them lead me straight to long-abandoned farmsteads where they had enjoyed apples years before. We found many long-dead trees, but also a few old survivors.

"It took me five years of searching to find 'Winter Banana', and even longer to find the 'Leathercoat' russeted apple mentioned by William Shakespeare. I am still looking for the 'Wasp' apple, also called 'Birdstow Wasp', and Thomas Jefferson's favorite cider apple, 'Talliaferro'. I keep hearing about an apple with the local name of 'Chuke', known in Great Britain as 'Chuket' or 'Teuchat Egg', but have yet to find a tree by that name. It was recorded in Scotland in 1768.

"The luckiest find in all my searching," Elwood said, "was a man who had served for many years as a judge at county fairs. He would ask entrants for cuttings of varieties that placed well in fruit exhibitions. He was ninety-six years of age when I ran across him, and still had twenty-two great old apple varieties, some of which I have found no place else.

"One of my other hobbies, bird watching, ties in beautifully with my searching for old fruit trees. I visit several areas in the mountains during the spring and fall to count or study migrating birds. While driving, I keep one eye peeled for fruit trees, or remnants of old homesteads. Whenever I spot something promising, I will mark it on a map for a visit on the way back home.

"For several reasons, I am having better luck in finding old apple varieties than other fruits," Elwood explained. "First, hundreds of apple varieties were planted in the Colonies; the settlers apparently learned from seamen that stored apples and cabbages could help prevent scurvy during the winter when greens were not available. Also, apple trees can survive longer than most other fruit tree species . . . sometimes more than two hundred years.

"Pear trees usually don't last as long as apples. They need good soil, and tend to be shorter-lived where soils are thin or infertile. Fire blight tends to debilitate and eventually kill trees, especially where bees can bring the bacterium in from other fruits," Elwood continued. "For that reason, the old varieties of pears I have obtained have usually gone through several cycles of renewal by rooted cuttings or grafts. Like apples, pears tend not to come true when grown from seeds. Apparently, their genetic makeup is so complicated from eons of hybridizing, that tremendous variation occurs among seedlings.

"Among the stone fruits, cherries are fairly long-lived," he said. "I've found some trees that must have been sixty to seventy years old. Up in the mountains where it is cool, they can grow the large sweet cherries as well as sour or pie cherries. Growers treasure them so much that they will graft desirable scions onto seedlings to keep the variety going.

"On the other hand," Elwood said, "the relatively short-lived stone fruits such as peaches, plums, apricots, and almonds usually produce pretty good trees when grown from seeds, and they resemble the parent tree fairly closely. The American Indians fell in love with the first peaches introduced by settlers, carried seeds with them all over the mountains, and planted patches which still survive. The red-fleshed 'Blood' or 'Indian' peach was one of their favorites."

Elwood caught my doubting look when he was describing the true-breeding character of peaches and plums grown from seeds. "Oh, yes!" he reassured me. "I've seen some seedlings from old greengage and French prune plums that were superior to the original." He showed me one of his selections, grown from a seed and code-numbered "EF-33-74." It certainly bore out his contention.

"American Indians and settlers alike," he said, "used fruits in a way not generally known today. They fed them to livestock. Lacking any means of preserving the stone fruits other than drying, they fed surplus peaches, plums, and apricots to pigs and cattle. Apples and, to a lesser extent, pears, were stored in caves, cellars, and straw-lined pits."

I asked Elwood about gooseberries and currants, of which he had several attractive varieties. "One of the great gardening disasters, in my opinion," he said, "was the misdirected eradication program against gooseberries and currants during the 1930s. I can recall crews of WPA men combing the hills, valleys, and home gardens to find and burn gooseberry and currant bushes because they were felt to be alternate carriers of white pine blister rust disease, which endangered this valuable timber tree.

"Our old German families were law-abiding, but not inclined to go along with edicts that didn't make sense to them. Consequently, they tended to dig up and store plants of currants and gooseberries and replant them after the eradication crews had moved on. Thanks to them, I have been able to find quite a few of the really old garden favorites. I expect to see more gooseberries and currants planted in gardens as people learn what delicious pies and preserves can be made from them."

1) 2) 3) 4) 5) 6)

Antique Fruit Varieties

Searching out and saving antique fruit trees, berry and grape varieties have taken much of Elwood's spare time and energy for more than twenty years. He continues his crusade largely because he is uniquely qualified to find and preserve old fruit cultivars such as those shown here: a seedling from an unnamed antique nectarine (1); 'General Hand' plum (2); 'Perfection' red currant (3); 'Medlar of Nottingham' (4); an antique crab apple grown for preserves (5); 'St. Edmund's Pippin' apple (6).

As Elwood's collection of fruit trees expanded, it became apparent that he would soon run out of room. His half-acre lot would hold only seventy-five or so mature fruit trees of standard size. Then, he made a decision that multiplied the capacity of his orchard severalfold. He began grafting several kinds of apples and other species on each of his existing trees, always tagging the grafted scion by cultivar name. He also began cordoning trees by the Belgian system to allow much greater planting density. Some trees were espaliered up walls or trained flat against trellises made by lacing and tying together canes of local bamboo. His trees are crowded, by any standard, and berry canes and bush fruits are chinked in wherever he can find a sunny spot. It isn't the optimum arrangement for growing fruit trees but it has enabled him to save countless cultivars that otherwise might have been lost.

Here and there among Elwood's collection of conventional fruits are oddities such as medlars, figs, almonds, nectarines, quince, and jujube (which grows into a good-sized tree at Victory Garden South). Someday, you might see jujubes on the gourmet produce counters; they are delicious little fruits the size and shape of a large date, apple flavored but rather dry in texture, tan to brown when ripe. Medlars will probably remain obscure; they look a bit like the fruit of quince but smaller. You have to develop a taste for them. Madge made a face when Elwood mentioned medlars. "The nearest next-to-nothing fruit I ever tasted!" she exclaimed. "You have to pick and store them until the pulp ferments before they are worth eating. When they are ready, you have to really work at it to get more than a taste of fruit." (Well, that pretty much explains why more people don't plant medlars.)

Elwood asked me to help him diagnose what was wrong with a medlar tree he had espaliered, for protection, in a corner between a brick wall and a chimney. The margins of the leaves were bleached almost white. I hipshot and guessed at overly high soil pH, which would tie up iron and perhaps other trace elements. This condition frequently occurs where lime from concrete foundations and walls gets into the root zone of nearby plants. Elwood agreed to apply a blend of chelated micronutrients in the fall to see if it restores the desired color to next year's foliage.

What really impressed me about Elwood's orchard was the extraordinary range of flavors in the old apples. Mind you, these were rather small fruits, some no larger than the crab apples you see pickled and colored red. We ate them warm, out of hand, peeling and all. I detected flavors I never knew came with apples: cinnamon, licorice, nutmeg, banana, pineapple (and, once or twice, worm). Elwood explained that certain tart varieties are preferred for cider-making, others for pie-making, still others for drying. You can use antique cultivars for other than their primary uses, but some of the fun in growing them is using them as their developers intended. Truly, gardeners are missing something good by settling for just the few modern cultivars that are sold for home orchards today, a sentiment to which Elwood added a heartfelt "Amen!"

"All told, I have nearly eleven hundred varieties of apples here," said Elwood, "plus three hundred pears, nineteen grapes, some fifty-seven cherries, twelve apricots, twenty-nine plums, several figs (including the hardy Siberian and one which is claimed to be seedless), and some thirty varieties of red, white, or black currants and gooseberries. I have several kinds of brambles but they tend to get out of hand. I don't know how much longer I can continue to grow them.

"I feed the whole neighborhood with fruits," he said, "but a lot of it goes to waste. I have to overpower my instinct to provide food, by reminding myself that my most important goal is to preserve the plants and not to save the fruit crop. But, at the same time, I feel I should learn how to thin, prune, and spray all the kinds I grow, in order to advise people on the best regimen for fruit production. I have an obligation to my neighbors to keep the place clean and not to have my orchard harbor insects or plant diseases that could spread."

We talked for a long time about ways he might reduce the dreadful number of hours he has to spend in the orchard spraying, often in the hot sun. Elwood is a highly conscientious man about protecting the environment but is reluctantly convinced, as am I, that a certain minimum of

Antique apple varieties are espaliered Belgian fashion atop a terrace formed by one of Elwood's stone walls.

Madge and Elwood Fisher gather apricots in a Welsh trug.

spraying is required to keep damage from insects and diseases at an acceptable level. Being a scientist, Elwood is extremely careful about spraying, and wears the full recommended regalia of rubber clothing and gloves, goggles, and respirator.

Madge is concerned about the effect on her husband of the heat and hard physical labor of spraying. Elwood uses a gasoline-powered "Solo Port 423" backpack mist blower, which is a great sprayer, but heavy to lug around. He is going to look at the electric-powered Atomist as a lighter, less noisy alternative, which uses less actual chemicals because it micronizes the spray.

Elwood's spraying program begins in the fall, after leaf drop, when he drenches all the trees with a dormant spray of Ferbam and dormant oil. This is his first line of defense against overwintering insects and the bacterial disease peach leaf curl. To control plum curculio and codling moth on plums and apples, he sprays with malathion at blossom drop and again later when the insects begin to emerge.

He sprays at full flower to prevent fire blight, which is destructive in Harrisonburg. He uses Agrimycin or a 4 percent solution of Chlorox. Later in the season, he "target sprays" spot outbreaks of such diseases as quince rust. The fungicide Polyram works well for him against scab, cedar-apple rust, fly speck, and sooty blotch. He also uses benomyl (Benlate) to control powdery mildew on apples, but only when necessary.

He advises using common sense in reducing brown rot damage by concentrating on early varieties of peaches, plums, apricots, and nectarines. Elwood has observed that the disease is much worse on later varieties that mature during hot, humid weather. On the few occasions when warm, humid weather has come at ripening time, he has used Benlate and Funginex to control brown rot on peaches and other stone fruits. "But, I have gone back to using old-fashioned Bordeaux mix on stone fruits and grapes we plan to eat," he said. "I feel it is safer. At times I have used Carbaryl to control Japanese beetles on grapes and roses."

Elwood realizes that thinning fruits, particularly peaches, apricots, and nectarines, would reduce the incidence and severity of brown rot. However, thinning an orchard the size of his is physically impossible for one person, part-time. He has to prop up many overloaded branches to keep them from breaking under the weight of fruit.

"One of my best weapons against the spread of diseases and insects, and the effect of drought," Elwood said, "is mulching between the rows of trees in my orchard. I have all my neighbors save leaves and lawn clippings and I sheet-compost them. I know that the trees are withstanding the drought better. Believe it or not, I didn't water once during our long drought, except when I transplanted new trees. I think that, being healthier, my trees suffer fewer disease and insect problems, perhaps because more predators can live in the mulch than in clean-tilled soil. I frequently bring in 'helpers': toads, salamanders, lizards, and their skink cousins."

Elwood explained "summer pruning" of apple trees to me. It must have seemed to him that I had been living on another planet because, literally, I had never heard of it, nor seen it done. He showed me how, come June 15, he cuts back each shoot with fifteen or more leaves on it. He takes off two-thirds of each shoot, being careful to disinfect his shears between trees or after pruning in an area that appears diseased. Then, in late July, he cuts back to two leaves, the growth put on since the first pruning. Finally, in late August, he repeats the procedure used for the second pruning. The technique, he explained, forces more fruit to form the next year, instead of excessive vegetative growth, and may prevent the tree from getting into the cycle of "biennial cropping," setting a heavy crop every second year.

Elwood is especially skilled at grafting. April is the time for cleft, bark, and whip grafting of scions collected during the winter. Then, from June through August, he does budding, or chip, grafting of both pome and stone fruits.

Cleft grafting is used mostly when topworking existing trees to replace all or part of the smaller limb structure with a more desirable cultivar. He cuts off limbs up to a size of about 1 inch in diameter, splits the ends, and inserts one or two short pieces of scion wood so that cambium meets cambium, and wraps the union and all the exposed cut with a rubber grafting band.

Bark budding is used mostly to start a new branch growing when a tree is lopsided, or to replace a broken branch. You have to wait until new growth is pushing out and make a tee-shaped slice in the bark. Insert a short piece of scion wood with the end trimmed into a "vee," and dab the exposed surface with grafting wax to prevent drying out.

Whip grafting is used to join a piece of scion wood to a slender branch of equal diameter. You can cut both pieces on a slant and join them so that cambium meets cambium or, if you are dexterous, you can match two sawtoothed cuts so that the graft won't slip. Wrap the whip graft with a rubber grafting band and tie snugly.

Budding is used to graft desirable scion wood to young seedlings with strong root systems, and is done by inserting a chip of scion containing a bud, into a cross or tee-shaped cut through the tender bark. Whip a wide rubber band around the graft and tie it snugly. Elwood prefers to do most of his grafting by the chip-bud method because buds done at the right time "take" almost 100 percent. Yet at the many grafting workshops he conducts, he demonstrates every known method because of the special situations which call for specific grafts. He isn't doing much grafting now, because he is concentrating on keeping his present inventory alive and healthy, rather than adding to it.

Although Elwood is an ace at pruning, he balks at trying to describe it, or how to graft, to anyone, other than at workshops where he can also demonstrate the procedures. "I've been pruning so long," he says, "that I do it automatically, like riding a bicycle or laying stone. Every tree of every variety of every kind calls for different pruning. It is an art that has to be explained to a person as you show him or her how to do it, just as my grandfather taught me."

Elwood smiled as he recalled three rigid rules of pruning given to him by Granddad Shuman all those years ago:

1. There are only fifty-two days of the year when you should not prune fruit trees . . . Sundays! (Grandfather Shuman was of the strict Dunkard faith.)
2. Never leave one limb superimposed over another; the bottom limb will be too shaded.
3. Open a tree enough that a bird can fly through it.

Elwood starts his pruning in the winter, right after Christmas, and continues through February. He prunes the older trees first, but waits until February to prune trees that are three years of age or younger. (These require minimal pruning.) Then he moves on to grape pruning and the special pruning required for cordoning and espaliering trees.

I asked Elwood how he felt about disinfecting shears and painting wounds on trees. He grinned and said that professional pomologists, Extension Service personnel, and he agree on disinfecting with Clorox or Lysol spray but disagree on wound paints. They maintain that paint is more cosmetic than effective, but Elwood says he suspects that decay organisms can enter wood at unprotected cuts, especially if the wound is large enough for the wood to crack. He applies a homemade mix of asphaltum diluted with xylene solvent or, in a pinch, a shot of cheap latex paint from a spray can.

Elwood glossed over his feeding program because, in his rich Shenandoah Valley soil, not much is needed. "Oh, I will scatter a little 19-19-19 corn fertilizer under a tree in late summer if it looks a little puny but, truly, I rely on the decaying mulch to supply most of the needs for nutrients. Too much vegetative growth results in poor production . . . the energy goes to shoots, not fruits."

Since Elwood and I are within a year of each other's age, we couldn't avoid the subject of what happens as he loses some of his stamina and when he is finally called to that great orchard in the sky.

"Madge and I have thought about selling this place and moving to a farm after retirement. It would take me about three years and a great deal of work to move all two thousand or so plants I have on this property. I would be willing to do it, if a way could be worked out for a

1)

2)

3)

4)

Grafting Fruit Trees

Elwood demonstrates his proficiency at grafting fruit trees. He prefers the chip-bud method because such grafts done at the right time "take" almost every time. He cuts a chip bud from scion wood (1). Then the chip is fitted to match a chip taken out of the understock branch (2). The bud graft is wrapped with flexible "parafilm" (3) to protect it, then labeled with the date and names of the scion and the understock (4). When slender branches are splice grafted (5), the cut surfaces of scion and understock must match perfectly. Whip the two pieces together with parafilm or a broad rubber band to secure and protect the splice.

5)

foundation to take over my collection for posterity. There isn't any point in moving it if it can't be carried on. I think it is crucial that this country protect the gene pool of its major food crops in the event the standard commercial varieties are attacked by a plague of insects or diseases, or unforeseen events such as destruction of ozone burn or acid rain . . . both of which are already real threats.

"A few others have collections of old fruit trees, grapes, and berries, including individuals such as myself, the restored garden and orchard at Monticello, the Luther Burbank Garden, the Colonial Williamsburg Foundation, and the American Museum of Frontier Culture at Staunton, Virginia. There are a few germ-plasm banks in Europe but they have had to turn to us for new starts on old varieties that have disappeared there.

"Cornell University has over thirteen hundred old apple varieties at their Geneva, New York station. I send them scions of the rediscoveries I have made, and I send scions to several collectors and breeders to reduce the risk of loss. Cornell is undertaking a valuable program of heat-treating and tissue-culturing old apple varieties to rid them of disease-causing viruses carried in their tissue."

I did convince Madge and Elwood to divulge the names of some of their favorite fruit varieties. Elwood winced when Madge chose the modern Japanese apple variety 'Mustu', a cross between 'Golden Delicious' and 'Indo'. Both like 'Tabarza' plum from Iran. Elwood likes the gooseberry 'Kathleen Olenberg' with large, red fruit, and the pearl-like white currant, 'White Imperial'. "My taste buds would soon tire of just one variety of a given fruit," Elwood commented.

After extracting my promise to return someday soon, the Fishers took me over to their regional airport. On the way, Elwood asked a favor. "Have anyone contact me," he said, "if they know anything about the history of the old apple variety named 'Walla Walla'. It has been grown in these parts since 1919 but no one has a record of it anywhere else. What's an apple named 'Walla Walla' doing in the Shenandoah Valley?"

More about Antique Fruit Varieties

You will seldom find antique varieties at retail stores. When you do, they might be labeled incorrectly, because synonyms are rampant among antique varieties. This is not due to deceptive trade practices but, rather, to the fact that original names of some varieties were lost years ago and local names assigned.

"Some of the supposedly 'lost' varieties have been rediscovered under synonyms," says Elwood Fisher. "For example, I have found very old English varieties, which have been lost over there, under different names in this country." Elwood is a bear on keeping fruit tree names straight and kindly gave me the names of reference books on antique fruit trees.

"These old books, plus some twenty others of the nineteenth century, help me key out unknown varieties. For example, the books describe the shape of the fruit: flat, conical, elongate, round, quadrate, etc. Then, I look up its color: red, yellow, green, blush, striped, spotted, solid, russeted, or smooth. If still in doubt, I can split a fruit and look at the core and the shape and color of the seeds. Even the calyxes, straight, reflexed, or absent due to aborting, can settle difficult identification questions. The season of ripening is also significant, though it varies, of course, from North to South."

Elwood is outspokenly critical of the books written for the general public on the subject of growing fruit trees. When I asked him to name good books on fruit culture he replied, "There aren't any!" Then, he went on to explain that fruits and berries are so regional in their adaptation and demanding in their requirements that no one has written a book which could apply to all climates. "It would take three or four volumes and several years of work to do it thoroughly," he said. "I think that gardeners would be further ahead relying on variety recommendations and pruning and spraying information from their State Cooperative Extension Service.

Terminology

A relatively modern innovation may complicate your ordering of antique fruit trees. Some nurseries, as a nod to the smaller gardens of today, graft antique scions onto dwarfing rootstocks. For your guidance, here are the terms used to describe the mature height of grafted and own-rooted trees, both antique and modern:

- *Dwarf:* 4 to 8 feet at maturity. (While most trees in this class will grow to 6 feet in height, the M-27 rootstock can produce 4-foot-high trees when grafted to certain scions.)
- *Semidwarf:* 8 to 12 feet.
- *Semistandard:* 12 to 20 feet.
- *Standard:* 20 feet or more at maturity.

The tree size should be listed as a part of the description of a fruit variety in catalogs or on tags. If not, don't buy the tree; you may be getting a full-sized tree when you have room only for a dwarf.

Dwarf Fruit Trees

A continuing decrease in the size of home gardens and yards has created a new demand for dwarf fruit trees. From the home gardener's viewpoint, the little fully dwarfed apple and pear trees may seem the most attractive, but the semidwarfs usually give greater satisfaction and can be controlled to some extent by pruning. In addition to the obvious advantage of being able to pick fruit from the ground or a short stepladder, you can also reach all parts of small trees with an ordinary pump-type sprayer. You are less apt to crowd small trees together, and the incidence of foliage and fruit diseases is lessened by the improved circulation of air. You can easily reach all parts of the tree for pruning, thinning, and summer tipping-back, which can prove especially important in years of heavy bearing. Without thinning and summer pruning, a feast could be followed by a famine. Finally, with a soft landing pad of a mulch under the foliage canopy, you will lose fewer fallen fruits to bruising. As with a child learning to walk, they don't have far to fall.

Peaches grow very fast, and are usually sold as standards, assuming that you will replace them when they overgrow or succumb to borer damage. Yet, certain plum tree stocks, when spliced in between the rootstock and the scion, can restrict top growth.

Cherries are also usually sold as standards although they can be dwarfed on G-9 rootstock. Of all fruit trees, cherries often suffer the worst from bird damage, and dwarfed trees can be reached for covering with bird mesh.

Plums are also susceptible to bird damage, and can be dwarfed with the 'Pixie' rootstock. Neither 'Pixie' nor G-9 are widely available, but are increasing in popularity. They are grown by a nursery called Oregon Rootstocks.

If you can't find dwarfed peaches, cherries, or plums, you can prune these trees relatively severely after two or three years of growth. You may suffer remorse after pruning, asking yourself, "What have I done!," but the tree will form more fruiting spurs and reward you for keeping it within bounds.

Care and Training

The care and training of young fruit trees soon after planting has changed drastically in recent years, due to new discoveries and new products. No longer do the experts advise gardeners to prune new trees severely at planting time. In fact, they advise minimizing pruning for the first two or three years after planting, except for training to a low head, because pruning very young trees can stunt a tree. By preserving the maximum amount of limbs, twigs, and foliage, you can increase photosynthesis and promote a stronger root system. Once the tree is settled in and growing strongly, you can begin a program of "tipping-back," or shortening limbs, as Elwood Fisher does with his summer pruning.

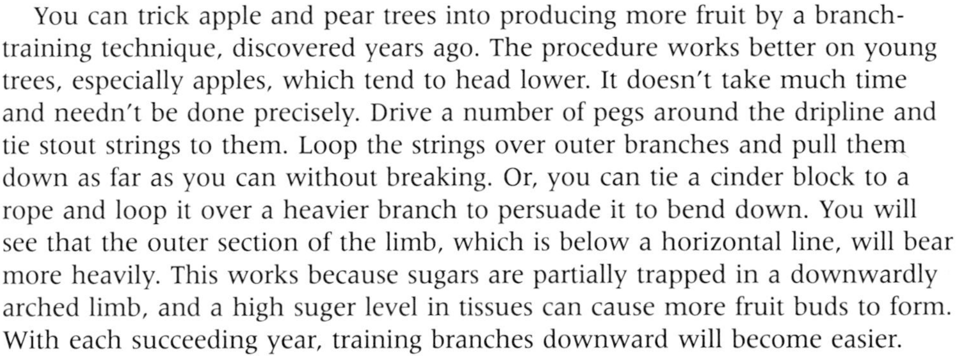

"Crop props" support heavily laden apricot branches and prevent breakage.

You can trick apple and pear trees into producing more fruit by a branch-training technique, discovered years ago. The procedure works better on young trees, especially apples, which tend to head lower. It doesn't take much time and needn't be done precisely. Drive a number of pegs around the dripline and tie stout strings to them. Loop the strings over outer branches and pull them down as far as you can without breaking. Or, you can tie a cinder block to a rope and loop it over a heavier branch to persuade it to bend down. You will see that the outer section of the limb, which is below a horizontal line, will bear more heavily. This works because sugars are partially trapped in a downwardly arched limb, and a high suger level in tissues can cause more fruit buds to form. With each succeeding year, training branches downward will become easier.

Home gardeners in the northern tier of states and at high altitudes have difficulty getting apple trees to survive. But they can copy a technique perfected in Siberia (apples in Siberia?) which results in a bizarre-looking but hardy tree. There, orchardists head the trees quite low and train the branches low to the ground and horizontally, supporting them with pegs and posts. As the tree grows, they train the limbs into a pattern like a four-leaf clover, so they can get into the center without stepping over branches. The trees survive extreme winters and bear good crops because the bulk of their top growth is down near the warming effect of the earth. Snow covers the branches and protects them from drying out and destruction from freezing and thawing.

Mulching

Landscape cloth, one of the new weed barriers developed for agriculture and home gardeners, and mulches of various kinds of organic matter combine to save labor and help trees grow and produce to their full potential. Commercial growers have long known that grass and weeds growing under fruit trees can compete for food and water, slowing growth and reducing yields. They are also aware of the damage done by cultivation, either to feeder roots near the surface, or accidentally to tree trunks. One of the saddest sights I know of is a poor little fruit tree with lawn grass growing right up to the trunk, whipped and nearly girdled by a string trimmer.

Commercial growers also know that mulches under the foliage canopy of fruit trees help growth and production in many ways: by keeping down weeds, reducing evaporation, and decomposing into humus while nurturing beneficial soil organisms. There is a downside to mulches such as hay or straw; they offer protection to meadow voles and pine voles as well as to rabbits, all serious pests in the eastern U.S. You need to protect the trunks of trees mulched with hay, straw, chipped wood, pine or fir bark, with a loose wrapping of half-inch-mesh hardware cloth. Commercial growers often protect trunks but don't mulch, mostly because of the cost of labor.

The ultimate mulch combines organic matter with an underlayment of landscape cloth under the entire area beneath the foliage canopy. The fabric looks like a thin blanket. No weeds can penetrate it except nutgrass, which is one of the sedges, and certain aggressive grasses. You could eradicate such ugly customers with a herbicide such as Roundup before planting. Here's the sequence for planting new trees and mulching:

Planting

After killing out aggressive perennial grasses and weeds, work lime and fertilizer into the soil according to soil test results.

Plant and water the new tree and wrap the trunk loosely with hardware cloth to protect against mechanical injury and chewing of bark by rodents. Tie the wire on with cotton string so, if you forget to loosen it later, the string will decay and prevent the wire from girdling the tree.

Spray the trunk and inner parts of lower limbs with cheap latex flat white paint. Technically, this isn't necessary except where sunscald or winter burn is a problem. But, why take chances? It won't hurt and, at the least, will keep the trunk from splitting on that warm day in midwinter when the sunny side expands rapidly while the shady side is still frozen.

Cut a square of landscape cloth and make a slit halfway into it. Slip it around the tree as a collar. Overlap strips of the fiber to enlarge the covered area. You can enlarge the mulched area as the tree grows.

Scatter a cup of vegetable garden fertilizer or organic equivalent over the landscape cloth and spread mulch 3 to 4 inches deep. The mulch will protect the fiber from ultraviolet ray deterioration. Don't draw the mulch up close to the trunk. Use pine or fir bark, hardwood mulch, or chipped wood, preferably precomposted. Let me caution citrus belt gardeners not to mulch around their citrus trees with organic mulch; it can encourage serious root and crown diseases.

The fertilizer should prevent nitrogen drawdown. However, if yellowing foliage makes you suspect a nitrogen shortage, drench the mulched area with manure tea or a liquid fertilizer. Don't fertilize late in the growing season; it can tenderize the young tree. Subsequent applications of fertilizer can be made as drenches or broadcast over the mulch and raked in. If you top-dress stable litter or manure over the mulch, you may introduce weed seeds and defeat the major purpose of the mulch.

As the tree increases in size, the layer of mulch can be made deeper to keep aggressive weeds under control by shading or smothering them out.

Buying

The selection of modern fruit trees for your home garden is more complicated than simply deciding which sorts you like to eat, and planting trees. You can start by visiting your Cooperative Extension Service office and picking up bulletins on adapted fruit tree varieties and their culture in your climate. Often, the value of Extension Service literature depends on the importance of commercial orchards in your state, and their recommendations will be tilted toward varieties grown commercially. For a balanced perspective, send for catalogs from fruit tree growers in your region, or one of the national suppliers. Here are a few of the things you will learn:

Fruit trees are indexed by the number of "chilling hours" (less than 40 degrees F.) required for blooming. Some with a high number of chilling hours will not bloom or bear fruit in warm climates with mild winters. Most catalogs cover this requirement by listing adaptation to the various climate zones on the U.S. hardiness zone map. The most reputable nurseries will not ship unadapted varieties, even if you ask for them.

While many tree fruit cultivars are moderately self-fertile, production can often be increased by the presence of another tree, of a kind known for good pollination and for flowering at the same time as your chosen cultivar.

Some kinds of fruit trees, notably cherries and Japanese plums, require "two to tango." If a neighbor happens to have a recommended pollinator in his yard, bees will probably carry the pollen to your tree. Or you can graft a piece of the recommended pollinator on the fruit-bearing tree. If fruit set is poor after planting two trees known to pair well for pollination, suspect lack of bees, due to indiscriminate spraying nearby, or rainy or cold weather when blossoms are open to pollen transfer.

Very early blooming cultivars should be avoided in areas prone to late frosts, as this can result in poor or no production.

Certain areas are "frost traps," where frost will occur even though surrounding areas are frost free. These can be basins caused by the topography, or traps caused by obstructions such as buildings, fences, or evergreen trees. Before planting, look all around and try to choose a spot where cold air will drain away rather than be trapped.

Each kind of fruit has distinct soil preferences. While all will grow well on deep, fertile soil, peaches and plums do better on comparatively poor sandy or gravelly soil. Of the tree fruits, pears show the strongest preference for fertile soil. Yet, on fertile soil, especially if forced with fertilizers, pears will produce soft, lush growth that may develop fire blight, if the disease is entrenched in that neighborhood. Few of the tree fruits, except certain plum cultivars, will tolerate poor drainage and, on dense clay soils, will do better if planted on low, wide mounds.

Care and Feeding

All new trees, and especially those of standard size, need a number of years to set the first significant fruit crop. You have to regard the care they need during those years as you would the feeding and training of a child. If you are faithful in your obligation, both tree and child should reach a healthy, productive maturity. Although early-bearing differs by cultivar, peaches, apricots, nectarines, and plums are generally the most precocious, followed by cherries, pears, and apples. Some apple cultivars don't hit their stride for six to seven years, and a few even longer. Elwood Fisher's experience with 'Northern Spy', for example, is that dwarfed trees should produce in seven to nine years, but standard trees not until fourteen years! I think that the definition of an optimist would be an eighty-year-old gardener planting standard trees of 'Northern Spy'.

All fruit trees need fairly frequent watering the first summer after planting and, later, generous watering when setting fruit. You can taper off for a short time, but resume watering again when trees are forming fruit buds for the next season. Water by flooding around the tree, rather than by a sprinkler.

All fruit trees benefit from yearly feeding at rates per square foot of soil comparable to those of large, greedy vegetables. From 2 to 3 pounds per 100 square feet of soil beneath the foliage canopy should be sufficient. Scatter the fertilizer around the dripline and slightly outside it, where the greatest concentration of feeder roots can be found. Spring feeding is preferred because late summer or fall feeding can tenderize the tree.

Pests and Diseases

The testimonials from gardeners who grow fruit without chemical sprays or dusts often neglect to mention the amount of fruit spoiled by insects or diseases, or damage to trees by borers. Even the most dedicated organic gardener will search out effective botanical and biological controls and acceptable mineral sprays such as Bordeaux mix and dormant oils. The amount of insect and disease controls you need is dependent on how much damage to trees and how much blemished or spoiled fruit you are willing to accept.

Insects such as borers, codling moths, plum curculios, and the various scales can weaken trees and damage fruit. Diseases such as brown rot, scab, rust, and bacterial leaf curl can have the same effect. If you are dead set against the use of proprietary insecticides or fungicides, ask around for the best organic fruit growers in your area and inquire how they manage it. Start with your local Master Gardeners Association. If you can accept the small amount of environmental impact caused by spraying a home orchard, ask your Cooperative Extension Service for a preventive spray program, scheduled for your area.

A growing trend, particularly at the universities, however, is the inclusion of nontoxic controls in "Integrated Pest Management" programs, which rely on a balance of predatory insects and biological controls. In the South and West, where nematodes are a problem on fruit trees, universities are researching green manure crops which either repel nematodes or will not harbor them.

If you'd like to try antique varieties of fruit trees in your garden, remember that they will grow into standard, full-sized trees. The options are to order antique varieties grafted to dwarfing rootstocks, or to graft scions of antique varieties onto existing trees of the same species. Any way you do it, the result will fully justify the effort.

Herbal Arts

Her love of growing and drying herbs for seasoning and crafts draws Maureen Ruettgers's family and friends into her hobby.

(Left) Drying herbs and everlasting flowers fill Maureen Ruettgers's antique barn.

Herbal arts is a new name for a very old pastime. To sit and weave wreaths from herbs or to dry and toss petals and flower heads into fragrant, colorful mixtures links you with a chain of humankind all over the world, back to the dawn of civilization. We have the leisure time now to practice herbal arts, which relieve stresses and satisfy our creative instincts by busying our hands and stimulating our senses. Ancient Greeks and Romans, Chinese philosophers, and medieval ladies might not have described their motives and gratifications in the same way but they, too, hung herbs and flowers to dry, wove them together with thread, and scented closed spaces with what we now call potpourris, and sprays of lavender, sage, and rosemary.

The herbal arts have advanced on the wave of interest in herbs for culinary, landscaping, and medicinal purposes. As gardeners experimented with herbs for seasoning foods, added silvery or gray-foliaged herbs to landscapes, and soothed upset stomachs with mint teas, they discovered that their attractive and durable flowers or seed heads could be dried for winter arrangements. And, as they grew in gardening, they evaluated garden flowers and wild species for drying and ranged out over the landscape to find natural materials to add variety to their dried creations. The result has been a vigorous revival of the ancient art of decorating with dried plant materials, only more eclectic and considerably faster, thanks to glue guns, monofilament line, desiccants, Styrofoam forms, and floral essences not available to previous generations.

The growing interest in country living and our colonial heritage has spawned research into the part played by herbal arts in the lifestyles of earlier days. Restored settlements such as Colonial Williamsburg, Old Sturbridge, Old Salem, and Plimoth Plantation reproduce the dried arrangements, swags, and fragrant mélanges of dried petals settlers made from the herbs and flowers of their day. All of this has raised our awareness of growing and utilizing herbs as a rewarding hobby, steeped in tradition and lore. Few other hobbies can call forth such strong images of families, on long winter evenings, clustered around lamps or hearths for light, busy with herbal crafts or capturing the images of flowers in needlework or quilts.

Always, there have been lively cottage industries associated with herbal arts. When practitioners reach a certain level of proficiency, and people begin to admire their handiwork, some decide to sell what they make. Today, herbal arts are often displayed at crafts fairs and harvest festivals. Thus it was, too, at medieval fairs and festivals. Lacking tools and the money to buy them, peasants made and marketed what they could from materials they could gather from gardens, fields, and hedgerows. Even the most highborn shopper must have reacted favorably to the cunning combinations of homegrown or found materials.

At herbal arts displays today, many of the hobbyist-exhibitors are well educated; some are trained in fine arts. But many are plain, everyday people with extraordinary talents in growing and utilizing herbs and flowers artfully.

Most of these hobbyists are good gardeners. They grow their own herbs and flowers for drying, and combine them with seed pods, vines, and flowers gathered from the wild. Some buy dried material and floral scents from florists and specialty suppliers at trade fairs or through the mail. They feel their way into the hobby, enticed by the beautiful creations they see at craft fairs and garden club flower shows. They ask questions, attend workshops and seminars, study how-to books, and practice with simple creations. All the while, the people who are good gardeners expand into

Maureen created this wreath from artemisia decorated with gomphrena and statice.

growing species and cultivars known to be useful in making wreaths, dried arrangements, bunched mixed herbs for hanging, collages, and potpourris. The more adventurous scout roadsides, stream banks, fencerows, botanical gardens, and vacant lots for weeds and wildflowers, vines, trees, and shrubs with decorative flowers or seed pods.

The typical herbal arts hobbyist does not have the dark, drafty barn so often featured in articles about drying herbs and flowers. Well-ventilated, dark barns are great for hanging hundreds of bunches of garden flowers or herbs for drying. Good ventilation reduces the incidence of molding, and gradual drying in the dark reduces fading and loss of natural fragrance. But, favorable drying conditions can also be created by darkening a room, opening a window from the top, and running an electric fan to keep the air moving.

The majority of herb hobbyists dry their herbs and flowers in darkened rooms, garages, or sheds, often with help from a small heater and a fan. Their gardens produce too much raw material for drying with silica gel, except for particularly fragile blossoms. Hobbyists use cookstove ovens set on the lowest heat, commercial dehydrators, and microwave ovens for drying during rainy weather or to speed up the process to meet show deadlines.

I know many gardeners who are deeply involved in herbal arts. Their hobby involves them year-round, yet accommodates time needed for work, family, or social obligations. Herbs and flowers for drying are easy to grow and don't demand harvesting within a tight time frame. Harvesting and preparing flowers for drying is especially enjoyable, and putting them together artfully can wait until you have spare time and feel creative. I know of no other hobby that has so many dimensions or that involves more sensory stimulation. The fragrances transport you to the garden or fields where you harvested the plants; the bristly textures and muted colors remind you of the fullness and brilliance of the fresh flowers and leaves.

A few miles out from Boston, in the countryside that sent militia for the first battles of the Revolution, and in a home occupied by three generations before the call went out from Lexington and Concord, lives the Ruettgers family. Without a doubt, families who tilled this farm in past years and gardened near the old white frame home grew herbs and flowers for drying, and used them artistically.

Perhaps emanations from generations past guided Maureen Ruettgers into herbal arts, or it could have been a near and dear role model, or an inborn and carefully nurtured artistic talent. Whatever the source, it has produced a good gardener with a gift for landscaping with herbs and flowers useful for drying, and for employing them in highly creative ways.

Maureen shows me how she selects materials for wreathmaking.

Maureen Ruettgers is living proof that a young woman can have a satisfying plant hobby while raising a family and doing community work. She and her husband, Michael, have gradually converted the grounds of an historic home into a large, beautiful, and functional garden for herbs and flowers for drying. The old barn that came with the place proved to be a perfect site for drying and storing herbs and dried flowers. Their three children grew up in the garden and at the feet of their mother as she worked away at herb crafts. They took to it naturally, much to the delight of their mother and father.

Michael shares Maureen's love for growing things but he describes himself as "more of an inside man." He loves to cook and preserve the vegetables and grapes he and their son Chris grow. Michael learned gardening from his father at their homes in England and, later, in San Diego.

Maureen is among the many herb growers who are enlarging the scope of the hobby to include herbs for seasoning, for medicinal purposes, and for inexpensive, fragrant decorations for the home. Although she considers herself an herb enthusiast, Maureen grows many annual and perennial flowers, and some wildflowers, for decorative flowers and seed heads. She uses them to enrich her materials for dried herb crafts: wreaths, swags, bunches, sachets, potpourris, and so forth. This infusion of nonherb plants adds color and texture to her garden, which, for much of the growing season, would otherwise show mostly the muted green, gray, and silver colors of her herbs. Maureen grows several of the healing herbs in her garden, not for medicinal use but because they look good in landscapes or can be used in herbal arts.

A tour of the Ruettgerses' garden is a learning experience because of the many uses to which Maureen puts her plants. We began our tour just outside their back door, in view of the kitchen windows:

"The first garden we built here was a 'ladder garden,'" Maureen recalled. "We laid an old ladder on prepared ground and planted in between the rungs with herb plants. We used it to teach visiting schoolchildren how to garden in small spaces: they loved to sample the herbs. The kinds of herbs vary from year to year but are basically the

The "ladder garden" makes a pretty display for French tarragon, center; 'Spicy Globe' basil, foreground; and chives and parsley in the background.

edible herbs that can be bought anywhere as plants . . . sweet basil, parsley, dill, spearmint, thyme, sage, rosemary, and chives. I was trained as an elementary school teacher and it did my heart good to see the difference that old ladder made in getting the story over. We still use the ladder garden with visiting school groups.

"Gradually, we expanded the herb garden to its present size of a quarter of an acre and added beds for perennials, mostly those with interesting flowers for drying, seed pods, or shade-tolerant cultivars. It is hard to find shade-tolerant plants with useful seed pods. I use pods of hosta, one of the best shade plants. Alchemilla, or lady's mantle, one of my favorites, withstands moderate shade and stands up well to wind and rain. It has greenish yellow blossoms that dry well, and the cupped leaves collect large, glistening drops of dew or rain. The drops slide over the leaves like quicksilver. I like to plant lady's mantle in drifts. Out in the sunny areas of the perennial beds, we grow the eryngiums, baptisias, verbascums, horehound, and butterfly weed for decorative seed pods which we combine with dried pods of annuals such as *Nigella damascena, Scabiosa stellata,* and Shirley poppy.

"There really is a fine line of distinction between what nurseries call 'perennials' and the perennial herbs. I suppose that what qualifies a plant as an 'herb' is its usefulness in flavoring, medicines, or scenting. Many herbs have decorative uses as well, and I will confess a fondness for them, but when it comes to choosing flowers for drying or for decorative seed pods I'm not so much of a purist that I discriminate against annual or perennial flowers. I need a wide variety of blossoms, seed pods, and dried foliage for my creations, as well as fragrant herbs.

Tall artemisia 'Silver King' stands guard for Maureen's drying barn in the background.

"Here's why I like lady's mantle," explains Maureen during a taping by The Victory Garden.

"Next to lady's mantle, cinnamon basil is my favorite plant in the garden. It is easy to grow in full sun, and quickly develops a mounded shape. The tip growth of each branch is purple green and the blossom scales are deep purple. The blossom spikes retain their color when dried and, being short, mix neatly in potpourris. The fragrance is intense and clovelike, fresh or dried."

Maureen has found it helpful and pleasing to the eye to divide her garden into two parts: one half, dubbed by the children "The Magic Garden," is planted with pastel colors of flowers for drying, and mostly silvery or gray herbs. The other half, "The Kitchen Garden," is reserved for brighter colored flowers, mostly grown for potpourris, and herbs that are blended in their manufacture. The garden is made up of raised beds separated by mulched walks; the perennial border is elevated two feet and surrounded by a wall of gray fieldstone.

Near the house is a forty-foot-long arbor for grapes, very ornamental and painted white. Maureen's father built it; he is a master woodworker and was restless in retirement. Michael's wine and jelly grape varieties are beginning to climb up and over it. The arbor is a work of art; it looks much like the one at the Victory Garden in Lexington, Massachusetts.

Maureen and her daughters, Polly and Abigail, and I had a great time touring the herb garden. Of all the plant classes, I suppose I know the herbs best, having grown the culinary herbs commercially for several years. Nevertheless, the Ruettgerses were growing several I'd never seen before. Their cooler climate and emphasis on decorative herbs has allowed them to collect and propagate some kinds you won't find outside of the catalogs of herb specialists. Odd species of salvia, thyme, artemisia, and mint kept me guessing, and rarely successfully. Maureen swapped what she knew about unusual herbs for what I knew about container growing, pest control without chemicals, and plant nutrition, in relation to herb growing. The children didn't say much but I could tell they were absorbing the conversation.

In the Ruettgers garden, the plant that impressed me most was the ambrosia, *Chenopodium botrytis*, also called feather geranium or Jerusalem oak. I know it can become a weed in some gardens, but growing it in the hot, dry soil of the South where I live is anything but easy. Maureen's garden was well stocked with ambrosia; she told me she has to thin out and discard surplus volunteer plants every year.

I was particularly interested in her collections of salvias for drying, including *Salvia hordeum* and *S. leucantha*, and numerous artemisias (wormwood). Unusual alliums were blooming all over the place; August is the time for these onion family relatives to shine. I saw yellow, white, pink, and purple varieties from 8 inches to 24 inches in height.

Here and there, around the garden, were herbs growing in containers. I asked Maureen which herbs, in her experience, do best in containers. "The shorter ones," she replied, "especially herbs that trail over the sides of containers; lemon thyme, oregano, and creeping rosemary are good. You need some erect plants of the shorter varieties for vertical accents and foliage or flower color: chives, lavender, or sage, for example. The gross feeders such as basil need larger containers, as does mint."

I was curious to learn if Maureen left any of her containerized perennial herbs out of doors during the winter. "No," she said, "not only because they would die from freezing, but also because the containers would break up from the pressure of expanding ice." Maureen uses terra-cotta containers to blend with her old-fashioned garden. She knocks the plants out of containers in the fall, heels them in for winter protection, and repots in the spring. She takes plants of the tender herbs indoors: bay, lemon verbena, rosemary, and such.

Maureen and I agreed on the difficulty of growing herbs on windowsills during the winter, despite the bland assurances in some books that it is easy. As you travel north, winter days grow progressively shorter and often more cloudy. Herbs have a hard time existing, let alone producing enough new growth for cutting. The overly warm, bone-dry winter atmosphere of many homes also works against plants. You can get around the problems by installing fluorescent lights in a cool room and enclosing the plant growing area with clear plastic sheeting. Under lights is a great place for starting seeds and saving plants and starts of your prized tender perennials.

Maureen's raised beds for herbs enjoy many of the advantages of containers, without the need for frequent watering. She fills them with moderately fast draining soil that holds moisture well, yet never becomes waterlogged. The porous soil is easy to cultivate and to keep free of weeds. Her raised beds reminded me of a similar arrangement for herbs at the Birmingham, Alabama, Botanical Garden. Volunteer herb enthusiasts had converted a steep slope into an outstanding herb garden by using weathered railroad ties to break the slope into level terraces. *The Victory Garden* taped the Birmingham "Herb Army" at work weeding and grooming their wide selection of improved cultivars.

Maureen gets her information on esoteric herbs from a large home library and from her association with the oldest group within The Herb Society, the Massachusetts chapter. "An office I held in the chapter proved invaluable to me," Maureen said. "I was elected librarian. That gave me access to 700 volumes on herbs, some very old and valuable." At one time, The Herb Society's national garden was nearby, at the Arnold Arboretum. It was a valued resource that assisted Maureen in learning the many genera and species that are called "herbs." Now, it has been moved to Holden Arboretum in Mentor, Ohio, near Cleveland.

At chapter meetings, Maureen has met many notables in herb growing: Madeline Hill, Joy Martin of Logee's Greenhouses, and Cyrus Hyde of Well Sweep Farm, to name a few. Some have visited her garden and have shared information and plants. I reminded Maureen of the several *Victory Garden* programs which have featured herbs, among them being visits to Caprilands in Connecticut, to the Denver Botanic Garden, and a wreath-making workshop at Callaway Gardens.

At the time I visited the Ruettgerses, they had just returned from a trip to Europe, and Maureen's daughter Polly was preparing to leave on another trip. Nevertheless, she took the time to show me the flowers and herbs she likes to grow, and how she makes potpourri by mixing dried herbs and flowers from the garden. She and her mother are keeping notes to establish the best stages of maturity for harvesting herbs and flowers for the best color, fragrance, and keeping quality.

I asked Maureen about sources for seeds, plants, and supplies for herb crafts. "You can avoid a lot of trial and error," she said, "by asking a member to recommend you for membership in a local chapter of The Herb Society. If there is no chapter nearby, you can network with other herb enthusiasts in horticultural societies, or within the Master Gardener organization; many of their members grow herbs along with vegetables.

"Some herb enthusiasts bring back seeds from foreign countries, of species not known in this country. Bringing in seeds is permitted, but importation of plants is so complicated that usually only botanical gardens are willing to make the effort. Once in this country, it is a slow process introducing a new species until one of the major herb seed and plant marketers gets behind it. Conversely, greatly improved cultivars can catch on rather quickly, as did 'Dark Opal' and 'Spicy Globe' basils. Also, the seed and plant companies seem to be making an effort to locate and market more flower varieties with potential for drying."

(Left) Polly gathers roses for potpourri while Abigail holds an armful. (Right) Abigail and Polly mix dried herbs to make potpourri.

We spent some time in the fragrant drying shed, already filling up with bouquets, swags, wreaths, and the makings of potpourri. "In about two weeks," Maureen said, "every tray in the big dryer will be covered with herbs and flowers, and every hook on the wall will be loaded with wreaths." She emphasized the necessity of darkening all the windows and maintaining good air circulation in the drying room, to retain color and fragrance. Slow microwaving or drying in ovens is being used by

1) 2) 3) 4) 5) 6)

Herbs and Flowers for Drying

A basic selection of herbs and everlasting flowers for drying includes florist's statice, Limonium statice (1); teasel, which is widely naturalized (2); matricaria or feverfew (3); *Gomphrena* 'Strawberry Fields' (4); *Salvia farinacea* 'Victoria' (5); yarrow, *Achillea filipendulina* 'Moonshine' (in the foreground); and ambrosia (6). All have versatile colors and textures that hold up well in dried arrangements. A variety of techniques, from air-drying to microwaving, are used by hobbyists. Experimentation will show you which method is most effective for you.

other enthusiasts for preserving herbs and flowers, but the Ruettgerses' production would overwhelm home units.

Maureen and Polly use silica gel to dry certain delicate flowers, and most species with blue or purple flowers, which tend to fade in air-drying. The silica gel helps to retain natural colors. Silica gel is a powdery substance. When flowers are imbedded in it, and the powder dusted in among the petals, the silica gel draws the moisture out of the tissues. It has to be shaken off the dried flowers, and can be reclaimed by heating to drive off the absorbed moisture. "We found that we could air-dry the blue flowers of 'Hidcote' lavender so perfectly that they could hardly be distinguished from the fresh. We can't grow and dry enough lavender to meet the demand at our annual sale," said Maureen.

"Members of the Massachusetts chapter come out and help us dig and pot up plants for the sale. We have many other herb enthusiasts in the area; they bring friends to see the dried materials and crafts and to pick up ideas. They especially like our wreaths and necklaces made of spices and can't seem to get enough of Polly's potpourri. We are very choosy about the essential oils we use to reinforce fragrance: some of the commercially available stuff is cloyingly sweet or offensively oily smelling. You can buy essential oils extracted from all the major herbs and fragrant flowers. They add life to potpourris; just stir the contents of the jar gently and the fragrance will come to life again and again.

"In wet years, we have had to cancel the sale. Continuing rains and damp weather can make drying of herbs and flowers difficult for everybody. What a difference a dry summer can make! In just two or three days, herbs can dry sufficiently to keep. Wet seasons have convinced me to install a warm air drying system in the barn similar to the one used here years ago to dry digitalis grown on the farm for pharmaceutical use. Also, the heat would let us work later in the winter here in the barn; without heat, it gets too cold by January.

"One little extra that makes our sales so successful is that we serve an herb lunch, along with herb teas. That alone has persuaded many customers to take up herb growing. It helps that we offer books on growing and using herbs. Books on birds and butterflies also sell well because they naturally go with herbs.

"Above all, I want to do everything I can to lead, but not push, our children into gardening with herbs and flowers. It has meant so much in my life and I hope it will in theirs. We were so proud of Polly for two term papers she did; they were on medieval gardening and heart drugs. She did all the research, including tracing how Mr. James Patch grew digitalis on our land years ago."

That her large garden is both beautiful and functional is a tribute to Maureen's dedication to the aesthetic values and country traditions that the herbal arts represent.

More about Herbal Arts

Herbal arts, the "craft" side of herbs, is one of many specialties open to the hobby herb grower. It attracts nearly as many herb growers as producing herbs for gourmet cooking. Both of these specialties lead medicinal herbs in popularity, but such has not always been the case. Mankind was using medicinal herbs when diagnoses were by supposition and treatment by trial and error. Scenting herbs were used not only for such civilized purposes as imparting a sweet smell to linens and clothing, but also for masking unpleasant odors and repelling insects. Herb uses are described at length in the writings of early physicians and philosophers, from Europe east through China. Some herbs were gathered from the wild but, as trade and commerce grew, seeds and plants helped gardeners everywhere to grow a broad range of herbs. Improvement by selection began more than two thousand years ago.

Now, gardeners can buy seeds or plants of herb varieties developed especially for drying. These hold their flower colors with little fading, and resist shattering during handling. For instance, the common purple-flowered oregano, *Origanum vulgare*, is no great shakes for flavor, but has superb color, holding power, and stem length for drying. Cinnamon basil, one of the recently rediscovered "rare basils," is perfect for potpourris, where its bronzy purple color and strong, clove-like scent will hold for several months.

The cultural methods for growing herbs for culinary uses are not always compatible with those for herbs to be dried. Herb cookery calls for tender vegetative tips. To produce new vegetative growth, you need to trim off the very flower heads and seed pods that are useful in herbal arts. For this reason, the herb specialist usually grows culinary herbs in the vegetable garden or dooryard plot, and isolates the herbs for drying in a special herb garden. This arrangement also makes best use of the landscaping value of the gray and silver herbs which are so important in herbal arts.

Most gardeners hate to waste the beautiful flowers and seed heads on their herb plants but, every year, many do. They might be pleasantly surprised at how easy and satisfying it is to work with dried materials, and at the extent of their own creativity. Herbal arts is not gender-oriented; many men are quite good at it. Their dried herb and flower creations tend to be large and robust and to include wild materials such as cattails, which can be collected only by slogging through marshes, and teasel weed and rabbit tobacco from the roughest terrain.

Starting Right

It is possible to throw yourself wholeheartedly into herbal arts—simultaneously to begin growing special herbs and flowers for drying, all the while scouting for wild seed pods and flower heads. I would counsel moderation. If you are already growing herbs, start evaluating a few new herbs every growing season; learn how to grow and when to harvest them for drying. Experiment with blending them with herbs you already know. Discard the varieties you don't like or which don't hold well when dried and move on to others.

Once you become proficient in herb growing, study the catalogs of seed companies and specialists in flowers for cutting. Select a few varieties which are adapted to your climate and which are specifically recommended for air-drying.

Watch this last point carefully; some suppliers recommend varieties which are so fragile that careful and tedious drying with silica gel is required. Grow a short row of a few new varieties each year, in your food garden, where cutting armloads of flowers won't disrupt the landscape. Anticipate that the colors, even after careful drying, will be subdued when compared to fresh flowers. Of all the colors, blue is the most elusive in drying and the yellows and oranges the least likely to fade. Good clear whites are rare; most dry to cream or dingy shades.

Drying Herbs

People who love to tinker can find plenty of room for their talents in techniques for drying herbs and flowers. First place in drying techniques is held by uncomplicated air-drying, using a dark area ventilated by fans. But, air-drying is speeded up considerably by drying for two or three days in a refrigerator, then hanging bunches in the dark to complete drying. Hanging lets stems and leaves assume a more or less natural stance, while laying them to dry on racks or layers of paper towels flattens them like herbarium specimens. Microwaving at low settings can preserve colors at exceptional levels of brilliance, but some flowers tend to collapse and lose their shape. You will have to experiment with settings and duration of microwave drying; it varies from oven to oven. Very slow drying in an electric oven with the door cracked works well; sometimes the oven pilot light alone will do the job in a gas oven. Commercial or homemade dehydrators are good for drying petals for potpourri and seed pods with short stems, but usually lack the capacity to handle long-stemmed flowers.

One of the best rigs for drying is a home greenhouse. Gardeners drape the houses with black plastic to exclude light, hang their harvests of herb and flower stems in bunches, crack the vents to let out moisture-laden air, turn on the fans, and, in less than a week, their plant materials are dried just right, pliable but not

These wooden drying trays were made by Maureen's father.

brittle and prone to shatter. Almost as good are large cold frames covered with black plastic, cracked for ventilation, and fitted with a fan in one corner to force out moist air. Such units can dry small wreaths made up from fresh vines, branches, and flowers, but the monofilament thread or thin copper wire used to hold them together should be tightened after drying.

Making Wreaths

Wreaths are probably the most popular herbal art. Most are made on Styrofoam or straw forms purchased at florist shops or specialists in flower-arranging supplies. Or, you can weave your own forms from kudzu, honeysuckle, and wild grape vines, or prunings from vineyards. Where I garden in the South, tall silver artemisia, lemon verbena, and anise-scented (licorice) basil grow so large that the limber branches can be half-dried, woven into wreaths, then completely dried before adding decorations.

There is an art to making wreaths perfectly round and symmetrical, or to other special shapes such as ovals and hearts. The professionals use jigs fitted with slots through which the monofilament, thread or wire can be passed for wrapping. But, the real art starts with the decoration; a well-made wreath is solidly covered with a mixture of dried flower and herb heads, frothy dried foliage, tiny conifer cones, seed pods in scale with the size of the wreath, and ribbons to suit your taste. It should be so securely wrapped with monofilament thread in a muted shade of gray, or fine wire, that it will stand up to handling. All decorations should be either firmly threaded into the base or stuck on with a glue gun so that they won't shake loose in handling.

Wreathmaking

Maureen demonstrates the art of wreathmaking, using artemisia, sage, and oregano. Using blue-gray thread, she ties the fresh artemisia to a wire ring (1). The real artistry begins with the decoration. Over the artemísia, Maureen arranges sprays of sage leaves with oregano flowers, and ties them securely to the wreath (2). Lamb's ear, gomphrena flowers, sage flowers, and gray santolina add their decorative effects (3). When the wreath is completely assembled, Maureen hangs it to dry.

1)

2)

3)

Making Potpourris

Potpourris also make excellent gifts when packed in the special decorative large-mouthed jars on sale at pottery outlets. Some gardeners use so many petals that they arrange with local greenhouses and public parks to deadhead their geraniums and roses. Not all dried flowers used in potpourris are fragrant; some are added for color and bulk. Herbal arts specialists are divided on the issue of using floral essences to enhance the fragrance and carrying power of petal and flower blends. Some use none at all. Some load their potpourris with perfume. Others compromise by using only highly refined natural floral fragrances discreetly, along with orris root as a stabilizer and extender.

Bunches of dried herbs are rather plain and simple, but are appropriate for hanging in kitchens. They look at home in kitchens with a colonial or country design but are not out of place with any decor. Sage, rosemary, common oregano, and English thyme cut at first flower stage look good and hold well. There is no denying how attractive mint looks when the stems are cut at the ground and dried when the first flowers are opening, but it tends to shatter, as does basil. Sweet marjoram can be cut when the little seed balls are still green. Common chives and garlic chives should be cut at full flower; garlic chive seed heads are also quite decorative. Ordinary garlic flower heads dry beautifully and don't smell rank. If you consider the many other alliums to be herbs, you add many excellent colors and blossom forms to your flowery workbasket.

Landscaping with Herbs

Some of the decorative herbs have potential as landscape subjects, as do some of the species grown mostly for medicinal purposes. Landscape architects have begun to appreciate certain of the herb species for their foliage, flowers, and fragrance. Some of the interest is due to the imaginative plantings in the National Herb Garden within the United States National Arboretum at Washington, D.C. Also, designers have seen how Europeans use herbs in conjunction with perennials, groundcovers, and shrubs, often to get special textural effects and silvery colors. Greenhouse growers who produce herb plants for sale often install demonstration gardens to show visitors how herbs will look at maturity in various landscaping situations. As yet, most full-service nurseries market herbs as a class and don't separate the species with special potential for herbal arts or landscaping. That day will come.

Once you get started in herbal arts, you may wish to attend one of the national seminars and trade shows for hobby and commercial herb growers and herb craft specialists. The Cooperative Extension Service at Purdue University and the International Herb Marketers Association sponsor yearly conferences. The lectures are superb and the trade fair attracts all kinds of suppliers and products for herb specialists. Your Cooperative Extension Service office will have dates and locations. Until and if the time comes when you head for the national herb meeting, there is plenty at home to feed your curiosity about herbal arts. Every town of any size has a hobbyist so good at herbal arts that they lecture and give demonstrations. Books on drying flowers and herbs are plentiful and well illustrated. Yet, the best way to learn is by growing and drying your own, and experimenting to make herbal creations that please you. You will seldom go wrong and, when you do, you simply take your less-than-a-masterpiece apart and do it better.

Dwarf Conifers

Ed Rezek gains international notice for his Long Island collection of dwarf conifers, miniature jewels of the evergreen world.

This corner of Ed's back yard displays his exotic-looking collection in an artful landscape.

Dwarf conifers are not a modern discovery. Interest in these slow-growing, miniature forms of standard plants goes back centuries. They are found in all the forms of standard conifers—ground-hugging, spreading, mounded, ball-like, vase-shaped, columnar, and conical erect plants, and special forms such as weeping and contorted—and in a wide range of colors including blue, variegations of silver, white, or cream-yellow, as well as every shade of green. Such myriad variations make the plants eminently collectible.

The early collectors of dwarf conifers were noblemen or traders with the time and money to devote to scholarly pursuits, including collecting plants from afar and learning how to identify and grow them. The first collectors were probably wealthy Chinese and Japanese hobbyists who, hundreds of years ago, gathered dwarf conifers from the wild to include in their bonsai collections. Though many of their bonsais, then as now, were normal plants artificially dwarfed by severe pruning and root restriction, these collectors sought out and cultivated true miniature conifers as well.

Interest in collecting dwarf and unusual forms peaked during the mid-nineteenth century as wealthy gentry in Great Britain and on the Continent vied with one another for exotic garden specimens. Sheltered courtyards, old walls, granite troughs, rock gardens, and alpine screes accommodated dwarf conifer collections naturally. When wars and hard times took their tolls on the estates, interest in dwarf conifers went into decline, but they were protected at botanical gardens and smaller private collections.

Today, as gardens become smaller in scale and gardeners become more discerning, dwarf conifers are increasingly prized for their beauty and longevity as well as for their compact size and slow growth habit in the landscape. The distinctive forms invite close inspection and contemplation, for many are best appreciated at close range. Landscapers think of them as "designer plants" because, as in designer clothing, their style, uniqueness, and finish are immediately apparent.

The term "dwarf" is a relative one and therefore somewhat misleading. A dwarfed forest tree might grow ten times as large as a dwarfed shrub. However, all dwarfed plants mature at smaller sizes than are normal or typical for the species. At maturity, dwarf plants can range from one-half to only one-twentieth the size of normal plants. Furthermore, dwarf plants grow very slowly, from less than one inch to five inches a year.

Some dwarf and unusual conifers come about as chance seedlings. Others are propagated by cuttings taken from a dwarfed branch of an otherwise normal plant. No one knows all the causes of spontaneous dwarfism in plants, but it may be due to air pollution, radiation, or viruses. Dwarfing anomalies may show up as:

Juvenile fixation. Ordinarily, the foliage of juvenile conifers differs from that of adult plants in form and color. Some plants never "shift gears"; they retain their juvenile characteristics at an advanced age. *Thuja occidentalis* 'Rhineglow' is an example. Others, such as *Chamaecyparis thyoidies* 'Andelyensis', may exhibit fixation, but become unstable later on and revert partially or fully to normal performance.

Witches' brooms. No causal organisms have been found to create these profusely branched and often low-growing malformations on conifers and deciduous plants. As the name suggests, they are congested and resemble brooms. You can reproduce them by cuttings or grafting, and they will often grow into dwarfed or unusual plants. Witches' brooms or grafted

Their distinctive forms, compact size, and slow growth habit make dwarf conifers the designer plants of the small landscape.

cuttings made from them rarely set seeds but, when they do, mutations can occur at a higher rate than with normal plants.

Grafting cuttings from witches' brooms to normal rootstock is one way to propagate these curiosities, but the plants sometimes suffer from incompatible grafts, due to different rates of growth of the scion and understock. The rate of growth of grafted specimens (dwarf scions grafted on normal rootstock) can depend on the vigor of the rootstock. Strong rootstocks can sometimes force dwarf conifers to grow too large. Grafts are unavoidable, because certain forms of dwarf conifers don't set good root systems when you try to make cuttings and root them.

Dwarfed or stunted alpine forms. Most of these will start to grow normally when planted in regular garden soil at low elevations. They can, with difficulty, be maintained as dwarfs by growing them as severely pruned bonsai. A good example is *Abies lasiocarpa* 'Sub-alpina' from the timberline in the Northwest.

An old, overgrown conifer has been opened up by pruning and clipped to train it into a pom-pom form.

Fastigiate (narrow, flattened, upright) forms of conventional conifers. These generally come about as chance seedlings and are identifiable at an early age. The flattening effect is most noticeable in the tips of the twigs, but can also show up as kinked branches.

Side shoots from erect conifers. If you have ever tried to root and grow a cutting from the tip of a side branch of a conifer, you doubtless found it to be stubbornly geotropic. They usually produce prostrate or descending forms that will not turn upright. However, if you injure one of these forms by severe pruning or mechanical damage, or if they are injured by freezing, they can revert to upright growth, resulting in a freakish-looking plant.

Many dwarf conifer specimens are not perfect miniatures of the standard version, but show the effects of the various conditions that dwarfed them. Early attempts at identification left a confusing legacy of mixed-up Latin and variety names. Now, a botanist or knowledgeable amateur can, after a brief inspection, identify each by its genus and species and make an educated guess as to its cultivar name. The shape and arrangement of the leaves, and, if available, cones and seeds provide the botanical "fingerprints."

What is it about these miniature plants that exerts such fascination? Aside from smallness, collectors look for forms that differ from the norm for the species. Whereas a normal tree might be conical in form, a dwarf offspring might grow into a weeping shape, or globose, drum-shaped, creeping, or spreading. Collectors look as well for color variations or variegations: a yellow-foliaged plant from a green parent, a silvery-blue plant from a green parent, a green and white or green and gold variegation from a solid green species. They look for curiously contorted plants resulting from the genetic aberration called "fasciation" or flattening of stems and terminal growth, for thread-leaved foliage where flattened foliage would be normal, and for mimicry of other species in leaves or needles.

Not content with variations from the norm, some advanced dwarf conifer specialists experiment with topiary effects, grafting ball-like or weeping forms onto tall, single trunks to get tree forms, and splicing variegated foliage among solid-colored growth. They prune larger specimens to imaginative designs: spirals, poodle puffs, mushroom shapes, tall columns, Medusa-like branching, and pearls-on-a-string fantasies. They interplant their dwarf conifers with choice small deciduous trees and perennials. They want to do more than simply charm visitors with their collections; they want to overwhelm them with effects not seen since royal gardeners sought to please their lords and ladies.

In the landscape, dwarf conifers are often combined with young specimens of Japanese maples, alpine plants, dwarf perennial flowers, and small-leaved groundcovers. With more commercial nurseries offering a wider selection, home gardeners can choose superior dwarf conifers to replace overgrown or overused shrubs. These plants hold great potential as container-grown specimens for decks, patios, and terraces, where space is valuable and every plant must have year-round impact. Both the visual effects and the maintenance are enhanced by grouping dwarf plants together.

Part of the challenge of growing dwarf conifers is in keeping the surroundings and accessories in scale with the plants, to emphasize their beauty and not purely their oddness. Skillful collectors, like Ed Rezek of Long Island, New York, can work magic in creating miniature landscapes that display their plants to perfection.

Ed created this spiral topiary form by clipping a Chamaecyparis pisifera *'Squarrosa Intermedia'.*

Ed Rezek of Malverne, Long Island, typifies the new breed of dwarf conifer collectors. Enthusiasts such as Ed can't stop with simply collecting new specimens: their love for their specialty plants compels them to master the art of displaying dwarf conifers. And it is an art, the art of illusion. When the *Victory Garden* crew arrived at Ed Rezek's home, they couldn't resist rubbernecking around the front, side, and back yards. I think it is safe to say that, in the many years of the show's existence, we have never seen such an extraordinary garden!

On a tour of the garden, my eyes told me I was looking at very young evergreens, but Ed told me they were up to forty years old! Tiny ball-like *Chamaecyparis,* wee spruces growing like hand-high Christmas trees, and sculpted miniature topiaries made a bewitching sight.

Ed's yard is the centerpiece of the neighborhood, immaculately kept, rising up in tiers from street level. The back yard is short from front to back but, by designing a peninsula to jut out from the side and past the center of the yard, Ed manages to convey an anticipation of what lies beyond. A tastefully constructed waterfall and pool catch your eye as you round the tip of the peninsula. By stair-stepping deep beds of plants down from slow-growing deciduous trees in the back, to waist-high dwarf conifers in the center and, finally, to very short dwarf conifers in the front, he creates a harmonious and totally artistic effect. The illusion is one of looking at a much larger landscape compressed to miniature scale.

Ed Rezek could sell the plants in his back, front, and side yards for several thousand dollars. But he won't—not the whole collection, not even a single plant. Monetary return never has been a consideration in his hobby of growing dwarf conifers. Ed is not a wealthy man; comfortably situated, yes, but living on retirement income. His wife of more than forty years, Maureen, plans to work a year or two longer before retirement. She is an excellent typist and helps Ed with his many compilations and reports.

"The day I start expecting money or recognition for my dwarf conifers is the day I begin losing the fun of it," Ed says emphatically.

Ed is an agile, energetic man, yet infinitely patient. His is a class of plants that you have to get on your knees to appreciate fully, and that require a full measure of faith from the grower. You'll never hear a dwarf conifer grower boast, "You can almost see my plants grow!" These diminutive plants grow so slowly that, years after the passing of the hobbyist, most will still be wee, little things as compared to the original, standard-sized species. Ed is so advanced in his hobby that the tinier and more difficult the plant, the more he likes it. He showed me a couple of seedling plants that, although several months old, had grown into little knots of foliage no larger than a pea seed.

His production of dwarf conifers, choice variegated conifers, and deciduous trees and shrubs could rival that of a commercial nursery. He grows from seeds and cuttings. Hundreds of plants, started in his ten-by-twenty Everlite greenhouse in pots, fill every spare inch of space in his yard. Prior to joining the International Plant Propagators Society, he learned to root cuttings and germinate seeds of dwarf conifers by trial and error. Now, he has excellent success, using sterile rooting media, mist propagation, and bottom heat in his greenhouse.

Some of his benches hold propagating boxes, filled with perlite and watered with an overhead mist system. At the time of my visit, they were full of recently stuck cuttings, stripped of lower leaves, dipped in rooting hormone, and plunged deep into the rooting medium. Other benches were covered with trays filled with deep pots of potting soil. He uses these to put a compact root system on the cuttings rooted in perlite. His greenhouse space is so valuable that, after a few weeks, he moves the tray of potted plants to a lath-covered holding area wedged in between the garage and the greenhouse.

"You might think I'd want to move to a home with a larger lot to hold all the dwarf conifers and special grafted plants I produce," he said. "But no, my neighbors have helped to keep me here. They have let me help renovate their landscapes with choice evergreens and dwarf conifers that have overgrown my space. I bet I've placed a thousand plants in good homes!"

You can see what Ed means when you drive down his quiet side street. Several of his neighbors have the most distinctive landscapes you ever saw, each bearing Ed's signature—multiple colors or forms of the same species grafted on one plant, elaborately trimmed topiaries, imaginatively trained creeping or prostrate plants, and, more than anything else, dozens of dwarf conifers that would make a retail nurseryman's mouth water.

Ed says, "I got hooked on dwarf conifers shortly after I moved into this house. The guy that built it hauled off the topsoil and sold it: I had to have thirty truckloads hauled in to raise the level of the ground in my side yard and to build up raised beds to hide the high walls of the base-

Ed's neighbors enjoy a garden landscaped with choice dwarf conifers. Some of these are more than twenty years old, yet are quite small.

ment. I had the usual 'quick and dirty' landscaping done: I didn't have the money to buy choice plants. So, I ended up tearing it all out about two years later.

"What happened is that I met Joe Reis at the printshop where I worked as an electrotyper. Joe was a true pioneer in dwarf conifers: he ate and slept dwarf conifers. He found out that, while stationed with the Marines in Peking in 1945, I had seen the 'Forbidden City' and had vivid memories of its old and fantastically trained bonsais. Joe showed me how to prune and train dwarf conifers to start bonsais and gave me starter plants for a new landscape." (Ed paused a minute to show me two dwarf Alberta spruces from Joe's original gift: they are now ten feet tall. Then he had to explain to me that some dwarf conifers grow rather large after several years, yet not near as big as the standard species.)

Ed continued his story . . . "Joe Reis was a scrounger. He had to be. The nurseries on the Island didn't handle dwarf conifers, except maybe a few Alberta spruces and other semidwarf cultivars. We'd get the bums' rush when we asked too many questions or wanted the nurseryman to order special stuff for us. One nurseryman said to us, 'This is the stuff

I've got to sell. If you want it, buy it. If you don't, I've got other customers to wait on!'

"So, Joe and I began sniffing out the few collectors on the East Coast and swapping what we had for what they had. We visited the Arnold Arboretum in Boston and Longwood Gardens in Kennett Square, near Philadelphia. Those were exciting days, not only discovering fascinating new plant materials but finding other specialists who were just as crazy about dwarf conifers as we were. When I look back on the dwarf conifers we perceived as outstanding in those days, I have to admit that, today, they'd be rated as rather ordinary 'Old Standards.'

"Other collectors and I had what amounted to a 'dwarf conifer underground' out here on the Island because, with our mild climate, we could grow plant material that would succumb to weather stresses on the mainland. And most variegated conifers won't sunburn or fade here. By word of mouth, we found several other private and commercial growers near enough to us to get together every now and then. All were knowledgeable about dwarf conifers: what one didn't know, another did. We had a ball, exchanging plant material, going plant hunting and bringing back cuttings in Wardian cases like those Darwin took with him."

Ed mused, "Some of the collectors in those days were secretive about their sources. I expect it was because they wanted first crack at anything new their sources might come up with. Other collectors would not sell starts of their plants to a plant propagator, protecting, I assume, their potential for profit. Other collectors, and they were in the majority, shared freely.

"Personally," Ed continued, "I think it is foolish to have a dog-in-the-manger attitude about a plant which you alone have. You could lose it and it could never be duplicated. Whenever I grow or discover a plant that seems to have potential, I propagate it and give a plant or two either to the National Arboretum in Washington, D.C., to the Planting Fields here on Long Island, to the Arnold Arboretum in Boston, or to close friends who are collectors. Should something happen to my original plant, it is not lost, never again to be cultivated. When I share with other collectors or arboreta, I often get something in return that I may prize. It is a two-way street.

"I also send rooted cuttings or scions to friends who operate large wholesale nurseries in Oregon; they specialize in dwarf and unusual conifers. One has a color picture of my garden in their catalog, and another grows many of my developments for retail nurseries." Ed showed me an inventory list from the commercial propagator: an outstanding number of dwarf cultivar names were followed by an I.D. for the source . . . "Rezek."

"It has taken all these years for dwarf conifers to be available in local nurseries on the Island, and I know that only a few old standard dwarfs are available in even the best retail nurseries in other states, except on the West Coast. Dwarf conifers haven't quite 'arrived' in much of this country. But, they'll become well known, just as they have in Europe."

Often, dwarf conifer enthusiasts also grow unusual forms of conifers, not dwarf, but standard-sized shrubs and trees with novel color forms, weeping or creeping habit, unusual leaf or needle formations, attractive bark, or with the potential for shaping into topiary forms. Ed's garden includes multiple-graft trees in various colors or growth habits of the same species and "multigeneric" plants with two or three plants of different kinds twisted and bound together so the trunks would apparently (but not actually) fuse. There are trees with kinks in their trunks, shrubs espaliered up trellises, and hundreds of offspring of dwarf conifers which Ed shared with commercial nurserymen years ago.

Nurserymen in the area regard Ed as some sort of phenomenon because he knows so much about his subject. He knows where and how to look up information on plants and propagation. Early on, he was accepted into the International Plant Propagators Society and attends their meetings in North America and abroad. He was a founding member of the American Conifer Society, and has served on its board since its inception in 1980.

Wherever he travels, Ed watches for aberrations in plants. A trip into a nearby town can turn into a collecting expedition. He is very good at spotting anomalies: color mutations, witches' brooms for dwarfing, growth habit mutations, anything that sets a conifer off from the "type" or standard for the cultivar. He soon discards any plants that lack grace or beauty. However, a sugar maple, *Acer saccharum* 'Monumentale', which grows in his side yard, is more startling than graceful. It is thirty feet tall and twenty inches wide, like a telephone pole with leaves. Ed loves to tell visiting kids that it is "Jack's Beanstalk." They believe it; so do I!

I was curious about how Ed has discovered so many oddities in his small back yard. It has partly to do with the fact that he is working with genetically unstable plants, but more to do with his daily prowling of a relatively small garden: weeding, clipping, and thinning. Nothing escapes his notice and he is out there every day during the growing season.

Right before our eyes, he pointed out a silver-fringed branch on an all-green dwarf conifer, a tightly clustered witches' broom on a tiny juniper, and a ground-hugging seedling grown from seeds harvested from an upright conifer. Later, we discovered that such mutations are more prevalent in urban areas, perhaps due to air quality.

Some of Ed's most productive seed parents are old dwarf hinoki cypress growing around the neighborhood, many from his collection. He gathers and plants the seeds, and watches for variations from the norm. The seeds have grown into many useful and beautiful variations on the

Two old specimens of Cedrus Atlantic *'Glauca Pendula', weeping blue Atlantic cedar, are trained on supports around three sides of Ed's house. Posts hold the limber branches clear of the path.*

original . . . the not-so-beautiful-nor-useful were discarded. Apparently, these old hinokis have an involved genetic makeup, which accounts for the wide segregation in offspring from seeds. Ed doesn't do any hybridizing, but relies on genetic anomalies to get new material from seed propagation.

Now that Ed has virtually no room to grow new plants, he is concentrating on making his old plants look better. Out front, he trimmed and trained two old and overgrown bird's nest spruces, *Picea abies* 'Nidiformis', into flat-topped pom-poms. From the street you can see the character of the old and twisted stems with their attractive mature bark.

Ed is changing the top growth of some old but not particularly valuable plants by grafting on new scions from desirable cultivars within the same species. Not content with that, he is tying knots in whippy *Chamaecyparis* suckers, plaiting trunks into incredible forms, and training procumbent plants like Atlantic cedar thirty feet around the sides of his house, where the twigs hang like green icicles.

Now that Ed is so sure of what he can do with plants he seems to be playing with them to amuse himself, his family, and neighbors. But, whatever he conceives has to look graceful, not grotesque, or he will prune it off and start all over. Harkening back to the plants he saw at the Imperial Palace in Peking, Ed grows bonsai and sets the containers wherever there is a little space in his crowded garden. Come winter, he sinks the containers in the ground and the warmth keeps the tiny, artistically trained plants from freezing. He has some bonsai that could grace any collection, including one cork-bark pine with an exquisite line, and a forest of Norway spruce seedlings.

Ed freely admits that three things have helped him to succeed in his specialty of dwarf conifers: an understanding and supportive wife, a job with regular hours (he worked for twenty years as a postman in Valley Stream after leaving the printing industry), and growing up in a family that loved gardening. He credits his automatic watering system for helping preserve domestic harmony: he and Maureen never feel trapped by their garden. They just set the automatic timers on the sprinkling system and the mist emitters and ventilators in the greenhouse and take off!

Ed is a natural teacher, gifted with enthusiasm and quick, sure hands. He taught a neighbor, Regina Scimeca, to graft trees. She showed me her Japanese maple with twelve grafts on it, all taking! Such multigraft trees, after you get over the shock of seeing several foliage and color forms on one tree, can be beautiful. More important, they give gardeners with small yards a way to enjoy several kinds of trees in a small area.

Always teaching, Ed showed me how to wait until axillary buds show on Japanese maples before taking cuttings, and to trim off all the leaves from the scion (the piece to be grafted on the understock, which is the bottom, or rooted, part).

Quick as a wink, Ed stripped the scion, carved the ends into a long "vee" shape, cut a cleft into the bark of the understock, inserted the graft, and whipped it into place with a wide rubber band. "New growth should start in two to three weeks inside this protective baggie," he said; "it maintains high humidity around the graft."

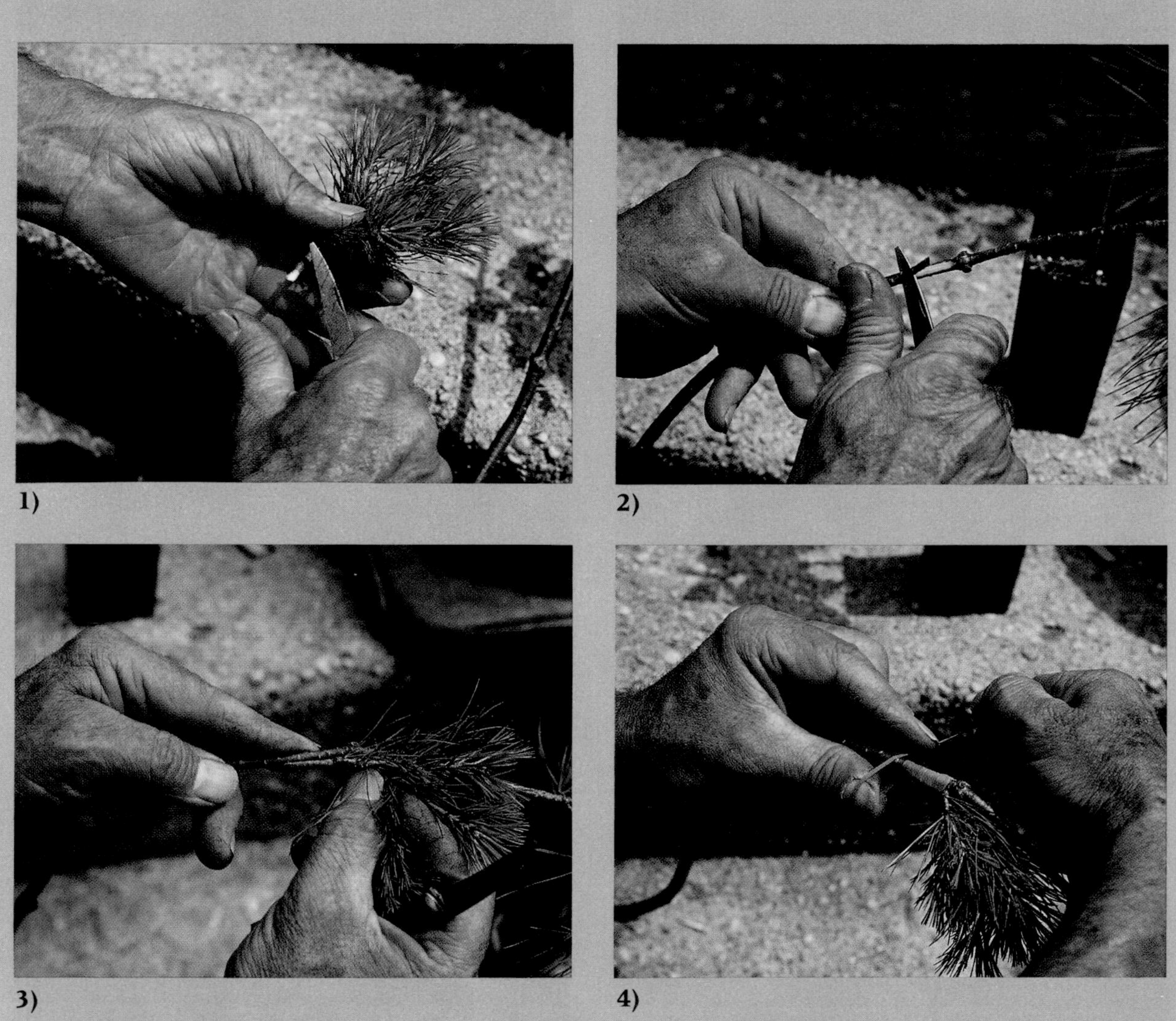

1) 2) 3) 4)

Grafting Dwarf Conifers

Ed explains the process of grafting dwarf conifers. He begins by trimming the tip of a scion branch into a vee shape (1). He cuts a matching slit through the bark of the understock (2) and slips the scion into the slit so that cambium meets cambium (3). A good bond will start the sap flowing from the understock to the scion right away. Finally he wraps a wide rubber band snugly around the graft and ties it tight (4). To maintain high humidity around the graft, Ed slips a protective plastic bag over it. New growth will begin in two to three weeks.

Some of the dwarf or compact conifers in front of Ed's home grew too large and dense for their settings. He gave the Chamaecyparis pisifera *'Compressa' a poodle cut and limbed up the golden* Taxus cuspidata *'Aurescens' into an umbrella shape to let more light in his windows.*

Ed matches the diameter of the scion to the diameter of the understock when cleft grafting, so that the connective tissue (the cambium) matches up. A good cambium-to-cambium bond will start the sap flowing right away from the understock into the scion, so it won't wilt. He prefers to work with small-diameter branches, less than ¼ inch in diameter. On deciduous trees, he uses new-growth wood from near the tips of branches.

The top growth of a sapling tree can be entirely changed by grafting a desirable scion on the stem of a vigorous but common seedling of the same species. That's the quick way to convert a cheap garden-variety tree into a choice specimen. Ed calls these "high grafts" and often uses them to replace the top growth of common green Japanese maple, *Acer palmatum*, with scion wood from a more valuable crimson or cutleaf cultivar. The branches of choice Japanese maples descend from the main trunk to form a flattened, pagodalike canopy that looks very good in the company of dwarf conifers, and which becomes picturesque with age.

I asked Ed to recommend a starter collection of dwarf conifers and choice, compatible Japanese maples for gardeners just entering the hobby. His list includes many colors, forms, habits of growth that lead to distinctive shapes, and novel foliage characteristics. These cultivars lend themselves to an infinite number of landscape situations:

- *Abies balsamea* 'Nana': Dwarf, globose, dark green, with stomatic lines on undersides of needles.
- *Chamaecyparis obtusa* 'Gracilis Nana' (Japanese hinoki cypress): Pyramidal, medium to dark green, obtuse leaf shapes.

- *Chamaecyparis obtusa* 'Lutea Nana': Dwarf, broadly pyramidal, bright gold, cup-shaped leaves.
- *Chamaecyparis pisifera* 'Golden Mop': Dwarf, mound-forming, with bright gold, threadlike foliage.
- *Chamaecyparis thyoidies* 'Little Jamie': Dwarf, dense, columnar, rock garden plant, purple cast in winter.
- *Juniperus chinensis* 'Procumbens Nana': Low-growing, groundcover-type juniper, ideal for overhanging walls.
- *Juniperus communis* 'Berkshire': Very dwarf, broadly globose, dark green, blue-striated foliage.
- *Juniperus communis* 'Compressa': Very dwarf, spirelike cultivar. Excellent for use in small-space gardens.
- *Juniperus scopulorum* 'Table Top Blue': Silver-blue foliage grows like a table top.
- *Juniperus squamata* 'Blue Star': Dwarf, mounding, with star-shaped, steel blue foliage, a recent introduction from Holland.
- *Picea abies* 'Little Gem': Very dwarf, dense, bun-form plant; diminutive, excellent for the rock garden.
- *Picea pungens* 'Globosa Glauca Nana': Dwarf, globose, dense shrub, with good blue coloration.
- *Picea pungens* 'St. Mary's Broom': Diminutive, mounding blue spruce with conspicuous buds; a real "mini-gem."
- *Picea sitchensis* 'Papoose': Dwarf, compact, broadly conical bush; fine needles with blue striation beneath.
- *Pinus parviflora* (Japanese black pine) 'Adcock's Dwarf': Diminutive, slow-growing, congested bun; a jewel for a rock garden or small area.
- *Pinus strobus* 'Nana': Dwarf, compact, spreading mound; long, soft, dense bluish-green needles.
- *Pinus sylvestris* 'Repens': Rich green, compact ground-hugger.
- *Tsuga canadensis* (hemlock) 'Cole's Prostrate': Dwarf, slowly creeping, well-branched mound; center wood is exposed; partial shade is best.

As taller companion plants for dwarf conifers, Ed suggests "high grafts" or four Japanese maple cultivars: 'Garnet', 'Crimson Queen', 'Ever-Red', and 'Filigree Lace'.

- *Acer palmatum* 'Garnet': Coarse, dissected, gem-red foliage on a broad, compact mound.
- *Acer palmatum* (Japanese maple) Dissectum 'Crimson Queen': Mounding, cascading form; deep red, finely dissected foliage and branches.
- *Acer palmatum* Dissectum 'Ever-Red': Leaves emerge with fine silvery hairs; retains good red color in hot weather.
- *Acer palmatum* 'Red Filigree Lace': Fine, threadlike, deep red foliage: the finest cutleaf red in existence.

A cork bark black pine, Pinus thunbergiana *'Corticosa Nishiki', has been trained into bonsai form.*

As companion perennials to cover the soil between dwarf conifers, Ed suggests: the compact sedums and sempervivums; *Lamium* 'Beacon Silver', and dwarf *Thymus* (thyme) cultivars. These are smaller than the culinary thyme cultivars. Miniature hostas and dwarf iris such as *Iris verna* and *I. cristata* are quite appropriate for interplanting among dwarf conifers.

As annuals for color spots among the dwarf conifers, he uses (discreetly): tuberous-rooted begonias, New Guinea impatiens, and wax begonias. When they grow so large that they begin to look out of scale, Ed pulls them out and replants with younger plants of annuals.

In his rich topsoil, Ed never feeds his dwarf conifers. His object is neither to starve his plants to retard growth nor to stimulate them into growing rapidly. Rather, he wants them to grow slowly but steadily and retain good foliage color. He has applied a light mulch of pine bark for several years and feels that the nutrients released during its decomposition are sufficient to nourish the slow-growing evergreens. They certainly looked well fed to me!

Red spider mites are a major problem on conifers everywhere; they can be troublesome in hot, dry weather. Ed is planning to use insecticidal soap to increase the effectiveness of his spray program. He is watching with considerable alarm a serious pest on other parts of the Island, the Adelgid hemlock scale. These armor-plated insects are difficult to control, except at the crawling stage. Then, insecticides mixed with spreader-sticker agents will penetrate and kill them.

Slugs are a minor problem, mostly on the hostas Ed uses in shaded areas. Squirrels try, and sometimes succeed, in digging up his precious plants. Ed captures them in a humane trap and carts them off to a large park some distance away.

In Ed Rezek's garden, it is easy to see why dwarf conifers are the designer plants of tomorrow. Experts like Dr. Henry Marc Cathey of the National Arboretum predict that the new American landscape will be composed of smaller, slow-growing, choice plant material, sited with care for maximum impact. Anyone looking for a prototype garden will find it in Malverne, New York.

More about Dwarf Conifers

Dwarf conifers have been selected from a number of genera. Most of these species are native to temperate climates and prefer rather moist soil conditions. With the growing interest in water conservation and xeriscaping, we may see more interest in selecting dwarfs from warm climates, plants which can tolerate dry soils:

Abies (fir)
Cedrus (true cedar)
Cephalotaxus (plum yew)
Chamaecyparis (false cypress)
Cryptomeria (Japanese cedar)
Juniperus (southern red cedar)
Picea (spruce)
Pinus (pine)
Podocarpus (southern or Japanese yew)
Pseudotsuga (Douglas fir)
Taxus (yew)
Thuja (arborvitae)
Tsuga (hemlock)

Dwarf conifers can be grouped into three divisions by size:

- *Pigmy:* Only one-twentieth the size of normal plants of the species at maturity, the specimens can be quite expensive because they grow so slowly.
- *Dwarf:* One-twentieth to one-quarter the size of normal plants of the species at maturity, these are usually easier to grow than the pygmy types, because of their vigor.
- *Compact:* One-third to one-half the normal size of the species when mature, these should not be confused with young plants of standard-sized shrubs, trees, and groundcovers, which grow considerably faster and up to three times as large.

Rate of Growth

The rate of growth of dwarf conifers depends not only on the length and warmth of the growing season but also on precipitation, irrigation, exposure to wind, nutrition programs, and underlying soil. Hobby growers make their soil well drained, and keep it on the poor side, although well fortified with organic matter for water retention and biological activity. Maintaining an organic mulch by adding to it each year or two is standard practice in most dwarf conifer gardens.

Rate of growth can also depend on the interaction of the scion and the understock of dwarfs grafted on normal rootstocks. Grafting is the only practical way to increase certain desirable specimens that may be difficult to root as cuttings, or don't set seeds. Much trial and error has gone into matching scions to understocks that won't force them to grow overly large and that weld into strong unions.

Buying Dwarf Conifers

Accumulating a dwarf conifer collection is usually a long-term proposition because of the care needed in acquiring compatible specimens adapted to one's climate. You often see rock garden enthusiasts evolving into dwarf conifer enthusiasts as well, for they already have the site and a feeling for working with small plants.

Use caution when planting balled and burlapped plants. Most sources offer dwarf conifers as balled and burlapped plants or containerized specimens. Generally, the slower-growing the plant, the costlier, because of the time it has to spend in the nursery growing large enough to be sold. Rezek told me that plants can be grown in fields with soils that are too sandy to retain a good, solid root ball, or sold before a new network of roots has proliferated inside the burlap. If the nurseryman knocks these around with careless handling, or if you rush the planting, you can end up with a bare-root plant that may not survive. Ed always leaves the burlap in place, but unties and folds back the top after he has pulled the backfill soil up and around the root ball. He firms the backfill thoroughly to eliminate air pockets that could let roots dry out. I might add that you should avoid plants that are balled in woven plastic; you must completely remove this stuff. Roots won't grow through it.

Ed uses a lath cover over plants in his holding area for winter protection and for summer shade.

Prepare the soil for dwarf conifers by thoroughly mixing in a 2-inch layer of moistened peat moss or finely ground composted pine or fir bark to spade depth. If your soil is heavy clay, also mix in 2 inches of sand. This will raise the level of the dwarf conifer bed 3 to 4 inches above the surrounding soil for good drainage. Raised beds give no particular advantage on deep, sandy soils.

Landscaping

Effective arrangements can be as simple as a small, uncomplicated combination of shape and colors for an intimate corner, a little colony of various shapes and colors among a cluster of large rocks, one or two in a stone trough interplanted with alpines, or on a gritty, gravelly, scree sloping down from a scattering of rocks that appear to have been deposited by a retreating glacier.

Group pygmy plants fairly closely: individual specimens tend to fade into the wallpaper. However, space dwarf and compact types far enough apart so that they do not become crowded with age. Leave generous spaces between groups of dwarf conifers and fill them with choice groundcovers and spring bulbs.

Between groups of dwarf conifers, establish mats of low-growing, nonaggressive groundcovers. You will have to hunt up suppliers of choice groundcovers to get cultivars to set off the color and texture of your dwarf conifers.

Care

You can keep the interiors of large plants free of accumulations of dead needles by shaking them and, if you can reach the interior, raking and disposing of needles. A few dead needles do no harm, but a deep layer can be unsightly, can shed water, and can actually become a fire hazard around smokers.

Some authorities recommend that you syringe plants with a fine spray of water frequently during warm weather. But Ed Rezek cautions you not to do it on new growth, not until after it has hardened. Water on tender young needles or leaves, followed by hot sun, can cook them. Some of the dwarf hemlocks are particularly susceptible.

Sharp, fine sprays of water can discourage spider mites. One of the best ways to do this is to use a backpack sprayer with plain water or insecticidal soap. Maximum pressure will blast many of the red spiders off, if directed up toward the undersides of leaves. It is difficult to get a sufficiently fine spray with a water hose without so much pressure that needles or leaves are damaged.

Propagation

Once you have developed the touch for siting and growing these fascinating plants, you may be inspired to try growing them from seeds, collecting them from abnormal growths such as witches' brooms, and propagating them by cuttings or grafting. Growing and propagating dwarf conifers from seeds or cuttings taken from growth anomalies is not really difficult, but it does require more attention and concentration than most other plant specialties.

You really need to see pygmy, dwarf, and compact conifers to appreciate their uniqueness and to get ideas on where and how to use them. Don't be overwhelmed by the complex plantings displayed at public gardens. Start with a small grouping of plants that please your sense of color and balance, and let your collection evolve from there. If you plan to grow your dwarf conifers in containers, select cultivars that are hardy in the next zone to the north to assure their overwintering reliably.

Peonies

With a good eye, a green thumb, and a little bit of luck, Wisconsin's Roger Anderson makes a breakthrough in peony breeding.

(Left) 'First Arrival' was Roger Anderson's first introduction from his efforts to cross tree peonies with herbaceous cultivars.

Peonies are legendary for their opulent, often fragrant flowers in luminous shades, from pastels to deep reds and creamy whites. The vivid hues of the emerging spring growth and flower buds provide color impact long before the blossoms open. After bloom, the foliage is clean and glossy, a handsome foil for later-blooming perennials. Peonies deliver an end-of-season gift; seed pods on long stems can be dried for arrangements. Peonies are long-lived, too; a mature plant can eventually spread to four feet, a commanding spectacle in the perennial border.

The range of peony flower forms include *single,* with the flower's center composed of stamens and pistils, and a single, daisylike layer of ray petals; *semidouble,* with two or more layers of petals in open blossoms, and with the stamens and pistils clearly visible at the center; *double,* or *"fully double,"* nearly ball-like, with many layers of petals concealing the stamens and pistils; and *"Japanese type,"* in which the single or semidouble blossoms have a distinctive crested, petaloid or staminoid "boss" in the center.

Most gardeners are familiar with herbaceous peonies, cultivars which freeze to the ground during the winter and regrow each spring from strong, deep rootstocks. All require a long winter dormancy and do not perform well south of zone 7B. Long-stemmed and fragrant, herbaceous peonies are one of the most desirable flowers for cutting. Though the double cultivars that look so spectacular in the garden can overpower arrangements, the single or crested anemone types combine well with other blooms. Early, midseason, or late-blooming cultivars provide an extended flowering season.

The relatively rare early-blooming herbaceous rock garden peonies, *Paeonia tenuifolia*, are very hardy. They average twelve to eighteen inches in height, with fernlike, deeply cut leaves. Some of the cultivars in this class have a blossom form not found in other classes, single with tufted centers.

More unusual are tree peonies, which actually resemble shrubs rather than trees and develop woody, persistent top growth reaching two to four feet or more in height. Their bloom period begins with the late herbaceous types, and extends two or three weeks thereafter. The flowers have distinctive frilled petals with dark "flares" at the base; in some cultivars, the petals are fringed with contrasting colors. In many parts of the United States, tree peonies are more difficult to grow than herbaceous types. The West Coast, Northwest, and protected East Coast sites provide the requisite mild winters and cool summers to produce the classic large, shrubby tree peony forms so coveted as landscape specimens. Where they can be grown, the dramatic size, fragrance, attractive foliage, and characteristic form of the blossoms rank tree peonies with rhododendrons and roses for sheer beauty.

A class recently expanded by breeders in the United States is one that crosses herbaceous peonies with tree peonies. These crosses resemble either true herbaceous or tree peonies, depending on the percentage of traits inherited from a particular parent. Their bloom period corresponds to that of tree peonies.

As a genus, the peonies number about thirty species, some of which are no longer found in the wild. Of these, six or eight have been extensively improved for garden use or incorporated into hybrids. Originally, peonies were brought to Europe from the Caucasus in the sixteenth century, and a different group of species from China and Siberia in the eighteenth century. The first mention of peonies in the United States was a listing of five varieties in M'Mahon's catalog in 1806.

American peony breeding was inspired by the progress made in Europe, notably by Lemoine in France, and by the English nurseryman James Kelway. Lemoine succeeded in crossing the Chinese peony with *P. Witt-*

Tree peonies flourish in light shade. 'Tria' is the yellow single; 'Joseph Rock' the white; 'Hana Kisoi' the pink.

manniana. The Chinese peony, *P. lactiflora,* is the ancestor of most herbaceous peonies and has long been cultivated in the Orient. Lemoine broke with the long-standing infatuation of European breeders with the indigenous *P. officinalis*. Lemoine's crosses became known as "European Hybrids." Kelway focused on selecting from the Chinese peony.

During the prosperous years of westward expansion following the War Between the States, keen American gardeners discovered how well the hardy herbaceous peonies grew in our northern climates. European travel grew, and gadabout gardeners saw and ordered the latest European peony hybrids. Interest peaked in the days of Queen Victoria, when spacious homes and yards provided room to grow large perennials and abundant domestic help freed genteel ladies to exercise their talents in making florid arrangements for their homes and churches.

'Coral Charm', an early, semidouble herbaceous peony, won a gold medal from the American Peony Society.

By 1903, interest in peonies was very high, and the first annual meeting of the American Peony Society commissioned Professor John Craig of Cornell University to plant and observe and standardize the many named varieties of peonies for sale in the United States and Europe. In addition, the Society had Craig rate peonies on a scale of 1 to 10 and recommended that the trade drop all varieties scoring less than 7.5.

During the 1930s, the foremost pioneer American breeder of peonies, Dr. A. P. Saunders of New York State, succeeded in crossing several species and made many desirable selections from the progeny. He also refined certain species imported directly from their native countries. Today, more than half a century later, eight of his herbaceous peonies, twenty-three of his tree peonies, and two of his rock garden cultivars are still being offered.

Between the two world wars peonies suffered a lag in popularity. In part this was due to certain limitations of the plants themselves. The blossoms of some of the older varieties are so large that they fill with water and tip face down during spring rains. The mature plants of some cultivars are simply too large for compact modern gardens, a far cry from Victorian times when tall peonies with blossoms as large as cabbages were in scale with homes. Moreover, the palette of traditional peony colors—shades of rose, magenta, lavender, and dark reds—has been subject to the whims of fashion trends.

Sluggishness among commercial producers contributed to public indifference. For various reasons, many commercial peony growers' offerings failed to keep pace with changing tastes. As their huge inventories of old favorites waned in popularity, these growers were slow to replace them with improved varieties, which tended to circulate within a small group of amateur breeders. Increasing stocks of new peony varieties is slow and expensive; it can be five years or longer between the evaluation of a deserving new hybrid and the production of an inventory sufficient for introduction. Good peony varieties are not cheap. Older varieties average ten to twenty-five dollars apiece, but new introductions, especially those which have received an award from the American Peony Society, can bring two hundred fifty dollars or more.

Even the way in which peonies are sold has held back their progress. Producers ship herbaceous peonies mostly in the late summer and fall, the traditional planting time. Yet, spring is the time when the mass of gardeners wish to buy plants. The peony plants offered for sale in the spring are mostly dormant root divisions, usually boxed in illustrated waxed-paper cartons and kept moist with shavings. If these are not sold within a few weeks, the warmth of the display area will wake them up and sprouting will commence. It is most difficult to transplant a sprouted peony root, with 3 or 4 inches of succulent growth, without its suffering considerable shock.

Several developments have pulled peonies out of their sales slump. Most important, devoted amateur breeders have risen to the challenge to improve the genus; their greatly improved cultivars and hybrids are becoming more widely available. The leading commercial growers of peony plants are now quick to react when an amateur hybridist develops a promising new seedling, by arranging for marketing rights. Some are also funding research and breeding programs of their own. Propagation by tissue culture promises to speed up the initial increase of these new varieties, and nurseries are beginning to grow and sell improved peonies in containers to make planting possible at any time during the growing season.

Yet, hobby peony breeders outnumber the professional plant breeders and, in the foreseeable future, will be having the greatest impact on improving the genus. One successful amateur breeder, Roger Anderson, feels there is plenty of room for more hobby breeders. His story will show you one way to get started in this fulfilling hobby.

Roger stands before the impressive array of his peony evaluation trials.

Each spring, the spacious, sloping front lawn of a farm home near Fort Atkinson, Wisconsin, undergoes a transformation. During the winter, little can be seen except long rows of tilled soil crossing the lawn on contour, and the glint of sun reflecting from plant tags. Then, with the melting of snow and warming of soil, strong spears, like bronzy-green asparagus, begin pushing up through the mulch. By late May, cars will be stopping on the farm-to-market road in front of the house to admire the rows and rows of flowers, breathtaking in their color. Roger and Sandra Anderson's peonies are doing their thing again, all twelve hundred plants, tall and short, single and double flowered, ruby-red or green leaved, moving with the slightest breeze, and, later, perfuming the air and exciting the senses.

The star of the peony show is a hybrid produced by Roger, a cross between an herbaceous cultivar and a hybrid with a tree peony as one of its parents. He named his hybrid 'Bartzella'. The plants are semiherbaceous in response to winter, yet the large, citrus-scented blossoms are like tree peonies, a lovely lemon yellow and fully double, with frilly-edged petals. Individual established plants of 'Bartzella' have produced more than sixty blooms each, up to six inches in diameter. The foliage resembles, at first glance, that of an herbaceous peony. A closer look reveals similarities with tree peony foliage. A cross between two species is difficult and unpredictable; that an amateur was able to accomplish it speaks well of Roger's self-taught skills.

The dense, compact plants of 'Bartzella' grow to a height of twenty-four to thirty inches and the sturdy stems won't gooseneck when weighted by rain. The petals have more substance than tree peonies. Plants have survived temperatures of 30 degrees below zero F. They froze back to about three inches above the ground but regrew strongly.

Roger didn't become a peony enthusiast and hybridizer overnight. His was a long and involved hegira, filled with summer romances with other plants, specialties which he explored then set aside to move onward. His journey began at Whitewater, Wisconsin, his boyhood home. All his people farmed, raised purebred Holstein cattle, and grew vegetable and berry crops to feed their families and to sell. His pragmatic father liked to kid

Roger about his fondness for flowers. His favorite line was, "When are they going to be ready to eat?"

It was Roger's grandfather who encouraged his involvement in flowers. Noticing the sturdily built toddler sniffing the gladiolus he raised for cutting, his grandfather nicknamed Roger "Ferdinand" after the famous bull in a children's story. Roger can still remember helping his grandfather harvest long gladiolus stems and seeing, around his yard, plants of old 'Festiva Maxima' peony.

After high school, Roger served a hitch in the military, then returned to truck gardening for several years, to supplement income from an eight-to-five job. They were good but hard years, with Roger and Sandra growing and selling many kinds of vegetables, fruits, and flowers for extra income. His interest in flowers led Roger to Bill Himmler, a local amateur plant breeder, who taught him how to hybridize gladiolus and grow them from seeds. Under Bill's tutelage, Roger learned how to evaluate new breeding lines critically. After taking a long, hard look at the limited market for new and improved gladiolus hybrids and the numerous breeders competing for the business, Roger went into other hobbies. He bred and sold black Labrador dogs, Golden-laced Wyandotte poultry, and Roller pigeons. A dog lover myself, I asked Roger why he moved from dogs to flowers. He answered "Well, I made money breeding Labs, but they tended to wander. I always knew where the flowers were at night!"

Along the way, Roger and Sandra were raising a family of four and making plans for their present hilltop home on ten acres just south of Fort Atkinson. To meet the needs of his growing family, Roger went to work as a purchasing agent for a local meat packing plant and, later, as a machinist . . . his present occupation. He still takes contracts for house painting. "Lets me make money to support my hobby," he says with a smile. (I know what he means.)

About fifteen years ago, Roger was introduced to peonies by his friend Carroll Spangler, who showed him photos of one of the first Itoh hybrid peonies from Japan. It was love at first sight! Roger scraped up forty dollars and sent to Gilbert H. Wild's nursery for plants to use for seed production. Roger told me that at the time, the forty dollars was his life's savings and he really felt guilty about spending the money on flowers. I'm sure that a lot of older gardeners who grew up during the Great Depression can relate to that feeling.

Roger had to wait several years for his small Itoh hybrid plants to produce flowers. They made such an impression that he has purchased more peony cultivars every succeeding year. His collection grew, and provided a large and diverse gene pool among his twelve hundred plants. As he mastered his specialty, Roger refined his objectives in peony breeding, foremost of which was the introduction of the yellow color into hardy herbaceous peonies. The way he got the female parent for the cross that produced his first breakthrough was serendipity itself.

One day, when Roger was visiting Carroll Spangler, he noticed a chance seedling peony in bloom. It was a plant Carroll had found years earlier, growing in an asparagus patch, apparently from a seed dropped there. Carroll took pity on the little plant and moved it to a peony bed where, at first, it produced double blooms. Thereafter, it always produced single blooms.

Roger looked beyond the rather homely single blossoms and saw possibilities for the plant as a parent in hybrids. It was vigorous, produced an abundance of pollen, and set loads of large, fat seed pods. Carroll saw no value in the blossoms for shows and was about to discard the plant when Roger intervened and asked to move it to his garden. He divided the crown of that vigorous seedling into three sections. Strangely, while one grew into a single flowered plant, two produced double pink flowers! Roger used the single-flowered plant not only as a female parent in crosses but also as a pollen donor. Roger has been very thorough about early removal of all anthers on female parents, and is positive that the resulting seeds from crosses with tree peonies have produced true hybrids and not "selfs."

Roger is not the first hybridizer to cross herbaceous and tree peonies. About forty years ago a Japanese (they are mad about tree peonies) named T. Itoh succeeded in crossing the herbaceous peony 'Kakodin' and a hybrid out of *P. lutea*, named 'Alice Harding'. Out of twelve hundred crosses he got nine plants: the offspring of four of these made it to the United States where they became known as the Itoh hybrids. As yet, they are curiosities to most gardeners except peony fanciers.

The Itoh hybrids are proving more valuable to gardeners than either of their parents, and should continue to attract interest for years to come. They are quite winter hardy, and resistant to wind and rain damage. To date, no problems with diseases have been noted. With their ease of growth and low maintenance requirements, they should be a landscaper's dream. Early in the season the bushes take on a symmetrical globe shape, which holds until late in the fall. The plants color up nicely after a light frost.

Actually, Mr. Itoh was only one of a line of peony breeders who sensed the commercial possibilities of transferring the yellow color of *P. lutea* to other peony species. The French breeder Lemoine and, later, A. P. Saunders crossed the Japanese tree peony with *P. lutea* to produce what became known as the Lutea hybrids.

Roger Anderson saw the Itoh hybrids as a means to an end. He felt that he could transfer their yellow, golden, and softer colors to herbaceous peonies, *P. lactiflora*, and retain the best qualities of the three contributing species. It took a few years, but he did it! A few other American

'Cora Louise', which Roger named for his grandmother, was his second tree x herbaceous peony hybrid.

hybridizers have succeeded with similar crosses: two named cultivars have come out of their efforts.

Rather than clutter the nomenclature, the American Peony Society has decided to list all Roger Anderson's cultivars and genetically comparable strains from other breeders with the Itoh hybrids. Roger commented, "I should have enough of my hybrids increased to begin selling small quantities on a first-come, first-served basis in 1992. Prices will be rather high, due to the limited number of plants available." Roger and Sandra have named their budding commercial peony plant enterprise "Callie's Beaux Jardin." Says Roger, "Out here in Holstein country that French name

These two unnamed seedling tree x herbaceous peony hybrids are under evaluation. Hybrid 81-08, left, and 81-18 are from crosses Roger made in 1981.

ought to be an attention-getter!" Visitors are welcome at Callie's Beaux Jardin during bloom season, by advance arrangement.

As we talked peonies, it began to emerge how Roger and Sandra have accomplished so much, with both working full-time jobs. An energetic and physically powerful man, with shoulders an ax handle wide, Roger has worked his way through several hobby plants and up through the ranks to the inner circle of peony breeders. (He would modestly decline the latter distinction, but I feel he deserves it.) Roger is a study in goal-oriented self-discipline.

His wife, Sandra, would like to see the day arrive when Roger will feel comfortable leaning on a hoe handle and admiring the fruits of their labors, rather than working harder every year. Much of her spare time has been spent in the garden with Roger, planting, weeding, labeling, and assisting him in evaluating experimental hybrids. "There are many days," Roger said, "when Sandra spends more time in the yard than I do, patrolling the peony beds, pulling and spraying weeds." But now, with an empty nest, Sandra is going back to school to get her degree in nursing, which has sent Roger scurrying to find herbicides to reduce the weeding problem.

Roger is a likable man but very serious about his work with peonies . . . so serious that he doesn't realize that he can now let up and take the time to extract more joy from every minute of his hobby. I think he realizes that he may be quite close to making his mark in the peony world and doesn't want to risk letting the opportunity slip from his grasp.

Sandra and Roger work together to grow peony seedlings from his precious hybrid seeds. After putting so much work and so many hopes into producing a few hybrid seeds, Roger wants as many as possible to grow and produce plants. Peony seeds germinate slowly, over a period of several months, and should be planted within two months after the pod turns color and before the seed coat dries hard.

Roger and Sandra pick off individual seed pods just before they become fully mature, shell out and label the seeds. He puts the fresh seeds in a plastic bag of moist sphagnum moss, in a warm corner near the furnace. This treatment produces roots on the viable seeds, but no shoots for a while.

As the roots show, Roger places the seeds in a refrigerator for two to three months, or until a growing point emerges. This satisfies their dormancy requirement. Then the seeds are potted in individual pots. When the shoot breaks through the surface of the soil, he sets the pots under fluorescent lights to hasten growth and development.

Their light fixtures can accommodate only about one hundred seedlings, so the Andersons hold back the remainder by sowing the seeds in boxes of growing medium made by mixing sphagnum peat moss with potting soil. In midwinter, they move the boxes to an unheated but sunny garage. Little happens until spring, when the seeds resume growing. By that time, Roger will have moved the indoor-grown plants to the outside to harden off, making room under the lights for additional seedlings. Seeds that germinate even later are potted up and grown outdoors.

The Andersons have almost an ideal situation for growing and evaluating peonies. Their house sits on a high hill, with their two-acre front lawn sloping down to a country highway. The land was once a dairy farm and the only trees are close to the house. The display beds, two to three hundred feet in length, run across the slope to minimize erosion.

The plants are in bloom from mid-May through late June, and attract visitors from all over the Midwest. When I phoned Roger during a dry September to check on how his plants were surviving, he told me, "Hey, don't worry, once peonies are well rooted, they are very drought resistant. And, Jim, I wish you could have been here in late August. My line of Itoh hybrids bloomed again, that late in the season! It was weird seeing peonies repeat!" he said. "I've never seen anything like it before . . . maybe the dry soil set up the situation."

The Andersons have very few problems with their peonies. Their rich, black soil seldom needs fertilizer or lime, and the carpenter bees which tunnel into peony stems elsewhere haven't yet reached Wisconsin. They spray occasionally during damp spring weather to control botrytis and other blights, with either captan or Bordeaux mixture, made by dissolving copper sulphate and hydrated lime in water: about a quarter pound of each in three gallons of water.

1) 2) 3) 4) 5) 6)

Hybridizing Peonies

Roger demonstrates his procedure for hybridizing peonies. He begins by removing the petals from the bud of the female parent's unopened flower (1). Then he emasculates the female parent by removing the anthers (2). With his finger, he dabs pollen on the receptive stigma (3). Good record-keeping is essential. Colored tape records the details of the cross for posterity (4). Covering with a paper envelope prevents contamination by pollen from other blossoms, carried by bees and other insects (5). Individual blossoms of the female parent peony, 'Martha W.', have been crossed with various pollen parents (6). Roger harvests the individual seed pods just before they are fully mature. The seeds are shelled out and labeled. Peonies germinate slowly, and the Andersons are careful to plant their precious hybrid seeds within two months after the pod turns color, before the seed coat dries hard.

Even though the peony beds are fully open to cold, drying winter winds, the Andersons never lose peonies to freezing. In severe winters, tree peonies freeze back nearly to the ground, but send up new wood from underground buds. These produce large, late blooms.

Roger feels that the good survival is due mostly to good drainage combined with very deep topsoil. He could use Snow Cones to protect flower buds, but doesn't because they would interfere with his getting a true measure of winter hardiness.

We talked for some time about why peonies had not taken off in demand like daylilies and hosta. Considering their beauty, adaptability, longevity, and freedom from problems, they should be ranked with the leaders. "Four things are holding them back," he said: "the slowness of propagation, unpredictable performance from the one-year-old grafted plants sold at retail stores, lack of promotion, and, more than anything else, lack of advanced, committed hobbyist hybridizers. I feel we are on the verge of breakthroughs in peonies that should make them the new frontier in perennial plants!

"We badly need to learn how to increase valuable new hybrids by tissue culture and to accelerate production. To my knowledge no one has succeeded at tissue-culturing peonies in quantities. Vegetative propagation is so slow that desirable new hybrids remain expensive for several years, and are known only to the fanciers who are accustomed to paying fifty to two hundred fifty dollars for a single plant. The cost of patenting a new peony is high; therefore, most new ones go unprotected. The breeder is lucky to recover his development costs.

"This situation produces no funds for promotion of peonies. Consequently, the growth of interest in peonies has been the result of one-on-one missionary work by the enthusiastic members of the American Peony Society, plus the exposure in a few national and regional mail-order catalogs.

"I think the situation is about to change," he continued. "Many other hobbyists such as myself have invested substantially in peonies. To date, it has been a labor of love for me, but my investment in plants is approaching ten thousand dollars. Some of us, myself included, will want to convert our hobby into retirement income and will go commercial.

"One promotion that is attracting attention from other gardeners are the flower shows put on by the American Peony Society. When we get together for annual meetings at various midwestern and Canadian cities, we hold shows in shopping malls, botanical gardens, and the like. We have a number of hobby growers of peonies in southern Wisconsin and hosted the 1989 annual meeting of the American Peony Society at Janesville."

I asked Roger what he had up his sleeve to follow his beautiful 'Bartzella'. "In 1988," he said, "I got my first look at a new batch of hybrids

Roger's prize tree x herbaceous peony hybrid, 'Bartzella', testifies to Roger's skill as a breeder. Large, citrus-scented blossoms, as many as sixty on an established plant, adorn the sturdy stems of this semiherbaceous peony.

between herbaceous and tree peonies. Two of them looked mighty good . . . doubles, with yellow blossoms, tinged coppery gold. They'll be increased, and evaluated elsewhere as well as in Wisconsin.

"Also," he said, "I'm trying to introduce the orange color into herbaceous peonies. I now have seven plants produced by crossing pollen from *P. lactiflora* (herbaceous) onto an orangeish Lutea hybrid tree peony. They are young now but should bloom in two years. I think I have something good, but time will tell. David Reath, over in Vulcan, Michigan, is on a similar breeding track.

"I continue to try crossing the various species to increase my peony gene pool. Sometimes it works, sometimes not. I tried *P. delavayi* but none of my crosses took. However, I did have success with using *P. Potanini* in a cross: it is a tall, shrublike peony with small yellow flowers.

One cross took: the female parent was *P. lactiflora*. The resulting hybrid was a fooler: the first-year plant produced small, dark pink, incomplete flowers. But, on the second year, it grew into a very nice plant, covered with bright red flowers. It could be the start of a new breeding line.

"And, I'm shooting for a true dwarf peony that can be containerized in an eight-inch pot and sold fully grown at four years of age. To get it, I'm using a double-flowered mutation from the fern-leaved rock garden peony *P. tenuifolia* and a dwarf *P. lobata* seedling which grows to a height of only seven to eleven inches. That's a tall order, and I probably won't succeed without several hundred experimental crosses. I won't quit until I get a dwarf with blossoms as large as teacups, even though I may have to wait from four to ten years to see the first flower on a hybrid seedling." (Note, some authorities question the existence of a distinct *P. lobata* species, but Roger and other peony hybridists will use the name to identify a generally recognized breeding line until the taxonomists agree on what it really is.)

"You can find dwarf herbaceous peonies listed now. They grow no higher than eleven to twelve inches and have blossoms about two inches across. But I want to improve on them."

As "starter" varieties for beginners, Roger recommends:

- 'Msr. Jules Elie': A double pink with good plant habit; very fragrant.
- 'Lord Calvin': Double, creamy white, accented with red candy stripes; fragrant.
- 'Wilford Johnson': Large, fragrant, dark pink.
- 'Karl Rosenfield': Double red.
- 'Paul M. Wild': Large, dark pink double; great for shows.
- 'Norma Volz': Large double, blush pink.
- 'Virginia Dare': Arrangers like it for its small white single blossoms.
- 'America': Dark crimson-red single hybrid.
- 'Sparkling Star': Pink single; looks good in flower shows.
- 'Sky Pilot': Pink, tall plants, up to 34 inches when well grown.
- 'Paula Faye': Semidouble, glowing pink; outstanding garden performer.
- 'Cytherea': Coral, cup-shaped.
- 'Eastern Star': White double.
- 'Shawnee Chief': For its red fall foliage color.

In addition, any of the 'Estate' cultivars, developed and introduced by the Klehm family, would be good prospects.

Looking forward to his retirement in a few years, Roger has already started hybridizing other garden plants, such as bearded iris, daylilies, and flowering crab apples. And, he has begun an ambitious program for renewing the landscaping around his house with choice trees and shrubs. Roger has completed putting in a water garden and will landscape it with peonies and amenable perennials.

I aked Roger what makes him so fond of hybridizing. "I guess I can't leave well enough alone," he said. "I love trying to do what no one has done before, or doing it better." You can't beat that for an attitude!

More about Peonies

I plant peonies partly because I remember the plants in my mother's garden in Memphis and in the cemeteries we visited on Confederate Memorial Day, and on Decoration Day. That's what we called the Memorial Day that everyone celebrates. The connection between peonies and Memorial Day is universal: before the days of plastic containers and plastic flowers, people used to cut armloads of peonies and stick them in half-gallon fruit jars of water to decorate the graves of their war dead.

One of our old family varieties, I believe, was 'Festiva Maxima', a fragrant white peony with crimson flecks. It was introduced in 1851!

People everywhere respond to the powerful nostalgic pull of peonies, to their bountiful beauty, their fragrance and long life as a cut flower. But some gardeners have given up after a brief fling with peonies because they don't understand that how you grow them depends largely on your climate.

Herbaceous peonies require a winter dormancy to rebuild the food reserves necessary to renew plants year after year. Therefore, they will not live for more than a year or two in mild-winter areas. There is no sharp line of demarcation, but the area where herbaceous peonies are difficult to grow corresponds roughly with hardiness zones 8 and 9. It starts at about Virginia Beach, North Carolina, and takes in the low country of the Carolinas and Georgia, including all of Florida, a strip about two hundred miles wide around the Gulf Coast, and all low-elevation areas in Arizona and California. Surprisingly, however, herbaceous peonies can survive for years in certain parts of northern California, perhaps because the summer dryness forces the plants into a pseudo-dormancy.

Planting

I asked Roger Anderson what advice he could give to beginners on growing peonies. "If possible," Roger said, "plant herbaceous peonies in the fall. If you have to start in the spring or summer, buy potted plants that can be set in the garden with minimum disturbance to the roots. Good-sized potted plants, when planted in early spring, will probably bloom the first year.

"The more advanced nurseries grow and ship tree peonies in containers from early spring through fall. The plants can be set in place in the garden at any time during the growing season but spring or fall planting, when it is cool and rainy, creates less stress on the plants.

"Peonies like loose, airy soil, with plenty of organic matter such as peat moss, rotted leaves, or pasteurized manure worked into the soil before planting, because the peonies are going to be there a long time," Roger said. "I don't like to use sawdust as a soil conditioner or mulch because it continues to cause nitrogen deficiencies in the soil.

"Planting depth is critical to the success of peonies. When planting herbaceous peonies in the northern states, locate the 'eyes,' which are the buds that produce the shoots for the coming year. Look for the tallest ones. These should not be positioned more than two inches below the surface of the surrounding soil, and preferably a bit less. If you plant the crowns deeper, chances are the plants will not bloom. Conversely, if you position the eyes level with the surface of the soil, they could freeze or dry out during a severe winter.

"However, in the South and West where winter temperatures don't drop much below 20 degrees F., plant herbaceous peony crowns so that the eyes are about level with the surface of the soil or slightly above. The shallower planting exposes the eyes to colder temperatures and helps to satisfy the requirement for winter dormancy. "Fall is the best planting time for herbaceous peonies because strong plants may bloom the following spring. However, many herbaceous peonies are sold bare-root in early spring for planting as soon as the soil can be worked. They may produce only vegetative growth the first season.

"I plant tree peonies deeper than herbaceous hybrids, and position the 'union' (where the rootstock joins the scion) 5 to 6 inches below the ground level. Where rainfall is heavy and soils are tight clay, be sure to raise the beds for tree peonies and modify the soil with organic matter.

"Plant bare-root tree peonies in the fall, between September and the end of November, or until the soil freezes. You can plant containerized tree peonies from early spring through fall. Here in Wisconsin the dates are April through November. I mulch fall-planted peonies to keep them from heaving out of the ground due to freezing and thawing.

"With herbaceous or tree peonies, the depth of planting is the same for both bare-root and containerized plants. You can't always go by the depth of the soil in the container. The sure way is to gently feel your way in from the side and brush away enough soil to see the eyes. Once you know where they are, you can position the new plant at just the right level.

"When planting any new peony, don't let the roots dry out while digging the hole, and settle it in with plenty of water. If there is no rain, give it water two or three times weekly. Spring-planted crowns will need watering several times during the first season, but fall-planted peonies develop a strong root system during early spring months to support the plants from then on.

Mulching and Fertilizing

"I use little or no fertilizer when planting because, for two or three weeks after planting, the roots can't take up fertilizer," Roger said. "The fleshy roots are busy sending out a new network of fibrous feeder roots to absorb water. At this stage they are very sensitive to excesses of fertilizer. In my rich soil, I work in a handful or two of bonemeal around each plant, about two weeks after blooming, or in the fall. On less fertile soil, I would recommend a standard commercial fertilizer of a low-nitrogen analysis, drilled in a circle around the dripline of the plant in the early spring, per manufacturer's directions. It has been my experience that feeding late in the spring, when plants are making new growth, can disturb flowering, and should be avoided.

"Wisconsin winters are severe, so I mulch new plants to prevent the soil around them from heaving due to freezing and thawing. Heaving can uproot plants and expose the roots to drying. Composted chipped wood from tree trimmings is good for mulching: it won't blow away like straw or settle into a dense layer like leaves. Piling the fresh-chipped tree trimmings with a little nitrogen and occasional sprinkling will start the decomposition process and prevent nitrogen drawdown. The pile should be started in the spring or summer and turned once or twice to prevent fermentation due to lack of oxygen.

"If you live where winters are severe, pull two or three inches of mulch right over the crowns after the ground starts to freeze and mice have found a home elsewhere. Remove the mulch in the spring when the worst of the cold weather is past but before sprouts show. If you forget and fail to pull the mulch away from the tops of crowns, the plants could suffer from excessive moisture and perhaps contract diseases. I like to use pine boughs for mulching; they stay put and are easy to remove. But, I don't always have them available.

Pests and Diseases

Roger told me: "In the North, the major pests of tree peonies are carpenter bees, deer, and rodents. I protect againt deer, rabbits, and mice by surrounding plants with fine mesh wire. Carpenter bees are not as easy to control. They enter peony plants through the scar left from cutting stems, and the young burrow down to the roots, killing the plant. You can prevent their entry by sealing cut places with soft wax or tape.

"Ants are often perceived as pests of peonies, when actually they do no harm. I can recall telling this to an older lady who, while an excellent gardener, was convinced that ants had to be on peony flower buds before they would open. Perhaps I was a bit less than tactful in telling her that it was 'nonsense and an old wives' tale,' because she took it personally and gave me a severe tongue-lashing.

"Maybe someone can suggest how to convince people that the ants aren't eating the peonies. If they'd just take a good look, they would see that the ants are merely tending aphids like we tend milk cows. They want the sticky honeydew the aphids excrete, or the droplets of sweet sap on the flower buds.

Care

"Peonies prefer full sun, except in the middle South and the West. My peony-growing friends there tell me that afternoon shade on peonies lessens the stress from intense heat and dryness. Also, tree peony blossoms hold up longer when they are protected from hot afternoon sun.

"There is little need to 'deadhead' spent blossoms except for cosmetic purposes," Roger continued. "I've seen plants grow to a great age with no one removing spent blooms. Flower arrangers would be happy to take all your long-stemmed seed pods. The pods split open when dry and are great for winter arrangements. However, you do need to remove the top growth from herbaceous peonies when it freezes back in the fall, to lessen problems with foliage diseases. The frost-killed tops twist off easily. Leave the tops on tree peonies or Itoh hybrids. After the new growth has started, you can trim the tops to about three-quarters of an inch above the topmost bud on each shoot, to tidy up the plants.

"Notice that I haven't talked about dividing peonies? You shouldn't do it unless a clump needs to be moved. New divisions can take two or three years to hit their stride. I've seen fifty-year-old clumps that have never been divided, still blooming vigorously."

Regional Differences

Let me add that peony culture in the South differs slightly from northern practices. Growing up in climatic zones 6 and 7, I saw my parents apply rotted manure two to three inches deep as a mulch on herbaceous peony beds after the tops had frozen. They were careful not to cover the crowns with it. The mulch seemed to slow the emergence of spring shoots by a week or so, just enough to keep the buds from being frozen during late cold snaps. Every two or three years they would apply a top-dressing of lime before mulching with manure, to keep the soil from becoming too acid.

Like Roger Anderson, we had few insect and disease problems with peonies. However, this was before Japanese beetles began invading the upper South. Unfortunately, the late-blooming peonies can still be in flower when the first of the Japanese beetles arrive. Now, we hang beetle traps 100 yards upwind from our peony and rose plants to trap as many as possible on the wing. We also patrol the garden mornings and evenings during the worst of the beetle season to handpick the critters. We drop them into a can of kerosene. Thankfully, the beetle season lasts only a month or so where we live.

Unlike Roger Anderson's rich, deep, black soil, southern soils are generally poor. To grow good peonies, you need to fortify the soil with organic matter to improve nutrient holding capacity and drainage. We feed peonies with a balanced garden fertilizer once, in late summer. Our soils are so low in nitrogen that a low-nitrogen fertilizer can't supply enough nitrogen to meet the needs of peonies. Deep, fast-draining, sandy soils have little capacity for nutrient storage and call for an additional feeding right after blooming is completed. We mulch peonies as Roger does, using compost or hardwood bark mulch.

If you like the idea of growing peonies and want to start out right, the catalogs of peony specialists would be a good place to get a feel for the cultivars, their classes, sizes, colors, advantages, and limitations. In surveying the catalogs, you may be attracted to the old standbys because of their modest price. Let me recommend that you consider buying fewer, but better, cultivars. The newer introductions are so dramatically improved, and peony plants last so long, that the additional cost for modern cultivars is an investment which will repay you many times over.

Wildflowers

It took thirty years of study and work, but now Weesie Smith's woods teem with choice southeastern native plants.

Great expanses of wildflowers in full bloom can knock your socks off with their vivid colors, movement in the wind, and the extra added attractions of butterflies, skippers, moths, and other colorful insects. These native or domestic stands of plantings are what "hook" many gardeners on wildflowers. But what keeps them involved has to do with the need to live closer to nature: if you can't go out into the woods and fields as often as you like, bring small reminders of the great outdoors into your garden.

Unlike garden flowers, wildflower plantings in full sun depend on a succession of bloom, one species overgrowing and following another, all season long, rather than a few kinds of highly selected flowers remaining in color for extended periods. Dominant species come and go, with pinks and blues much in evidence in the spring, followed by earthy yellows, reds, and mahoganies; and white, purple, and gold in the fall. Almost always, the annual grasses are very much a part of the scene; you learn to view them not as weeds but as a foil for the flowers.

(Left) A trail mulched with wood chips leads from the forest and up stone steps to the Smith home.

The past two decades have seen an enormous growth of interest in native stands of wildflowers and in bringing wildflowers into home gardens. The crossing over of many gardeners into conservation and restoration of wildflower sites has swelled the ranks of wildflower enthusiasts. Any meeting of native plant hobbyists will be a happy jumble of home gardeners with no training in horticulture, nurserymen with a special interest in wildflowers, and botanists and naturalists, either professional or self-taught.

Planting wildflowers in gardens and tended woodlands is not a new idea. After all, the first garden flowers were transplanted from the wild or grown from seeds or bulbs found in the wild. It is safe to say that the first flowers were domesticated because they were the prettiest plants around, at the least prettier than weeds, and perhaps fragrant. Some would have been "bee plants" grown to supply foraging bees with a nearby source of nectar and pollen.

Home gardeners have an easier time than botanists when it comes to distinguishing between wildflowers and weeds. To nonprofessionals, if a native North American plant is showy in bloom or graceful in foliage, even for a short period of time, it is a wildflower. Most nonprofessionals would expand the usual definition of a weed as a "plant out of place" to include all plants with tiny, nondescript flowers and awkward growth habits, even when they are part of the native plant population. Botanists prefer not to use the pejorative term "weed": they tend to group all wild, nonintroduced flora as "native plants." They refer to all introduced plants as "exotics."

All garden flowers were at one time wildflowers but have been so extensively hybridized and improved that they would have a hard time surviving if transplanted to the wild. Many have been so dwarfed and loaded with flowers that they are dependent on gardeners for supplementary plant food and water.

(Right) One of Weesie's "affinity groups" incorporates blue Phlox divaricata*; white foam flower,* Tiarella wherryi*, the Japanese Solomon's seal,* Polygonatum odoratum *'Variegatum'; the groundcover* Epimedium x warleyense *and, foreground, hardy cyclamen.*

By definition, wildflowers are unimproved species. Plants within species are not as alike as peas in a pod. Individual plants or isolated populations often show quite a bit of variation from the plant designated as "typical," or "the norm," which has caused great confusion in nomenclature. This gene pool diversity is one of nature's devices for insuring survival of the tens of thousands of species in the wild. It also provides sharp-eyed plant breeders candidates for improvement and introduction as garden flowers or landscape specimens.

Always, there have been nature-oriented gardeners who prefer wildflowers "as is" . . . who appreciate their often spartan simplicity and informality. Almost as soon as the first colonists arrived here, these early naturalist-gardeners began moving wildflowers into their gardens by seeds, bulbs, cuttings, and transplants. Those with talents in botany began active seed, bulb, and plant exchanges with the Old World and with other parts of the Colonies. Some North American species were instant "hits." Others

became the stuff of legends, such as the beautiful flowering shrub *Franklinia alatamaha*, sent to Europe and no longer found in the wild.

Native North American wildflower history and lore is really more about people than plants because it concerns the early plant explorers such as John Bartram, who gathered and sent seeds, plants, and bulbs to foreign collectors. In some instances, plants and seeds were collected on research, military, or strategic explorations of middle America and the West, by Audubon, Lewis and Clark, Fremont, and others. European plant explorers came over, either out of scientific curiosity or on commissions from wealthy collectors. Catesby, Michaux, and others are remembered by species they discovered. Thomas Jefferson broke with the reliance on exotic flowers for gardens and tried our native wildflowers at Monticello.

The incredibly rich and varied flora of the New World has enchanted European gardeners since the first boat returned with glowing descriptions of our plants and animals. To this day, interest in propagating North American wildflowers for garden plantings is stronger in Europe than in the United States. Our wildflowers are capable of getting started, surviving, and multiplying despite wide fluctuations in temperature and rainfall. Except for dryland species, ours are easier to grow in Europe than some of their more temperamental species are here.

The early involvement of Europeans with our wildflowers explains why, in colonial days, seeds of some North American species were shipped back to us for planting in gardens. The Europeans were growing species from all over North America, including Mexico, at their botanical gardens when our own garden seed industry was limited to a few industrious Shakers in the East. Some of the varieties had been selected for uniformity, larger flowers, and a better range of colors, but many looked essentially as they did growing in the wild. Thereafter, for many years, the emphasis among European and American seedsmen was on converting American wildflowers into improved garden flowers rather than on propagating wildflowers as Nature put them on this earth.

Wildflowers deserve all the attention they are now receiving, and more. Some rival garden flowers in beauty, durability, and ease of growth. They can add character and interest to otherwise bland seasonal grasslands, forests, and rocky slopes. With all of this going for them, why do so many gardeners slight them in favor of named cultivars of garden flowers?

Some of the resistance is the result of the "regionality" of wildflowers. Each species or subspecies gradually evolved to fit a certain rather narrow ecological niche, and some are not happy unless the grower can provide a similar environment in his garden or woodlands. You have to devote more thought to planting wildflowers and native trees and shrubs than to establishing garden flowers. You have to think of wildflower plantings as "restoring an original picture" rather than "creating a new picture," as you do with garden flowers.

Four developments during the last two decades have conspired to simplify the growing of wildflowers. First, several regional greenhouse-nurseries have begun to produce plants of a wide range of species of native wildflowers, trees, and shrubs for sale. They have worked the kinks out of propagation and can offer sound advice on landscaping with native plants. Second, certain wildflower groups have worked hard to popularize native plants, such as prairie wildflower associations in the Midwest, mountain wildflower groups in the Appalachians, and horticultural societies everywhere. Third, seed companies are promoting mixtures of wildflower seeds as an alternative to large expanses of high-maintenance turf grass. Last but not least, easy-to-follow books on propagating native wildflowers from seeds, cuttings, and division are becoming available.

More and more Americans are becoming concerned about preservation of the environment and the conservation of resources, including native plants. Some are concentrating on protecting or enhancing wildflower sites; others on establishing sanctuaries for wildflowers in their private or public gardens and woodlands. Others are pushing officials to establish wildflowers on roadsides and large open sites such as the land around airfields.

Before the term "conservationist" became stylish, Weesie Smith of Alabama combined her love for wildflowers and gardening with an intense and active concern for preserving irreplaceable sites. Her knowledge of southeastern wildflowers is so vast, her motives so simple and straightforward, and her personality so warm and sharing that it rubs off on everyone she meets.

Weesie's steep land features rock outcroppings that she has planted with native ferns and flowering plants.

It is hard to envision Weesie slogging through the swamps of Alabama, or picking her way through deep, brush-clogged ravines to find and identify wildflowers. A tall, slim, gracious lady of great beauty, she charmed the *Victory Garden* audience when we featured her garden. With her education, energy, and natural talents, Weesie would have had little trouble running a sizable business. But she chose family life, gardening, and wildflowering.

In 1957, Weesie and Lindsay Smith built their present home on a deeply wooded, steeply sloping lot of more than four acres on the outskirts of Birmingham, Alabama. She laughed when she recalled how they had to convince their contractor that they really wanted to build on such rough terrain, and that they had to insist he remove only the trees that were in the way of the lane and the house. (In those days, contractors preferred to clear and flatten building lots.)

For a while, Weesie gardened conventionally, landscaping mostly the sunny areas around the house. She had already been bitten by the wildflower bug, but now she had the space to bring them into her garden. Over the years, she and Lindsay constructed winding paths throughout the heavy woods on her property, and removed dead trees to open up the dense canopy of foliage. Then began a continuing wildflower planting program that includes native plants from all over the Southeast and some related wild species from afar.

The *Victory Garden* TV crew taped Weesie Smith's wildflower garden at peak bloom time. I saw species that were new to me, including the forest understory tree, *Stewartia malacodendron*, also called the silky camellia, and *Luecothoe populifolia.* She had great swatches of the common herbaceous wildflowers such as deciduous ginger, and little clumps of rare plants such as terrestrial orchids. Down in a deep ravine, she had sunk plastic bags in the ground to create a boggy environment for southern rain orchids, *Habenaria clavellata.*

Weesie's gardening interests include more than native wildflowers. "Years ago," she said, "Lindsay and I built a 'pit greenhouse,' sunken into a hillside, with the south side open to the sun. We installed drainage tiles and insulating glass slanting toward the winter sun. Down in the concrete block pit, it is cool and dry, and almost never requires heat. I start seeds of wild species and cultivated plants under banks of fluorescent lights over benches, then move the seedlings to a bench beneath the slanted window to grow to transplanting size.

"That ten-by-thirty-foot greenhouse," he continued, "has the propagation capacity to quickly overload our property with wildflowers. So, I use much of the space to force cool-loving, winter-blooming pot plants such as freesias into bloom to use as holiday gifts."

Downslope from the Smiths' house are several terraces, supported by boulders removed during construction. On these contoured banks, Weesie has planted exotic rock garden plants and perennials such as tree peonies and the "roof iris," *Iris tectorum*. Odd little bulbous plants spring up through the rock walls, but she often has to replace them because of the depredations of chipmunks, mice, and voles.

Weesie refers to these areas as her "cutting gardens" because she relies on them to produce sprays for arrangements throughout the growing season. She calls a similar garden nearer the house her "cottage garden"; it receives more sunlight than any other site on the property.

"These tightly managed gardens look okay where I have them," she said, "but I choose carefully the wildflower species I plant close to the house. To me, most wildflowers look best in a natural setting, away from manicured lawns and flower beds . . . out where they appear to have been 'born free.' Conversely, I am very careful not to turn aggressive cultivated ornamentals loose in my wildflower area. The shade-loving woody and herbaceous exotics can become real pests, competing with native wildflowers. Two of the worst in our area are the ivies and vine myrtle."

Weesie was drawn into wildflowers in the late 1950s when her children were still small. She and Lindsay were, and still are, avid hikers and canoers and felt at home in the outdoors. Identifying wildflowers came naturally to Weesie, and during the first years of their marriage, she grew a few without knowing much about them. But she felt the urge to learn more about the environment, and especially Alabama soils, how they were formed, and how they influence plant populations. So, she completed several courses in natural and physical sciences, beginning with geology.

That was the scene when a wildflower enthusiast entered Weesie Smith's life—the late Eleanor Brakefield, a pioneer in the "dig and save" movement for conserving wildflowers threatened by construction projects. Eleanor persuaded Weesie to come along on a wildflower rescue expedition. In those days, dams were going up all over Alabama, often flooding priceless ecological niches; suburbs were expanding; freeways were being pushed through. Irreplaceable wildflower sites were being drowned, bulldozed, or asphalted over.

"I soon found myself caught up in the race to save whole populations of wildflowers from being wiped out," said Weesie. "From the beginning, I centered on saving shade-loving species of herbaceous wildflowers, shrubs, and small trees and transplanting them to our lot. Our property is heavily wooded and bringing in more sun-loving species than we could accommodate in our few patches of sunlight would have been pointless. I was already an experienced gardener, but I soon found that I had to learn a lot about each wildflower to succeed with it."

So began the gradual conversion of the Smiths' wooded lot into a wildflower garden. Weesie's studies in geology helped her to analyze native plant sites and to approximate them in her home garden. Cleaning out the invasive Japanese honeysuckle, muscadine grapevines, and catbriers from four acres by hand-pulling familiarized her with every square inch of the property. She probed here and there and located dry, rocky outcroppings, moist seeps, and areas of deep, fertile loam.

"There were virtually no understory plants worth saving," she said. "So it simplified the removal of about four hundred dead pine trees, killed by pine bark beetles. Later, I contacted the city and commercial tree companies and found them only too happy to dump chipped wood and leaves on our property. I wheelbarrowed it into areas I had marked for planting wildflowers. It wasn't long before I had a deep layer of decaying organic matter over much of the forest floor, and was building paths of chipped wood.

"Our five children were busy being kids," said Weesie: "they helped a little, but I couldn't expect them to share my commitment to wildflowers. I tried taking them on wildflower digs, but found the two incompatible. Instead, Lindsay and I diverted their energy into exploring northern Alabama.

"Lindsay helped by clearing honeysuckle and fallen tree limbs, but he was working long hours building his practice and couldn't go along on dig-and-save missions. After a while, I realized that wildflowering is basically a solitary pursuit, except when you are on field trips with like-minded enthusiasts. You can enjoy wildflowers without knowing much about them, but there are so many species that really knowing them can become a lifelong learning experience. Many gardeners have never ventured deep into woods and wetlands, and are more familiar with the bright annuals and perennials that grow in full sun. The rugged roadside flowers pretty well take care of themselves, but not the forest understory species. You can't just plant them and let them grow wild: they require varying degrees of management.

"When I advise gardeners on starting wildflower gardens," said Weesie, "I take them through a short checklist. I suggest that they first consider the duration and density of sunlight that falls on the site. Any site that receives a half day or more of full sunlight should be planted with

Weesie gathers fragrant freesias in her pit greenhouse.

sun-loving meadow flowers. The shade-tolerant species will do better beneath deciduous trees, but some have a tolerance for sun that doesn't appear in catalog descriptions. Densely shaded areas can be improved by limbing up trees or dropping and chipping unthrifty specimens."

Weesie has formed a conclusion about "shade-loving" wildflowers that has a lot of merit. She feels that many species are found only in the woods in the wild because of heavy competition from other plants out in the sun. She has found that many forest species will adapt to situations where they receive morning sun, and afternoon and evening shade. "But," she says, "they won't survive in the sun unless the soil is rich in organic matter and is kept moist." I think that Weesie's discovery opens up many possibilities for gardens that have little shade.

"Beginners need to locate different soil types on their property. Dig into the soil at various places on the site. If the soil is uniformly heavy, you may have to modify some spots with sand to suit the preference of some species for fast-draining soil. Southeastern soils are almost always acid and relatively poor, which suits most wildflower species just fine.

"There isn't much you can do to prepare soil beneath trees for planting wildflowers, other than raking the leaf litter to the side, spreading a two-inch layer of composted wood chips or pulverized pine bark as a mulch, planting through it, and pulling the dry leaves around the plants.

"Competition from tree roots is fierce; wildflower plants need help to get started on the forest floor. Fall is a good time to transplant wildflowers to wooded sites because the trees are going dormant, and rains will lessen the watering chore while getting plants established and well rooted. Spring is a poor time to transplant because the trees are leafing out and roots are competing for soil moisture.

"The forest landscape will become more natural looking as the stands of wildflowers thicken and spread from the few plants you plug in beneath trees. Contented wildflowers set seeds and reproduce abundantly.

A pea gravel walk leading to the pit greenhouse is bordered with the azalea R. *'George Taber' and* Phlox divaricata.

Some species have backup systems for reproduction, rhizomes or bulbs as well as seeds.

"The big difference in just growing wildflowers and gardening with wildflowers," said Weesie, "is using landscaping skills to enhance their natural beauty. For example, whenever I acquire a new species, my first priority is to choose for it the best possible site, one with the proper amount of shade and moisture, and the most appropriate soil. We have both heavy clay and sandy soil on the place, which gives me some flexibility. Then, I look up at the forest canopy and down at the soil, and try to sense the effect of wind and winter exposure on the site. My aim is to do everything I can to start that new plant off right, because, once it is planted, I can't change its surroundings.

"I don't wish to make wildflower gardening seem difficult," she said, "because it is as simple as growing zinnias and tomatoes. It is just that the needs of most wildflowers are different from those of garden flowers. If beginners will take a little time to try to understand wildflowers, they won't be disappointed in their attempts to grow them. In the wild, each species adapts to certain soil, climate, and exposure situations; the trick in growing them is to try to duplicate those conditions in your own garden or woodlands.

"Let me back up," Weesie said, "and remind beginners in wildflowering never to remove plants or seeds from national or state parks or nature preserves. Actually, it is best to defer collecting until one knows for sure whether a species is abundant or rare. Generally, the summer-flowering meadow and roadside wildflowers are fairly abundant: collecting a few seeds shouldn't hurt. Just leave a few heads to drop seeds for next year's plants.

"I have to caution beginners about the 'localness' of many wildflowers. Only a few, and they are meadow flowers such as gaillardia, coreopsis, liatris, and phlox, will grow in varied locations around the country. For example, in Birmingham, we are on the southern edge of adaptability for species that are more at home in northern Alabama, Georgia, and Tennessee. We know from experience not to go into southern Alabama and bring back wild plants. They are accustomed to mild winters and more rainfall. Rarely will they survive our cold winters, tremendous variations in winter temperatures, and periodic droughts.

"This is why the first wildflower books you buy should be publications of your state wildflower or horticulture society or, at the most, books published for a discrete climatic region such as our Southeast. As you get deeper into the subject, you may wish to buy one of the college-level books published for each state or region, bearing the title of *Flora of* a particular state. These are heavy books, but you will need them when you begin delving deeply into wildflowers. They list and describe many species not found in general garden encyclopedias."

Two treasures from Weesie's woodland garden: Cypredium kentuckiense, *a recently named species of lady's slipper orchid (left); and the adaptable forest floor native bloodroot,* Sanguinaria canadensis.

I asked Weesie which "surefire" wildflowers she would recommend as starter plants for woodlands. She reminded me that her recommendations would stand only for the Southeast and told me that the first plants she moved to her woods were:

- Bloodroot, *Sanguinaria canadensis*
- Blue phlox, *Phlox divaricata*
- Liverleaf, *Hepatica spp.*
- *Trillium spp.* (she now has fifteen species)
- Jack-in-the-pulpit, *Arisaema triphyllum*
- False Solomon seal, *Smilaceae racemosa*
- Solomon seal, *Polygonatum biflora*

I certainly concur with her choices, because the woods around my farm are rich in these species. One more I would add is a sun-tolerant plant with yellow and green daisylike flowers, *Chrysogonum virginianum*, usually found where a fallen tree has opened the forest canopy to let sunlight through. And the wild deciduous azaleas: they especially like moist soils along creeks and around seeps.

Weesie has mixed feelings about the current rage for "wildflower meadows." These are areas planted with mixtures of flower seeds made up of sun-loving native American species and exotics from other parts of the world, often laced heavily with grass seeds. "I would feel better about them," she said, "if they were made up totally of North American wildflowers, because I am wary of introducing species which could become invasive weeds, such as cornflowers. They are probably okay for yards where they are not likely to escape, but I'd rather see only natives planted along highways, where roadside plants might escape into agricultural land."

Weesie offered this advice to gardeners trying to propagate wildflowers or to increase stands on their property. "With my greenhouse and banks of fluorescent lights, I have an ideal setup for starting seeds and growing plants of wildflowers. However, a beginner could get by with one fluorescent light fixture in a cool corner of a basement or unheated room. Get fresh seeds if possible. Fresh seeds of many wild species will germinate within a week or two, but let them dry out and turn dark, and they may not come up for six to twelve months! If your supplier ships plants or bulbs, query them on the source; buy from only the specialists who propagate their plants and not from those who take them from the wild."

Weesie doesn't shy away from being called a "conservationist" as well as a wildflower gardener. "It took only a trip or two with experienced wildflower specialists," she said, "to convince me of the scope of ecological loss we were facing in Alabama. It was abundantly clear that very few people seemed to understand that it was irrevocable. And even fewer were doing anything about it. In all of northern Alabama, not more than a dozen of us were fighting for conservation. But we pulled others into a loose-knit coalition and began to press for the protection of significant sites. We began to log the locations of scarce species of wildflowers and, in the process, discovered some that were previously unknown.

"One of our most significant accomplishments was protecting unique ecological niches along the ravines in the northern sector of the Sipsey River wilderness. Lindsay and I had hiked through them and were convinced of their value. With help from all over the state, indeed from the entire United States, our coalition of concerned citizens was able to have some deep ravines set aside as wilderness area. These were all in the northern sector of the Bankhead National Forest; we were too late to save similar ravines in the southern sector; they were flooded by a dam impoundment.

"We hadn't been as successful in getting the ear of highway officials," she said. "Until recently, they seemed more interested in subduing the environment with herbicides than in putting wildflowers to work in beautifying roadsides." Fortunately, this is beginning to change.

Weesie told me that her wildflowering trips were fewer nowadays because of the demands her home gardens place on her time and energy. When we taped the *Victory Garden* show there, we were amazed that one person, with occasional help for heavy jobs, could manage such a large area of wildflowers. Weesie admitted ruefully that she is no longer expanding the garden but is concentrating on maintaining it. "There are days," she said, "when I think about removing trees to let in more sunlight for my wildflowers, then I remember that we need the shade to keep the house cool and to discourage sun-loving weeds from coming in. It's a trade-off.

"Nowadays, rather than rushing out on dig-and-save missions, I find myself spending more time at home, protecting my weak wildflowers from the more aggressive species, replacing plants or stands that have been damaged or wiped out by voles. Much of my time is spent pulling out and composting ferns. I think that, if I left our woods unattended, ferns would take over and run out most other species.

"Every now and then I get a pleasant surprise like a little patch of three birds orchids, *Triphora trianthophora*, which apparently came up from seeds. They grew in chipped wood I had spread on a path. The seeds may have been picked up in the bark of a tree dragged across the land during harvesting. The little orchids seem willing (or able) to grow only in the path, perhaps because no other plants are growing there. They come up, bloom, set seeds, and die back in five or six weeks, so I don't try to move them. I just block off a four-foot section of the path in late July."

Weesie shared with me some of the challenges and triumphs of collecting and moving wildflowers. "When the children were small," she said, "we had one of those huge station wagons. We'd load it with newspapers and canvas carrying bags and head for a dig-and-save site. We always asked permission to enter such rescue sites, unless the bulldozers were already going. Then, we'd try to get ahead of them.

"One of the conservationists active then, Eleanor Brakefield, taught me how to move wildflowers at any time of the year. She would worry a plant out of the ground to save as much as possible of the root system, lay it on a newspaper, fold the paper over the root ball, roll it up, soak the wrapped roots in water from a creek or seep, label the plant by species and location, and stand it up in a canvas bag. Sometimes we lugged plants for miles, sweating and swatting at mosquitoes, gnats, and ticks. It was thrilling when we crept down steep inclines on rough, rocky roads that were more like trails, but there were times when, with tires spinning and throwing gravel, I doubted if we would make it back up those hills!

"I had a good eye for spotting wildflowers . . . still do," said Weesie. "But another conservationist, Josephine Henry, beat us all. It would be fair to call her a plant explorer because she traveled all over the country identifying plants, recording their locations, and profiling their sites. On the few occasions I was lucky enough to travel with her, she would use binoculars to locate spots of color at great distances. When you are in such rough terrain that each step is work, being able to go straight to a patch of plants is a lifesaver."

1) 2) 3) 4) 5) 6)

Southeastern Wildflowers

A gallery of typical southeastern wildflowers from Weesie's collection: the Atamsco lily, *Zephyranthes atamasco* (1), grows from bulbs and likes light shade and moist soil. The Florida flame azalea, *R. Austrinum* (2), brightens open woods in midspring. *Phaecelia bipinnatifida*; the celandine or woods poppy, *Stylophorum diphyllum*; and the cinnamon fern, *Osmunda cinnamomea* (3). *Trillium luteum*, one of Weesie's fifteen trillium species (4). Green and gold *Chrysogonum virginianum* tolerates sun (5). *Hepatica americana* (6), liverleaf, a widely known early spring flower. Weesie reminds beginners that success with wildflowers depends on respecting their often limited adaptability. Most species are suited only to the particular conditions of soil, climate, and exposure of their region.

I asked Weesie about memorable "digs." She recalled the day she and Lindsay whizzed past a clump of wild red lilies on a bank alongside the interstate freeway they were traveling. She fixed the spot in her mind and determined to come back and see the lilies. So, the next morning, she told Lindsay she'd be right back and took off for the remembered spot. When she sighted the lily, she realized that it was just past an exit. She kept on going to the next exit, which proved to be eighteen miles down the road! Thirty-six miles later, she found the lilies, dug up just one, wrapped it in sphagnum moss, and sent it to a botanist friend, Joab Thomas, at the University of Alabama. He pronounced it to be a previously unknown species, more like *Lilium michiganense* than *L. canadense* or *L. superbum*, yet resembling all three. After more study, it will be classified. Perhaps it was fateful that Weesie dug that one bulb. The clump on the highway has disappeared, but their salvaged specimen is reproducing through stolons and can be perpetuated.

Weesie also recalled collecting on a 100-degree day near Peterson, Alabama. The site had long been used for field trips by university students in botany but was slated for obliteration, due to the construction of a new lock and dam. "We carried heavy canvas bags of plants for what seemed like miles through that heat and humidity. But it was worth it! We were saving plants of Alabama croton, a relic from the Silurian geologic era, and snow wreath, *Neviusia Alabamensis*, a beautiful little deciduous shrub.

Accustomed to such feats on her collecting missions, Weesie adroitly walks a fungus-fringed log over a deep ravine.

"Later, I had to travel into central Alabama to rescue from a scheduled spraying with herbicide a plant I consider the star of my garden, a rare yellow ladies slipper orchid, *Cyprepedium kentuckiensis*. It has larger, slightly later flowers than the more abundant yellow ladies slipper, *C. pubescens*, and is lighter yellow in color. In my garden this precious plant has thrived and is multiplying nicely."

Weesie paused and, with a concerned look, told me, "I hope I'm not giving you the idea that I'm rushing around Alabama ripping off rare wildflowers. For many years, I got my plants solely on dig-and-save missions, where the plants would have been destroyed, along with their site. In those days, thirty years or so ago, virtually no nurserymen propagated wildflowers. Every now and then, I'd see advertisements in our *Alabama Farmer's Bulletin* for wild plants being sold by farmers. Usually, I would drive out to see the plants to assure myself that they were not an endangered species and, if not, that they were dug in a way which would insure survival.

"We in Alabama owe a debt of gratitude to two nurserymen for promoting nursery-grown wildflowers. Years ago, commercial 'collectors' would raid wild plant populations and sell them by mail or to pharmaceutical companies or mail-order nurseries. Some still do, and I deplore it. That's why I feel so grateful to my nurseryman friend, Tom Dodd, for popularizing all sorts of woody native Alabama plants, especially the azaleas and rhododendrons. And Dan Coleman, even though he never seemed to have enough plants in his nursery to meet the demand, brought several choice species into public notice. At first, they propagated the traditional ways, by cuttings and layering. It was so slow. Now, they use mist propagation and container culture to reduce the time from cuttings to sales size. Tom Dodd grows most of his native shrubs from seeds to maintain a wide gene pool and has evolved into a wholesaler."

I asked Weesie what advice she had to offer people who are just becoming interested in wildflowers. "The single most important step is to find a local wildflower society or a wildflower group in a local horticultural society. Then, begin going on field trips with them. At first, you may feel totally out of place, listening to the botanists and old-time wildflower specialists reeling off latin binomials and reminiscing about great field trips they have taken. They will be patient and sharing with you, and will show you how to use the picture book guides to identify species.

"Books and seminars are just fine, but they aren't sufficient unto themselves. I've never met an armchair wildflower specialist who knew what he or she was talking about. There is simply no substitute for time in the field, in the company of knowledgeable specialists. Most of these specialists are not botanists or biologists but come from all walks of life. Anyone who loves nature can fit into these groups.

"I wouldn't even dream of trying to plant wildflowers in my garden before seeing or studying how they, or a closely related species, actually grow in the wild. From that, I can make educated guesses on the type of soil, level of acidity, soil moisture preference, and sun or shade requirements of the plant."

Weesie Smith is grateful that getting to know wildflowers led her into the preservation movement. She feels that the two are inseparable; no one can know and love wildflowers without being concerned about their shrinking habitat. She feels blessed that her hospitable land provided a safe harbor for many wildflowers that would otherwise have been lost. But most of all, she values the person/plant interdependence that grows out of wildflower gardening—the pleasure they bring to her, year after year, in return for the time she took to learn their likes and dislikes.

More about Wildflowers

Most wildflower beginners aren't ready to become activists in wildflower conservation, and they aren't up to the more challenging aspects of propagation. They want to start with something simple, sure-fire, and inexpensive. Growing wildflowers from seed mixtures is the answer.

Planting Wildflower Seeds

One of the best ways to get to know the common varieties of sun-loving wildflowers is to plant a row or two in your food or flower garden, using a wildflower seed mixture. Start with at least an ounce or two of seeds to be sure to get a good stand and a representative number of plants of each species in the mixture. Sow the seeds in a row or band so you can tell where the flower seedlings leave off and the weeds begin. The mixtures contain both cool-weather and warm-weather annuals. Plant them in the fall or spring; summer planting won't give the cool-weather annuals a chance to show off before hot weather burns out the plants.

A gardening encyclopedia or a wildflower reference book will help you learn the names of the flowers in the mixtures: the references with color pictures will give you a better batting average. Some are common American wildflowers but many are rather obscure European species. Let the plants dry up at the end of the season; then pull them and scatter the seeds over the row. You should get a good stand of the stronger species the following year and another opportunity to identify those which baffled you at the first try.

Establishing large meadows of wildflowers from seed mixtures is a bit more complicated because you have to eliminate heavy stands of grass and weeds to get a good stand. Flower seedlings are small and comparatively weak, and strong grass and weeds can swamp them before they develop plants large enough to compete.

The success of wildflower seedings depends partly on the soil being rather poor, and not heavily loaded with seeds of grass that spread from stolons to make dense mats. Wherever the soil is naturally fertile, moist throughout the year, and seeded with grass, the grass will soon push out all the wildflowers, except the rugged species with large-enough plants to overgrow or thrive between tufts of annual grasses. Casual observers can get the impression that wildflowers prefer poor, dry soil. Not true. They grow there because Nature has adapted many species to grow on soils too poor, dry, or infertile to support a thick stand of stoloniferous grass. Some western wildflowers survive by growing in the open areas between clumps of bunch grasses.

Start a year ahead, during the summer. Plow and rototill the soil. Fumigate the soil to kill weeds, grasses, seeds, and root-rot organisms. Use a chemical such as Vapam or methyl bromide when the soil is warmer than 60 degrees F. If you are an organic gardener, cover the moist, tilled soil with clear plastic, batten it down tightly, and let the accumulated solar heat of summer kill most of the weed seeds. Allow six to eight weeks to "solarize" the soil. Alternatively, soak the area a few times and rototill when the soil is dry enough to work. Several tillings will kill many sprouting seedlings and greatly reduce the weed seed count. Planting thickly and tilling under a summer green manure crop such as soybeans will also help reduce the weed population. During soil preparation, incorporate limestone as indicated by soil tests, and a phosphate source. Incorporate a balanced fertilizer only if the soil is exceedingly poor or if it is raw subsoil. Supplementary nitrogen has a way of encouraging the bad guys to take over.

During the past few years, *The Victory Garden* has taped programs at several botanical gardens where wildflower meadows have been established. Consistently, the thickest stand of wildflowers, the greatest range of species, and the fewest weeds and aggressive grasses were seen where the soil had been fumigated. Furthermore, fumigated plots repeated better and longer; one still looked good after three years, requiring only the pulling of a few aggressive weeds before they set seeds.

After fumigating or "solarizing" large areas, work the soil into a seedbed and use a disc, spring-tooth harrow or rake to make furrows about 2 inches deep across the area. If you garden in zone 7 or south, scatter seeds at the recommended rate in late summer or fall, then drag the soil with a square of cyclone fence to cover seeds lightly with soil. You can either "water up" the seeds with a sprinkler or let them emerge with the fall rains. Either way, they will go through the winter as small seedlings and bloom the following year.

In zones 6 and north, get the soil ready and delay seeding until late fall, just before the soil freezes or early spring. Broadcast the seeds and cover them lightly with straw, not weed-infested hay. The mulch will prevent seeds from washing away and will reduce the loss to foraging birds. Few seeds will come up until late spring; the freezing and thawing will hasten and improve germination. The meadow will bloom the following season. However, some of the slow-growing perennials may form rosettes and not bloom for yet another year.

Starting and Transplanting Seedlings

An even better way is open to gardeners who are prepared to start wildflower seeds in flats. At the time you begin preparing the soil, fill shallow plastic or fiber "seed flats" with planter mix and plant them with seeds of wildflower mixes or individual adapted wild species. You don't need a greenhouse: start them under the shade of a tree, up on a table out of reach of pets and mice. Once the plants have grown enough to fill the flats with a mat of roots, and before they bloom, plant entire flats by scraping shallow holes into the prepared soil. Soak the holes before setting-in the flats. Consider the flats as "islands" of flowers scattered randomly across the prepared soil.

As the islands of flowers grow, water occasionally and cultivate in between them to kill emerging weeds and grasses. By late summer, many species will have completed flowering and will have set seeds. Discontinue cultivating and let the seeds drop or blow onto the bare soil surrounding the islands. Scatter a few wildflower seeds on the loose, bare soil to hasten the process of filling in. Wildflower islands can be transplanted in early spring, but this means you have to start seeds in a greenhouse or under lights in late winter.

A few enlightened nurseries have begun to grow what they call "plugs" of wildflowers, which are similar to the flats previously described, and are planted in the same way. They know how to start the species that are difficult or slow to germinate. Some offer plugs of individual wild species as well as mixtures of adapted species.

Some of the widely available North American species are easy to start and dependable in wildflower meadows: coreopsis, *Gaillardia*, *Rudbeckia*, *Ratibida*, *Bidens*, *Echinacea* or coneflower, *Liatris* or gayfeather, *Helianthus* or sunflower, *Phlox drummondi* and *P. subulata*, various lupins and fall-blooming asters are good examples. You can buy seeds of them from wildflower specialists, grow plants, and set them in colonies in meadows, the way they would grow naturally. This is the best way to establish a meadow of purely American wildflowers.

Planting in Shady Areas

A wooded landscape presents a different set of challenges and calls for a different group of wildflower species than sunny meadows. In nature, some forest floors seem hostile to wildflowers; others teem with them. In my climate zone 7, the richest concentrations of hardwood forest-floor flowers are on steep hillsides away from the afternoon sun, and they always seem to be thicker toward the base of the hill. Scientific research indicates that the degree of shade is not nearly as important as root competition for water. Slopes away from the afternoon sun don't dry out badly, and flowers on the lower end of the slope benefit from water seeping from in-soak higher up the hill.

This information suggests how you could grow wildflowers under trees with aggressive surface roots which suck the water out of soil. Rake the area free of leaves and loose duff and lay down a layer of spun-bonded synthetic "landscape cloth." Buy the cloth as wide as you can, because you will need to overlap joints 6 inches. Shred the leaves with a rotary mower and mix them with finely pulverized pine bark and moistened peat moss, mixed on a 3:1 ratio. Include a few shovels of topsoil from beneath the trees. Add a phosphate source but no limestone, and no nitrogen or potash fertilizer. Spread the organic mulch 3 to 5 inches deep over the landscape cloth, and you are ready to plant.

Planting seeds under trees is futile. Start with adapted plants purchased at a native-plant nursery. Spring or early fall transplanting should give you the best results. The landscape cloth should prevent tree roots from competing with the wildflowers until they get a good start. After three or four years, tree roots will find a way to grow into the moist mulch and you may have to fish around, find the heaviest of them, and snip them off with pruning shears.

Generally, the best competitors for forest-floor plantings are the hardy perennial species that come on with a rush in early spring, bloom, and restore their stored carbohydrates before the forest canopy shuts out the sunlight they need for growth and reproduction. In my climate, wild ginger, hepatica, blue-eyed grass, anemone, bloodroot, several species of wild violets, and two species of dwarf iris like hardwood forest situations. Several species in these genera will grow as far north as zone 4.

Some of the most hospitable forest situations are moist glens between trees where the light or dappled shade excludes most grass but allows summer-blooming wildflowers to thrive. The steep banks of healed ravines are ideal for plants such as *Trillium, Dodecatheon,* or shooting stars, which need more moisture than most wild species.

Landscaping with Wildflowers

An increasingly popular use of native plants is for surrounding intimate garden rooms, retreats, or sanctuaries in landscapes. You can go all the way and transform a thoroughly domestic garden by landscaping it entirely with native plants. Use shrubs for screening, medium-height to tall wildflowers for color, and low-growing wildflowers for groundcovers. Look for slow-growing plants that mature at small sizes. In the trees and shrubs you may have to settle for improved cultivars of native species. Your Cooperative Extension Service can supply you with a list of adapted native trees and shrubs. If the list seems uninspired, check your library for books on native plants of your region. Most of them will be about herbaceous wildflowers. Only a few will instruct you in landscaping with larger native plants. These definitive books will tell you how large a tree or shrub will grow at maturity, its rate of growth, and its soil preference.

When searching for native plants, write down a few facts about each contender: mature height and spread, season and duration of bloom, fragrance, attractiveness to butterflies or their larvae, fruit or berries for wild birds, fall color, winter bark and form of branches, special soil requirements, and water needs. If you live in an acid-soil area, stick with the species that like acid soil. Concentrate those which like moist soils around ponds or streambanks or near a water faucet. Make raised beds for the species such as azaleas that need perfect drainage. Leave generous spaces between trees and shrubs: give them room to grow. You will enjoy watching plants develop their natural form, and they will be healthier.

One of the easiest ways to use wildflowers is to set plants into mixed borders of perennials, shrubs, and roses. Many of the native wildflowers are just as beautiful as exotic cultivars; their inherent vigor enables them to survive where exotics could succumb to insects, plant diseases, and weather stresses. Collectively, more herbaceous wildflowers are planted in this fashion than in any other way. Gardeners usually start out with rugged species that will adapt to almost any garden situation, then gradually work their way into more demanding flowers. The lists given previously for meadow and forest floor plantings are good starting points. Native orchids and plants which require hosts to thrive are not for beginners.

Most nurseries display wildflower plants among other perennials and sort them out by sun- or shade-loving species. When you do find a native American species, it may very well qualify as a wildflower by definition, but won't naturalize well over much of the United States.

With this in mind, if you like the looks of flowering meadows planted with exotics, by all means plant them. But, not if your garden is near agricultural land; exotics can escape and become pests. Personally, I'd rather be selective and use only North American wildflowers, especially those native to my region.

I am optimistic that gardeners in the United States and Canada will come to appreciate the incredible variety and beauty of our native North American wildflower species and will demand plants or seed mixtures only of species native to their regions. When that day comes, the seed companies will be forced to mass-produce seeds of native North American wildflowers instead of garden flowers originally from other parts of the world.

If you want to know and grow wildflowers, it has to be more than a summertime romance. You can learn a bit by growing and observing a few species each year and you can benefit from seasonal wildflower walks sponsored by your state parks system. But you will become proficient by attending meetings of your local wildflower society or horticultural society. Go along on their walks in the woods and meadows. They know what is blooming, and where to find it. Hardly a bush, tree, vine, or groundcover escapes their notice. They exclaim just as jubilantly over common Jack-in-the-pulpit as they do over showy orchids. A plant doesn't have to be in flower for them to know it. They are naturalists as much as gardeners and will help you through the most difficult part of wildflower gardening . . . getting to know the plants. In their company it will be a pleasant voyage of discovery.

Lilies

Ruth and Hugh Cocker find southern Minnesota just right for their hobby of breeding and showing hybrid lilies.

Perhaps it is fragrance that makes lilies seen years ago linger in your mind like the memory of a lost love. Or their compelling presence: they draw attention away from lesser flowers by grace and perfection, by colors that make catalog pages pale by comparison. There is no blue lily, nor black, and I would hope never to see one. Give me, instead, the sunny yellows, strawberry and candy-apple reds, delicious pinks, and waxy whites. Throw in a few stripes, penciled or picoteed petals, spots and aureoles . . . and you have enough variety to fill a lifetime of gardening with joyful discoveries.

Combined with other flowers, groundcovers, or dwarf shrubs, or displayed against a hedge of conifers or hollies, lilies display their charms to best advantage. Their graceful flowering stems, elaborate as chandeliers, move in the slightest breeze and animate gardens. Some lilies have been refined so much that you can barely see the foliage between the flowers, but some blend into surroundings like a fawn in a sun-dappled glen.

(Left) The Cockers' lily evaluation plot dazzles the beholder on a summer day.

Were you to gather and plant bulbs from each of the ninety-odd lily species, then label each with its flag of national origin, your garden would look like a gathering of the United Nations. Then, you would discover that Northern Hemisphere nations from around the globe would be represented, but there would be not one flag from south of the equator!

About half of the species are native to the Asian landmass, about one-quarter from Europe, several to North America, and a few to Japan. One, the southernmost in origin, is native to the mountains of the Philippine Islands and was not discovered until the late 1940s. Doubtless, a few species remain to be discovered.

This enormously varied gene pool has given us some of the most beautiful plants in the world, so spectacular that the flowers were offered to propitiate the gods of ancient civilizations. But, secular needs were fulfilled as well as sacred: the bulbs were used for food and, later, for their medicinal properties. As human cultures mingled through trade and conquest, lilies began to cross boundaries. The Romans introduced Asian and Middle Eastern lily species to Europe as they fanned out to establish forts and footholds for the Christian religion. During the Dark Ages, monastery gardens sequestered the bulbs, which might otherwise have been eaten. Literature of the 1500s mentions *Lilium martagon*, a Turk's cap lily, and *L. chalcedonicum*.

In the 1700s, the eastern American natives, *L. canadense*, *L. superbum*, and *L. philadelphicum*, made their way to Europe. Importation to Europe of Japanese species such as *L. japonicum* did not begin until the 1800s. The lilies native to the western United States were little known until after the Gold Rush, but created a sensation when they arrived in Europe. Unfortunately, because of their demanding cultural requirements, they proved difficult to grow in Great Britain.

Plant explorers found and introduced *L. Henryi* and *L. leucanthum* in the early 1900s: the dauntless E. H. Wilson brought back *L. regale*, *L. Sargentiae*, and *L. Davidii* from Asia between 1905 and 1908. Shortly thereafter, *L. amabile* was introduced from Korea. Many bulbs perished in transit, forcing plant explorers to retrace their steps hundreds of miles back into mountainous terrain, to dig and ship replacements.

Early lily breeders made some significant crosses but lost them to diseases transmitted through vegetative reproduction. Had they known that disease-free lilies can be grown from seeds, more long-term hybridizing successes might have been reported during the 1800s and early 1900s, when other specialty plant species were rapidly being improved.

(Right) These unnamed Asiatic hybrid lily seedlings bred by the Cockers are still under evaluation.

The Japanese had been improving their indigenous species all along, but mostly by selection, until they crossed. *L. martagon* from Europe with their own *L. hansonii*, to create the first of the Martagon hybrids. The hybrids had larger individual flowers, more of them, a wider range of colors, and extended life due to thicker petals.

The Boston nurseryman Charles Hovey reported making crosses in 1843, and the renowned plant breeder Francis Parkman made a three-way cross in the 1860s, using *L. speciosum, L. auratum,* and *L. candidum.* The Bellingham hybrids, incorporating mostly western North American species, were made in 1899 by Robert Kessler of Los Angeles, but languished until 1932 when they were introduced by the USDA.

Perhaps the most severe obstacle to the improvement of lilies was the lack of a strong, skillful, committed, and well-financed breeder/grower/marketer. But such a man, Jan de Graaf, came along in the late 1920s. He began working for, and later bought, Oregon Bulb Farms in the fertile Willamette Valley.

With so much untapped potential to exploit, Jan de Graaf set about directing the work of a crew of skilled plant breeders in making up to thirty thousand crosses every year. Prior to that time, no other lily breeder had made crosses on such a large and organized scale and embracing so many species. In the process, Jan de Graaf's hybridizers helped to establish the chromosome counts of the various species and to perfect ways to save pollen from early bloomers for use on late-flowering species, and vice versa.

The various lily species are relatively easy to cross. For some reason, they have not developed the elaborate defenses against cross-pollination that complicate the cross-breeding of other genera. In fact, the only defense of lily flowers is against self-pollination, undoubtedly Nature's scheme to prevent the gene pool from shrinking. Lily flowers display their reproductive organs with the innocence of little children and readily accept bee- and wind-delivered pollen from other flowers.

With Jan de Graaf, as with other breeders, success came as much from the courage to discard good, but not great, hybrids as from the ability to recognize and propagate the pivotal selections. He employed European know-how in freeing his foundation bulbs of viruses by production from seeds and popularized the term "strains" of lilies, meaning sibling bulbs grown from seeds. Strains produce lilies that are reasonably similar to each other, but not as alike as peas in a pod. De Graaf also produced cultivars of lilies by what we now call "cloning," vegetative reproduction from scales, bulblets, or stem cuttings. Cloning is mandatory in new award-winning cultivars, where each bulb has to produce a plant and flower almost exactly like every other one bearing the name.

De Graaf seemed to have a sixth sense for the colors, flower and plant sizes, and plant habits that were desired by both home gardeners and commercial growers of pot plants. Beginning with 'Enchantment' in 1942, De Graaf's "Jagra" line of hybrids became world famous. More than any other cultivar, 'Enchantment' marked the turning point in lily breeding. It remains the most popular lily hybrid worldwide. Among other famous Jagra cultivars and strains are the trumpet type Aurelian hybrids and the late-blooming Oriental hybrids. His 'Pink Perfection' strain, 'Red Band' hybrid, and 'Golden Splendor' are popular around the world.

In 1968 Jan de Graaf sold his business and, in succeeding years, the company lost momentum. Numerous smaller companies in the northwest United States, the Great Lakes area, and southern Canada moved in to capitalize on the swelling demand. Dutch bulb producers began growing the cultivars needed for the American market. At the same time, some private lily hybridizers began licensing bulb producers to increase their backyard businesses. Other lily enthusiasts, with promising seedlings from their own hybridizing, elected not to expand, but to keep their hobby secondary to growing and showing lilies.

The decision to begin breeding a specialty plant marks a turning point in the lives of hobby growers. Successful plant breeders have a special status at plant society meetings because other advanced hobbyists know how much forethought, work, and determination is required in crossing, evaluation, and follow-through. For Ruth and Hugh Cocker, lily breeding sets the pace of their days, the rhythm of their seasons, and most of the goals for their gardening.

Hugh and Ruth collect pollen from choice male parents to be saved for hybridizing.

On a breezy June day, I visited Ruth and Hugh Cocker at their five-acre farmstead on the outskirts of Rochester. Their comfortable home is shaded by trees they planted shortly after buying the place in 1950. Black walnut and butternut trees line the approach drive. The most obvious feature is an impeccable half-acre patch of closely spaced lily beds in the side yard and another smaller field of lilies and perennials in the back. Hugh told me that, if all the rows in the beds were lined up end to end, they would measure amost two and a half miles!

Anchoring the farmstead is a neat red haybarn built by Hugh . . . an artifact from the days when he raised and showed Shetland ponies. More than two dozen grazed their pasture at one time. Now, the barn comes in handy for storing lily bulbs in sand over winter.

The Cockers have always been hard workers. At his boyhood home in Canton, Minnesota, Hugh helped his parents with general farming as well as with their spring business of growing and selling bedding plants, perennials, and gladiolus bulbs. Moving to Rochester after finishing high school, he went to work part-time for Ruth's parents in their business, Whiting's Flowers. Ruth and Hugh married while he was serving the air force as a gunnery instructor in B-17s in Florida. The noise battered his hearing. Hugh jokes, "The phone keeps ringing in my right ear, but I've learned not to answer it."

Home again, Hugh worked full-time at Whiting's and after-hours did carpentry. In 1973 he was employed by the city of Rochester as head gardener for the Plummer House estate garden. He and his crew brought the neglected grounds back to their original beauty. He retired in 1986 to devote full time to growing and hybridizing lilies.

Ruth is a small, wiry, brisk woman who chuckles a lot as she recalls her lifelong involvement with plants. "There were few child labor laws in the late twenties and early thirties," she said. "My parents were good to me but, as soon as I was big enough to help, they put me to work with an older brother delivering vegetables to rooming houses in Rochester. Even back then, Rochester was a national medical center, and families would stay in the rooming houses to be near loved ones. We would wash and trim radishes, carrots, onions, and rhubarb, and load them into a coaster wagon. Dad would give us a ride in the morning on his way to work. We would make the deliveries door to door, and there were lots of rooming houses in Rochester. When we were down to odds and ends, we'd pull the wagon home.

"At age eight, I was assigned one street corner adjacent to a Rochester hospital, my older sister another. Every weekday during the summer, I would make up bouquets from buckets of flowers my parents grew, and sell them for twenty-five cents to people visiting patients. Early on, I learned not to put fragrant flowers in hospital bouquets, because the scent can bother sick people. To this day, I have to force myself to recognize fragrance in lilies as a trait desired by most people."

Ruth never lost her interest in growing flowers for florists. Today, sales of stems of lilies, coral bells, balloon flowers, baby's breath, and statice help to pay for their lily hobby.

In the early 1960s, Ruth had become interested in hybridizing daylilies and had worked up to twelve hundred experimental hybrids in her trials. Then, their orbit intersected that of lilies.

"Mentally," she said, "we had been preparing to explore lilies for some time. Back in 1967 we had joined the North American Lily Society. A friend, Louise Koehler, cemented the decision when she gave us eleven of her unnamed hybrids. We loved them and still do. But, it was Earl Tesca, a crusty, opinionated hybridist, who showed us how to recognize potential in lilies and to settle for nothing but the best."

Ruth and Hugh loved working with the lilies. Eventually they offered to move Earl Tesca's collection to their farm. Until his death, Earl continued to work in the lily trials, teaching the Cockers what he knew about hybridizing and lily culture. His breeding emphasis had been on the early "Asiatics" which he felt had the greatest potential for northern home gardens and for cutting. Ruth and Hugh offered to register any of Earl's hybrids in his name, and have honored their promise.

The sudden acquisition of several thousand lily bulbs, representing more than four hundred species and crosses, forced Ruth to make a wrenching decision. "I knew I couldn't work with both: one had to go," she said. "When I made up my mind to get out of daylily hybridizing, I sat down in the middle of my 'babies' and had a long cry. Then, I got up, and dug and bagged all my plants of 'Hems', fifty plants per bag. I hauled those bags all over town and gave plants to schools, county and city parks, and 4-H clubs, hoping to create an interest among youngsters in growing daylilies. And, do you know that, to this day, I can still recognize my hybrids growing around Rochester public gardens and homes!"

Ruth and Hugh gradually transformed what they had learned from Louise Koehler and Earl Tesca into their own set of criteria for breeding lilies. Each breeder has his own vision of "the perfect lily" and, realizing that it is not likely to be achieved with one masterful stroke of the pollen brush, settles for a long-range program of gradual improvement.

The secret of successful lily breeding is to recognize good parents and to know the traits they pass on to progeny. It isn't as simple as it may appear. Some characteristics are linked to others; some are recessive, others are dominant. You can even get entirely different results when you make a "reciprocal cross" by changing roles between the male and female parents.

The time-honored route to gradual improvement is to start with a desirable parent that has a particular shortcoming. The breeder tries to replace that trait with a more desirable characteristic from another species or hybrid by crossing. If the result is promising, but not sufficiently attractive, the breeder may "backcross" to intensify the desirable trait. All of this takes time, careful and critical note-taking, and a great deal of luck. Yet, it is infinitely superior to random crossing.

I asked Ruth if there is a shortcut to recognizing good parents for hybridizing. "If there is, I wish someone would tell me," she said. "I know that certain lines set seeds well and I tend to use these as female parents. And I know that certain lines produce lots of variation when used as male or pollen parents. I don't mind sharing that kind of information with other lily hybridizers because, even if they duplicated my crosses, they would probably get different results. Any new lily hybridizer is going to plow old ground for a while until he or she discovers parent lines that 'notch' and produce interesting offspring."

Ruth took me through the steps of hybridizing lilies, a simple operation because the reproductive parts are so large and easily accessible. She forced apart the petals of a nearly open flower, reached in with her fingers, and pulled off the anthers with their load of unripe pollen, to emasculate the flower. Then, she covered the female stigma with a little square of aluminum foil and squeezed down the corners to form a cup. "Easier and faster than bagging to keep out foreign pollen," she explained, "and hardly visible except from close up.

"In two or three days the stigma will be covered with stigmatic fluid and sticky—receptive to pollen," Ruth explained. "I harvest pollen from desirable male parents just before it is mature enough to shake loose. I catch it in little rectangular snap-top plastic boxes like those used for faucet washers. After the pollen has dried for a day or so, I outfit each box with its own short-handled cotton swab. The pollen will keep all season in the refrigerator; I understand you can freeze it, but I've never needed to do that."

Ruth showed me how to hybridize by transferring dried pollen from one of the storage boxes to a receptive stigma. She removed the protective aluminum foil, pollinated the stigma, and replaced the foil to exclude windblown or insect-vectored pollen from a different source. I

1) 2) 3)

4) 5) 6)

Hybridizing Lilies

The Cockers demonstrate the steps of hybridizing lilies. Pollen from desirable male parents is collected, labeled, and boxed, then stored in the refrigerator (1), where it will keep all season. The female parent's receptive stigma is swabbed with pollen on a Q-tip (2); afterward Ruth covers the stigma with a square of aluminum foil to keep out foreign pollen. The cross is labeled with the code numbers of the parents (3), then Ruth records the cross in the "Stud Book" (4). When the pods are nearly ripe, the seeds are shelled out (5). The seeds from one hybridized pod are planted in a single pot (6). These seedlings are ready to be separated and transplanted into garden rows for growing to evaluation stage.

thanked her and started to move on, but Ruth stopped me and said, "Hold on, Jim; we're not through yet." She wrote on the tag the date of the cross and the code numbers of the female plant and the pollen donor, then looped the tag over the completed cross.

She told me that she goes back later and looks for crosses that have "taken," those that show swollen ovaries, indicating successful cross-pollination. Only about one-third of Ruth's crosses take; these are entered into her "stud book," a permanent record of pedigrees. For ease of retrieval, crosses are entered alphabetically and numerically. Regrettably, some of the seeds from crosses don't germinate: these failures are also noted in the stud book for future guidance.

I asked if they have tried any hybrids between species. "No, we leave that to the scientists who understand how to manipulate genes and germ plasm. Interspecific crosses are difficult. We find plenty of potential for improvement just in crossing within the same species," said Ruth.

When I asked the Cockers for their checklist for evaluating new hybrids, they told me that "everything was in their heads," and commenced pouring out information as fast as I could take notes:

"We look first for color and flower form. You might describe it as 'overall impact.' This first screening can be done on the first or second year of bloom and will eliminate 90 percent of the hybrid seedlings. An entirely new color is highly unlikely, so we look for clarity of straight colors and new combinations of markings and background colors. Earl Tesca preferred only a few strong colors, and 'spotless' at that, with no markings or spots on petals. We don't have a bias against any color, and our taste runs toward the modern bicolor or tricolor patterns and spots.

"We look for symmetry, width of petals, lively texture, and number and conformation of flowers that is new for that particular class. There are places in every garden for upright, outfacing, and nodding blossoms; open-faced, flaring, or reflexed. Size isn't everything; the maximum overall impact can also be attained by greater numbers of rather small individual blossoms. Bright colors aren't everything; we've found some lovely pastels.

"Plant height has to be in scale with the 'inflorescence,' or the total frame of flowers. Short plants tend to be more wind-resistant but, if they are dwarfed too much, you can't cut the inflorescence without weakening the bulb. So, our preference is for vigorous, medium-height plants.

"Our experience in flower shows and selling cut flowers conditions us to look for flower substance and holding power. We want flowers that look crisp week after week in the garden and that will hold well when cut for arrangements. The thickness of petals has a lot to do with this.

"Flower colors should not fade with age or sunlight; we call this trait 'color-fastness.' We grow all our lilies in full sun so we can judge this factor critically.

Hugh and Ruth show me their early-flowering Martagon hybrid lilies. Note the pendant blossoms.

"Of late, we have been breeding for more flowers per stem, that open sequentially. Some of our lines have as many as five buds per stem branch, as opposed to the usual two or three. This means that lilies will continue to bloom longer and, with deadheading of spent blossoms, will last longer in arrangements.

"We watch for endurance of bulbs; they should come back year after year, increase strongly, and not tend to die out. With this screening, we also cull out the hybrid seedlings that tend to be severely hurt by late spring frosts.

"Out in the open, and not staked, out lilies are exposed to high winds and thunderstorms. We look for strong stems that don't break or topple, and that recover quickly after being bowed down by rains. We don't have many lily diseases in Minnesota and, with our preventative spray program, we don't let virus-carrying aphids get a start. Consequently, most of our selection for disease resistance is done by eliminating the lines that show susceptibility to leaf spots and bulb rotting.

"As for earliness . . . at first, we were taken with the extra-early Asiatics but found that they emerge too early in the spring. The growing point can be frozen so badly that the bulb will not bloom or even may die. Consequently, we are gravitating toward second-early and later types to lessen the damage from late spring frosts.

"Most of our breeding is with the Asiatics and the Martagons, neither of which has much fragrance, if any. To introduce fragrance to these lines, we would have to cross them with the later-blooming Trumpets or

Orientals and backcross to restore earliness. We don't have the time for such an ambitious project."

Actually, Earl Tesca's passion for perfection has, in a way, delayed the introduction of a line of lily hybrids under the Cocker name. "We respected Earl so much," Hugh said, "that we felt obligated to continue evaluating his hybrids and to register the outstanding lilies after his death. That took several years.

"We have registered only one of our own hybrids, 'Carolyn Marie', named after one of our daughters. We have six or so more ready to register with the Royal Horticultural Society in England but have been vacillating. Now we are sure enough of our own judgment in lilies to say, 'Okay, this is the best we can do in improving this class . . . perhaps the best anyone in the world can do. The time has come to register our own hybrids, increase and introduce them.' Meanwhile, we will continue hybridizing in other classes."

I asked Ruth and Hugh how many lily awards they had won. Ruth gave one of her chuckles and asked, "Do you really want to know?" Then, she proceeded to drag out enough silver to start a mint, plus a cut-glass award from Czechoslovakia, a bronze medal from Poland, and fancy porcelain plates in presentation cradles. Ribbons were laced together like fish on a stringer; they weighed so much that Ruth grunted when she hoisted them up to show me.

"It has gotten to the point that people expect Cocker seedlings to win in the classes where we specialize," said Ruth. "We never take lily shows for granted, however. We are fortunate to have thousands of lilies from which to choose, and we cut and condition stems carefully. For local or regional shows, we cut stems early in the morning, tag them with cultivar names or code numbers, stand them in glass milk bottles filled with water, bag each head, and load them into our van for transport. National conventions of the North American Lily Society are another matter. When we have to fly, we reduce the number of stems over what we usually show, pack the stems carefully, and check them as baggage.

"As for stem length, it doesn't hurt the bulb to cut stems. Just leave about a third of the stem and leaves for photosynthesis. We have cut stems from the same bulb year after year and have noticed only a slight decrease in the size of the plant and spray of blossoms. However, you can kill bulbs by taking the entire stem when cutting. We had a severe hailstorm one summer, which stripped some plants of leaves. We lost a number of these, and the damage would be comparable if you cut off stems at ground level.

"When we are setting up for shows we cut off a bit of each stem to balance the stem length to the size and optical weight of the blossom truss. We advise home gardeners to nip off the anthers of lilies they bring in the house because the pollen can stain clothing and tablecloths. We

Ruth loads up for a show. The carrying trays hold lily stems in bottles of water.

The Cockers have amassed an impressive collection of trophies from their participation in lily shows.

don't do that for shows, of course, because blossoms must be complete for judging. We find that sun-warmed water is taken up by cut stems faster than cold water right out of a tap.

"Our satisfaction really doesn't come from winning lily shows. Sure, we'd like to win "Best in Show" at the NALS someday, but aren't going to fret if we don't. We get our kicks out of renewing old friendships at local, regional, and national shows, including many lily people from Canada and other foreign countries. We love shoptalk and sharing lily know-how with people just getting into lilies as a hobby plant."

We talked about the place of lilies in landscaping. The Cockers' home landscape reminded me of "the shoemaker's children." It is neat and attractive, but includes no lilies. "We forget about taking care of the lilies we plant around the house," explained Hugh, "so we concentrate our lilies in the test plot." But, they have a good feel for how to use them massed in exhibition beds, or mixed with perennials and annuals for flowering borders. Their lectures on lilies explore the many ways lilies can be used in home gardens.

"In lectures," said Ruth, "I always tell home gardeners that they shouldn't believe everything they read in garden books. For example,

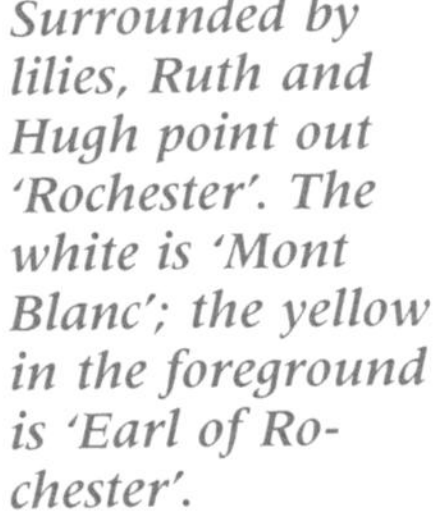

Surrounded by lilies, Ruth and Hugh point out 'Rochester'. The white is 'Mont Blanc'; the yellow in the foreground is 'Earl of Rochester'.

books will tell you to group three to five bulbs of the same lily cultivar to make 'drifts' of the same height and color. That's good if you can afford it. But, good lily bulbs are not cheap. If you are on a tight budget, you can buy one each of several kinds, space them widely, and let each bulb increase to make a drift. Sure, the recommendations for planting tall kinds in the back and shorter kinds toward the front always apply, and you shouldn't mix colors indiscriminately. But, it's no problem if you make bad combinations; just wait until late fall and move the bulbs."

Ruth added, "I prefer to see lily bulbs interplanted with low-growing annual flowers or nonspreading perennials. Lilies don't really hit their stride until the second or third year after planting. The filler flowers help to cover the bare dirt while the lily clumps are thickening, then the lilies begin to shade the ground around them. This serves to keep down weeds and reduce evaporation of water."

The Cockers are blessed with deep, fertile, sandy loam soil. Much of their nutrient supply comes from decaying organic matter. Ruth and Hugh gather and work in leaves saved by friends in Rochester; consequently, their soil is in beautiful condition. However, to maintain a good level of mineral nutrients, they top-dress a light application of balanced fertilizer around April 1, before the lilies begin to emerge.

The high level of organic matter may explain why they have been able to replant the same area in lilies for several years with no outbreaks of bulb diseases. It also increases the speed and depth of in-soak of rain-water and encourages root proliferation by bulbs. On the flip side, it also encourages all sorts of rodents: moles, voles, gophers, mice, and shrews. But their talented cat, Dixie, kept them under control until her demise. Even the abundant rabbits gave their yard a wide berth. Deer are all around but have bothered them only once, when they browsed a few seed pods. Then, Ruth got some human hair from the beauty shop and tied balls of it around the lily plots; it did the job.

Hugh offered this advice to gardeners who are just beginning to grow lilies: "In the North, the weather in late fall may be so wet and cold that planting becomes impossible, and you will have to store bulbs until spring planting time. When it happens to us, we store our common bulbs in boxes of sand in the barn. They freeze solid but it does no harm. However, we pack our most valuable bulbs in plastic bags without holes, fill them with moistened peat moss, and seal them tight. We store the bags in a refrigerator in the basement, set at about 40 degrees F. to keep the bulbs from freezing. In tight bags, the bulbs hold without sprouting until we can prepare the soil in April.

"Spring planting works fine for us," said Hugh, "but there is a solid reason for planting in the fall when possible. Lilies have contractile roots that anchor them like holdfasts. Being accordion-pleated, contractile roots can increase or decrease in length. They can pull shallow-planted bulbs down to a depth where the bulb feels comfortable. I think that adjustment goes better in the fall, when the soil is loose and moist."

The Cockers use Treflan pre-emergence herbicide to maintain clean beds, and mulch with pine needles. In our walk through their plantings I saw Ruth remove only three weeds, all so small that I didn't notice them until she stooped to pull them out.

"You have to keep an eye on the clumps," Ruth cautioned. "After a few years, five on the average in Minnesota, the clumps will thicken up so much that they will begin to run down in vigor. The stems will be shorter than is normal for the cultivar, and look puny. The plants are doing everything but waving and shouting at you to signal that it is time to lift, divide, and replant them. We wait until the frost has killed the tops in the fall before digging and replanting."

Hugh grinned at that thought and said, "Some of those big old clumps of lilies will give you a struggle, especially if the soil is wet. A big clump can weigh twenty pounds, dirt and all. You have to lay it on the grass and blast the soil off with a spray of water before you can see and get at the individual bulbs. I can usually pull the bulbs apart but sometimes have to use a sharp knife. We don't have bulb disease or nematode problems in southern Minnesota, so there is no need to dip or dust our bulbs with fungicides or insecticides."

As we walked through their lily trials, the Cockers pointed out plants with brown lower leaves, evidence of late frost damage. Some plants were oddly stubbed-off, their flower buds apparently blasted. "It's the very early ones that get hurt badly by late frosts. They look unhappy, but will survive and develop new flower buds for next year," said Hugh. "That's one reason why we like the mid-season Asiatics; they emerge a little later and usually escape frost damage."

Ruth and Hugh pondered and waffled for a long time before answering my request for a short list of starter varieties for beginners. (When you know and love so many cultivars, it is genuinely difficult to boil down the list to a few.) At last they agreed on these selections:

- 'Connecticut King': Yellow with orange center, midseason.
- 'Black Beauty': Dark crimson with white edge, late.
- *Tsingtauense:* A species lily, orange, early; it prefers partial shade.
- 'Henryi White': Blooms just after midseason.
- 'Carolyn Marie': Wine-colored, midseason.
- 'Claude Shride': A dark red, early Martagon hybrid.

"Where winters are severe, stay away from the class of lilies called Oriental; they are not hardy. Avoid the unusual species lilies until you get a feel for lilies; with certain species you have to practically duplicate the conditions under which they grow in the wild."

Ruth gathers lily trusses to be sold to local florists.

With their tremendous and varied experience, the Cockers have long held memberships in local, regional, and national organizations, and have served them well. Hugh was President of the Northstar region of NALS for two years and served two three-year terms as a Director. Ruth was Secretary of the Northstar region for two terms. Over the years, their lily patch has given the Cockers rest from their busy schedules and restored their psyches.

Thomas Jefferson said, "The greatest service which can be rendered any country is to add a useful plant to its culture." Perhaps the Cockers' deep enjoyment of their hobby springs from the value their work will have for future gardeners.

More about Lilies

Buying Bulbs

The first order of business, if you are interested in growing lilies as a hobby plant, is to send off for catalogs from specialty suppliers of lily bulbs. Freshness of bulbs is very important to success in growing, and the best place to get fresh, carefully harvested bulbs is from mail-order suppliers.

Specialty bulb growers will ship you new crop bulbs as soon as possible in the fall or early winter, after digging. They can't do it any earlier, because bulbs shouldn't be lifted until the foliage has turned color. The major United States producers of lily bulbs are in the Northwest, where digging of the Asiatics doesn't begin until late October and, for the later Orientals, not until well into November.

Gardeners in northern states are then faced with shipments that come in after the ground is frozen. Experienced lily growers anticipate the late delivery. They prepare lily beds in advance, dig the holes, cover the soil with mulch to keep it from freezing, and slip the bulbs in the holes when they arrive.

Growers in Holland, where lily bulbs mature even later than in the United States and Canada, have to wait until spring to ship and sell over here. This causes no great problems with home gardeners because, when spring-planted, good-quality bulbs will bloom the same growing season. However, the plants won't be quite as vigorous the first year as those grown from fall-planted bulbs. Gardeners should be wary of bargain-priced lilies, for while mail-order lily specialists price their bulbs according to size, small bulbs can be sold at retail to novices without their knowing that they will take longer to measure up to their bred-in capacity.

Lily bulbs are a difficult product for mass marketers to sell in the spring, because the bulbs begin to sprout shortly after they are displayed in a warm area. They are sometimes packed in plastic bags, which force the sprouts to turn and twist. Such distorted growth will usually produce a stunted plant that will rarely bloom the first year.

Experienced local nurseries know to pot up lily bulbs when they show signs of sprouting in the package. Some will offer plants in full bloom for transplanting to the garden, but these are not a good buy. All that top growth will stress the root system when the plant is set in the garden, and the plant may not survive. Young, green containerized lilies will adjust much faster and better when transplanted.

Lily Classifications

Lily enthusiasts have organized lily hybrids and species into ten "divisions," which are internationally accepted. Ideally, all catalogs and labels should carry the name of the division, because the excellent European books on lilies refer to them frequently and they are used in lily shows. Of the ten lily divisions, five are important in North America. If you have only the cultivar or strain name, here are some hints on finding its proper division:

Asiatic Hybrids. Most of this germ plasm is from species originally from Asia. The goal of hybridizers has been to create early-blooming, adaptable, short-to-medium-height, disease-resistant plants. The colors range from pastels to bright and include a few dark shades. The only shortcomings of this division are lack of fragrance and a decided preference for the cooler weather of the northern and midwestern states. The NALS describes these as "the early-blooming and easy hybrids."

Martagon Hybrids. Taller than most of the Asiatics, the Martagon hybrids have pendant Turk's cap blossoms and whorled leaves. In favored locations, the Martagons will spread into large colonies and naturalize. Colonies have been known to live for more than a century. Slower to get started than the Asiatics, the Martagons prefer about the same climatic conditions.

Trumpet and Aurelian Hybrids. These generally tall, magnificent lilies bloom after most of the Asiatics are spent, and are second only to them in popularity.

The powerfully fragrant Trumpets are recognizable more by their petals than by blossom form. The petals have a waxy sheen and dark-colored outer surfaces: purple, brown, or green. The newer Trumpets, especially, are easier to grow than the Orientals. Within this division are cultivars with blossoms that look not at all like trumpets, that are, instead, bowl-shaped and outfacing, pendant, or nodding. Some have open-faced flowers, with petals flaring back from the center attachment.

The early Trumpet hybrids utilized *L. regale* × *L. sulphureum* crosses to get golden and sulfur-yellow colors. Jan de Graaf made hundreds of selections from *L. leucanthum* (centifolium), then crossed the best of these with *L. Sargentiae, L. sulphureum,* and *L. Brownii.* The most significant results were the cultivar 'Pink Perfection' and the large, varied class called the "Aurelian hybrids." This division of lilies is intermediate in hardiness between the Asiatic and Oriental hybrids. Most cultivars are fragrant; the flowers are borne in large trusses.

Oriental Hybrids. Easily recognizable, these have enormous individual blossoms. The first crosses were between *L. speciosum* and *L. auratum,* and many hybrids have since been developed from this approach. Later, *L. auratum* was crossed with *L. japonicum* and *L. rubellum* to get plants with less massive frames. Out of these crosses came the "Imperial Strain," which added gold center bands to petals, expanding the color range of the basically deep red, pink, or white flowers. The most recent hybrids within the division include genes from disease-resistant species or from the short, large-flowered, upfacing *L. nobilissimum.*

In North America, the Oriental hybrids perform best on the West Coast and in favored locations in the East and Upper South. They grow well in warmer parts of Great Britain but even better in New Zealand and cool zones of Australia. They are not nearly as cold hardy as the Asiatics, but will tolerate hot weather better, if given afternoon shade. Their elegant presence brings entirely different reactions from viewers than do the saucy, bright-faced Asiatic hybrids. They have an innate dignity. Thus, they have to be sited with greater care in the landscape than do the Asiatics.

Species Lilies. If you could see the species lilies growing wild in native populations, you could understand why you cannot satisfy the requirements of all species with one garden soil, one site, one feeding and watering regimen, and one schedule and method of propagation. Most grow in rather cool areas, at specific latitudes, altitudes, and sun exposures. The North American Lily Society recommends that, despite the fact that some of the true species lilies are easy to grow, novices should start with the hybrids, which are less demanding. The species lilies range in size from miniature to head-high and require research to appreciate the great range of choices. A good place to look up species of native American lilies is in wildflower books for your region.

Planting

Have your soil tested before preparing soil for lilies. Most lilies prefer a soil pH range of 6.0 to 6.5, but the Oriental hybrids prefer somewhat more acid soil in the range of pH 5.0 to 6.0. The pH of soil can be lowered (made more acid) by working in 1 pound of agricultural sulfur per 100 square feet of sandy soil, or twice as much for heavy clay soil. Apply yearly until the desired pH level has been reached. Except on vegetable garden soil, which contains residual nutrients from fertilizers, mix in 3 pounds of 5-10-10 fertilizer per 100 square feet.

Lily bulbs can be sunk into the soil in open spaces between low-growing conifers, dwarf rhododendrons, or groundcovers, where they will benefit from the organic litter and from their roots being in the shade. Incorporate a little fertilizer and, if needed, lime, before planting.

When your bulbs arrive, you can dust them lightly with captan fungicide or dip them in a Benlate solution. If they look dry and a bit shrunken, put them in a sack of moistened peat moss for a few days until they plump up. If your bulbs arrive with the roots trimmed off or rotted, send them back. Well-rooted bulbs will start off much faster and give better first-year performance.

Follow the directions received with the bulbs for spacing and planting depth. The rule of thumb is to cover the bulb with soil to a depth twice that of the *diameter* of the bulb. (Lily bulbs are usually rather flattened from top to bottom.) When you see recommendations to cover bulbs with 6 to 8 inches of soil, they are the type that forms a root system on the stem above the bulb, as well as contractile roots below the bulb. Conversely, when you see directions to cover bulbs with 2 to 4 inches of soil, they are the type that forms roots only at the bottom of the bulb, or are of a species that will rot if planted deep.

If you decide to plant "on the flat," you will discover that the bottom of your planting holes will be below the level of the surrounding soil, not the best situation for drainage. Instead of digging holes, work up the soil in the bed and buy some bags of planter mix. Set the bulbs on the top of the prepared soil and pour the planter mix over them to cover the bulbs to the recommended depth. This is a fancy way of building a raised bed, but it elevates the bulb to warmer, drier soil levels where the drainage is better.

As you plant each bulb, mark it with a more or less permanent label. Drive in a stake 3 to 5 inches away from each bulb of taller varieties.

Fertilizing

A preplant application of fertilizer won't be enough to feed lilies through the growing season unless your soil is quite fertile. Typically, lily enthusiasts side-dress a low-nitrogen fertilizer on the soil around lily plants as soon as new growth begins to show: 2 to 4 tablespoons per plant should suffice. Be sure not to get any fertilizer on the foliage. One or two foliar feedings with water-soluble fertilizer before flower buds form may work better on sandy soils.

Pests and Diseases

Several minor leaf spots may attack lilies in zones 7 and 8, and elsewhere during wet summers. They are not critical but can disfigure foliage. In northern and midwestern areas the only major fungus disease is botrytis or gray mold, a muggy weather problem, which starts as spots on the leaves and gradually involves flower buds. Micronized copper sprays are effective. Wide spacing between plants and siting lily beds out in the open helps lily foliage to dry faster and to minimize foliage disease.

Even more important, spray at the first sign of aphids. Keep weeds pulled too; some weed species can harbor cucumber mosaic virus and transmit it to your lilies through aphid vectors. If any foliage looks mottled, light green against dark, dig out and discard the bulb without delay. Mosaic virus symptoms are nothing like nutrient-deficiency signs, light or off-color foliage. Try supplemental feeding if you are in doubt: foliar feed or drench around plants with fish emulsion or one of the water-soluble fertilizers high in potash; they are labeled for feeding ornamentals.

Dividing and Transplanting

Don't move or divide lilies unless there is a good reason for it. However, taking up lilies to speed up increase is a different matter. As plants mature, young plants will begin to come up, growing from new bulbs that form around the mother bulb. In the fall, you can dig these young bulbs and spread them out in drifts or use them to start new lily beds. Tiny new bulbs may get lost if you transplant them into the landscape, unless you label them carefully.

The stems of some lilies run for some distance underground before turning up one to two feet away from the old bulb. This is an especially good habit among low, rather open shrubs, which act as an understory, even giving stems some support. These are called "stoloniferous" lilies after their underground stems. The American lilies with stolons form new bulbs on the ends.

Some species, such as *L. tigrinum*, set numerous bulbils—little dark, shiny beads—in leaf axils. These can be taken when they begin to loosen prior to dropping off, and rooted to make new bulbs. Or when the foliage turns brown, you can bend the stem over at the base, cover it lightly with soil, and new lily plants will grow along the stem the following year. You may see small bulbs forming right at the surface around stem-rooting hybrids; if so, heap up a few inches of soil to cover them until they are large and well-rooted enough to take up for division.

Certain lilies can be increased from bulb scales. Plunge the scales with the scar down, in trays of moist vermiculite to root, or alternate layers of scales with layers of moist vermiculite in a plastic bag. Bottom heat will speed the process but, since you will be doing it in late summer, you probably won't need extra heat. Tiny bulblets will form around the scale and, when these begin to show green shoots, detach and pot them up in a seed flat mix to grow to the size of a quarter before setting them out in a nursery row.

Hybridization

Watching lilies develop and bloom from bulbs you planted and nurtured is thrilling, no doubt about it. But, the ultimate thrill is to become the proud hybridizer of a seedling lily that is more beautiful than either of its parents. Don't bother with haphazard crossing; instead, start with one of the newly introduced polyploids. They have extremely complex genetic backgrounds, which enhance your chances of developing a fine new hybrid. Just make sure that the catalog listing says that they are fertile.

To succeed in crossing polyploid lilies, you need to play a little "numbers game." The chromosome number of the gametes of most lily species is 12. Normal or standard lilies are diploid; that is, they have a chromosome number of 24. Triploid lilies have a chromosome number of 36, and the chromosome number of tetraploids is 48. Your best results will come from crossing diploids with diploids, triploids with triploids, and tetraploids with tetraploids.

Lily catalogs lump all cultivars with more than the normal chromosome number under the catchall term "polyploid." This classification developed only recently and includes some of the most exciting new lilies seen in many years.

Peppers

Fun, fellowship, community service, and creative satisfaction are harvested along with Ann and John Swan's Pennsylvania pepper crop.

Peppers are one of the most important food crops in the world, but you'd never know it from looking at typical produce counters. One small bin of green stuffing peppers and a few jalapeños in the gourmet section would be representative. However, as you travel south through Mexico and into the Caribbean and Central America, you enter the homeland of peppers. Peppers everywhere! Fresh, dried, pickled, roasted, fried . . . mostly hot, but many with subtle flavors that are wasted on us Norte Americanos.

(Left) The colorful sampler shown here displays some of the sweet, mild, pungent, and hot peppers grown by the Swans.

Whoever first referred to the genus *Capsicum* as "peppers" started a confusing situation that seems insoluble. The name "pepper" was already being applied to *Piper nigrum*, the tropical spice pepper, before explorers brought back garden peppers from the New World. Most Europeans refer to garden peppers correctly as "*Capsicums*," but it seems doubtful whether the Latin name will ever catch on here.

Collectively, sweet and hot peppers may rank second only to tomatoes among garden vegetables worldwide. In many nations, hot peppers are the single most important condiment. Use of garden peppers in the United States, mostly fresh in salads, is "small potatoes" compared to other parts of the world. The use here is increasing, thanks to the promotion of golden and mature red sweet peppers and the increasing interest in Mexican, Southeast Asian, and Pakistani cuisines, which call for hot and mildly hot peppers.

Peppers spread all over the tropical and semitropical parts of the world with the early explorers. The seeds are easy to keep and transport, and will remain viable for several years. Curiously, the "hottest" cuisines in the world are not found in the New World, where garden peppers are native, but in Africa, Pakistan, Thailand, and China. Many countries offer side dishes of fiery pepper sauces and vinegars, so that diners can season foods to individual tastes. It is possible that the bland taste of the basic foods of these countries led them to welcome the addition of hot peppers for seasoning.

Early explorers reported that Amerindians grew peppers for more than flavoring. They appreciated hot peppers as an appetite enhancer, an aid to digestion, an expectorant, and an aphrodisiac. When the Europeans arrived, peppers had long been domesticated. However, a few wild stands survive, and are harvested annually for vine-dried hot peppers. Old-timers in the South maintain that homemade sausage made with hot peppers keeps better and that peppers tame the taste of wild game. No self-respecting truckstop in the deep South is without bottles of red "Louisiana hot sauce" and pickled hot peppers on every table. The hot, vinegary juice from pickled peppers is used mostly to flavor boiled mustard and turnip greens.

Peppers were first reported in North America in the Florida and New Mexico gardens of Spanish garrisons. Soon thereafter, numerous varieties of both sweet and hot peppers arrived with planters from the Caribbean settling in the South. Yet, seeds of sweet peppers had arrived early with colonists from Great Britain, France, and Holland, and spread south and east with frontier expansion. This may account for the overwhelming national preference for sweet peppers.

Thomas Jefferson planted peppers at Monticello, perhaps ordering seeds from Bernard M'Mahon's catalog. In his 1806 offering, M'Mahon states: "The capsicums are in much estimation for culinary purposes . . . the 'Large Heart-shaped' is the best." He named other varieties: 'Cherry', 'Bell', and 'Long-podded'.

Taxonomists have squabbled over the botanical arrangement of the genus *Capsicum* for centuries. One of the major drawbacks to classifying the various varieties by species was that most of the United States taxonomists and agricultural botanists were at northern universities. In short-season

A harvest of "hots." Clockwise from the top: 'Anaheim TMR 23', 'Tabasco', 'Frogmore', an unidentified wild species, 'Habañero', 'Hungarian Yellow Wax'; center, 'Jalapeño M.'

areas, culture of the late-maturing sweets and hots was difficult, and growing of the true tropicals was impossible. However, in recent years, with the aid of laboratory techniques such as electrophoresis, taxonomists have been able to distinguish the subtle differences among species.

Classifying peppers is difficult partly because pepper plants cross so readily. Fortunately, wild specimens of certain pepper species can still be found, which gives scientists a starting point. They have been able, working with ethnobotanists, historians, and archaeologists, to project the centers from which the various *Capsicum* species spread throughout the world.

Hortus III lists only two *Capsicum* species as important in North America, *C. annuum* and *C. frutescens*. Five "groups" are listed under *C. annuum;* these include virtually all the sweet and nontropical varieties of hot peppers. Within *C. frutescens* is the Tabasco pepper, the source of the heat for the best-known brand of Louisiana hot sauce, which is fermented for a year before bottling. Vinegar-pickled hot peppers are often of the 'Serrano' variety or of 'Tabasco'. Certain of the tropical species or forms won't grow well in this country because they developed under specific conditions of night length, duration of season, and day and night temperatures that we can't duplicate in continental United States gardens.

Everyone, it seems, is more aware of peppers these days. The press coverage generated by the many chili cookoffs, which have now spread coast to coast from the original in Terlingua, Texas, has helped. People everywhere are recognizing and using sweet peppers as well, to add color and flavor to salads, and for their high vitamin content. Still, we have only just begun to appreciate the great variety and potential of the many easily grown pepper varieties and hybrids. Elizabeth Snyder, in her book *Uncommon Fruits and Vegetables*, puts it this way: "With the Mexican and Southeast Asia food explosions in this country of late, we had best begin to make an effort to understand which [pepper] is which and how to use them."

A good place to start would be the produce stand of a grocery serving Mexican-Americans or Southeast Asians. You'll see fresh fruits of the bluntly conical, black-green 'Jalapeño'; the slender, twisty 'Red Chili'; the considerably longer and milder 'Anaheim' or 'New Mexico Chili', or the variably hot, horn-shaped 'Hungarian Yellow Wax'. Dried pods of 'Ancho' and 'Poblado' will be for sale for making powders, and the small, pungent, fruits of 'Serrano' and 'Bird Pepper'. Few of the varieties popular in Southeast Asia and Pakistan are seen here; emigrants from those countries have adapted pretty well to the Mexican varieties.

There is, as well, a big difference in flavor of the various kinds of sweet peppers. Connoisseurs agree that the best flavors are not to be found in the big, blocky bell peppers sold on produce counters, but rather in the medium-sized tapered or horn-shaped peppers such as 'Gypsy' hybrid or the sweet strains of 'Hungarian Yellow Wax'.

Each sweet, mild, or hot pepper variety has its own distinctive flavor; these flavors change with maturity, and in cooking, drying, or pickling. Pepper enthusiasts have learned to tune their tastebuds to the nuances. For John and Ann Swan, a flirtation with peppers more than thirty years ago has blossomed into an infatuation that adds zest to their lives.

John and Ann prefer to allow their sweet peppers to ripen red before picking.

John and Ann Swan of West Chester, Pennsylvania, are the kind of people who have fun growing any kind of plant, be it a flower, vegetable, tree, or shrub. They are good-natured, sharing people who have developed into crackerjack home gardeners and are enjoying every minute of it. Peppers are one of the plants that add spice to their lives and those of everyone around them. Red, yellow, green, purple . . . sweet, mild, hot, and fiery peppers; name a variety and chances are they will have grown it. In their big garden, their pepper patch dominates.

Plunked down in the middle of a large raised-bed food garden, their pepper patch gives the Swans room to try a few new varieties each year, while supplying pecks of peppers of their favorite varieties. The food garden is only the beginning of a beautifully integrated landscape. Flanked by huge, curving beds of perennials and decorative herbs, their side-yard area melds into spacious peninsulas planted with shade-loving species, mostly native plants. In the background are great trees. Atop a rise above the food garden are a culinary herb garden and a sizable wildflower meadow garden. All around the house are choice shrubs, groundcovers, and bulbous plants. The Swans are serious gardeners, no doubt about it!

English born and brought to the United States in infancy, John credits some of his love for flowers to his mother, "who loved to gather and arrange great armloads of flowers, like a proper Englishwoman." Not so with Ann Tucker Swan. Born in Bermuda of an English mother and a Bermudian father, she came to the United States with John as a war bride after World War II. (John was stationed in Bermuda with the U.S. Army Air Corps.) Ann, who describes with relish her growing up as "the only girl on an island with a school for boys," came by gardening from both sides.

Ann's father founded and headed up the Nonsuch Island Training School for wayward boys. They were taught numerous skills, and gardening was, perforce, high on the list. Imported food would have been too costly to satisfy the appetites of growing boys. Her parents taught Ann how to prepare the eclectic foods of Bermuda, reflecting cuisines that merged on the island: British, African, Portuguese, and Caribbean.

In particular, Ann learned how to use peppers to make food more interesting.

"Our friends in Bermuda included people from many parts of the world," recalled Ann. "Each grew his or her own kind of heirloom peppers, sometimes several kinds per family. They pickled the small, red, very hot 'bird peppers' in sherry or rum and used them as condiments for fish chowders and stews. A dash of either of these hot sauces made a memorable Bermuda version of the Bloody Mary. Bermudians grew and used lots of cucumbers, as do I, and put them up as spicy pickles, sometimes with hot peppers. In Bermuda, all surplus vegetables were preserved; the cost of imported food provided incentive."

Gardening had to wait while John finished his degree in English at the University of Pennsylvania and Ann began a career at Smith Kline Laboratories in Philadelphia. "I wasn't good at waiting," said Ann; "I soon had an office full of plants!" John went to work in marketing communications at the DuPont Company. Thirty years ago, they bought a lot near West Chester, Pennsylvania, and later expanded it to three acres. They named their mini-estate "Frogmore" after a famous manor house in England.

"It was not until we began building our house that we took a close look at the land," said John. "We had wondered why the property was strewn with rocks and was rougher than the surrounding farmland. Then, an old farmer in the neighborhood told us that our land was the site of an abandoned dump for rock rubble blasted from a serpentine stone quarry. Ever since before the American Revolution, and up until the early twentieth century, chunks of rock had been hauled from the quarry to our lot. In some areas of the lot, rock was thirty feet deep! We had been unable to recognize the extent of it because of a tangle of underbrush, vines, shrubs, briars, and trees. The saving grace was a cart trail that wound through the piles at ground level, and a more or less rock-free area where we built our home. The old trail, which led down to a creek in the back, became our woodland garden.

"My back still aches," said John, "at the memory of the rocks Ann and I removed and piled aside to make room for our first food garden. That experience taught me why the settlers in this area built homes of stone . . . they needed a place to put them when clearing their fields!" Ann added: "We hauled in soil and dumped it over the rocks; we grew beans and corn at first, stuff we could direct-seed. Neither of us had done large-scale gardening, so we began with simple crops. Our first failure was asparagus; it just didn't produce well for us. Early on we began composting, as my father had taught the boys to do on Bermuda. John and I could get lots of manure locally, loads of leaves from our trees, and field hay from our open pastureland. Years ago, we began saving and recycling all garden refuse and kitchen scraps."

In their then-new garden, Ann could hardly wait to get started growing her fondly remembered peppers, especially the tiny, very hot bird peppers. She sent to Bermuda for seeds and began what has proven to be an absorbing hobby of evaluating hot, mild, and sweet peppers in the garden, and preparing or preserving them in many ways.

"Our friends considered me slightly balmy," Ann said, "until they tasted my bird peppers pickled in sherry. Just a few drops turns bland dishes into party foods!" Her days of sailing a ketch from Nonsuch Island to mainland Bermuda for shopping showed in her description of refilling empty pepper-sauce bottles. "As the tide goes out, pour in more sherry. The flavor will hold through one complete refilling."

A plant of 'Cubanelle' pampered by the Swans with a plastic pot reservoir, a wire cage, and salt-marsh hay mulch.

"I can't get the same kind of sherry we used years ago on Bermuda, but from all the kinds I've tested, one seems to approximate the taste I remember . . . Taylor's Golden Sherry. It is neither too dry nor too sweet.

"John helped me so much with my pepper hobby and, later, as I branched out into herbs," Ann said, "he built a thousand-square-foot vegetable garden on a slope so steep that he had to terrace it with railroad ties, three high at each step. I wheelbarrowed and dumped in soil mixed with spent composted manure from a nearby mushroom grower.

"After we completed that job, he and I tackled the piles of stones around the place." As Ann spoke, I tried to imagine the number of man and woman hours needed to load, move, offload, and set the thousands of stones in evidence. They were neatly laid without mortar, in backsloping walls. I estimated the walls at about five hundred feet total, ranging in height from two to four feet. The stones have begun to collect a patina of moss, lichen, and ferns. Here and there, choice perennials are chinked in. Carefully chosen prostrate shrubs and creeping groundcovers break the stark gray-green lines.

"If only we had been able to afford a tractor and a scoop loader," John added, "we could have finished the job in a year or two. But, we were young and strong. The hard work, year after year, may have been a blessing. We still have the energy and endurance to do whatever we wish, be it gardening, volunteer work, or travel."

Their shared excitement crackled as they told how they discovered a wild pepper on an island in the Galapagos Archipelago. "On the side of a still-active volcano, at some distance, partly hidden by tall grass, we caught a glimpse of pepper red. We picked our way through the underbrush and, sure enough, found a tall, shrubby, pepper plant with small pods. It was the first wild pepper we had seen in our travels and we had to have it for our pepper trials.

"We brought seeds home and grew plants, only to find our Galapagos pepper was a promiscuous little devil. After only one generation, we lost the original line due to natural crosses with other varieties. One of those accidental crosses, it turned out, was a 'keeper,' a small-fruited pepper we named 'Frogmore' after an estate in England. We are still growing it.

"Many of the exotic pepper varieties are available from seeds ordered from specialty catalogs. We've picked up seeds of local varieties in Ecuador, and have found a few more wild kinds," says John. "Friends give us some; that's how we got started with 'Rocotillo'; it came from Puerto Rico. We order seeds of Mexican and southwestern specialties from Seeds and Plants of the Southwest, in Santa Fe, New Mexico, and from Horticultural Enterprises in Dallas. Stokes Seeds in Buffalo is another good source with a wide selection of sweet and mild peppers. The Pepper Gal in Largo, Florida, has an interesting list as does Park Seeds in Greenwood, South Carolina."

The Swans' pepper patch, which is planted on terraces, ascends a steep slope.

Ann is delighted with an heirloom pepper they were given by a friend who found it in South Carolina. It is one of the distinctive small-fruited hot peppers native to the tropics and has adapted to temperate climates. It is a different species from standard hot peppers: the foliage is smaller and the plants bushier. No one knew its name, so they dubbed it 'Ethel Jane' in honor of the person on whose property it was found.

"Space is limited in our garden," John said. "Before we order seeds, we decide how many fruits of each variety we will need to grow for our own kitchen and for the Pennsylvania Horticultural Society's 'Harvest Show.' Then, we project how many plants we'll need to produce them. Finally, we add a few varieties that we've never grown before. After dropping the varieties that were unsatisfactory or indifferent the previous year, that brings us up to twelve to fifteen varieties, three to ten plants per variety. That's all we have room for in the food garden. Ann plugs a few plants of the more ornamental hots into sunny perennial beds, and that relieves a bit of the pressure for space.

"I always draw a plot plan of the vegetable garden so we can rotate crops," John continued. "We don't like to plant peppers in the same location two years in a row. We don't rely on memory; a plot plan reminds us of what we planted, when and where, from year to year."

John does most of the propagation for the Swans' garden. "I start pepper seeds in the basement beginning the second week in March," he said. "I plant three seeds per cube in Jiffy 7s, which I buy a thousand to the case to save money. When the seedlings have their first set of true leaves, I scissor out the surplus and leave one strong seedling per cube. Pepper seeds germinate best at 70 to 75 degrees F. I get good results by setting trays of moistened and seeded Jiffy 7s in the furnace room for germination. I cover the trays with sheet plastic to keep moisture in and marauding mice out.

"As soon as the seeds show green sprouts, I remove the plastic and move the trays of Jiffy 7s to fluorescent-lit shelves and grow the plants to the six-leaf stage at about 65 degrees, 60 at night. Then, I do something that I feel makes a real difference in pepper growing. I pot up the Jiffy 7 plants in four-inch plastic pots filled with a half-and-half mixture of screened soil from the vegetable garden and a potting medium named 'Pro-Mix.' I don't sterilize the soil used in the mix; so far, we've been lucky not to have any root rot in our plants.

"After three or four weeks, the seedlings will have filled the pots with roots but, in an average spring, won't be pot-bound. At that season of the year, we begin listening to the weather-band radio. We really need to get our pepper plants in the ground around May 15, after hardening off for two weeks, in order to maximize production. So, around May 1, weather permitting, we begin setting trays of plants outside, along a sunny, sheltering wall. Wind is the real villain; if it kicks up during the day, we cover the plants to keep the stems from being damaged. If the temperature drops, we bring them indoors. Every cold night we bring them in. We have learned that you must not allow pepper plants to become shocked by cold temperatures or whipped and weakened by drying winds.

"We can actually see the plants changing as they harden off. The stems and leaves thicken and become stiffer. The leaves turn dark green. New internodes are short. We know that, when we set a hardened-off pepper plant in the garden around May 15, it won't be shocked by transplanting.

"We've developed a system of transplanting that works for us. Our soil is fluffy and weed-free from tilling in late fall and adding composted manure from a mushroom grower. We line out rows three feet apart and set pepper plants thirty inches apart, to get the maximum number on each terrace. How we set them in makes a big difference, we feel.

"Hooeee!" I sample Ann's dried and powdered hot peppers for the TV cameras during The Victory Garden*'s visit.*

"We mix a handful of 5-10-5 granular fertilizer into the quart or so of soil excavated to make a planting hole. We set the plant in just deep enough to match its soil line with the surface of the garden soil, perhaps half an inch higher. If the plants are overgrown due to weather delays, we straighten out girdling roots before planting and backfilling.

"Next, and we may be the only gardeners doing this, we cut the bottoms out of six-inch nursery pots and set them around the pepper plants, small end down. We twist them this way and that to sink the bottom rim one and a half to two inches deep into the soil. These pots shelter young seedlings not only from cutworms but also from stem-whipping winds. They reflect and concentrate heat, and give us a reservoir for watering. We pour water into them slowly, to avoid washing soil around. Those bottomless pots are one of our 'secret weapons.'

"Another secret weapon is a stack of large, rigid, empty three-gallon plastic nursery pots we stow in the garden house. If night temperatures threaten to fall below 50 degrees, we cover pepper plants with inverted pots. We're not so much concerned with frost after May 15 as we are with the chilling effect of cold wind and cold rain. We didn't have to buy the containers; they came with perennials and shrubs we purchased.

"As anyone knows who has grown peppers," John said, "they sit still for two or three weeks after planting, regardless of the weather. Nothing

Protecting Peppers

The Swans employ an arsenal of techniques to protect their peppers until harvest. Bottomless plastic one-gallon pots shelter new transplants from wind and cutworms, as well as reflecting and concentrating heat (1). Baskets and nursery containers cover pepper plants against late spring frosts (2). Old shutters supported above plants reduce the stress from extremely hot weather (3). Old madras bedspreads pulled over cages protect plants against fall frost (4).

you do will make them add size. I think that the plants are developing roots like crazy. When the soil warms in June, the plants take off and grow with a rush. Some of our hot varieties don't put on much growth until late July.

"When fast growth starts, we set a cage around each pepper plant. The cages serve three purposes: they keep plants from toppling in windstorms, they minimize breakage of brittle limbs, and they keep our feet from compacting soil near the plants. We have tried growing peppers without cages but lose production to toppling and breakage. We like red-ripe peppers and let so many fruit hang on the plants that they are especially vulnerable to breakage.

"We make pepper cages of the reinforcing wire mesh used to strengthen concrete; it works much better and lasts longer than the thinner, less substantial fencing such as dog wire. All our cages are eighteen inches in diameter. We make some of them thirty inches high for short varieties and some forty-eight inches for taller peppers. The net height is six inches less because we snip out the cross wires on the bottom ring. That leaves spears that stick into the ground to prevent the cage from tipping over in a storm. The cylinders last for nearly ten years; we're on our second set. In late June we dress two to three inches of salt marsh hay over the entire vegetable garden, for moisture retention, weed control, and reduction of soil temperature. Salt hay is particularly good because it holds up for a long time, contains no weed seeds, and does not support fungus diseases."

It's important not to cultivate around pepper plants. Instead, hand-pull weeds growing around the plants and rake soil out of the walkways to pull up around the plants and to bury weed seedlings.

John continued: "The mulch really helps our plants to withstand extreme heat and dryness. During a heat wave, some of our sweet varieties, especially 'Gypsy' and 'Cubanelle', looked as if they were about to die. Watering kept them barely alive but didn't seem to help the problem. We laid old louvered shutters across the tops of the cages and the shade saved the plants. Hot weather always reduces fruit set, except on the hot varieties, even though we water deeply every two or three days. Peppers can stand only so much heat and dryness."

The Swans rarely find it necessary to give their peppers supplementary fertilizer. "The 5-10-10 we mix in at planting time is enough to produce a good crop on our soil," said John. "The mushroom compost, being composed mostly of straw and horse manure, probably contributes most of the other nutrients needed by vegetables. If I see an occasional plant growing slowly, I will give it a shot of liquid plant food, but never of a high-nitrogen analysis."

I asked Ann how many peppers they harvested from the seventy plants in their garden, and which was the most prolific variety. "I have no doubt we lose some production," she replied, "by minimizing picking until the 'Harvest Show' in late September. Even so, we get up to five pounds of fruit per plant, especially from 'Cubanelle' and 'Gypsy'. Some of the hots such as 'Bird' pepper, 'Thai Hot', and 'Tabasco' have hundreds of fruits but they are so tiny and hard to pick that we are lucky to get half a pound per plant.

"Personally," Ann said, "I much prefer red-ripe sweet or mildly hot peppers over the immature green fruit. The flesh is sweeter and thicker. And, since I roast, sear, or sauté most fruits rather than eating them raw, the thick mature skin slips right off. I am willing to sacrifice yield for such quality. As it stands, the day before the 'Harvest Show,' every inch of space on the basement floor and the family room is covered with baskets of ripe peppers, labeled by variety. By the way, I clip off large-fruited peppers with a pair of sharp Felco shears. Snapping or twisting them off can break limbs.

"After the show, we concentrate on preserving all the peppers we can before hard frost," Ann said. "Light frosts don't worry us because we lay old cotton bedspreads over the crops. The Madras spreads are rather light, but rarely blow off, and they dry out quickly after a rain. We've tried the new spun-bonded floating row covers, but they tear on the cages and are hard to anchor. I hate the way they feel when they are wet! I'd rather dry the bedspreads on the vegetable garden fence, fold and store them between frosts."

The plants' heavy foliage canopy in the fall tends to shield the lower half of the plant and, often, the fruits that are borne down low. Even though a light frost can blacken the outer shell of foliage, you can continue to pick peppers for a while. But frost makes a warm-weather vegetable act like a wounded deer; it may run for a while but is doomed to a short life. You'd be better off either picking all the fruits before a frost and freezing them, or pulling the entire plant and hanging it in a cool basement to supply you with fresh peppers for up to a month.

"A killing frost doesn't ordinarily come before mid-October, so we have about three weeks to harvest and preserve our pepper crop. We freeze 'Gypsy' or 'Canape' diced, or halved and seeded, along with whole fruits of the pungent 'Rocotillo'. The 'Jalapeño M' fruits, we pickle. We lay fruits of the thin-fleshed hots on old window screens and dry them in the furnace room. Fortuitously, we turn on the house heat at the same time we need heat for drying.

"I hate the dry hot pepper flakes served in Italian restaurants and pizza parlors!" said Ann. "I prefer a powder I make by grinding and mixing selected hot and mild peppers to taste. I try to make my mixtures hot, but not so hot as to kill the flavor."

She showed me how she prepares hot pepper powder for the Philadelphia unit of The Herb Society, which sells it as a fund-raiser. She combines flavorful mild peppers such as 'Fushimi' and 'Zippy' and removes the calyxes (caps) from the dried fruit. Then she adds about 10 percent by volume of a very hot dried pepper such as 'Thai Hot', 'Bird', or 'Tabasco'. She runs these through her food processor, tastes the mixture to be sure it has the right degree of heat, then runs it through her blender to make a fine powder. She seals the powder tight in small bottles to preserve the flavor, labels and dates them, and they are ready for use. I tasted some of Ann's blends and, to this old hot-pepper lover, they seemed just right!

I asked Ann if she wore rubber gloves when working with hot peppers. "No," she replied, "the flush of heat I get from the active ingredient makes my arthritic hands feel better. But I always take out my contact lenses because the flying powder will bring tears, despite my laying a damp towel over the food processor and blender."

For her pepper jelly, another fast-selling item for their fund-raisers, Ann prefers to use mature red fruits of 'Gypsy' and 'Canape' hybrids, or 'Hungarian Yellow Wax'. They tried the paprika variety 'Szegedi', but it lacked production. They shy away from the large-fruited bells because

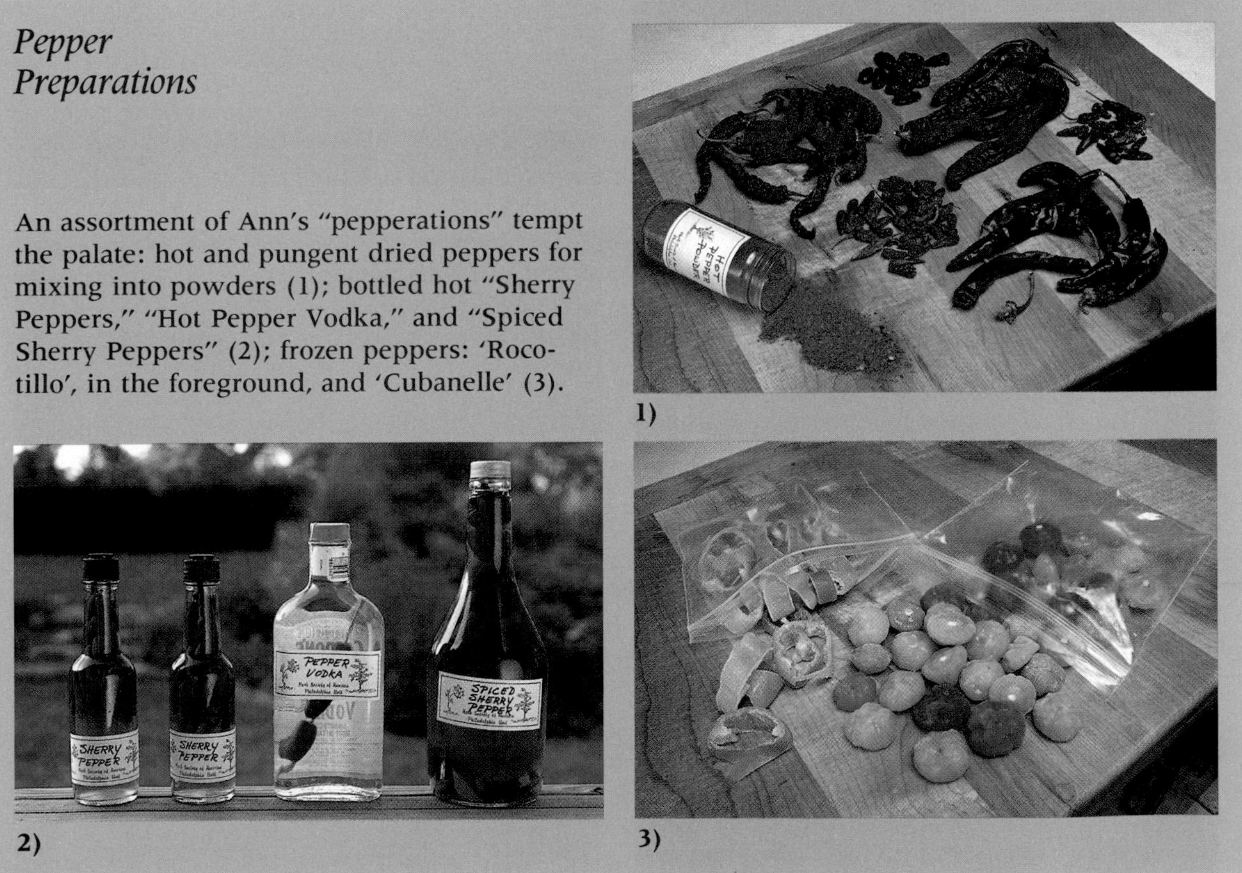

Pepper Preparations

An assortment of Ann's "pepperations" tempt the palate: hot and pungent dried peppers for mixing into powders (1); bottled hot "Sherry Peppers," "Hot Pepper Vodka," and "Spiced Sherry Peppers" (2); frozen peppers: 'Rocotillo', in the foreground, and 'Cubanelle' (3).

1)

2)

3)

the flat-topped fruits tend to catch water and rot. She finds other uses for mature red peppers; for her, 'Gypsy' makes fine pimiento peppers for canning. Others, such as the mildly pungent 'Anaheim TMR 23', she chars, removes the skin and seeds, stuffs into pint plastic containers, adds a pinch of salt, applies lids, and freezes. Thawed, they are in a handy increment for adding to cooked dishes.

One of Ann's newest but most popular productions are pickled cocktail peppers of the 'Rocotillo' variety, flavored with dill. These are funny little pungent, but not fiercely hot, peppers, flat like flying saucers. Green when immature, they turn yellow, then red when ripe. She mixes the three colors for pickles.

Also new are experimental hot mustards made with powdered dry 'Habañero' and 'Thai Hot' peppers. Ann is perhaps best known for the Bermuda specialties, sherry pepper and rum pepper. To make them, she stuffs tall, slender jars one-third full of red-ripe fruit of small, thin-skinned hots such as 'Bird', 'Tabasco', 'Thai', and 'Ethel Jane', fills them with sherry or rum, caps them, and lets them sit in the dark for at least a month before use.

Ann gave me two more pepper recipes before I left their pleasant company. "For breakfast, try 'Cubanelle' peppers sautéed in light olive oil. Serve them with grilled tomatoes. And for a pepper jelly that will take the blue ribbon, use red-ripe bell peppers and add either horseradish or freshly ground ginger."

The Swans' hobby has given a new focus to their travels and has attracted a new and expanding circle of friends who swap pepper seeds and stories with them. They have been at it so long and have researched peppers so thoroughly that they just might be the best-informed amateur pepper growers in the country. I think they are, and I hope they keep on growing and sharing for many years.

More about Peppers

What's in a Name?

The names of the *Capsicum* species and groups are complicated, but there is a reason for it. Long ago, seeds were transported from centers of origin in the New World to distant points where distinct "varieties" evolved or emerged from selection by man. If you could grow plants of a taxonomic variety side-by-side with representatives of its original species, you would see few differences except for those achieved by primitive methods of selection. Plant scientists can make the connections, however, despite the differences, by comparing similarities that only taxonomists can appreciate.

Eventually, when a taxonomic "variety" becomes sufficiently uniform and true to type, it may be given a "cultivar" name, which is botanical argot for "cultivated variety." Were you to compare cultivars with their original species side-by-side, you might see great differences in the size, shape, and number of fruit, plant habit, season of production, and disease resistance. Yet, taxonomists can look closely at antecedents and descendants and see their relationship.

So, there may be types of peppers for which three entities exist: the original species, the crudely improved and variable variety, and the greatly improved modern cultivar.

For maximum clarity, cultivar names should always appear in single quotation marks such as 'Yolo Wonder' or 'Anaheim Chili'. Few seed catalogs follow this modern nomenclature and prefer merely to capitalize the first letter of the cultivar name or to print it in boldface. Further confusing the issue, seedsmen also prefer to refer to their open pollinated strains of vegetables as "varieties" rather than cultivars.

Dr. Jean Andrews's book, *The Domesticated Capsicums*, contains a chart of domesticated pepper varieties which could be considered a *Capsicum* family tree. The apparent redundancies in naming are unavoidable. Explanatory notes have been added.

- *Capsicum annuum* var. (variety) *annuum:* Representative cultivars would be 'Jalapeno', 'Gypsy', or 'Park's Whopper'. Most of the sweet and hot peppers popular in temperate climates are in this group.

- *Capsicum annuum* var. *aviculare:* A representative cultivar would be 'Chiltecpin'. The bird peppers are in this variety. The plants are generally tall, open, and rather small-leaved, and the fruits are tiny, variable in shape, and very hot.

- *Capsicum baccatum* var. *pendulum:* 'Kellu-uchu' and 'Pucauchu' would be representative. These varieties do not perform well at our latitudes.

- *Capsicum chinense* var. *chinchi-uchu, habañero,* and *rocotillo:* Habañero and rocotillo are late maturing, but can be grown at our latitudes. The plants are rangier but otherwise superficially similar to popular varieties of *C. annuum*.

- *Capsicum frutescens:* Representative varieties would be *tabasco* and *uvilla grande*. Both have erect, quite hot fruit on large, late plants.

- *Capsicum pubescens* var. *rocoto:* No mistaking these plants: the leaves have a faintly furry look and appear thinner than those of our garden peppers. Not well adapted to temperate climates.

The *Capsicum* family trees don't show 'Habañero' and 'Rocotillo' as cultivars, even though seeds are available under these names. I believe it is because these are primitive and highly variable varieties from which other named cultivars were later selected. Any Jamaican, for example, can tell you that their version of *habañero* — some call it 'Scotch Bonnet' — can differ in hotness and flavor from village to village.

You won't find many hybrids among the hot peppers, but you may encounter the term "strains." A given variety may have several different strains, depending on who grows the seeds. Each producer has his own specifications for the variety, and selects toward it, when choosing seed parents. After a few generations of selection, his strain may differ from the original, yet will still look enough like it to pass. For example, certain strains of 'Hungarian Yellow Wax' are distinctly nippy while others are perfectly sweet. You can't tell the difference without tasting them. Sometimes, strains become accidentally mixed by field-crossing with another variety. That can result in mild-flavored peppers in a supposedly hot variety or—surprise!—hot peppers in a supposedly sweet variety.

Adaptability

I can remember when peppers were the prima donnas of food gardens. Those old varieties sulked in hot weather and cold: if the temperature didn't suit them, they would blossom, but wouldn't set fruit. The new hybrid peppers perform well in all the contiguous states, but the bearing season in the northern tier of states, even with the aid of heat-trapping mulch, is rather short.

When you order pepper seeds or plants, remember that peppers originated in or near tropic latitudes. If you garden in an area with short or cool summers, choose the early varieties or hybrids, those that will mature in sixty to sixty-five days. This means you can't grow the great big stuffing peppers because they mature rather late. Take heart: the smaller-fruited hybrids are more productive anyway, and often are better flavored.

Mulching

Peppers respond well to mulches but what you use depends on the average soil temperature in your garden during the summer. Peppers like warm soil, but not hot. The hot varieties of peppers can tolerate hot soil, but would yield better if mulched to hold down maximum soil temperatures. This is why John and Ann Swan's salt marsh hay mulch produces good results for them. Such organic mulches are recommended across Middle America and farther south and west, rather than plastic.

Plastic mulches, however, work better in northern zones such as 4 and 5 and the upper edge of 6. They trap solar heat and keep the soil warmer than in surrounding areas. Experiments in Duluth, Minnesota, confirm that clear plastic mulch is most effective in their cool climate, applied after the soil warms up, and covered with organic mulch later for shading. Weeds will grow beneath clear plastic due to the warmth, humidity, and transmitted light, but the organic mulch will shade them out.

Black plastic mulch is not recommended for zones 7 and south, unless you run drip irrigation tubes under it and spray-paint the areas over root zones with flat white. In warm climates soil temperatures can rise alarmingly beneath black plastic, particularly on dry, sandy soil, and can stress plants by killing the roots in the surface layer beneath the plastic. The white paint reflects sunlight and reduces soil temperatures. White plastic mulch is available but is expensive.

Buying Seeds and Plants

Pepper enthusiasts soon learn to order pepper seeds from companies that conduct field performance trials in a climate similar to theirs. Their "average plant height" figures can be relied on. Field trials also reveal the varieties or hybrids that are more tolerant of heat, cold, drought, or wet soil than others, and resistance to locally serious plant diseases.

Pepper breeders believe there is a genetic linkage between the ability of peppers to set fruit at low temperatures and at high. One appears to go with the other, to a point. There is a threshold of heat, about 86 degrees F., beyond which the bell or sweet peppers won't set fruit. You can expect peppers not to set fruit, when temperatures remain cooler than the low 60s for extended periods.

Pests and Diseases

Certain pepper hybrids have been bred for resistance to locally prevalent plant diseases. Your State Cooperative Extension Service will list these in their "Recommended Varieties" publications. They name resistances to specific diseases rather than, as some seed catalogs do, merely using the general and not particularly enlightening term "disease resistant."

One of the features we at *The Victory Garden* advise new gardeners to look for in pepper varieties is resistance to tobacco mosaic virus disease, TMV. This virus can cripple pepper plants, shut down their production, and make the plants look distorted and mottled. Many old bell pepper varieties have no resistance whatsoever, but most hot peppers have high levels of resistance. There are degrees of resistance: steer clear of any variety or hybrid labeled as "Tolerant of TMV"; you need maximum resistance in peppers, not merely tolerance.

Peppers have few problems with insects, but leafhoppers and thrips can rasp foliage and cause fruiting buds to drop. These can be controlled by spraying with insecticidal soap. A few species of larvae such as tomato fruit worms can bore into peppers; these are more difficult to control; your County Agent can suggest spray programs.

Planting

Peppers benefit from 2 to 3 percent organic matter in the soil, just enough to make it accept and store water, and to keep it biologically active. Too much organic matter can result in runaway release of nitrogen in warm weather, with resultant lush growth and inhibited fruit set. Peppers also like raised bed culture and drip irrigation; during dry seasons, drip irrigation can produce significant yield increases over watering by sprinkler.

Don't overplant peppers. Two or three plants will keep the average family in salad and stuffing peppers all summer long, and one plant of hot peppers will suffice. That leaves room to try new varieties and hybrids, and I hope you will. The incredibly beautiful ornamental peppers make fine heat-resistant plants to set among your garden flowers. Not all catalogs will tell you whether their ornamental varieties are hot or sweet; most are hot.

Boosting Yields

You can increase pepper production in many ways: by wrapping pepper cages with clear plastic for a few weeks after planting (leave a chimney for warm air to escape), by picking fruits weekly to reduce the drain on plant vigor, by installing drip irrigation, and by growing them with the aid of plastic mulch in cool climates. Some gardeners save plastic milk jugs, cut out the bottoms and remove the caps, and set them over young plants. The idea is to shield the plants from cold wind and rain and to accumulate a little heat to make them grow faster than unprotected plants. It works, and it also keeps out cutworms.

Most people miss out on one of the major advantages of peppers. They are so productive that only a plant or two of each variety can give you all the fruits of one kind that you can eat or put away for winter. Why plant several bushes of one variety of pepper when you can mix them up and have many different fruit sizes, shapes, colors, and flavors? Just one season of growing peppers will convince you that they really are easy to grow, and will inspire you to experiment with a wide variety. You'll have the makings for international cuisines and good old American cooking right at your fingertips!

Index

Page numbers in *italics* refer to illustrations

NUTRITIONAL HEALERS

How to Eat Your Way to Better Health

Carlson Wade

Parker Publishing Company, Inc.
West Nyack, N.Y.

10 9 8 7 6 5 4 3

This book is a reference work based on research by the author. The opinions expressed herein are not necessary those of or endorsed by the publisher. The directions stated in this book are in no way to be considered as a substitute for consultation with a duly licensed doctor.

DEDICATION

To a Longer and Healthier Life...
Filled with Youthful Happiness

Library of Congress Cataloging-in-Publication Data

Wade, Carlson.
Nutritional healers.

Includes index.
1. Diet therapy. 2. Nutrition. I. Title.
[DNLM: 1. Diet Therapy—popular works. 2. Nutrition—popular works. WB 400 W119n]
RM216.W29 1987 613.2 87-1373

ISBN 0-13-627233-9

ISBN 0-13-627225-8 PBK

Printed in the United States of America

Foreword by a Medical Doctor

In my medical practice, I see many health-conscious people who are concerned about the use of drugs for such conditions as arthritis, high blood pressure, cancer, cardiovascular disorders, allergies, and gastrointestinal problems. My patients want to feel good and look youthful while healing many common and uncommon disorders. They frequently ask if there is an alternative route to possibly addictive drugs and surgery. Happily, I am able to recommend highly the use of nutritional therapy as researched by the highly respected medical reporter, Carlson Wade.

This new guide to total healing of body and mind with the use of nutrition is designed for the complete person. The programs show you how to use everyday foods and nutrients to allow your body to initiate healing from within. These programs may be considered "natural medicines" because they work so effectively, but unlike chemotherapeutic drugs, they are free of side effects. Neither are they habit forming. They work on an entirely new set of principles of healing as revealed by Carlson Wade, namely, an inner transformation. Nutritional healers promote internal rejuvenation and stimulation of the immune system to overcome stubborn conditions.

This book is on the latest scientific findings about the effective treatment of many illnesses with the use of everyday foods. It takes you by the hand and guides you through the inner workings and mechanisms of a specific condition, then it gives you highly workable nutritional programs you can use in the privacy of your own home as a means of fast and effective healing. Often, the programs can give you lifetime freedom from problems you thought were hopeless!

With simple, easy-to-follow programs, you have a personalized nutritional healing prescription to help you to overcome debilitative conditions and boost the strength of your immune system to enjoy total health in the many years ahead. And thanks to the powerful and workable nutritional therapies presented by Carlson Wade, you will look better and feel better. This book should be in *everyone's* hands. It is the key to total rejuvenation and healing with the use of corrective foods. You will live longer and much, much better with Carlson Wade's highly recommended book. It works!

H. W. Holderby, M.D.

What This Book Will Do for You

A set of eight major diseases take 160 lives an hour. In the struggle for survival against killer illnesses, we see more than 4,000 Americans die every single day. The modern-day plagues—heart trouble, cancer, cerebrovascular disease, lung problems, respiratory disorders, diabetes, liver troubles, kidney failure—have proved to be among the most ruthless killers in our country. Even with high-tech science and computerized medicine, the fatalities still mount.

Additionally, there are crippling ailments that include blood pressure trouble, excess fatty accumulation, arthritis, allergies, stress, osteoporosis, the fear of memory loss via Alzheimer's disease, and nagging digestive disorders such as painful ulcers or irritating heartburn. We are troubled with obesity as well as everyday headache, muscle, or stress pain. The greatest problem is that of unwarranted premature old age.

In researching for therapies that would ease distress, promote healing, and give hope for a cure, I came across a treasure of nutritional therapies. The comparatively young science of using foods as medicine is being utilized and recognized by leading medical experts as a means of boosting the body's own immune system. The reaction is to fight illness from within and invigorate the body so it can recuperate and cast out infectious threats.

Gathering these latest nutritional doctrines in a book became a dedicated goal in my profession as a medical researcher and reporter. Not only did I criss-cross the country in search of answers to nutritional healing questions, but I talked to countless people, including experts in the field of health and nutrition. The purpose was to offer an alternative to drugs for more than the nation's most deadly killer diseases, that is, for just about any common disorder. Gradually, the book began to take shape as the nutritional therapies were outlined just as they had been used to snatch many from fatality or lifelong disability.

This book is a compendium of the best medical minds in the field of nutritional healing from all parts of the country. The programs use *no* drugs, *no* confinement, *no* unusual or costly devices. Many of the ingredients are in your pantry right now, or else they are available at your nearby food outlet. Many of the healers are so simple, they can be used in a matter of moments. Healing is just as swift, according to the researchers.

Why is nutrition so vital as a healing method? We currently spend some $2 billion a year searching for cures but 100 times more on treatments. It costs us upwards of $200 billion annually, or about $1,000 for every man, woman, and child in the country, for sick leave, doctors, hospitals, drugs, and surgery to treat these chronic killers. After years of investigation, it has been found that there are many opportunities to prevent such illnesses, and even more nutritional programs to help bring about effective treatment. The cost would be a fraction of spiralling hospitalization or lifetime drug taking. The book you now hold in your hands is a breakthrough in the search for alternatives to costly, painful, and often fatal consequences of conventional chemotherapy and surgery.

If you or anyone you know is troubled with any of the eight major diseases of the 1980s, this book is for you. For problems of stress, stiffness, poor memory, gastritis, heartburn, muscle or neurological pains of any sort, hypoglycemia, prostate trouble, menstrual syndrome, poor blood health, and premature aging, this book will share the findings of top nutritional and medical sciences the world over.

The very new science.of the immune system is also discussed with a variety of newly discovered nutritional methods to help boost resistance against a variety of assaults on your mental and physical heatlh.

The use of just one program may well save a life...of someone you know, or even your own!

You can win the battle against major and minor illnesses with the use of nutritional therapy. This book will show you how to reverse the tide of aging and tap the wells of healing with drugless methods. Thanks to this new research, it is possible for you to protect yourself against killing or crippling ailments—become totally healed and enjoy the best that is to come, with the use of nutritional healers.

Carlson Wade

Contents

1

How to Ease and Erase Arthritis Distress with Healing Foods

"Arthritis? Why me?"

This question is asked when an apparently healthy person is told that arthritis has taken hold and may worsen as the years go on. The traditional answer is either "heredity" or else "trauma" of one sort or another.

"Can my arthritis be cured?"

It is only natural for the patient to want to live *without* arthritis. This question shows a desire to want to heal and erase this health threat. The usual answer is that arthritis has no cure and that the most that can be done is to submit to various types of drug therapy and medication. It may be an occasional drug. It usually means a lifetime of chemotherapy. There is little hope beyond being drugged so that the pain of arthritis is not felt. But it increases in silent or drugged intensity because medications are directed at *symptoms,* not at the *causes* of arthritis. Under this regimen, *arthritis may well be forever.*

With the newer knowledge of nutritional science, you do have an alternative. You can find relief from pain and even healing of this threatening crippler with the use of newly discovered nutritional therapy. A dietary approach can be aimed at correcting the *cause* of this distress; once this *metabolic error* has been corrected, the symptoms subside and you may look forward to a life that is free of arthritis.

Before You Begin

There are different nutritional therapies. You may respond better to one program than to another. Since each person is different, each one will have a different response to the dietary program. You need to pursue the different therapies until you find one that offers you the relief you seek. When you feel the long-term control of symptoms because of one or more nutritional therapies, then you will assume that you are on the right track and look ahead to freedom from arthritis. It is up to you, with the help of your medical nutritionist, to find the proper program for your specific needs.

Arthritis: Something You Ate... Or Didn't Eat?

Is Arthritis a Food Allergy?

Something you ate may trigger arthritis flare-up. There are certain foods that upset the metabolic balance and can be blamed for causing an allergic reaction with the symptoms of arthritis! In particular, scientists have found that one group of foods, the *nightshade plant group*, can cause painful arthritic flare-ups, even if taken in small amounts. Eliminate these foods, and you may be able to eliminate arthritis.

What Are the Nightshade Foods?

These include four basic everyday foods: *white potato, tomato, eggplant,* and *red pepper.* They may be healthfully, nutritious foods for many people, but for others, they tend to trigger an allergic reaction that erupts as arthritis flare-up. By absolutely avoiding these four foods, you may well be able to turn the tide and bolster resistance to arthritis distress.

The Toxic Trigger in Nightshade Foods. Nightshade foods contain an ingredient identified as *solanine,* a bitter, toxic, crystalline alkaloid that causes a metabolic shock to trigger arthritic distress. It is a saponic like glycoalkaloid that irritates by destroying red blood cells to cause a general breakdown.

Solanine is an inhibitor of cholinesterase, an enzyme that provides agility of muscle movements. This toxic trigger can destroy the important enzyme and make you vulnerable to stiffness, sluggish muscle movements, painful spasms. If you are troubled with arthritis, check your nutritional program. If you eliminate the four foods of the nightshade family, you may well free your body from the destructive solanine toxic trigger and enjoy freedom from arthritis!

ERASES "HOPELESS" ARTHRITIS IN NINE DAYS WITH SIMPLE DIET CHANGE

Martha A. was so troubled with cripplinglike rheumatoid arthritis she could hardly hold a spoon in her pain-wracked hand. Housework was agonizing. There was no relief from stubborn pains, especially in the morning. She was told to "live with it" because chemotherapy offered partial help but could not heal arthritis. But Martha A. was determined to find an alternative or natural therapy for her condition.

A medical nutritionist prepared a complete dietary and physical profile for her. She was told to self-test by eliminating the four nightshade plants from her diet. Here response would be monitored to see if her arthritis was due to an allergic reaction to these solanine-containing foods. Martha A. followed this simple diet change. No white potato, no tomato, no eggplant, no red pepper in any form. Results? Within four days, her hands and fingers felt more flexible. In seven days, she could move around the house and grounds with youthful agility. By the ninth day, she was pronounced "free" from the formerly "hopeless" arthritis. Martha A. became so energetic by this nutritional therapy, she soon took on a full-time job because she liked being active. It was her way of celebrating her freedom from arthritis!

Be Alert to "Hidden" Forms of Nightshade Foods. These four "no-no" foods that may be responsible for allergic reactions of arthritis are found in packaged products. You may be eating them in the form of starch, filler, flavoring, spices, coloring, vegetables, without knowing it. Be sure to *read labels* of any packaged or processed foods. Be aware of seemingly innocent listings such as "starch" or "fillers" which are often made of these nightshade foods.

Eating Out?

Restaurant eating calls for planning. Salads, soups, stews, casseroles, baked foods, meat or vegetable pies, even sandwiches may have one or more of these four "no-no" foods, either as part of the original recipe or adding during preparation. Even a small portion could cause an arthritis flare-up, *if* you are allergic to these foods. Be prepared *before* you eat out to protect yourself.

Whole Foods Are Safe Foods. When eating out, select whole foods that will be free of these nightshades. *Examples:* consider a lean cut of meat, slice of seafood, dairy-based entrée, steamed fresh or raw vegetables, and freshly prepared legumes. *Careful:* beware of stews, burgers, and canned or frozen foods. You will be less likely to have an arthritic-allergic attack due to the solanine toxic trigger if you stick to whole foods.

Yes, the nightshades are nutritious foods. For many people, they can build health without arthritic or other allergic reactions. But for others, they can cause distress. If you belong to this latter group, try a simple elimination diet. The vitamins, minerals, and enzymes found in these "no-no" foods are easily obtainable in most other fresh fruits, vegetables, and whole grains. This easy diet change may well help you enjoy arthritis-free health.

Arthritis: The Current Problem

More than 36 million Americans have some form of arthritis. Each year, 1 million people will learn they have some form of this threat. About 250,000 children have juvenile arthritis. It is estimated that arthritis costs our country over $13 billion yearly in hospitalization, physician visits, drugs, nursing home care, lost wages and homemaker services, and earnings lost because of premature death.

We cannot put a dollar figure on the emotional and physical effects of living with this chronic and serious disease. Nor can we include many other costs such as those spent on disability payments to people whose arthritis has left them unable to work for a living. The problem knows no limits.

What Is Arthritis?

The word arthritis literally means "joint inflammation." That is, *arth* means "joint" and *itis* means "inflammation." It is not a single disease, but rather a symptom that can occur in more than 100 acute and chronic conditions. Two basic forms of arthritis appear to respond to nutritional correction:

Osteoarthritis. Considered the "most common form," it involves the breakdown of cartilage and other joint tissues. It causes little or no inflammation and does not affect the whole body. Probably every person over age 60 has it to some degree, but only a few have it badly enough to notice any symptoms. These usually begin slowly. One or two joints may ache or feel mildly sore, especially with movement. There may be some constant nagging pain. Usually, symptoms are their worst after the joints have been overused or have remained still for a long period. While osteoarthritis can occur in any joint, those most commonly affected are the fingers, hips, knees, and spine.

Rheumatoid Arthritis. An inflammation of the joint membrane. If neglected, outgrowths of the inflamed tissue may invade and damage the cartilage in the synovial (joint-lining) joints. This injury may change the shape of the joints, causing them to become deformed. Early in the condition, most people feel tired, sore, achy, and stiff. The joints stiffen, then swell, and become tender, later making full motion difficult and painful. The symptoms are often worst in the morning and after long periods of sitting or lying still. The knees, hands, and feet are commonly involved. Often, the joints on both sides of the body are affected. That is, both feet, or both hips are involved. In some people (about one out of six) the condition becomes severe, causing aches, pains, and badly affected joints. For example, the fingers may become crooked and deformed; movement is painful and difficult.

Juvenile Arthritis

Not exclusively an "old person's condition," we have identified several forms of juvenile arthritis. The condition may appear any time after birth, often before the age of 7. In most cases, it first affects a child's knees. The effects can change from day to day, even from morning to afternoon.

Affected children may experience skin rash, fever, inflammation of the eyes, slowed growth, swelling of lymph nodes, fatigue, and swelling and pain in the muscles and joints. Either a few or many joints may be afflicted. Some youngsters recover completely. Others may be troubled with it during their adult lives.

With the use of corrective nutritional therapy and an improved lifestyle, a youngster can be given hope for a lifetime that will be free of arthritis.

A Doctor's Nutritional Therapy for Healing Arthritis[1]

For several decades, an arthritis medical clinic has used nutritional therapy as part of a total body healing program to treat over tens of

[1]Robert Bingham, M.D., Desert Hot Springs Medical Clinic, Calif., press release, 1984.

thousands of arthritics with much success. Founder–medical director, Robert Bingham, M.D., a certified member of the American Board of Orthopedic Surgery and Fellow of the American Academy of Orthopedic Surgery, explains that by making changes in the diet, taking prescribed amounts of vitamins and minerals, there is hope to block rheumatoid arthritis and reverse degenerative forms of this disease.

The Diet Connection in Arthritis

Dr. Bingham explains, "Nutritional science teaches us (1) how crucial the internal environment of our body cells and tissues is; (2) that the nutrition we receive in food may shape and build our entire lives; and (3) all kinds of diseases and malformations such as arthritis are rooted in poor internal environment from dietary deficiencies."

He adds: "Medicines and drugs interfere with metabolism, but nutrients make metabolism possible. They are the raw materials from which metabolic machinery is built. Life cannot exist without them.

"The intricate balance of nutrients in the body involves the interrelationships among forty or more such substances. *An extremely poor nutritional balance may result in deficiency diseases;* a poor or mediocre balance yields at best sub-optimal health and vigor.

"Nutrition has been in lethargy for too long. It needs to be taken seriously by biochemists, medical scientists, medical educators, and family physicians.

"Vast human betterment—including substantial relief from coronary heart disease, birth defects, arthritis, mental disease, alcoholism, dental disease, muscular dystrophy, multiple sclerosis, cataracts, glaucoma, cancer, and many other diseases—must await the day when nutrition comes alive and reaches out to new horizons."

The Step-by-Step Nutritional Therapy for Arthritis

At his world-famous arthritis clinic, Dr. Bingham offers a program that, he says, could also be followed to a lesser degree at home to help reverse the tide of this condition. Here is this step-by-step nutritional therapy plan that has helped tens of thousands free themselves from arthritis.

1. Avoid all refined flour products, refined sugar, or sweets.

2. Daily, increase well-absorbed calcium to 6 oyster shell tablets a day. For osteoarthritis, Dr. Bingham recommends 1,000 units daily of vitamin D from a natural source such as halibut liver oil. Take this with 25,000 units daily of vitamin A. *Note:* This combination is for the treatment phase. For prevention, the doctor suggests half this amount.
3. Increase water consumption to 8 or more glasses a day.
4. Put yourself on a high-protein diet.
5. Eat only fresh, raw, natural fruits and vegetables—use a blender or grinder to prepare as needed. Cook only if absolutely necessary.
6. Eliminate tobacco, alcohol, refined carbohydrates, and saturated fats.
7. If overweight, lose the excess poundage. But be careful to get adequate protein from skim milk dairy products, lean poultry, fish, and lean meats as well as nuts, whole grains, and seeds. A blender and a grinder are beneficial in maximizing the use of such fresh, natural foods, says the doctor.
8. Ask your medical nutritionist for specific nutritional potencies for your personal condition. Generally, the arthritic is in need of additional vitamin B-complex, vitamin C, vitamin D, and iron. Drugs taken for arthritis tend to deplete these nutrients, compounding the problem.
9. Drink fresh milk as it offers a number of important vitamins and minerals, especially calcium, that helps to ease arthritis distress. "Certified raw milk, if available, is highly recommended," says Dr. Bingham. "It is higher in enzymes, hormone growth factors, protein, available minerals and fats and natural vitamins than pasteurized milk. It is especially valuable for those with a tendency to arthritis. Buttermilk has the same protein value as whole milk and contains no more fat than skim milk. Certified raw milk has the Wulzen factor or an antistiffness benefit that is important for easing arthritis distress."
10. Keep yourself physically active so that nutrients can perform their healing therapy. Many people are deficient in bone and muscle protein, bone calcium, and good joint cartilage, with excessive fat deposits in the tissue, body organs, and the arteries. Activity helps to put nutrients to active use in correcting arthritis distress.

With the assistance of a medical nutritionist, this 10-step program, as prescribed by Dr. Bingham at his arthritis clinic, may help to reverse the tide of this insidious and often-crippling disease.

Dr. Bingham asserts that not only is arthritis preventable with nutritional therapy, but it can be curable, too.

How to "Oil" Your Joints and Ease Arthritic Pain

For many arthritics, the ingestion of fish liver oil eases arthritic pain. What began as a folk remedy is now being seen as possibly having a biochemical basis. In studies, it was found that 1 or 2 tablespoons of cod liver oil, taken with milk at bedtime, was able to help ease joint stiffness and erase much arthritic pain.

"Secret" of Cod Liver Oil as Nutritional Therapy

Cod liver and most fish oils are prime sources of essential fatty acids such as linoleic and linolenic acids. These nutrients cause the outpouring of prostaglandins; these are potent hormonelike substances that are able to help block pain receptors, especially in the joints. The oil acts as a spark plug to promote the release of the important prostaglandins that will help to soothe the spasms of joint pain. This is the "secret" of any effectiveness noted from taking fish liver oil.

Simple Nutritional Therapy: About two hours before bedtime, take 2 tablespoons of fish liver oil with milk for easier digestion. You may be able to sleep better and awaken with less of the morning stiffness that is the curse of so many arthritics.

Instead of Aspirin, Try a Nutritional Pain Killer: Phenylalanine

If you are cautious about using chemicals to mask arthritis pain, you will want to use a nutritional alternative. It is a simple amino acid: *phenylalanine.*

What Is It?

Phenylalanine is one of the essential amino acids your body cannot make but must be obtained from your diet or a supplement. It does not exactly kill pain. Instead, it protects your body's own source of pain relief—*endorphins* (Greek for "the morphine within"). These are morphinelike substances produced by your body that block pain signals moving through your nervous system.

During the natural process of digestion, there is some destruction of these endorphins. You become more vulnerable to arthritic and other pains. You need to shield and protect these pain-killing endorphins. You can do it with *phenylalanine,* which is considered a *natural aspirin.*

Eases Pain, Cools Inflammation

This amino acid works speedily to guard the life span and effectiveness of the small endorphins, or enkephalins, which will ease your pain and cool the painful inflammation of arthritis.

More Benefits from "Nutritional Aspirin"

Phenylalanine is not a drug, but it performs like chemicalized aspirin *without* side effects. It is nonaddictive, nontoxic. It acts as a moodlifter. It relieves the depression that often accompanies arthritic suffering. This "nutritional aspirin" has the unique ability to block certain antagonists in the central nervous system from degrading (breaking down) pain-killing endorphins and enkephalins and allows them to act as natural and potent analgesics. It may well be the best "nutritional aspirin" available for relief of arthritis and other painful disorders.

How Much to Take?

A general rule of thumb calls for taking 375 milligrams with your breakfast, another 375 milligrams with your noonday meal, and a third 375 milligrams with your evening meal. Your nutritional health practitioner can recommend specific dosages for your needs.

Caution: Phenylalanine should *not* be taken by pregnant or lactating women or anyone who has the genetic condition of phenyketonuria (PKU) because these people cannot metabolize the nutrient normally. This also applies to those on a phenylalanine-restricted diet. Neither should it be given to children under the age of 14, except under prescribed dosages by the consulting health practitioner.

Where to Find This Nutritional Aspirin

Here are some food sources for phenylalanine and their potencies (Chart 1-1).

Chart 1-1: PHENYLALANINE CONTENT OF EVERYDAY FOODS

	Serving Size	*Milligrams of Phenylalanine*
Whole milk,	3½ ounces	170
Dried, nonfat milk	3½ ounces	1,724
Cheddar cheese	3½ ounces	1,244
Egg	1 large	739
Beef, chuck	3½ ounces	765
Chicken, fryer	3½ ounces	811
Turkey	3½ ounces	960
Codfish, fresh	3½ ounces	612
Haddock, fresh	3½ ounces	676
Halibut, fresh	3½ ounces	690
Salmon, Pacific, fresh	3½ ounces	646
Peanuts	3½ ounces	1,557
Peanut butter	3½ ounces	1,510
Pecans	3½ ounces	564
Walnuts	3½ ounces	767
Oatmeal, rolled oats	3½ ounces	758
Rice	3½ ounces	382
Farina	3½ ounces	579
Macaroni, spaghetti	3½ ounces	669
Shredded wheat	3½ ounces	755
Beans, lima	3½ ounces	197

Your Pain-Fighting Food Plan:

You can easily plan your daily menu to include just a few (or even one) of the preceding high-phenylalanine–containing foods. This will release a good supply of this valuable amino acid that will protect your endorphins and thereby help your body to unleash them to ease pain and elevate your mood.

PAIN FREE IN SIX DAYS

John R. developed arthritis in his knees five years ago. Not too painful at first, he took aspirin occasionally. Then the arthritis spread to his shoulders, hands, and left elbow. He took more aspirin and prescribed codeine, but these drugs made him feel sick, even if they did soothe the pain. Then he was advised by a physiotherapist to try phenylalanine supplements. He took about a total of 1,000 milligrams a day, in three divided doses. He also began to include foods high in this amino acid. Almost at once, the painful swelling subsided. Within six days, his knees, shoulders, hands, and arms were free of swelling and pain. He discontinued the supplement but continued the food sources of this amino acid. He gave up aspirin and drugs, too. He was soon free of arthritis pain, thanks to the soothing benefits of phenylalanine, which he calls his "food aspirin."

The Doctor Prescribes a Nutritional Therapy Program for Arthritics[2]

A noted physician, Leo V. Roy, M.D., of Toronto, Canada, has found that when arthritics follow a total nutritional therapy program, there is much hope for relief of symptoms and eventual elimination of this condition. Dr. Roy offers this total program to his patients which can be followed at home.

Basic Therapy:

Eat as many fresh raw fruits and vegetables as possible. Chew thoroughly so that saliva is mixed with foods and better utilized. Eat slowly. Avoid large quantities.

Food Program

1. *Proteins:* Every meal should contain a protein. One-fourth of daily food intake should be protein. Best sources: fish, nuts, cheese, eggs, raw certified milk.
2. *Meats:* Use internal organs, rich in vitamins and minerals. Avoid all canned and processed foods. Poultry, lamb, steak are good.
3. *Dairy products:* Eat all cheeses, natural and fermented; yogurt and natural buttermilk.
4. *Raw vegetables:* All are recommended, especially celery, cucumbers, and carrots. Make salads using oils for dressing.
5. *Cooked vegetables:* Baked potatoes and brown rice are nutritious. Use raw bean sprouts and other sprouts. Do *not* overcook any vegetable. Steam, bake, broil, or use as little water as possible.
6. *Fruits:* All are recommended, especially apples, grapes, bananas, or local varieties.

[2]Leo V. Roy, M.D., press release, 1985.

7. *Juices:* Drink freshly-squeezed or bottled grape juice, no sugar added. No tomatoes. No citrus fruits except as flavoring. Maximum of 1 teaspoon lemon juice for salad dressing.
8. *Cereals:* Try the fresh-ground combination—wheat, rye, sesame seed, flax, and millet. Do not boil. Soak 15 to 20 minutes in hot water over a double boiler, or soak overnight and warm. Raw sunflower seeds, raisins, or shredded coconut may be added before eating.
9. *Bread:* Use sparingly and only stone-ground fresh whole wheat or rye.
10. *Soups:* Bouillon or consommé is allowed.
11. *Acid drink:* Where there is insufficient acid or where there are calcium deposits, use 1 tablespoon apple cider vinegar to 1 glass of water (with or without honey, 1 teaspoon) at least twice daily.
12. *Oils:* Consider especially sesame, safflower, and sunflower oil and all seeds and raw nuts.

Avoid all the following:

Tea	Commercial cereals	All hydrogenated (hardened) fats
Coffee	Processed foods	Roasted nuts
Alcohol	Canned meats	Stale nuts
Canned foods	White flour	Stale wheat germ
Stale foods	White sugar	Stale wheat germ oil

Avoid overcooked and reheated foods, jams, jellies, syrups, ice cream, soft drinks, and tobacco; avoid all chemicals added to your food such as sweeteners, emulsifiers, thickeners, and fluoridated water. *Read your labels carefully.*

The therapeutic benefits of this program lie in its ability to help uproot and cast out corrosive or irritating waste products that could be at the root of the arthritic disturbance. It calls for a total nutritional cleansing, which is believed to be the key to healing of arthritis upset.

The preceding program of nutritional therapy has reportedly helped countless arthritic victims find relief from their disorder. You, too, may be able to reverse or, at least, halt the ravages of arthritis with such a program. The sooner you begin, the sooner you may see (and feel) the benefits.

Arthritis may be traced to something you should eat, and other things you should not eat. With these nutritional therapies, you may well be able to learn how to live *without* your so-called "hopeless" arthritis.

HIGHLIGHTS

1. You have an alternative to drugs in finding relief and escape from arthritis in the form of nutritional therapy.
2. Is your arthritis due to an allergic reaction? Eliminate the four "no-no" nightshade foods, and you may well eliminate your arthritis.
3. Martha A. was able to erase her "hopeless" arthritis in nine days with a simple nutritional adjustment.
4. Become familiar with the different forms of arthritis and their causes to help you understand how to cope with this condition.
5. A California doctor has healed thousands of arthritic patients with a nutritional therapy program that is outlined for home use.
6. Fish liver oils may hold the key to pain relief.
7. John R. became pain free in six days with the use of a common nutritional pain killer.
8. A Canadian physician has a nutritional therapy program that helps to relieve symptoms and offers hope for elimination of arthritis. The program can easily be followed at home.

2

Lower Your Blood Pressure with "Control Foods" and Nutritional Therapy

Your doctor has confirmed that your blood pressure is too high for your health. You are given prescribed medications. These are usually "water pills" or diuretics that help to wash out sodium from your body. Other nutrients may also be unwisely eliminated, and this could cause deficiency symptoms. A problem is that drug taking may become a permanent way of life. It may often interfere with body and, perhaps more seriously, with everyday foods. It becomes a dangerous "tug of war" in the battle to help lower your blood pressure.

A Nutritional Approach

To help correct your erratic or runaway blood pressure, your goal is to get to the cause: a metabolic error in your body. With the use of corrective nutrition along with "control foods," you can help keep your pressure in healthy check.

A Doctor's Eight-Step Program for Drugless Treatment of Mild Hypertension[1]

This approach has a double benefit: it lowers the blood pressure and it helps to control other risk factors for coronary heart disease, such as high blood cholesterol levels, adult-onset diabetes, and obesity. It could also save the person with slightly elevated blood pressure from a lifetime dependence on antihypertensive drugs, which often have troublesome side effects.

[1]Norman Kaplan, M.D., press release, May 2, 1985

This is the finding of Norman Kaplan, M.D., professor of internal medicine and chief of the hypertension unit at the University of Texas Health Science Center at Dallas. "I believe a non-drug approach should be the first treatment of mild hypertension, where the diastolic blood pressure is between 90 and 100 mm. Hg."

Dr. Kaplan bases his belief on the results of research done at the University and on a review of more than 160 published studies of the effects of weight loss, diet, mineral metabolism, exercise, and relaxation techniques.

Drugs: Proceed with Caution...Know the Risks Ahead

Dr. Kaplan explains, "The steadily growing tendency to treat even mildly hypertensive patients with drugs is bringing millions of non-symptomic people into lifetime drug therapy. For some, the risks of the drugs, as we have used them, may outweigh the benefits that can be gained from lowering the blood pressure," he warns.

"It is true that anti-hypertensive drugs will control the blood pressure. And that they have been shown to lower the death rate from stroke and heart failure that sometimes result from high blood pressure.

"But anti-hypertensive drugs have only spotty effects against what is by far the most serious and common complication of hypertension—coronary artery disease. I think we should consider all risk factors, along with the level of the blood pressure, before making the decision to use drugs."

The Doctor's Program You Can Follow at Home

Dr. Kaplan offers this eight-step drugless "prescription" for treating mild hypertension that he has found can work effectively for many people:

1. *Weight loss.* For the overweight, reduction should be the primary goal. The frequency of hypertension is about twice as high in the obese as in the nonobese; furthermore, even a small weight loss will often lower the blood pressure. The dual benefits of lowering blood

pressure and losing weight should provide incentive to stay on a weight-loss program.

2. *Sodium restriction.* For all hypertensive persons, salt in the diet should be restricted to 2 grams a day (about ½ teaspoon). This can be accomplished simply by leaving out salt in cooking and avoiding heavily salted foods such as smoked meats, pickles, and most canned and processed foods. After a few months on a lower-sodium diet, the taste preference for salty foods will decrease. However, to maintain calcium intake, the consumption of low-fat, low-sodium milk and cheese products should be continued.
3. *Fiber/fat in diet.* More high-fiber foods and less saturated fat in the diet are recommended for cholesterol-lowering diets. They may also help to lower your blood pressure.
4. *Alcohol.* In moderate amounts (less than 2 ounces a day) alcohol appears to protect against coronary heart disease. In larger amounts, it may raise the blood pressure enough to make it the most prevalent cause of reversible hypertension. Studies suggest that alcohol is responsible for at least 10 percent of hypertension in men and 1 percent of hypertension in women. A reasonable position would be to allow up to, but no more than, 2 ounces a day.
5. *Exercise.* After isotonic exercise such as walking, jogging, bicycling, or swimming, blood pressure falls as much as 25 percent and remains lower for at least 30 minutes. However, blood pressure may rise alarmingly during isometric exercise such as weight lifting. Regular active exercises of the isotonic type should be encouraged.
6. *Potassium.* For mild hypertension, potassium supplements are usually unnecessary. Potassium intake tends to increase when sodium is reduced, particularly by the substitution of natural foods for canned or processed foods.
7. *Other minerals.* Magnesium and calcium supplements should be given only to those who are deficient in the minerals until there is more evidence that they produce the desired results.
8. *Relaxation therapy.* Unfortunately, only a few hypertensives will choose to try relaxation therapy, and even fewer will stick with it. Most of those who do will achieve some lowering of blood pressure. A few will show a considerable decrease. In addition, they may be less anxious and feel better.

An Effective Pressure-Lowering Program

Dr. Kaplan notes, "This drugless therapy may lower the blood pressure to a level below 140/90 for a significant percentage of the large population with mild hypertension. Yet some patients may prefer treatment with drugs because it is easier and less expensive.

"Initial visits to a medical nutritionists and, for those older than 40, an exercise stress test before beginning a strenuous exercise program could make the expense of non-drug therapy slightly higher than medication.

"While the overall expense may be higher," says Dr. Kaplan, "the potential for improvement in overall health makes the cost seem trivial. Whether hypertensive patients take drugs to lower their blood pressure or not, they still need to lose weight, exercise regularly, eat a prudent diet and learn to relax. Non-drug therapies have a place in the treatment of all hypertensive patients."

LOWERS "DANGEROUS" BLOOD PRESSURE IN ELEVEN DAYS ON DRUGLESS PROGRAM

Oscar B. was examined by his company physician and told the startling news that his blood pressure reading was a dangerously high 160/95. He was put on diuretics without delay but was sensitive to side effects such as an increase of uric acid in the bloodstream and also upset in blood sugar that could predispose him to diabetes.

Oscar B. wanted quick but safe treatment. He sought the help of a local nutrition-minded cardiologist who put him on the preceding eight-step drugless "prescription." Within four days, his pressure began to drop. By the end of the month, it had reached the safe reading of 120/80. Without drugs. Without the risk of side effects that could make the "cure" worse than the condition. It was with the use of this nutritional therapy program that helped to correct the metabolic disorder so that the body could become self-cured of this malfunction. He had been saved from this sneaky illness, thanks to nutritional therapy.

"Silent Executioner": The Misunderstood Illness

Hypertension is a condition without symptoms, a "silent executioner." It threatens the life and health of more persons than cancer. It is the nation's number two killer after heart disease. And one-half of those who have this disease are unaware of it.

The Numbers Game! Are You One of Them?

At least 40 million Americans have hypertension and over 20 million do not know it. It is aptly labeled a "silent executioner" because it does not make you feel sick. You may have it for years while it worsens until it strikes you down, often, in the prime of life!

No Relation to Tension

The name is somewhat of a misnomer. Hypertension is not nervous tension or anxiety. A very calm person may have the condition. The word is simply a medical term for high blood pressure.

What Is High Blood Pressure?

Blood pressure is the force of blood against the walls of the arteries and veins created by the heart as it pumps blood to every part of your body. When arterioles (small arteries that regulate blood pressure) contract, blood cannot easily pass through them. When this happens, your heart must pump harder to push the blood through. This increased push increases the blood pressure in your arteries. If the blood pressure increases above normal and remains elevated, the result is high blood pressure (hypertension).

How High Is Too High? As stated earlier, the danger is that you may have high blood pressure for years and never know it, because usually there are no symptoms. But pressure can be measured with a quick, painless test. The doctor uses a sphygmomanometer, a rubber cuff that is placed around your arm and then inflated with air. The cuff squeezes against and compresses a large artery in your arm, momentarily stopping the flow of blood.

As the air is released in the cuff and the blood begins to flow, the doctor listens with a stethoscope to the sound of the blood pushing through the artery. While listening and watching a gauge, the doctor records two measurements: (1) the pressure of blood flows when the heartbeats (systolic pressure) and (2) the pressure of the flow of blood between heartbeats (diastolic pressure).

Both numbers are then recorded as the blood pressure measurements, 120/80, for example, being considered a good reading: the first number listed is the systolic pressure (heart beating); the second number is the diastolic pressure (between beats). *Danger:* The more difficult it is for the blood to flow, the higher the numbers. You have hypertension if either number is consistently too high. *Example:* If the systolic pressure is over 160, it is considered elevated. If the diastolic pressure is above 90, you may be diagnosed as having high blood pressure.

Checklist of Danger Zones

Because both numbers go up and down together, most doctors and patients find it simpler to talk about just the diastolic reading. Here is a checklist of numbers designated as either "too high" ranging to "normal."

115 or above: you have severe hypertension, highly dangerous.

105–114: moderate hypertension.

95–104: mild hypertension.

90–94: borderline hypertension afflicting three out of every four people with high blood pressure.

80–89: a safe and normal zone, but new warning flags about a diastolic in the 80s could be a signal to start doing something now to prevent any increases.

Why Does It Happen?

It happens when there is too much pressure in your circulatory system. Your body has about 60,000 miles of blood vessels. Each time your heart beats (about 70 to 90 times each minute), blood is pushed through arteries, capillaries, and veins. The pressure of your heart's pumping action creates force on the walls of these vessels. Normal pressure pushes blood through the blood vessels. *Problem:* When arterial muscles tighten throughout the body and stay that way, or when "corrosion" such as cholesterol deposits accumulates on the inside walls, the result is high blood pressure.

What's the Blame?

It is found to be one's life-style. Possible causes include overweight. The more you weigh, the more cells your circulatory system must feed. This means it must work harder, under greater pressure, causing a rising in the numbers game.

Another cause is excess fat in the diet that leaves a coating of cholesterol on the blood vessel walls, which narrows the pathways through which the blood travels. As the coating builds up, it raises blood pressure and the risk of heart trouble.

Is Stress to Blame?

While seemingly calm people can have high readings, it is noted that unrelieved stress can be a culprit in elevated pressure. In reaction to daily stress, your mind sends your body into high gear. The higher your pressure at the onset, the higher the gear you go into and the greater the strain on your system. *Danger:* Untreated, this can cause a weakening of your arteries and lead to "brain overload" or stroke. Your heart or kidneys may rebel against working under this excessive pressure and fail! So we see that unrelieved or consistent stress could be a life-threatening risk.

The Risks You Face

When blood pressure is too great, blood vessels burst. If it happens in the heart, you may have a heart attack. If it's in the brain, you have a stroke. Blood on the brain has the same effect of turning a water hose on a pile of sand—the surface is rearranged and damaged. Continued pressure may also cause progressive damage to the kidneys. As arteries thicken and narrow, the amount of fluid the kidney can filter out is reduced. Some of the waste the kidney ordinarily would filter out into the urine will accumulate, eventually causing kidney failure.

We see that hypertension is the root cause of many premature deaths. But we are not without hope. The severity and fatality rate from all these hypertension-related afflictions may be lessened and, it is hoped, reversed and eliminated, with correction of molecular-biological errors of daily living. You *can* turn back the tide of mounting pressure and become a winner in the numbers game. Here is a set of nutritional therapies that could very well be a lifesaver in terms of bringing your pressure readings under control and into the safe zone.

The Magic Mineral That Controls Blood Pressure

The evidence is small but dramatic—and growing. There is a link between blood pressure and the amount of calcium in your system. In various studies, it was found that if the diet contains adequate or abundant amounts of calcium, pressure readings are in the safe zone, even if the people are genetically disposed to the condition or are not salt watching. This "magic mineral" may well be a "natural medicine" to control your pressure readings.

How Calcium Keeps Pressure in Check

Calcium helps to modulate pressure by stabilizing the arterial blood flow. It exerts a bimodal benefit by balancing the rise in parathyroid hormone to regulate vascular smooth muscle tone and consequent blood pressure. Calcium has interactive aspects of metabolism with other nutrients. These responses tend to regulate blood pressure.

Salt-Washing Benefit

Calcium, together with potassium and other minerals, helps your body to slough off excess sodium or salt and protects you against an overload that could be a "nervous" trigger finger threatening to explode at any moment. Calcium also helps to wash salt out of your system. Calcium may be considered a "natural diuretic."

Calcium Balance = Pressure Balance

Calcium balance is the net of processes through which calcium enters and leaves your body. If you take in and absorb more calcium than you lose (through wastes), you are in *positive* calcium balance. If, on the other hand, you lose more than you take in, you are in *negative* calcium balance. *Danger:* if you remain in negative calcium balance for very long, your metabolism may accumulate sodium and deprive your circulatory system of the ability to maintain a safe and healthy arterial blood flow.

Nutritional Therapy:

Aim for a daily intake of adequate calcium from foods and/or supplements of 1,000 to 1,400 milligrams a day. (The recommended daily allowance or RDA of calcium for adults is 800. It is generally agreed that for safety's sake, boost intake to the 1,000–1,400 daily range.) Chart 2-1 presents some food sources of calcium.

You will do well, pressurewise, to plan your daily menu to include a variety of these foods to give you the needed calcium that will help to protect against an increase in life-threatening numbers.

Chart 2-1: FOOD SOURCES OF CALCIUM

Food	*Serving Size*	*Milligrams of Calcium*
Skim milk	8 ounces	302
Low-fat (2%) milk	8 ounces	297
Whole milk	8 ounces	219
Buttermilk	8 ounces	285
Low-fat yogurt	1 cup	415
Low-fat yogurt with fruit	1 cup	314
Frozen yogurt	1 cup	200
Cottage cheese, creamed	1/2 cup	116
Swiss cheese	1 ounce	272
Parmesan, grated	1 ounce	390
Cheddar	1 ounce	204
Mozzarella	1 ounce	183
American cheese	1 ounce	174
Sardines with bones	3 ounces	372
Salmon with bones	3 ounces	285
Bean curd	4 ounces	154
Collards	1 cup	357
Turnip greens	1 cup	267
Kale	1 cup	206
Mustard greens	1 cup	193
Dandelion greens	1 cup	147
Broccoli	1 cup	136

CALCIUM THERAPY LIGHTENS PRESSURE, LENGTHENS LIFE SPAN

When told that her pressure was not only "moderately high" but "continuously climbing," Janet L. agreed to take chemical diuretics to wash out salt accumulation. This offered partial help but gave her side effects such as dizziness, irregularity, and nervous tremors. She sought the help of an endocrinologist who said that she could be able to lighten her pressure with the use of calcium. Janet L. gradually reduced diuretic use as she started to increase her calcium consumption. By aiming for 1,000 milligrams a day, she created the metabolic reaction that helped control her pressure. Within 16 days, she not only brought her pressure into the "safe zone" but was told her electrocardiogram showed she had the reading of a "young heart" at her age of 56 years! It was calcium that acted as a nutritional therapy to give her the blood pressure of a youth.

The Salt-Free Way To A Lower Blood Pressure

Keep salt consumption under control, and you may well help develop immunity to high blood pressure.

The Salt Connection

There is a saying, "Water goes where the salt is." Because sodium clings to water, when an excessive amount enters the cellular fluid, it carries extra liquid with it. This extra liquid increases the volume of the plasma. To distribute the expanded blood, the heart must create additional pressure. It is forced to pump harder. This can elevate your pressure.

Taking a diuretic that pulls sodium and fluids from the tissues is one means of therapy. Anyone who has been on diuretics will complain of various side effects, of having sleep frequently disturbed by an emergency call from the bladder. This causes stress and a risk of pressure rise. To protect against this vicious cycle, it makes better sense to cut down or eliminate salt. This is a simple but effective nutritional therapy for high blood pressure.

How to Get Off the Salt Tightrope and Lower Your Pressure

You'll discover new tastes formerly masked by salt. Your taste buds will sense the delicate variations of flavor in infinite and exciting varieties that have been lying undetected in your food, smothered by salt that formerly dominated the delicate character of food.

How Much Is Too Much?

The RDA for sodium is 1,100 to 3,300 milligrams (1/2 to 1-1/2 teaspoons) for adults. One teaspoon of table salt (5 grams) contains 2,200 milligrams of sodium. Therefore, your goal is to consume no more than about 1-1/2 teaspoons each day. Better yet, you will be doing your pressure a nutritionally therapeutic favor by adding *no* salt to your foods, before, during, or after cooking!

How to Shake the Salt Habit

- Add fresh grated lemon peel and herbs to plain yogurt as a dip for crisp raw vegetables.
- Blend lemon and/or orange juice with Neufchatel cream cheese and chopped ginger or unsalted nuts for an appetizer.
- Add citrus fruit juice and float thin lemon slices in vegetable-based soups and in beef, chicken, or tomato bouillon (no salt added).
- Add grated citrus peel and chopped parsley or chives to yogurt for garnish on broths or soups.
- Peel and slice or section fresh oranges or grapefruit for a fresh lettuce–onion salad.
- For oil and vinegar dressings, substitute 1/2 lemon juice and 1/2 herb-flavored vinegar for regular vinegar.
- Add thinly sliced unpeeled lemon to marinated cucumber salad.
- Blend orange-lemon juice with honey for fruit-cabbage combination.
- Blend lemon juice, dry mustard, and freshly ground black pepper. Serve as a spicy hot sauce for roasts, steaks, or chops.
- For marinades, blend lemon juice with herbs and honey.
- Add citrus juice to a barbecue sauce made of salt-free tomato paste, chili powder, honey, garlic, and onion.
- For baking or broiling, brush with a blend of oil, lemon juice, and poultry seasoning (salt-free); then dust with paprika.
- For baking whole fish, sprinkle inside and out with fresh lemon juice; then baste with lemon juice, chopped parsley, and unsalted butter or margarine.
- Dust fish pieces with flour mixed with grated lemon peel and herb mixture of sesame seed, oregano, basil, and thyme.
- For broiling fish, brush with melted salt-free butter or margarine, lemon juice, dill weed, or tarragon.

- Eating out? For a main dish, choose broiled, grilled, or roasted meat, fish, or poultry. Try to avoid those prepared or served with a sauce or gravy. Ask for a wedge or two of lemon for seasoning meat. Order plain steamed brown rice or a baked potato. Ask for salt-free butter or margarine, which many restaurants have on hand.
- When eating vegetables away from home, leave the juice in the bottom of the dish and eat only the solid pieces of vegetable to keep the salt to a minimum. *Tip:* A squeeze of juice from a lemon wedge also brings out flavor in most vegetables, including potato.
- At lunch time, roasted, broiled, or grilled meat, chicken, or turkey sandwiches will have minimum amounts of salt. *Avoid* pickles, olives, potato chips, and ketchup or other salty sauces.
- If you want a salad, ask for the chef's salad to be made with turkey or chicken meat only (omit highly-salted ham or cheese) and mix your own oil and vinegar or lemon juice dressing. If ordering the Diet Plate, ask for some fruit in place of the cottage cheese frequently provided. Avoid salted crackers or wafers.
- In someone's home, avoid the salted snack foods. If possible, tell the hostess you prefer not to have cured or salted meats or salted vegetables, but can have baked or broiled foods.
- Always, always read labels of packaged or prepared products. Many list sodium content. In many outlets, low-salt or salt-free products are available. If you must use such products, begin by reading labels and selecting salt-free items.

Throw Away the Salt—But Save the Shaker

Visit your local health store, herb and spice shop, or the spice rack at your market. Stock up on a variety of flavorful herbs and spices. Again, read labels, and avoid any product that contains salt. Get the smallest containers. Keep them in a cool, dry place. Use your shaker for garlic or onion powder (not salt!) which can be just as tasty as salt.

Salt-DANGER

Think of salt *not* as a flavoring but as sodium, a dangerous and potential detriment to your blood pressure and general health.

Chart 2-2 lists the average sodium content in a number of everyday foods. Plan ahead. Your blood pressure will be all the more grateful for it.

Chart 2-2: SODIUM CONTENT OF EVERYDAY FOODS

	Serving Size	Milligrams of Sodium
Beverages and Fruit Juices		
Cola, regular	1 cup	16
low calorie	1 cup	21
Coffee or tea	1 cup	1–2
Apple juice	1 cup	5
Orange juice, frozen	1 cup	5
Tomato juice	1 cup	878
Dairy Products		
American pasteurized processed cheese	1 ounce	406
Cheddar cheese	1 ounce	176
Cottage cheese, reg. and lowfat	1/2 cup	457
Swiss cheese	1 ounce	74
Milk, reg. and lowfat	1 cup	122
Pudding, instant chocolate	1/2	445
Yogurt, fruit flavored	1 cup	133
Eggs, Fish, Meat, Poultry, and Prepared Main Dishes		
Whole eggs	1 large	59
Black sea bass, raw	3 ounces	57
Mackerel, raw	3 ounces	40
Lake trout, raw	3 ounces	67
Tuna, light meat		
chunk canned in oil	3 ounces	303
white meat, low sodium	3 ounces	34
Shrimp, raw	3 ounces	137
canned	3 ounces	1,955
Beef, cooked, lean	3 ounces	55
Lamb, cooked, lean	3 ounces	58
Pork, cooked lean	3 ounces	59
bacon, cooked	2 slices	274
ham	3 ounces	1,114
Chicken, roasted		
drumstick with skin	1 drumstick	47
breast with skin	1/2 breast	69
Bologna, beef and pork	1 slice	224
Frankfurter	1 frankfurter	639
Chili con carne with beans canned	1 cup	1,194
Beef frozen dinner	1 dinner	998
Pizza with cheese	1/7 of 10″ pie	367

Chart 2-2: *(continued)*

	Serving Size	Milligrams of Sodium
Fast Foods		
Cheeseburger	1	709
Shake	1	266
Fruit		
Apple	1 medium	2
Banana	1 medium	2
Orange	1 medium	1
Cantaloupe	1/2 melon	24
Peach	1 medium	1
Pineapple	1 cup	1
Watermelon, diced	1 cup	2
Grain Products, Breads, and Cereals		
White bread	1 slice	114
Whole wheat bread	1 slice	132
Cream of wheat cereal, reg.	1/4 cup	1
Mix'n eat	3/4 cup	350
Oatmeal, reg. or quick	3/4 cup	1
instant with maple and brown sugar	3/4 cup	277
Raisin Bran	1/2 cup	209
Corn Flakes	1 cup	256
Puffed Wheat	2 cups	2
Rice, regular white	1/2 cup	3
quick	1/2 cup	7
Rice, brown	1/2 cup	5
Stuffing mix	1 cup	1,131
Legumes and Nuts		
Baked beans, canned	1 cup	928
Dry, cooked navy beans	1 cup	3
Peanuts, dry roasted,		
salted	1 cup	986
unsalted	1 cup	8
Peanut butter, smooth or crunchy	1 Tbsp	81
Pecans	1 cup	1
Walnuts	1 cup	3
Soups		
Beef broth, cubed	1 cup	1,152
Chicken noodle condensed with water	1 cup	1,107
Mushroom, condensed with water	1 cup	1,031
Tomato condensed		
with water	1 cup	872
dehydrated with water	1 cup	943

Chart 2-2: *(continued)*

	Serving Size	Milligrams of Sodium
Vegetable condensed with water	1 cup	823
dehydrated with water	1 cup	1,000
Vegetables		
Beans, snap, cooked	1 cup	5
frozen	3 ounces	3
canned	1 cup	326
Broccoli, raw	1 stalk	23
frozen plain	3.3 ounces	35
Carrots	1 carrot	34
Corn cooked	1 ear	1
Frozen	1 cup	7
canned, cream style	1 cup	671
Lettuce	1 cup	4
Potatoes, baked or boiled	1 medium	5
Spinach cooked	1 cup	94
Squash, summer, cooked	1 cup	5
winter, frozen	1 cup	4
Tomato, raw	1 tomato	14
stewed	1 cup	584
Peas, frozen	3 ounces	80
Condiments, Fats, and Oils		
Baking powder	1 tsp	339
Baking soda	1 tsp	821
Catsup	1 Tbsp	156
Garlic powder	1 tsp	1
Garlic salt	1 tsp	1,850
Meat tenderizer	1 tsp	1,750
Monosodium glutamate (MSG)	1 tsp	492
Olives, green	4 olives	323
Pickles, dill	1 pickle	928
sweet	1 pickle	128
Barbecue sauce	1 Tbsp	130
Soy sauce	1 Tbsp	1,029
Worcestershire sauce	1 Tbsp	206
Vinegar	1/2 cup	1
Butter, regular	1 Tbsp	116
unsalted	1 Tbsp	2
Margarine, regular	1 Tbsp	140
unsalted	1 Tbsp	1
Oil, vegetable	1 Tbsp	0
Salad dressings		
blue cheese	1 Tbsp	153
French, bottled	1 Tbsp	214
Italian, bottled	1 Tbsp	116
Mayonnaise	1 Tbsp	78

Source: USDA Home & Garden Bulletin #233.

How Potassium Tames Your Runaway Blood Pressure

While you need to restrict sodium to soothe your blood pressure, these same "no-no" foods have potassium. This mineral is needed to maintain a normal flow of nerve signals and muscular contractions. Potassium plays an important role in energy release from carbohydrates, proteins, and fats. *Caution:* If you are taking diuretics or water pills, not only is sodium washed out but potassium is also eliminated. A deficiency could cause erratic heartbeats as well as disturbed blood pressure.

Nutritional Therapy

Plan for about 3,500 milligrams of potassium daily to help tame your runaway blood pressure. This magic mineral will enable your heart to pump blood with adequate force. Potassium will also strengthen the cellular walls and membranes to permit easier transportation of fluid and guard against water overload or edema. Keep your blood pressure in check with adequate daily intake of potassium-containing foods! This mineral may well be an all-natural "medicine" to protect against hypertension.

STABILIZES "THREATENING" PRESSURE IN SIX DAYS WITH POTASSIUM FOODS

When Martin J. was told he had a dangerously high pressure reading of 170/105, he followed a nutritional program as outlined by his doctor of osteopathy. But he still showed a too high reading. Further tests showed he had a serious potassium deficiency. To meet the "threat" of the "exploding" high pressure, he was told to boost intake of high-potassium foods. This simple nutritional therapy brought his pressure down to 130/90 within three days. By the end of the sixth day, his osteopathic physician happily told him the "wild" pressure was controlled and now he was at a more healthful 125/85. This *pressure-lowering mineral* snatched him from certain "jaws of death" with spiralling hypertension.

Had Your Potassium Today?

Chart 2-3 lists a variety of tasty everyday foods that are prime sources of this pressure-lowering mineral. Plan them as part of your daily menu, and you may well be master of your blood pressure, not the other way around.

Chart 2-3: POTASSIUM CONTENT OF EVERYDAY FOODS

Most of the items listed are good sources of potassium. A few such as fats, oils, processed cheese, eggs, and pizza are listed to show types of foods that tend to be low in potassium. The breads and rice are listed to show the difference between whole grain products. Note that a few items contain added salt and therefore are not recommended for sodium-restricted diets.

	Serving Size	Milligrams of Potassium
Beverages and Fruit Juices		
Grapefruit juice, frozen	1 cup	420
Orange juice, frozen	1 cup	503
Tangerine juice, frozen	1 cup	432
Tomato juice, low sodium	1 cup	549
Prune juice	1 cup	602
Dairy Products		
American pasteurized processed cheese*	1 ounce	23
Milk, whole	1 cup	351
skim	1 cup	355
Eggs, Fish, Meat, and Poultry		
Egg, whole	1 large	65
Tuna, chunk style, in water	3 ounces	237
Chicken, lt. meat without skin	3 ounces	369
Ground beef, lean, cooked	3 ounces	221
Pork loin, lean, cooked	3 ounces	280
Sirloin steak, lean, cooked	3 ounces	307
Fast Foods		
Pizza, frozen, cheese*	1/7 of 10″ pie	65
Fruits		
Apricots, fresh, dried	3	301
	10 medium halves	343
Avocado	1/2	680
Banana	1 medium	440
Cantaloupe	1/2 melon	682
Dates, with pits	10	518

Chart 2-3: *(continued)*

	Serving Size	Milligrams of Potassium
Prunes	10 medium	448
Raisins, dark, not packed	2 Tbsp	138
Watermelon, diced	1 cup	160
Grain Products		
Bread, white*	1 slice	29
whole wheat*	1 slice	68
Oatmeal, cooked	1 cup	146
Rice, brown, cooked	1/2 cup	69
Rice, white, cooked	1/2 cup	29
Spaghetti, cooked	1 cup	103
Wheat germ	1 Tbsp	57
Legumes and Vegetables		
Broccoli, cooked	1/2 cup	207
Brussels sprouts, cooked	1/2 cup	212
Cauliflower, cooked	1/2 cup	129
Lentils, cooked	1/2 cup	249
Mushrooms, raw	1/2 cup	145
Peanuts, roasted with skins jumbo in shell	10	127
Potato boiled in skin	1 medium	556
Spinach, cooked	1/2 cup	292
Sweet potato, baked	1 large	342
Winter squash, baked	1/2 cup	473
Fats, Oils, and Sweets		
Butter*	1 Tbsp	3
Margarine*	1 Tbsp	3
Molasses, light	1 Tbsp	183
Oil	1 Tbsp	0

*These products contain significant amounts of added salt—see sodium listing.

Source: USDA Handbook #456.

How Onions and Garlic Create Freedom from High Blood Pressure

Two tangy vegetables have long been used as folk remedies to help keep blood pressure in check. With the new knowledge of medical science as part of nutritional therapy, there is a sound basis for using these foods to protect against high blood pressure.

The Nutritional Therapy of Onions

A chemical analysis of onions will confirm the presence of prostaglandin A1, a hormonelike substance that definitely does lower blood pressure. This odoriferous root vegetable has oils that inhibit tumor growth in the laboratory. Onions also help to slow down platelet aggregation or clumping, which can lead to deadly blood clots or aneurysms traced to very high pressure.

The Nutritional Therapy of Garlic

This tangy vegetable is a concentrated source of allicin, a soothing ingredient. It is also rich in biologically active selenium, a mineral that prevents platelet adhesion and clot formation and thereby normalizes your blood pressure. Garlic has a dilating effect on the blood vessels, thereby causing a decided drop in the pressure. The aforementioned allicin is an active sulfur-containing compound that is changed into diallyldisulphide in the system to reduce the lipid (fat) levels in the serum (bloodstream) and liver and cause a biological chain reaction to bring down pressure.

Had Your Garlic and Onions Today?

Make it a daily program to include these two pressure-reducing vegetables in your nutritional plan. Since you will also be omitting salt, you will easily be able to substitute garlic and/or onions as a spicy substitute—and a pressure-saving combination, also!

Take charge of your blood pressure. Correct the nutritional errors with the use of these healthful foods and programs. You can make yourself immune to this "silent executioner" and avoid becoming one of the fatalities. Stabilize and keep stabilized your blood pressure readings with nutritional therapies.

IN REVIEW

1. A simple eight-step doctor-prescribed program, easily followed at home, can help to lower your blood pressure to a safe level, without any drugs or medications.
2. Oscar B. used this drugless "prescription" and normalized his "dangerous" pressure in 11 days.
3. Recognize the threat to your health that is caused by hypertension, the misunderstood illness that has no symptoms. No warning signs!
4. Go through the checklist of risk factors and make remedial adjustments.
5. Calcium is a "magic mineral" that helps to keep your pressure in check.
6. Using calcium foods, Janet L. lowered her pressure and lengthened her life span within 16 days.
7. Salt is a "no-no" on your pressure-lowering program. Follow the easy steps to getting off the salt tightrope and regulating pressure.
8. Potassium helps to tame your runaway blood pressure.
9. Martin J. stabilized "threatening" pressure in 6 days with tasty and lifesaving potassium foods.
10. Onions and garlic contain scientifically identified nutrients that expand blood vessels and control your pressure.

3

How to Feed Yourself a Forever Young Skin

Your skin is a reflection of your nutritional life-style. If you center your diet around fresh, wholesome foods, your skin is likely to radiate a youthful glow from within. If you upstage healthful foods with processed, chemicalized munchies, your skin loses its fresh appearance and looks as artificial and lifeless as the synthetics it is being fed. A forever young skin that is reasonably free of wrinkles, age spots, and sags is an inside job. By putting the proper foods and nutrients into your metabolism, you are able to nourish your skin so it glows healthfully. At any age!

Problem: Aging Wrinkles.
Solution: Nutritional Therapy

When skin becomes dry and loose, it shows creases that deepen into aging wrinkles. A lack or deficiency of oil production will dehydrate cells, and tissues beneath the surface of your body envelope to give your skin a parched appearance in the form of aging lines and wrinkles. To make up for deficiencies of important moisturizing sources, you need to use nutritional therapy from common everyday foods. You can then plump up and nourish your thirsty skin cells to give your face and body a youthful firmness, free of wrinkles.

Foods That Keep Your Skin in the Prime of Life

A number of everyday foods are brimming with nutrients that are able to perform a form of natural "face lifting" from within. Enjoy them daily and enjoy a skin that is kept in the prime of youthful life.

Vitamin A Will Erase Wrinkles

This nutrient helps protect against the clogging of pores that leads to blemishes and wrinkles. Vitamin A makes the cells lining the pores less sticky. It makes the surface layer of the skin less "tough" or keratinizing and speeds up the life cycle of the cells, creating a continual sloughing effect to keep pores open.

Skin Rejuvenating Therapy. Vitamin A increases blood flow to the skin and stimulates skin cells (called fibroblasts) to make new connective tissue called collagen. This is the key to wrinkle prevention. Collagen is found in the supporting tissue just under the thin surface of the skin. A wrinkle is actually a crease in the collagen and skin. With vitamin A, the tiny creases and deep wrinkles may be erased, and your skin will take on a rejuvenating look.

Antiwrinkle Foods: Enjoy sweet potatoes, milk, carrots, winter squash, cantaloupes, liver, cheese, and eggs. These are prime sources of this valuable wrinkle-erasing vitamin A.

Nutritional Therapy: In a blender, combine 8 ounces milk, 4 ounces diced carrots, 2 teaspoons zucchini squash, 4 ounces cantaloupe. Whiz for 1 minute. Drink slowly to enjoy good taste. *Benefits:* the vitamin A will soon initiate the manufacture of collagen to plump up and firm your skin, to help protect against wrinkles.

Vitamin C for a Youthful Complexion

This nutrient is valuable for stimulating the growth of collagen, the cementlike substance that binds cells together to give you a firm skin. It also helps to strengthen elastin, the fiberlike substance synthesized by the body. It decreases and loses tone or elasticity as you age or when exposed to various stresses. It is vitamin C that helps to nourish the elastin and promote its continuous manufacture to help give you a youthful complexion even in later years.

Food Sources: Enjoy green peppers, kale, broccoli, oranges, grapefruits, strawberries, lemons, and limes.

Nutritional Therapy: Daily, have a fresh fruit salad with the important vitamin C foods. Also include the vegetables throughout the week. *Tip:* Break several vitamin C tablets (from health store) and sprinkle over your salad.

Vitamin E: Antiaging Therapy

The power of this vitamin is in its role as an antioxidant. It neutralizes harmful age-causing particles called free radicals and helps to wash them out of the system. Vitamin E has a biochemical ability to strengthen the tiny blood vessels in the lower layers of the skin. It constricts these capillaries, reduces their permeability, so less fluid leaks into surrounding tissues, and less aging occurs. This action also reduces surface skin temperatures by several degrees to create a slight, cooling effect. By helping to reduce the soft tissue damage by scavenging the free radicals, this vitamin helps to keep your skin (and body) younger and healthier.

Food Sources: Consider wheat germ oil, soybean oil, corn oil, safflower oil, and whole grain products such as whole wheat, bulgur, buckwheat, barley, oats, and wheat germ.

Nutritional Therapy: Switch to whole grain products and nonprocessed oils. *Tip:* Over a raw vegetable salad, sprinkle wheat germ and 2 tablespoons of oil. You will be giving your skin cells and capillaries a supercharging of vitamin E to cleanse away the age-causing free radicals and give you a youthful glow.

Zinc Zaps Age Signs

This lesser known mineral packs a powerhouse of rejuvenation for the skin by acting as a catalyst (helper) in many biological reactions. It boosts protein metabolism and makes the skin cells less likely to stick together, so there is a greater exchange of nutrients. It, too, performs as an antioxidant to devour and cast out the harmful age-causing free radicals. Zinc will help knock out and defuse aging signs from within your skin. It rebuilds collagen-elastin fibers to help give you that firm look of youth.

Food Sources: Consider wheat germ, wheat bran, cowpeas, skim milk, cheddar cheese, and nuts.

Nutritional Therapy: Blenderize 8 ounces of skim milk with 1 tablespoon wheat germ and 1 tablespoon wheat bran. Drink one glass each day to help put age-zapping zinc into your metabolism. *Tip:* Enjoy cooked cowpeas (blackeye) at least once a week with your regular salad or vegetable dish. Also have some nuts each day. A cheddar cheese sandwich several times a week is still another tasty way to give your metabolism the important zinc (and other vitamins and minerals) needed to rejuvenate your skin.

SIMPLE FOODS CREATE "NATURAL FACELIFT" IN NINE DAYS

When Grace O. heard herself being cruelly called "prune face" behind her back by snickering coworkers, she decided to do something about her deep furrows and wrinkles. She had tried everything, but the wrinkles just stared back at her in the mirror. She discussed plastic surgery with her dermatologist who suggested first trying nutritional therapy. She needed to correct the cause of her skin aging, namely, deficiencies of important cell-feeding nutrients.

Grace O. gave up processed foods and switched to wholesome, freshly prepared items. She boosted intake of the four wrinkle-erasing nutrients: vitamin A, vitamin C, vitamin E, and zinc. Within four days, her skin showed a more youthful color. At the end of two weeks, the crease lines and furrows became invisible. By the fourth week, this 56-year-old woman looked 20 years younger! Her coworkers wondered about her "secret," but she would keep it to herself. She had used nutrition to give herself a "natural facelift."

How to Drink Your Way to a Refreshingly Youthful Skin

Dry skin is a major cause of premature and unnecessary aging of the skin. You rarely find it on any chart of daily nutritional requirement, yet water is your body's most vital nutrient. Every cell in your body needs water to perform. Water helps to detoxify your body and skin of pollutants while providing essential moisture.

After the age of 35, skin becomes drier as the oil glands slow up activity. There is less oil-holding water in your cells. You need to protect yourself against this deficiency by drinking at least six to eight glasses of water each day.

Nutritional Therapy:

Increase intake of fresh fruits and vegetables (they range from 80 to 95 percent water), their juices, and herbal teas. In hot weather, drink an additional amount of water. You will be quenching the thirst of your cells, keeping them from dehydrating and giving you aged skin.

"No-No" Beverages

Be cautious about caffeine and alcohol. They are diuretics and cause you to lose water. Beverages high in sodium such as diet soft drinks or club soda (unless labeled caffeine and salt-free) can also raise your need for water because your body must maintain a constant balance of salt and water. *Best suggestion:* Ordinary water may well be your best moisturizing beverage.

HOW WATER THERAPY CORRECTED "GRANNY" SKIN

As a computer operator, Edna McG. was always kept busy. She may have neglected water intake, as her company physician suggested when she complained that while she was hardly in her fifties, her face and hands had "granny" skin. That is, wrinkled folds. She was advised to consume at least six glasses of water daily. "Make regular visits to the office water cooler" was the prescription! Edna McG. began this water program, stepped up with fresh fruits and vegetables. Within one month, the skin started to smooth out. Her face, throat, and hands, became youthful again. She could now pass for the thirties as a "young again" cover girl...thanks to water therapy!

How to Use Foods as Age-Reversing Skin Cosmetics

To give yourself the natural look, use wholesome foods as cosmetics and skin lotions. Here is a collection of nutritional therapies that work on the *outside* of your body to help reverse the aging process and give you the look and feel of youth.

Skin Toner

Clean your face well and rub with egg white. It will tighten on your skin and require plenty of rinsing, but it leaves your complexion rosy, glowing, immaculate, youthful.

Pore Cleanser

If you use powder or make-up base, be sure to remove it well before bedtime. Stale make-up clogs your pores and causes wrinkling and blemishes. Just use baby oil for removing makeup. It helps to moisturize your cells at the same time.

Enlarged Pores

Make a paste of oatmeal or cornmeal by mixing with a little water. Spread on your face and let remain for at least 15 minutes. Rinse with warm water and then cool water.

Oily Skin

Blend avocado to a paste and apply to your oily skin. Let remain 30 minutes and then splash off.

Wrinkled Eyelids

If too much work or television has your eyes feeling tired and your lids showing wrinkles, soak gauze in freshly squeezed orange juice and apply to your lids. Keep the gauze wet with juice and let remain on your lids about half an hour.

Crease-Age Lines . . . Anywhere

Cucumber turns up over and over as a nutritional therapy for skin. It is used as an ingredient in some expensive modern creams. Fashion models have this face-saving secret: rinse your face with cool water in which you have mashed some cut-up cucumber. It's refreshing and nutritious to the skin.

Dry Skin

Rub your face lightly with olive oil.

Wrinkles

The juice of a honeydew melon applied to wrinkles has been known to soften, moisturize, and smooth out the folds. Or mix mashed melon with petroleum jelly and spread on your face to fortify natural moisture.

Rough Hands

Wet oatmeal to paste consistency, rub over wrinkled parts of your hands (top or bottom), and let remain 20 minutes. Wash off.

Rough Elbows

Rest each elbow in half a grapefruit for a half hour.

Body Soak

Oil baths have been used by famous beauties for centuries—the ancient Greeks and Romans especially loved scented oils. Just pour 2 ounces of any oil in your bath water and luxuriate for a half hour. *Careful:* Avoid water that is too hot or too cold. Temperature extremes may shock your system and cause dryness too. Tepid water is best.

Fruit Facial

Rub a half lemon on your face and anywhere that you need firming up. It leaves your skin looking and feeling tingly clean and helps to remove excess oil.

Pep-Up Your Complexion

Lightly beat an egg white. Mix in 1 tablespoon of mayonnaise and 1 tablespoon of lemon juice. Spread over your face and throat and allow to dry. Rinse with warm water.

Wrinkle Eraser

Mix 1 egg white and ½ cup lemon juice with sufficient dry oatmeal to make a paste. Apply to face and neck and allow to dry. Rinse with warm water.

Dishpan Hands

Rub your hands with lemon juice after dishwashing to help restore the natural acid mantle of the skin which is removed in dishwater. (Without this natural acid condition, certain types of bacteria can grow and causes aging or dishpan hands.)

Dry, Scaly Skin

Lemon oils from the peel are perfect for helping to restore your skin to a silky soft feeling.

Face Scrub

Peel and mash a ripe avocado (one-half should be enough). Mix it with a half cup of yellow or white fine-grind cornmeal. Wash your face first, then apply the avocado-cornmeal paste onto the trouble spots. Gently rub in the mixture for a few minutes. Remove with a damp washcloth and splash off with witch hazel.

Night Cream

Work a piece of avocado (about the size of a strawberry) in the palm of your hand until it has a buttery consistency. Then take an equal amount of any night cream and mix the two together, blending well. Apply this vitamin-rich cream to your face and throat, massaging with your fingers. Let it remain overnight. Next morning, your skin will glow with vitality and freshness.

Watermelon Lotion

Cut a slice of chilled, ripe watermelon, force it through a sieve and catch the juice in a bowl. Strain and put the liquid in a jar. Pat on your face and neck. Let remain until dry, about 5 minutes; then splash off with cool water.

These nutritionally therapeutic creams and lotions will help reverse the aging tide and give your skin a second chance to recover and retain its second youth!

"Forever Young Skin Food Tonic"

Troubled with dark circles under your eyes? Worried about deepening lines and creases on your face, throat, and elsewhere? Skin starting to sag? Do you look and feel old before your time? The reason may be in a deficiency of a vitamin group that stands head and shoulders above all others in terms of keeping your skin young.

The B-Complex Vitamin Family

A deficiency of just one of these vitamins can give you blotchy, lifeless, or blemished skin. The B-complex vitamins are needed to protect against scaly conditions of the skin and nerve deterioration. These vitamins activate enzyme systems required for the complete metabolism of carbohydrate foods needed to energize your skin and body cells. The B-complex family will activate metabolic reactions involved in oxidation-reduction processes to help give you a youthful skin.

If your skin looks older than you want it to, you could be in need of these vitamins. You can give your entire metabolism a supercharging of energy to firm up your skin cells with a simple but powerfully effective Forever Young Skin Food Tonic. Just drink one glass a day. See the results almost from the start.

The "Tonic"

Combine 8 ounces of orange juice with 2 tablespoons brewer's yeast powder; add 1 teaspoon lecithin granules, 1 teaspoon wheat germ, 1 teaspoon vegetable oil. Blenderize for 2 minutes. Drink slowly *before* breakfast so nutrients can work without interference from other foods.

Skin-Saving Benefits:

The vitamin C from the orange juice activates the B-complex treasure from the brewer's yeast and lecithin to combine with the vitamin E from the wheat germ and vegetable oil. In combination, this tonic will nourish your membranes, strengthen the cartilage and connective tissue, preserve oxygen within your skin cells, improve collagen-elastin stability, and lubricate and regenerate your entire skin.

The rich concentration of B-complex vitamins in this Forever Young Skin Food Tonic makes it a powerhouse of nutritional therapy from within.

LOOKS 10–20–30 YEARS YOUNGER WITH TONIC

When Helen LaR. was mistaken as the older sister of the three at a high school reunion (she was the youngest by nine years!), she decided to do something about her prematurely aging skin. She sought the help of a nutritionist who was known for aiding others who had skin disorders. The nutritionist suggested a return to fresh, wholesome foods and the use of the Forever Young Skin Food Tonic. Each day, for three weeks, Helen LaR. followed this easy plan. Quickly, her sallow complexion became fresh and young looking. Wrinkled folds started to smooth out. Crease lines just went away. Even more astounding was her boosting of energy in body and mind. She not only looked younger, but she felt more vibrant and alive. By the end of the month, she had such a young looking skin that radiated freshness, she was again mistaken by a neighbor, but this time, she was thought to be a "daughter" of one of her sisters!

Problem: Unsightly Red Veins on Skin

Nutritional Therapy: Turn to bioflavonoids

In this condition, tiny red threadlike veins have laced themselves across the face, most often on the lower cheeks. The cause may be traced to capillary fragility which creates these small red veins, running like wheel spokes beneath the skin. This suggests a weakness in your blood-carrying veins. Because of the damaged walls, fluid leaks through into areas beyond the veins.

To correct the problem from a nutritional view, the bioflavonoids (vitamin C complex with rutin, another nutrient) are needed to help strengthen this entire area.

Dietary Improvement

Boost your intake of bioflavonoid-rich foods such as citrus fruits, rose hips, turnip greens, green peppers, cabbage, and buckwheat (a prime source of rutin). *Tip:* The stringlike netting found near the inner peel of grapefruits, oranges, and tangerines is a concentrated source of bioflavonoids. Eat the whole fruit, including these strings to give your capillaries a powerhouse of bioflavonoids and protect against as well as reverse your problem of unsightly red veins.

How Oils Can Rebuild Your Skin from Head to Toe

With the use of fish liver oils, you can give your entire body a youthful skin all over. Fish oils are prime sources of vitamins A and D and contain the essential fatty acids that exert a powerful influence within your metabolism to prime your youth pump. This can be seen if you are in your late thirties and are concerned about aging skin. Let us see how this works.

Why Your Skin Ages

Your dermis (the supporting tissue lying beneath the paper-thin top layer of skin) contains water, fat, and spindly, star-shaped cells called fibroblasts. These cells act to support your network fibers, collagen, and elastin, to give your skin firmness and elasticity. But starting in the thirties, your dermis absorbs less water and fat. Your skin loses its firm and plump appearance. Oil-producing cells start to slow down. Your skin gets drier. Cell renewal begins to slow down, particularly in the menopausal stage. New cells do not develop as quickly. The older ones remain longer on your skin surface. Fibroblast cells produce fewer supporting fibers. Whatever is produced has less resiliency than in young skin. Your body envelope receives less oxygen and fewer nutrients as small capillaries beneath the surface start to close off.

Nutritional Therapy

Aging alone is not the cause of skin changes. Rather, how fast and how strong such changes occur depend largely on your nutritional intake. If you are adequately nourished, you may be able to cope with changes with fewer age signs. With the use of specific nutrients, vitamins A and D and essential fatty acids, you may be able to meet the challenges—and win. You can do it with fish liver oils. They contain these valuable nutrients which are able to stimulate your fibroblasts to create more essential fibers to support your skin structure. These vitamins combine with the fatty acids to provide valuable moisture to guard against dryness. They further introduce important oxygen so that your small capillaries can remain open and function to admit the free passage of nutrients. With the use of fish liver oils, you may well help rebuild your skin from head to toe.

Take Two at Bedtime...Look Younger in the Morning

About 30 minutes before bedtime, take 2 tablespoons of fish liver oil with water, milk, or citrus juice. Feel yourself relax. Then turn in. Throughout the night, your metabolism will seize hold of the important fibroblast-strengthening nutrients and begin to rebuild and repair your skin. This is an inside job. By morning, you should start to look and feel younger. Sagging skin, bags under the eyes, wrinkles, and unsightly blemishes will gradually ease and soon become erased with this inner rebuilding process.

Fish liver oil may well be the most valuable skin-feeding nutritional therapy you will need to help give your skin a second start in life!

Put the Skin-Aging Process on Hold

You have seen the reactions when former classmates get together at a class reunion after 20 years. As you greet a long-absent friend and notice the lined face, the changes that have made her look "so old," you cannot help but ask yourself silently, "Do I look that old, too?" The answer is in an honest self-appraisal before the mirror. The next step is to decide to put your aging process on hold as you begin a program of nutritional therapy. You do *not* have to accept your face and body skin the way it is. You *do* have an alternative with the use of corrective nutrition, inside and outside. You *can* have a younger skin, at any age!

WRAP-UP

1. Vitamin A has antiwrinkling and skin-rejuvenating powers that work swiftly.
2. Use a vitamin C boost to give yourself a youthful complexion.
3. Halt skin aging with the use of vitamin E.
4. Zinc will zap age signs and rebuild collagen-elastin fibers, the key to a youthful skin.
5. Grace O. used everyday foods to give herself a "natural facelift" in a short time.
6. Water therapy corrected Edna McG.'s "granny" skin very quickly.
7. Simple foods can be used as cosmetics to cleanse pores, correct dry-oily skin, smooth wrinkled eyelids, erase crease-age lines, soften rough hands and elbows, and brighten complexion.
8. The Forever Young Skin Food Tonic is a powerhouse of nutrients that firm up your skin, almost immediately.
9. Helen LaR. took 10-20-30 years off her face with the tonic.
10. Fish liver oils are rich, concentrated sources of nutrients that guard against and reverse the aging process. Just 2 tablespoons at bedtime and you wake up looking and feeling younger in the morning.

4

Cancer: How to Use Nutritional Safeguards to Build Your Resistance

Can vitamins halt the growth of tumors or shrink existing ones? Can nutritional therapy be used to keep cancer patients alive longer? Can specific foods be used to build immunity to cancer?

Chemoprevention—the use of nutrition to resist the start of cancer—is making it possible to fight back against this threat and win the battle with the use of a group of potent nutrients in foods. By making some simple adjustments in your daily food program, you can reduce the risks of developing cancer. You also can help to turn around certain existing cancer growths, block its spread, and resist the threatening consequences.

A major breakthrough in the search for dietary correction of the cancer threat has been announced by the National Academy of Sciences in a major report.[1] Nutritional therapies call for eating less fat; very little of salt-cured, pickled, and smoked foods; and more fruits, vegetables, and whole grains. The panel of experts from the Academy further urged daily consumption of fruits and vegetables rich in beta-carotene, the predecessor of vitamin A as well as vitamin C, which was found to inhibit the formation of certain cancer-causing substances and also lower the risk of cancers of the stomach and esophagus. With this set of guidelines, it was noted in various tests, that nutrition would be able to protect against specific cancers. It could also help undo much damage if cancer already did take hold. Nutritional therapy could even heal or "cure" some cancer.

[1]*Diet, Nutrition and Cancer,* National Academy of Sciences, Washington, D.C., 1982.

Correct Nutrition Can Give You Immunity to Cancer

Scientists have noted that:

1. Eighty percent of all cancers may be related to the environment, and to things you eat, drink, or smoke rather than to factors you cannot control such as family background. If you change the things you can control, there is strong evidence you can reduce your risk of getting cancer.
2. Thirty-five percent of all cancer deaths may be related to the way you eat. Make an adjustment in your dietary program, and you have build stronger resistance to cancer. You may even be able to knock out and defuse the cancer infestation and win the battle against this major killer.

Based on evidence at hand, you may win the battle by following a set of simple guidelines as issued by the American Cancer Society.

Seven-Step Nutritional Program to Build Cancer Immunity

1. *Avoid obesity.* Sensible eating habits and regular exercise will help you avoid excessive weight gain. There is a higher cancer risk among overweights, particularly if you are 40 percent overweight. Your risk increases for colon, breast, and uterine cancers. Tests indicate that the incidence of cancer is reduced and the life span lengthened by maintaining an ideal weight. Are you obese? Shedding those excess pounds may be one way to lower cancer risk.
2. *Cut down on total fat intake.* Excess intake of fats increases the chances of developing certain cancers like the breast, colon, and prostate cancers. Americans consume about 40 percent of total calories as fat. A decrease in the amount of fat to 30 percent of total calories, on the average, will help protect against this threat. You will also be able to control your body weight more easily.
3. *Eat more high-fiber foods.* Fiber is a term used to cover food components not readily digested in the human intestinal tract. These substances, abundant in whole grains, fruits, and vegetables, consist largely of complex carbohydrates of diverse composition. It

is believed that bulky, undigested food residues make quicker passage through the intestines, thus reducing the time in which bacteria or other cancer-causing substances could be in contact with intestinal tissues. (Fiber is also defined as the residue of plant cells after digestion by alimentary enzymes.) If bile acids or their breakdown products might be involved in causing cancer, the high-fiber diet with its larger bulk would decrease the time such agents could be in contact with intestinal tissues. Fiber may change the composition of bacterial flora and its interaction with carcinogens.

4. *Include foods rich in vitamins A and C in your daily diet.* Dark green and deep yellow vegetables and fruits such as carrots, spinach, yams, peaches, apricots, tomatoes, and cantaloupes are rich in beta-carotene, a form of vitamin A, that may reduce the risk of cancers of the larynx, esophagus, and lung. Second, oranges, grapefruit, strawberries, green and red peppers, lemons and melons contain ascorbic acid or vitamin C, which inhibits the formation of nitrosamines in the stomach. (Nitrosamines are powerful carcinogens formed when nitrates found in pickled items, in cured and preserved meats, combine with protein.) These two nutrients appear to offer protection or modify the incidence of stomach and esophageal cancer.
5. *Include cruciferous vegetables in your daily meal plan.* Cruciferous vegetables belong to the mustard family, whose plants have flowers with four leaves in the pattern of a cross. Some epidemiologic studies suggest that daily consumption of these vegetables may reduce the risk of cancer, particularly of the gastrointestinal and respiratory tracts. These vegetables include cabbage, broccoli, Brussels sprouts, kohlrabi, cauliflower, rutabaga, and turnips. These same cruciferous vegetables are prime sources of fiber as well as other vitamins and minerals, making them all-around healthful foods.
6. *Eat moderate amounts of salt-cured, smoked, and nitrate-cured foods.* Conventionally smoked foods such as hams, some varieties of sausage, and fish absorb some of the tars that arise from incomplete combustion. These tars contain numerous carcinogens that are similar chemically to the carcinogenic tars in tobacco smoke. The risks may apply primarily to conventionally smoked meats and fish. These processed foods may increase the risk of cancer of the esophagus and stomach. There is evidence that nitrate and nitrite can enhance nitrosamine formation, both in foods and the digestive

tract. Nitrate is used for meat preservation to prevent botulism (food poisoning) and to provide color and flavor.

7. *Keep alcohol consumption moderate if you do drink.* The heavy use of alcohol, especially when accompanied by cigarette smoking or chewing tobacco, increases risk of cancers of the mouth, larynx, throat, esophagus, and stomach. Alcohol abuse can result in cirrhosis, which may lead to liver cancer.

With the American Cancer Society's seven-step guideline, you may well be able to use nutritional therapy to prevent cancer or reverse its spread and free yourself from becoming another statistic in the list of fatalities.

Cancer: What Is It? Who Gets It? Who Will Survive?

What Is It?

Cancer is a disease characterized by uncontrolled growth and spread of abnormal cells. If the spread is not controlled or checked, it can be fatal.

Who Gets It?

It strikes at any age. It kills more children 3 to 14 than any other disease. It strikes more frequently with advancing age. Over 450,000 will die yearly of cancer—1,266 people a day, about one every 68 seconds. About 71 million Americans now living will eventually have cancer. Over the years, cancer will strike in approximately three out of four families. In an average year, about 910,000 people will be diagnosed as having cancer.

Who Will Survive?

Over 5 million Americans today have a history of cancer, 3 million of them with diagnosis five or more years ago. Most of these 3 million can be considered cured, while others still have evidence of cancer. By "cured" is meant that a patient has no evidence of disease and has the same life expectancy as a person who never had cancer. Today, about 340,000 Americans, or 3 out of 8 patients who get cancer, will be alive five years after diagnosis.

(The decision as to when a patient may be considered cured is one that must be made by the physician after examining the individual patient. For most forms of cancer, five years without symptoms following treatment is the accepted time. However, some patients can be considered cured after one year, others after three years, whereas, some have to be followed much longer than five years.)

THE SEVEN-STEP NUTRITIONAL THERAPY PLAN TO PROTECT AGAINST COLON CANCER

When Andrew J. was told by his proctologist that since several family members had colon cancer, he was at high risk, he understandably became frightened. He had three youngsters in school, a newly purchased home, a supervisor's job with a future. Would he face the hereditary risk of being cut down in the prime of his life? Colon cancer caused about 60,000 deaths in a typical year, second only in incidence to that of lung cancer. What were his chances?

His proctologist eased his panic by explaining that the proctosigmoidoscopy exam showed he could build a form of immunity if nutritional therapy were begun. He gave Andrew J. the American Cancer Society's seven-step plan and suggested he add another step by eliminating smoking and also cutting down all drinking. Eager to avoid the risk, he followed the program. Four months later, a new exam showed his colonic area to be in the best of health. The seven-step nutritional therapy plan now became his permanent way of life. It also gave him permanent life, he would say happily.

How Nutrients Build Immunity to Risk of Cancer

To build resistance to the risk of cancer, consider nutritional therapy. Some nutrients appear to act as anticancer fighters to correct the malfunction responsible for molecular chaos. You may want to build immunity with emphasis on one or more of these individual groups. This form of nutrition may well turn the tide against the risk of the spread of cancer and build a form of natural immunity.

Vitamin A or Beta-carotene

A report issued by the Nutrition Support Service of the Hospital of the university of Pennsylvania offers hope for immunity with this nutrient.[2] Robert C. Fried, M.D., explained that beta-carotene is called a provitamin because, once ingested, it is converted to vitamin A by the body's

[2]Clinical Nutrition Newsletter, University of Pennsylvania, Philadelphia, August, 1984.

tissues. It acts as a cancer inhibitor in many situations. It nourishes the epithelial varieties of tissues (those involving the cellular covering); it helps to shrink tumors, especially in epithelial cancer; additionally, beta-carotene offers defensive immunity to protect against the recurrence of the same cancer.

Vitamin C

Dr. Fried also explained that the risk of developing certain cancers (particularly gastric and esophageal carcinogens) could be reduced with regular intake of this vitamin. It inhibits the formation of carcinogenic N-nitroso compounds that have been found to be the villain in gastrointestinal cancers. It also appears that indols (a protein product containing tryptophan) from vegetables stimulate the increased manufacture of aryl hydrocarbon hydroxylases, which act as barriers to various cell-damaging chemicals. The doctor feels that boosting intake of vitamin C from vegetable sources is one way by which you can fortify yourself with internal protection against cancer. Typical food sources include turnip greens, kale, broccoli, green peppers, Brussels sprouts, cauliflower, cabbage, and tomatoes.

Vitamin E

"With various nutrients, we have for the first time in human history a biological tool to prevent cancer," says Kedar N. Prasad, Ph.D., a researcher at the University of Colorado Health Sciences Center and president of the International Association for Vitamins and Nutritional Oncology. "And the prospects for treatment with nutrients look promising as well. It will take a long time before we have conclusive evidence of all the anti-cancer properties of these substances, but we've made a good start."

Investigators at the University of Colorado have discovered in laboratory tests that vitamin E may halt the growth of prostate cancer cells. Test tube research had already shown that vitamin E could kill or inhibit other kinds of malignant cells, but this study zeroes in on vitamin E's impact on cancer of the prostate.

"Our data suggest," says Dr. Prasad, "that vitamin E may be useful in the treatment of patients with prostate cancer. After all, compared to cancer drugs, vitamin E is very low in toxicity so it can be easily incorporated into chemotherapy treatments. It simply will not interfere with standard therapy."[3]

How Vitamin E Builds Immunity. By helping cell membranes remain healthy, this vitamin appears to guard genetic material from damage that could lead to cancerous changes. Vitamin E intercepts and neutralizes dangerous molecular fragments, called oxidants, that might otherwise penetrate the nuclei and alter the DNA of healthy cells. This could predispose one to dangerous forms of cancer. It is vitamin E that acts to build internal immunity against the risk of this molecular damage. It has been found that this vitamin helps to prevent chromosome damage in cells exposed to certain chemicals. It also appears to be beneficial in building resistance to a common breast disease called fibrocystic cancer, affecting about 50 percent of all women who have a two- to eightfold greater risk of developing breast cancer.

Selenium

This mineral is a potent antioxidant that protects the cell membrane from free-radical or oxidant attack. Dr. Richard A. Passwater hails this mineral in his book, *Selenium as Food and Medicine,* as a barrier against the risk of cancer.[4] Selenium helps to produce an enzyme called glutathione peroxidase, or GSH-Px, for short, notes Dr. Passwater. He explains that here is a valuable antioxidizing enzyme that protects your body from damage by free radicals—the substances that bombard and break down cells and may trigger cancer. Selenium comes to the rescue by entering your red blood cells. It stimulates your immune system. It further alters the workings of carcinogenic substances, protecting against an accumulation of dangerous free radicals. The current RDA for selenium is 50 to 200 micrograms a day. You may want to aim for about 150 micrograms as a protective supply of needed GSH-Px. You will find 102 micrograms in ½ cup of water-packed tunafish. (The same serving packed in oil gives you only 55 micrograms.) One slice of whole wheat bread has 18 micrograms. Other rich sources are liver, kidneys, Brazil nuts, and brown rice. *Caution:* because of the potential toxic risk of selenium overdose, the *medically*

[3]*Prevention* magazine, Emmaus, Pa., June 1985.

[4]*Selenium as Food and Medicine* by Dr. Richard A. Passwater, Keats Publishing Co., New Canaan, Conn., 1980.

unsupervised use of selenium as a food supplement cannot be recommended.

HOW MIRIAM F. USED NUTRITIONAL THERAPY

Miriam F. became understandably concerned when her gynecologist, who had learned of her family's history of breast nodules, told her she would have to build resistance to cancer without delay. Miriam F. discussed nutritional therapy with the surgeon who explained that tests showed she had low levels of both vitamin E as well as selenium. By boosting intake of foods containing these nutrients, Miriam F. could help build immunity to offset the risk of so-called heredity cancer.

She followed a simple program that called for an increased consumption of vitamin E foods from unrefined wheat germ oil, whole grain breads and cereals, nuts, and seeds. She also consumed more brown rice as well as about 2 cups of water-packed tunafish throughout the week. A few diced Brazil nuts mixed in a whole grain cereal would give her both these nutrients. Results? By the end of the month, these immunity-building nutrients helped to improve her resistance. A new exam showed Miriam F. to be in excellent health and not the slightest risk of growths.

Two Potential Immunity Builders

Both vitamin E and selenium help the workings of an intracellular messenger, cyclic AMP, to become broken down by an enzyme, phosphodiesterase, as soon as signals are sent into the cell. These nutrients protect against any blockage of the cyclic-AMP signal, thereby guarding against the runaway proliferation of tissues.

How To Plan Your Food Choices To Help Build Your Resistance Against Cancer

Here is a set of dietary guidelines that will help to prevent and treat certain types of cancer. Nutritional therapy is one part of your total health picture. Daily exercise, not smoking, maintaining ideal weight, keeping yourself safe on the job, and having regular physical checkups add up to total resistance to cancer and other illnesses.

Dietary Fiber

Choose more often whole grain products such as:

- Bakery products, including whole wheat crackers; bran muffins; brown, rye, oatmeal, pumpernickel, bran, and corn breads; whole wheat English muffins, bagels.
- Breakfast cereals such as bran cereals, shredded wheat, whole grain or whole wheat flaked cereals, others that list dietary fiber content.
- Other foods made with whole grain flours such as waffles, pancakes, pasta, and taco shells.
- Foods made with whole grain such as barley, buckwheat groats, and bulgur wheat.
- Fruits such as apples, pears, apricots, bananas, berries, cantaloupes, grapefruit, oranges, pineapples, papayas, and prunes, raisins.
- Vegetables such as carrots, broccoli, potatoes, corn, cauliflower, Brussels sprouts, cabbage, celery, green beans, summer squash, green peas, parsnips, kale, spinach, other greens, yams, sweet potatoes, and turnips.
- All dry peas and beans such as black, kidney, garbanzo, pinto, navy, white, and lima beans.
- Lentils, split peas, and blackeyed peas.
- Snack foods include fruits and vegetables, unbuttered popcorn, whole grain and bran cereals, and whole grain breads and crackers.

Choose less often:

- Refined bakery and snack products such as refined flour breads, quick breads, biscuits, buns, croissants, snack crackers and chips, cookies, pastries, and pies.

Your Fat Program

Choose more often:

- Lower-fat poultry such as chicken, turkey, and Rock Cornish hens (without skin).
- Fresh or frozen fish or water-packed canned fish.
- Beef, veal, or lamb with little or no marbling (visible intermixed fat) and trimmed of all fat.
- Peas and beans such as pinto, black, kidney, garbanzo, navy, white, lima beans; lentils; and blackeye and split peas.

- Lower-fat dairy products such as skim milk and buttermilk, low-fat yogurt.
- Skimmed evaporated milk, nonfat dry milk.
- Low-fat cheese such as ricotta, pot, farmer, or cottage, and mozzarella, or cheeses made from skim milk.
- Sherbet, frozen low-fat yogurt, and ice milk.
- Low-fat salad dressings.
- Low-fat margarine.

Choose less often:

- Higher-fat poultry such as duck and goose, chicken with skin.
- Frozen fish sticks, tuna packed in oil.
- Fatty luncheon meats, bologna, hot dogs, and sausage.
- Beef, veal, and lamb cuts with marbling, untrimmed of fat.
- Peanut and other nut butters.
- Trail mix.
- Full-fat dairy products such as whole milk, butter, and yogurt made from whole milk.
- Sour cream, sweet cream, half and half, whipped cream, and other creamy toppings (including imitation).
- Full-fat soft cheeses such as cream cheese, cheese spreads, Camembert, and Brie.
- Hard cheeses such as cheddar, Swiss, bleu, American, Jack, and Parmesan.
- Ice cream.
- Coffee creamers, including nondairy.
- Cream sauces, cream soups.
- Shortening, lard, meat fats, salt pork, and bacon.
- Mayonnaise.
- Margarine.
- Gravies, butter sauces.
- Snacks such as donuts, pies, pastries, cakes, cookies, brownies, and croissants.

- Potato chips and snack crackers.
- Canned puddings, icings, candies made with butter, cream, and chocolate.
- Avoid food preparation methods such as batter and deep-fat frying or sauteeing. Avoid use of fatty gravies and sauces. Do not add cream or butter to vegetables.

Your Vitamin A and C Program

Choose any of the following:

- Dark green leafy vegetables such as broccoli, Swiss chard, kale, spinach, romaine, endive, chicory, escarole, watercress, collard, beets, turnips, and mustard and dandelion greens.
- Vegetables such as asparagus, green and red peppers, cauliflower, cabbage, Brussels sprouts, bean sprouts, mushrooms, squash, green beans, onions, okra, and tomatoes.
- Yellow-orange vegetables such as carrots, sweet potatoes, pumpkins, and winter squash.
- Yellow-orange fruits such as apricots, cantaloupes, similar melons, cherries, papayas, peaches, prunes (even though they are not yellow in all forms), berries, pineapples, plums, strawberries, and watermelons.
- Citrus fruits like lemons, limes, oranges, tangerines, and grapefruit.
- Juices made from any of the foregoing.

Your Vitamin E Program

Choose any of the following:

- Wheat germ oil, whole grain products, vegetable oils, sunflower seeds, raw or sprouted seeds, nuts and grains, and green leafy vegetables.

Your Selenium Program

Choose any of the following: tunafish, water-packed; fresh garlic; barley; whole wheat bread; egg noodles; brown rice; beef liver; beef kidneys; Brazil nuts.

Can Nutritional Therapy "Knock Out" Cancer?

Can nutritional therapy disarm dangerous cancers? The new knowledge of using nutrients as weapons does suggest you can help to build immunity to the risk of the formation of misshapen cells and the onset of cancer. These same nutrients are able to "knock out" enemy cells and mend injuries to help free you from cancer.

Your Hope for Health

The facts show that about 3 out of every 10 cancer deaths are traced to poor diet. Fortify your resistance with the use of the preceding seven-step program and you will enjoy better health and freedom from the risk of cancer.

SUMMARY

1. Since 8 out of all 10 cancers are environmentally related and 3 out of 10 cancers are diet connected, you can build immunity with proper self-care.
2. The easily followed seven-step nutritional program should be your foundation of better health.
3. Andrew J. was able to resist colon cancer with this improved program.
4. Boost intake of four nutrient groups to build an inner fortress against cancer.
5. Miriam F. used two nutrients in everyday foods to build immunity to the threat of heredity-caused breast cancer.
6. Plan your anticancer diet program with suggested guidelines.
7. You can be victorious in the threatening battle against cancer with nutritional therapy.

5

The Low-Fat Way to a Healthier and Younger Heart

When you hear the saying, "The way to a person's heart is through the stomach," do you immediately plan imaginary menus? Do you think of rib-eye steak, baked potato with cheese and bacon, vegetables with hollandaise sauce, and cheesecake? Or do you think of chicken-fried steak with cream gravy, fresh snap beans flavored with salty fat, and banana cream pie with whipped cream?

The condemned man's last meal! Either menu could lead to a man's heart—or his heart attack! Both are laden with cholesterol-rich foods and saturated fats that could trigger heart disease. It could very well be the man's last meal.

Cholesterol and Fat—Are You Eating Too Much?

All persons 2 years of age and older need to make nutritional adjustments to reduce the risk of heart trouble, according to a panel of experts at the National Institutes of Health (NIH). In particular, it is lifesaving to control intake of both cholesterol and fat.

Cholesterol-Control Goal

Lower your blood cholesterol to the NIH-recommended 180 milligrams or less for those age 30 and younger; 200 milligrams or less for those over age 30. Reduce your blood cholesterol by about 10 percent. Consume no more than 300 milligrams of dietary cholesterol each day.

Fat-Control Goal

Lower total fat levels by limiting fat intake to no more than 30 percent of total calories. Plan to consume one-third from animal sources and two-thirds from vegetable and plant sources. *Example:* on a 2100-calorie-a-day diet, as much as 630 calories may come from fats. (Because 1 gram of fat contains 9 calories, fat intake comes to 70 grams, or 2.5 ounces.)

How to Reach a Fat Balance. According to the NIH guidelines, no more than 10 percent of the total calories intake (about 210 calories) should come from saturated fats, found mostly in animal and dairy products. The rest, about 420 calories, should be shared between polyunsaturated fats, such as vegetable oils, and monounsaturated fats such as olive oil.

Fat and Cholesterol Go Together

The catch here is that few foods (except some shellfish and egg yolks) are high in saturated fat without also being high in cholesterol. This means that the most efficient way to lower blood cholesterol is to decrease the amount of saturated fat in your diet. You cannot reduce one without reducing the other at the same time.

Fat City: Making Your Way Through the Crowded Saturated and Polyunsaturated Pathways

It can be a maze of fats! Which way to turn? Which ones to avoid? Fat can be a detour or roadway in your search for a healthier and younger heart system. You can go in the right direction toward a longer lifeline, with a better understanding of the fat picture. Let's talk the language of these necessary and unnecessary "evils."

Cholesterol

A waxlike compound (sterol) found in all animal cells, including those of the human body; it is part of the cell membrane and a building block for bile salts and sex hormones. Produced by most body cells, but especially by the intestine and liver, it influences digestion because it is needed for bile production.

Dietary cholesterol. This is found only in animal foods and products such as meat, fish, poultry, and egg yolks and foods made from animal products.

Blood cholesterol. This is found in the blood and is strongly linked to risk and incidence of coronary heart disease. Eating too much cholesterol and saturated fat raises blood cholesterol levels, which causes cells to become overloaded in the blood vessel linings. This leads to atherosclerosis or hardening of the arteries. (Atherosclerosis refers to the clogging of blood vessels by deposits of cholesterol and other minerals which may lead to a heart attack or stroke or aggravate arterioscleoris, which is a thickening-hardening of the arteries.)

Fats

Saturated Fats. Found mostly in meat and dairy foods, saturated refers to chemical bonds; saturated fats contain more hydrogen atoms than do other types of fats. These are usually solid at room temperature. These fats are constituted chemically so that they cannot absorb additional hydrogen.

Polyunsaturated Fats. Found mostly in vegetable foods such as liquid oils; these fats consist of molecules that have one or more double bonds that are capable of absorbing more hydrogen. They are liquid at room temperature. Polyunsaturated fat helps to clear saturated fat from the body.

Monounsaturated Fats. These come from vegetable sources and contain one hydrogen atom less in their structure than saturated fats. This type of fat does not appear to raise total blood cholesterol levels. It may be as effective as polyunsaturated fats in reducing the levels. Sources include olive and peanut oils.

The Good Versus the Bad Cholesterol

When you stand at the crossroads of "fat city" and wonder which way to go, you need to know that there are three avenues to explore. One will lead to a younger heart. The other two could lead to a collision! Let's look in these directions.

High-Density Lipoprotein

HDL, as it is called, is the *good* fat. It is considered protective because it helps to remove cholesterol from your body.

Low-Density Lipoprotein

The most common type of fat, LDL, tends to pick up cholesterol and deposit it for storage in various cells throughout the body.

Very-Low-Density Lipoprotein

VLDL is an even more hazardous fat that can cause accumulations of more cholesterol than the LDL and can be responsible for a serious overload.

Make Your Selection with Nutritional Therapy

You will be giving your heart and circulatory system a new lease on life with increased amounts of HDLs through more polyunsaturated fats and fewer saturated fats. You will help protect yourself against a collision and pile-up of accumulated debris of cholesterol blockages. You can use nutritional therapy to go down the pathway of HDLs to reach your goal of a healthier and younger heart.

Go Slowly with Polyunsaturated Fat Increase

Caution: Granted, polyunsaturated fat will help clear the saturated fat from your blood and lower cholesterol levels, but you need to proceed with caution. Excessively high levels of polyunsaturated fats may work too powerfully and *reduce* HDLs—that protective fatty substance that acts as a cholesterol sweeper. So proceed slowly and within reason.

Simple Nutritional Therapy Goal

It takes 2 grams of polyunsaturated fat to counteract the effect of 1 gram of saturated fat on blood cholesterol. Therefore, decreasing saturated fat will have a greater impact than will increasing polyunsaturated fat. You can do it by changing your meal program to meet the percentages given in Chart 5-1.

Less Cholesterol = Less Heart Disease

For each 1 percent reduction in blood cholesterol levels, there is a 2 percent drop in the risk of developing heart disease. Furthermore, according to NIH researchers, even if you have had one heart attack, you will be protected against a recurrence if you control your diet. Your goal is to help wash out excessive cholesterol and protect against further pileup of this risky blood fat.

Chart 5-1: THE BALANCING ACT: Common Foods and Their Proportions of Saturated and Polyunsaturated Fats

Experts advise counting total fat calories and also watching the ratio between polyunsaturated fats (found largely in plant and vegetable scurces) and saturated fat (mainly in animal products).

Since it takes 2 grams of polyunsaturated fat to counteract the effects of 1 gram of saturated fat, experts suggest you eat foods with a 2:1 ratio or better of polyunsaturated to saturated fat.

Food	*% Total Calories From Fat*	*% Calories Saturated Fat*	*% Calories Polyunsaturated Fat*	*Polyunsaturated To Saturated Fat Ratio (Ideal = 2:1)*
Cheddar cheese	74%	47%	2%	2:47
Swiss cheese	76	43	2	2:43
American cheese	75	47	2	2:47
Edam cheese	70	44	2	2:44
Creamed cottage				
cheese (regular)	39	25	1	1:25
1% fat)	13	8	less than 1	less than 1:8
Whole milk	49	31	2	2:31
2% Milk	34.6	22	1	1:22
Skim milk	4.6	3	trace	trace:3
Nondairy creamer	58.5	54	trace	trace:54
Half and Half	80	50	2.9	2.9:50
Yogurt, lowfat	13	8	less than 1	less than 1:8
Ice cream, vanilla	48	30	2	2:30
Ice milk, vanilla	28	17	1	1:17
Sherbert, orange	13	8	less than 1	less than 1:8

Chart 5-1: *(continued)*

Food	*% Total Calories From Fat*	*% Calories Saturated Fat*	*% Calories Polyunsaturated Fat*	*Polyunsaturated To Saturated Fat Ratio (Ideal = 2:1)*
Peanut butter	78	14	26	26:14
Tofu (bean curd)	52	8	27	27:8
Bologna, beef	81.5	33.5	3	3:33.5
Beef hot dog	82	33.4	3	3:33.4
Chicken hot dog	68	19	14	14:19
Turkey breast (no skin)	5	1.6	1.3	1.3:1.6
Turkey leg	21	7	6.3	6.3:7
Chicken breast (roasted, no skin)	19.5	5.5	4.2	4.2:5.5
Roast beef (eye of round, lean and trimmed of fat)	34	14	1.4	1.4:14
Ground beef (Lean, well-done)	57	23.5	2.3	2.3:23.5
Tuna (in soybean oil)	37	10	7.7	7.7:10

Source: U. S. Department of Agriculture.

The Simple Oil That Helps to Clear Away the Cholesterol Threat

Olive oil is a powerful monounsaturated oil that helps to control and wash away cholesterol in the blood. It protects against any accumulation of fatty deposits that might threaten to narrow the vessels, reduce blood flow to the heart, and pose a risk of cardiovascular disease.

Olive oil helps the HDLs to transport cholesterol from the body's tissues to the liver where it can be either converted for use by the body or processed for elimination. Furthermore, olive oil is a monounsaturate that has a more stable shelf life, so it does not go rancid nearly as fast as the polyunsaturates.

Nutritional Therapy

Use olive oil as part of a salad dressing, mixed with various herbs, every day. Use the same olive oil in cooking for any recipe that calls for oil. You will be supercharging your cholesterol-cleansing HDLs to give you a clean heart and a healthier body, too.

Fish Oils Will Cleanse Arteries and Strengthen Your Heart

Eating fish and using fish oils several times a week may significantly reduce fatty accumulations on your arteries and make you less likely to risk heart disease.

New epidemiological studies show that there is a much lower incidence of atherosclerosis in some populations that eat larger amounts of cold-water fish and fish oils.

The protective effect appears to be in the oils which seem to prevent the formation of artery-blocking deposits much better than vegetable oils.

The Heart Benefits of Fish Oils

The secret of the fat washing and heart saving is the unusual ingredients found in fish oils: *eicosapentaenoic acid* (EPA) and *docosahexaenoic acid* (DHA), two long-chain fatty acids. There are also some amounts of vitamins A and E. Between 5 and 40 percent of the fat in seafood consists of these omega-3 fatty acids, as they are called. In contrast, polyunsaturated vegetable oils are rich in omega-6 fatty acids such as linoleic acid. (The number refers to the location of the first unsaturated bond in the fat. In the omega-3 fats, the bond occurs between the third and fourth carbon; in the omega-6 variety, it occurs between the sixth and seventh.)

What's the Difference?

Researchers suspect that omega-6 fatty acids predispose to substances that encourage platelets to stick together. But in omega-3 fatty acids, the platelets are kept cleansed, and there is less of a tendency to congeal. So it seems that the omega-3 fatty acids protect the platelets against clotting. These substances make the platelets less sticky, and this protects against the threat of atherosclerosis. This can be a lifesaver!

In brief, the more omega-3 you consume, the less likely you are at risk of heart disease.

Where to Find Omega-3

The leading sources would be cold-water fish (and their oils) such as salmon, mackerel, sardines, cod, halibut. You can hook into these heart-protecting sources of EPA and DHA by planning your meal program to include at least 6 to 8 ounces of seafood four or five times a week. Boost the action of cleansing HDLs by taking fish liver oils, 1 tablespoon every day. This bountiful catch from the sea may well foil cardiovascular disease.

WINS HEART BATTLE—HOOK, LINE, AND SINKER—WITH FISH OILS

An electrocardiogram showed that factory foreman Victor DeN. had a fluttering heart. Blood tests showed he had a risky cholesterol reading of 350 milligrams per deciliter. Dangerous! Life-threatening! And he was only 52 years of age! He asked his cardiologist for a diet program to help bring readings under control. He was put on a low-animal-fat and higher-polyunsaturated-fat menu. In four weeks, his reading was down to 320. Too slow, his cardiologist observed. Swifter and safer action was needed. The doctor then made a simple nutritional therapeutic prescription: eat seafood from salmon, mackerel, sardines, cod, halibut throughout the week. Use seafood as a replacement for animal products. Each day, take 2–3 tablespoons of fish liver oil with either citrus juice or with some herbs as part of a raw vegetable salad. Results? In seven days, his reading was a safer 210 milligrams. His new cardiogram showed a steady beat. His pressure, too, was stabilized. The fish oils had rescued him from the threat of atherosclerosis and heart trouble. Victor DeN. considers his seafood program to be a lifesaver that brought him to safety.

Say "No" to Three Items; Say "Yes" to a Healthier Heart System

Your nutritional program should be planned to avoid three items that can be deleterious to your heart and health. These are

1. *Salt.* Because it absorbs water, salt can cause edema, which is a threat to the health of your heart. *Avoid* salt either from the shaker or in cooked foods as well as in packaged products.
2. *Caffeine.* For some people, caffeine stimulates the central nervous system, makes the heart beat faster, stirs up the metabolism, and plays havoc with the blood vessels. It may widen some but choke others. It could cause heart flutters. *Avoid* caffeine whether in coffee, tea, soft drinks, medications, even some confections.
3. *Sugar.* It can cause the rise of a lesser known blood fat called triglycerides. Sugar seems to build up excessive amounts of this fat, and this could cause a heart risk. *Avoid* sugar from the shaker or in cooked foods. Read labels of all packaged products to see if sugar is contained—along with salt or caffeine. If in doubt, pass up the product.

You can help keep cholesterol and fat in check and your heart in better shape by eliminating these three "no-no" items from your food program.

Triglycerides—The Sneaky Blood Fat You Need to Control

Triglycerides is the technical term for fats and oils. Your body's fat stores are triglycerides. Although your bloostream always contains some triglycerides, if they are elevated, they may be implicated in atherosclerosis, the disease process that leads to heart disease.

Triglycerides are often upstaged by cholesterol. They do not take such a bad rap, but a high level of these lipids (fatty substances) in your blood should not be disregarded. True, there is no *direct* link to cardiovascular disease as there is with cholesterol, there is an indicator of risk. Triglycerides can be sneaky and if allowed to become overloaded, might cause problems.

Nutritional Therapy

It is believed that sugar tends to predispose accumulation of triglycerides. So will animal fats. Avoidance of sugar is one important step in controlling the levels of this blood fat. Moderate animal fat intake is another decisive step. Control caloric intake along with saturated fats. Eliminate alcohol. These factors can help keep triglycerides in check and give further protection against atherosclerosis and heart disease.

WOMAN OVERCOMES "HEREDITY" WITH NUTRITIONAL THERAPY

Joan Y. came from a family that had many heart problems. Her parents and two older sisters had such difficulties and faced a shorter life span. But Joan Y. resolved not to follow in their ill-fated footsteps. She consulted a clinical heart specialist who would use nutrition as the first line of defense against such difficulties. Joan Y. was put on a fat-controlled eating program. She was told to avoid salt, caffeine, sugar totally. Also, she would take 2 tablespoons of fish liver oil daily. Together with prescribed exercise, she resisted the risk factors of fatty deposits on and within her arteries. Her cholesterol level was a constant 175 milligrams per deciliter. Her heart was in tip-top shape. This simple program of fat control and saying "no" to salt, caffeine, and sugar, and taking 2 tablespoons of fish liver oil daily helped her remain heart-healthy...for her entire life! She had won against predictions that "heredity" would end her in the early forties. She celebrated her seventy-eighth birthday—hale and hearty!

Garlic—Relieves Chest Pains

The old-time remedy of using garlic to ease chest pains is an important part of the nutritional therapy program for a healthier heart.

Garlic eases plaque formation in arteries; it is a prime source of allicin, an active sulfur-containing compound that is changed into diallyldisulphide in the system; this helps to liquefy cholesterol deposits, loosen plaque, reduce lipid (fat) levels in the blood and liver, and improve the action of the heart. Garlic also improves the flow of oxygen into the bloodstream, thereby relieving chest pain associated with heart conditions. (Medically, the condition is called angina pectoris, in which the heart muscle receives an insufficient blood supply, causing pain in the chest and often in the left arm and shoulder.) It is garlic that may well help to dilate the blood vessels, allow a better exchange of oxygen, and relieve pain.

GARLIC AS HEART "MEDICINE"

Philip K. was troubled with recurring chest pains. He feared the use of nitroglycerine, which would dilate the blood vessels but would also cause dizziness, loss of some of his senses, nervous tremors, and gastrointestinal upset. He asked a homeopathic physician if a less risky treatment could be found. He was told to eat at least four garlic cloves daily, along with a fat-controlled and salt-free program. Philip K. chewed the cloves together with parsley to ease the strong scent, on a daily basis. In 11 days, his chest pains were gone. No longer did he awaken in the middle of the night, terrified, clutching his pain-filled chest, gasping for air. Now, he felt brand new, thanks to garlic. He even took a few cloves at night as his "sleeping medicine," so he could sleep well and awaken with hearty good health!

How to Feast High on a Low-Fat Food Program

You want to enjoy taste in your foods. You have a right to favor taboo fat. You can be satisfied with fatty good taste, but with these simple adjustments. They get the fat out of food, but leave behind the taste! (See Charts 5-2, 5-3, and 5-4 for guidelines.)

Meats

Select the leanest cuts. Avoid those with marbling. Grind lean beef at home to prepare hamburger. *Caution:* commercially ground hamburger contains about three times as much fat. Before cooking, cut away as much fat as possible. For example, the fat pads under the skin of poultry and game.

Panbroiling: Use a heavyweight pan. Do not add oil or fat. Add meat. Cover pan and broil over low heat, turning meat once or twice. After meat is cooked, turn up heat the get browning effect of a broiler. Drain off all fat drippings (see below). Fish and organ meats do not panbroil well, but you can poach them over low heat by adding skim milk or water. Season liquid with a small amount of lemon juice, vinegar, or a dry wine. Add herbs and spices to taste.

Fat-Free Broths, Gravies, and Sauces: If you chill drippings, drainings, and commercial sauces after cooking, the fat will rise to the surface and solidify for easy removal. To remove fat while broth is in original pan, skim ice cubes through it. To prepare brown gravy from fat-free broth, add 1

Chart 5-2: FAT AND CALORIES FROM SOME FOODS

If you choose to reduce the fat in your diet to 30 percent of your daily calories, for a 2,000-calorie diet that is about 67 grams of fat.

Food	*Serving*	*Calories*	*Grams of Fat*
Dairy Products			
Cheese			
American, pasteurized process	1 ounce	105	9
Cheddar	1 ounce	115	9
Cottage			
Creamed	½ cup	115	5
Low-fat (2%)	½ cup	100	2
Cream	1 ounce	100	10
Mozzarella, part skim	1 ounce		5
Parmesan	1 Tbsp	25	2
Swiss	1 ounce	105	8
Cream			
Half and half	2 Tbsp	40	3
Light, coffee, or table	2 Tbsp	60	6
Sour	2 Tbsp	50	5
Ice cream	1 cup	270	14
Ice milk	1 cup	185	6
Milk			
Whole	1 cup	150	8
Low-fat (2%)	1 cup	125	5
Nonfat, skim	1 cup	85	trace
Yogurt, low-fat, fruit-flavored	8 ounces	230	2
Meats			
Beef, coooked			
Braised or pot-roasted			
Less lean cuts, such as chuck blade, lean only	3 ounces	255	16
Leaner cuts, such as bottom round, lean only	3 ounces	190	8
Ground beef, broiled			
Lean	3 ounces	230	15
Regular	3 ounces	245	17

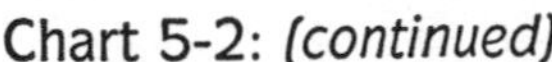

Chart 5-2: *(continued)*

Food	*Serving*	*Calories*	*Grams of Fat*
Roast, oven cooked			
Less lean cuts, such as rib, lean only	3 ounces	225	15
Leaner cuts, such as eye of round, lean only	3 ounces	155	6
Steak, sirloin, broiled			
Lean and fat	3 ounces	250	17
Lean	3 ounces	185	8
Lamb, cooked			
Chops, loin, broiled			
Lean and fat	3 ounces	250	17
Lean only	3 ounces	185	
Leg, roasted, lean only	3 ounces	160	7
Pork, cured, cooked			
Bacon, fried	3 slices	110	9
Ham, roasted			
Lean and fat	3 ounces	205	14
Lean only	3 ounces	135	5
Pork, fresh, cooked			
Chop, center loin			
Broiled			
Lean and fat	3 ounces	270	19
Lean only	3 ounces	195	9
Pan-fried			
Lean and fat	3 ounces	320	26
Lean only	3 ounces	225	14
Rib, roasted, lean only	3 ounces	210	12
Shoulder, braised, lean only	3 ounces	210	10
Spareribs, braised, lean and fat	3 ounces	340	26
Veal cutlet, braised or broiled	3 ounces	185	9
Sausages			
Bologna	2 ounces	180	16
Frankfurters	2 ounces (1 frank)	185	17

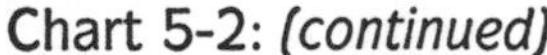

Chart 5-2: *(continued)*

Food	*Serving*	*Calories*	*Grams of Fat*
Pork, link or patty, cooked	2 ounces (4 links)	210	18
Salami, cooked type	2 ounces	145	11
Poultry Products			
Chicken			
Fried, flour-coated			
Dark meat with skin	3 ounces	240	14
Light meat with skin	3 ounces	210	10
Chicken, roasted			
Dark meat without skin	3 ounces	175	8
Light meat without skin	3 ounces	145	4
Duck, roasted, meat without skin	3 ounces	170	10
Turkey, roasted			
Dark meat without skin	3 ounces	160	6
Light meat without skin	3 ounces	135	3
Egg, hard cooked	1 large	80	6
Seafood			
Flounder, baked			
With butter or margarine	3 ounces	120	6
Without butter or margarine	3 ounces	85	1
Oysters, raw	3 ounces	55	2
Shrimp, French Fried	3 ounces	200	10
Shrimp, boiled or steamed	3 ounces	100	1
Tuna, packed in oil, drained	3 ounces	165	7
Tuna, packed in water, drained	3 ounces	135	1
Grain Products*			
Bread, white	1 slice	65	1
Biscuit, 2½ inches across	one	135	5
Muffin, plain, 2½ inches across	one	120	4
Pancake, 4 inches across	one	60	2
Other Foods			
Avocado	½	160	15
Butter, margarine	1 Tbsp	100	12

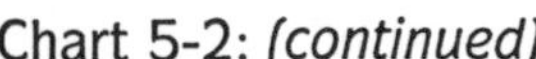

Chart 5-2: *(continued)*

Food	*Serving*	*Calories*	*Grams of Fat*
Cake, white layer, chocolate frosting	1 piece	265	11
Cookies, chocolate chip	4	185	11
Donut, yeast type, glazed	one	235	13
Mayonnaise	1 Tbsp	100	11
Oils	1 Tbsp	120	14
Peanut butter	1 Tbsp	95	8
Peanuts	½ cup	420	35
Salad dressing			
Regular	1 Tbsp	65	6
Low Calorie	1 Tbsp	20	1

*Most breads and cereals, dry beans and peas, and other vegetables and fruits (except avocados) contain only a trace of fat. However, spreads, fat, cream sauces, toppings, and dressings often added to these foods do contain fat.

Source: Human Nutrition Information Service, U.S. Department of Agriculture.

tablespoon of flour and one (salt-free) bouillon cube dissolved in ⅔ cup of water.

Browning Mushrooms and Onions

For better flavor, brown without fat by using just enough salt-free soy sauce or Worcestershire sauce to wet them. Cook in a covered pan over low heat.

Desserts

To make fruits without syrup tastier, add lemon juice, clove, or ginger. Since ½ cup of regular prepared gelatin has 70 calories, use dietetic gelatin and flavor with fruit or fruit juice.

Salad Oils and Dressings

Use polyunsaturated salad oils or margarine for seasoning, cooking, and baking instead of shortenings, butter, lard, and salt pork.

Chart 5-3: GUIDE TO REDUCING DIETARY FAT

This guide shows the amount of fat in diets with different proportions of calories from fat. For example, a 2,000-calorie diet calculated to have 30 percent of calories from fat has a total of 67 grams of fat or 600 calories from fat. Food labels can help you find how many grams of fat are contained in packaged foods.

Percentage of Calories Desired from Fat (%)	*Total Calories From Fat Should Not Exceed (calories)*	*Total Grams of Fat Should Not Exceed (grams)*
For a 1,500-calorie diet		
40	600	67
35	525	58
30	450	50
25	375	42
20	300	33
For a 2,000-calorie diet:		
40	800	89
35	700	78
30	600	67
25	500	56
20	400	44
For a 2,500-calorie diet:		
40	1,000	111
35	875	97
30	750	83
25	625	69
20	500	55

Chart 5-4: CHOLESTEROL CONTENT OF COMMON MEASURES OF SELECTED FOODS (in ascending order)

Food	*Serving Size*	*Milligrams of Cholesterol*
Milk, skim, fluid, or reconstituted dry	1 cup	5
Cottage cheese, uncreamed	½ cup	7
Lard	1 Tbsp	12
Cream, light table	1 fluid ounce	20
Cottage cheese, creamed	½ cup	24
Cream, half and half	¼ cup	26
Ice cream, regular, approximately 10% fat	½ cup	27
Cheese, cheddar	1 ounce	28
Milk, whole	1 cup	34
Butter	1 Tbsp	35
Oysters, salmon	3 ounces, cooked	40
Clams, halibut, tuna	3 ounces, cooked	55
Chicken, turkey, light meat	3 ounces, cooked	67
Beef, pork, lobster, chicken, turkey, dark meat	3 ounces, cooked	75
Lamb, veal, crab	3 ounces, cooked	85
Shrimp	3 ounces, cooked	130
Heart, beef	3 ounces, cooked	230
Egg	1 yolk or 1 egg	250
Liver, beef, calf, hog, lamb	3 ounces, cooked	370
Kidney	3 ounces, cooked	680
Brains	3 ounces, raw	1,700+

Source: "Cholesterol Content of Foods,"" R. M. Feeley, P. E. Criner, and B. K. Watt, *Journal of the American Dietitians Association*, Vol. 61 (1972), p. 134.

Low-Calorie "French" Dressing: Mix 1 cup of tomato juice and ¼ cup of apple cider vinegar or lemon juice. Add chopped onion, garlic, pepper, or any desired seasonings such as mustard, green pepper, celery seed, bay leaf, chili pepper, or Worcestershire or Tabasco sauce. For even lower calories, thin a mayonnaise-type dressing (not mayonnaise) with equal portions of apple cider vinegar or lemon juice and evaporated skim milk. Stir until smooth and let stand to thicken. Can be used on fruit, tuna salads, or cole slaw.

Low-Fat Whipped Cream: Mix 2 cups of evaporated skim milk with 1 teaspoon of lemon juice, or use 1½ cups of powdered skim milk reconstituted with ½ cup of water. Add a bit of honey. Chill and whip until thick.

"Creamed" Cottage Cheese: Add skim milk to dry cottage cheese and mix to get desired consistency. Cool overnight and flavor with buttermilk, spices, or vegetables when the curd is soft.

Sour Cream: To ½ cup plain "creamed" cottage cheese, add 1 tablespoon of apple cider vinegar or lemon juice. Blend or strain and beat mixture until fluffy. Add pepper, spices, or herbs, if desired.

Cream Soup

Use skim milk, dry skim milk, or water as recipe requires. Or thicken 1 cup of skim milk with 1 tablespoon of flour. You can also use the cooking water from boiled meats. Flavor with vegetables and add meats as allowed.

White Sauce

Thoroughly mix 1 tablespoon of flour in 1 cup of skim milk.

Egg Recipes

Substitute egg white for yolk in the following ratios: 1 egg white for 1 egg yolk, 2 egg whites for 1 whole egg, and 3 egg whites for 2 whole eggs.

Read Labels Carefully

Even low-cholesterol foods may have high amounts of saturated fats. A product may say that it contains "all" vegetable shortening. It may still have high saturated fat if it contains coconut or palm oils. Avoid these two "vegetable" oils. Hydrogenated vegetable oils are to be limited or avoided. Hydrogen is percolated back into these fats, transforming them from a polyunsaturated to saturated fat.

Oat Bran "Soaks Up" and "Dissolves" Cholesterol

Oat bran is a grain that is a rich source of dietary fiber, especially cellulose, hemicellulose, and pectin. It has been reported that this grain has the ability to "absorb" cholesterol and wash it out of the system. The reason is in its water-soluble properties. It acts like a sponge in absorbing the excess cholesterol and preparing it for elimination. If you enjoy a bowl of hot oat bran cereal several times a week, you may well be helping to keep cholesterol-fat levels under control. The mechanism is believed to be in oat bran's knack for binding bile acids in the intestines, breaking down cholesterol into more bile acids and helping to eliminate them. It is a natural way to keep your cholesterol in control.

The Spice That May Prevent a Blood Clot

You may be salt-restricted, but you can enjoy another tangy spice that is good for your heart! Meet capsicum or the familiar hot pepper. It contains an unusual ingredient that increases fibrinolytic activity that could well prevent thromboembolism (blood clot) among many people.

It is estimated that 8 out of 10 heart attacks are the result of development of blood clots on top of diseased blood vessels. Fibrinolytic action refers to clot-dissolving activity. A substance that can disolve the clot can save a life.

Capsicum is a prime source of a protein-substance that activates plasminogen, an item in the blood vessel walls that is needed to dissolve clots. It is capiscum that creates this process to activate the plasminogen to protect against vascular obstruction. You may consider it a built-in process to dissolve the threat of a heart attack.

Tangy Suggestion

Use a modest amount of capsicum in cooking as a seasoning to help maintain active levels of clot-dissolving plasminogen to keep your heart (and yourself) alive and healthy.

Take heart! Use nutritional therapy, along with better living habits such as exercise, stress reduction, emotional happiness, and you will give your heart its chance to live its maximum nine lives!

WRAP-UP

1. Keep your fat levels under control. Know the different types of fats and how some are helpful, others hurtful.
2. Slowly increase polyunsaturated fat intake at a 2:1 ratio over that of saturated fat to improve your heart's health.
3. Olive oil helps to control cholesterol in daily usage.
4. Fish oils can help you to win the battle against cholesterol.
5. Victor DeN. lowered cholesterol and stabilized heart health on a fish oil program.
6. Avoid salt, caffeine, and sugar, and you may well avoid a heart attack.
7. Be alert to triglycerides, a sneaky blood fat, boosted by sugar and animal fats as well as alcohol.
8. On a fat-controlled, fish oil program, Joan Y. celebrated her seventy-eighth birthday with a healthy heart; even when her parents and two older sisters had "inherited" cardiovascular disease.
9. Garlic is a natural chest pain antidote.
10. Philip K. used garlic to soothe his angina pain.
11. Oat bran is a spongelike cleanser of fat and cholesterol.
12. Capsicum, a hot pepper, may help to prevent a blood clot.

6

Allergic? Breathe Easier with Therapeutic Foods

Wheezing, sneezing, coughing, choking. These are the symptoms of an allergic attack. At work, at play, or in the middle of the night, the onset of such an attack can make you feel as if you're going to pass out. Until the frightening episode passes and you can breathe easier again, you feel that you have had a narrow escape. After all, life begins with breath; take away oxygen and you take away life! During an allergic attack, you have the terrifying fear that your breath of life will expire.

Allergy: What Is It? Why Does It Happen?

An allergy is an unhealthy reaction to substances normally harmless. These may be taken into your body by being inhaled, by being swallowed, or by contact with the skin. Such sensitizing substances are called *allergens.* Common allergens include pollens, molds, house dust; animal danders (skin shed by dogs, cats, horses, rabbits); feathers (as in feather pillows); kapok, wool, dyes, chemicals used in industry; pollution; and medicines and insect stings, to name the most common.

How Allergen Triggers Attack

When the allergen is absorbed into your bloodstream, it stimulates certain small white blood cells (lymphocytes) to produce special substances known as allergic antibodies. These allergic antibodies react with the allergen and produce allergic inflammation and irritation in particularly sensitive areas of the body—the nose, eyes, lungs, digestive system.

This sensitivity may not be present at first contact with the allergen; it may develop after repeated exposure. *Example:* A new cat may not cause allergy until it has been living in a household for many months, and then the susceptible person becomes sensitized and develops a stuffy nose and sneezing or wheezing on further contact with the cat.

"Why Me? Why Does It Happen?"

This is asked when you find yourself allergic to substances that may not affect others in your midst. One answer is that your respiratory system may be malnourished so that offending substances are able to penetrate your bronchial breathing apparatus to cause distress. Your protective barrier has become fragile, your bronchial cells are easily invaded by irritants to cause the allergic reaction. The problem is compounded when antibodies attach themselves to certain cells—called mast cells—in the nasopharynx, lungs, lining of the body cavity, or the skin. When these mast cells become saturated with antibody complexes, a reaction takes place.

Histamine Is Released. This is a natural body substance that tells you an allergy attack is on the way. Histamine dilates your blood vessels, slows circulation, and lowers blood pressure; it causes runny eyes and nose, bronchial asthma, and headaches from dilation of blood vessels in the brain. Your levels of immunity have been reduced because of the bronchial fragility and the outpouring of an excess amount of histamine.

To help strengthen resistance to this sensitivity, certain foods and nutrition programs can act as "natural medicines" to rebuild your breathing apparatus and act as a fortress against allergic reactions.

How Beta-carotene Helps You to Win Battle Against Allergies

Beta-carotene is the predecessor of vitamin A, found in everyday fruits and vegetables. This preformed vitamin A is taken by your digestive system and is metabolized so that the retinols or molecules are transported to your bronchial tissues to strengthen and fortify the cells and tissues. Beta-carotene dispatches molecules to the critical points of your breathing segments, nourishing the walls and rebuilding the collagen, so that offending allergens are not able to penetrate easily. In effect, it is beta-carotene that will help give you immunity to allergies.

Beta-carotene Food Sources

Red, yellow, and dark green vegetables such as carrots, deep yellow squash, dark salad greens, sweet potato, broccoli are fine sources. Good fruit sources are the apricot, cantaloupe, peach, nectarine, and mango.

By boosting intake of these beta-carotene foods, you will be strengthening the mucous membranes of your respiratory system, building an inner fortress against the invasion of allergens; the same beta-carotene also buffers the outpouring of histamine which helps to ease and erase many of the symptomatic reactions of an allergy attack. In effect, beta-carotene is a form of natural therapy against allergies.

OVERCOMES "HEREDITY ALLERGY" IN THREE WEEKS WITH BETA-CAROTENE AS NUTRITIONAL THERAPY

The slightest dust would provoke a wheezing-choking attack in Walter G. until he would feel the breath of life being squeezed out of his chest. When the attack was over, he needed a half hour to recover and gasp precious air to replenish the lost supply. He was resigned to lifelong allergies because it "ran in the family." Because medications made him drowsy, caused headachelike side effects, as well as mental sluggishness, Walter G. decided to try an alternative treatment as suggested by a local nutritionist.

Walter G. was told to boost intake of beta-carotene foods. He switched to freshly prepared vegetable salads including greens, broccoli, yellow squash, and carrots. Desserts were always beta-carotene fruits such as cantaloupe, peaches, apricots.

Within ten days, he noticed he was becoming more resistant to offending dust or pollutants. By the fifteenth day, the beta-carotene program had so strengthened his breathing system so that he scarcely had an allergic attack when they were as common as twice a day, sometimes more. By the twenty-first day, Walter G. was completely free of allergic reactions. His medical nutritionist explained that the beta-carotene had rebuilt his fragile bronchial system so that offenders could not easily penetrate the tissues to cause distress.

Heredity? His nutritionist explained that allergies do run in the family but they can be controlled and corrected with therapy. Walter G. is now free of allergies, despite the heredity "theory," thanks to beta-carotene, which he calls his "natural allergy medicine."

Bioflavonoids Will Ease and Even Erase Allergic Episodes

Lesser known, but dynamically effective as an allergy fighter, are the family of substances known as bioflavonoids. These are natural ingredients found in specific foods, especially in the weblike inner netting of citrus fruits. Bioflavonoids are valuable in strengthening the permeability of capillaries so they resist invasion of irritating allergens. For many victims of allergies, bioflavonoids may well be the most powerful nutritional therapies needed to help ease and erase attacks.

Corrects Weakness, Strengthens Barriers

Bioflavonoids have the unique ability to increase capillary strength, regulate their permeability. There are millions of miles of tiny blood vessels, capillaries, that connect the arteries and veins in the tissues. Bioflavonoids work with vitamin C in keeping collagen, the intercellular cement in a healthy condition by correcting weaknesses and strengthening resistant barriers.

Bioflavonoids prevent breakage, so-called hemorrhages or ruptures in the capillaries and connective tissues, which might otherwise admit viral and bacterial infections. By correcting the disturbances in capillary permeability, by restoring strength and stability in the cells of the bronchial and entire respiratory tract, bioflavonoids become an effective therapy in the correction and prevention of allergic reactions.

How to Eat Your Way to Allergic Healing

Bioflavonoids are found in green peppers, citrus fruits, grapes, rose hips, apricots, black currants, acerola cherries, apricots, and strawberries. *Caution:* Because these allergy-fighting nutrients are water-soluble and heat-sensitive, these foods must be eaten *raw.* The bioflavonoids are largely destroyed by cooking or preserving.

Simple Nutritional Therapy Program

Keep a variety of the bioflavonoid foods in your refrigerator. Daily, especially in the morning when allergic resistance is low, have a platter of these various fruits. *Benefit:* Within moments, the bioflavonoids will exert prophylactic and therapeutic properties to boost the intercellular network of your breathing system so that offenders are resisted or "defused" to have much less distress.

Eat the Whole Fruit

Because bioflavonoids are so richly concentrated in the white pulp of the fruits and in the sheaths separating the sections in citrus, the whole fruit is your most potent source of a nutritional therapy. *Juices?* They are quick acting because they are concentrated, but when you squeeze the fruit, you leave most of the bioflavonoids in the peels. *Balance:* Emphasize whole fruits in the morning. Drink a glass of juice in the afternoon. Have a whole fruit in the evening to help build respiratory resistance so you are less likely to have a night attack. It is this balance that should form your basic nutritional therapy program against allergies.

FRUITS ARE MY ALLERGY MEDICINE

Antihistamines made Dorothy W. so dizzy she could hardly concentrate on her driving, let-alone exacting work at her video display terminal in the large corporation where she was employed. Yet she always insisted she was "hooked" on her drugs because without them, she would continuously erupt into choking spasms and hacking coughs without any advance warning. Her health and her job were both threatened. How could she free herself from the slavery of the medicines along with allergies?

The company nurse, also a dietician, suggested she try boosting bioflavonoid intake to build resistance from within. She provided a list of the proper fruits and recommended ample amounts on a daily basis. Dorothy W. felt she "had nothing to lose but the allergies," so she started enjoying the raw fruits.

Within six days, she felt better able to breathe. What triggered the choking attacks was less frequently pulled. Taking less medication, Dorothy W. still had fewer allergic reactions. By the end of the second week, she was able to do without her drugs and experience almost no symptoms. But when she discontinued the tasty bioflavonoid-rich fruits, she had itching, runny nose, constant sneezing, and coughing. Now she knew that the bioflavonoids were working. She eventually made a healthy changeover and took just the fruits as natural therapies. She could boast to family and coworkers that the fruits were her allergy medicines. They helped her become free of breathing disorders.

Garlic—The Quick-Acting Allergy Healer

A "wonder food" that has been found to possess nutritional and medicinal properties, garlic is a quick-acting allergy healer.

Garlic is known as being an antitoxin; that is, it defends and strengthens the body against allergens. It neutralizes toxins present in the system and "knocks out" their irritating threats to protect against respiratory attacks.

Garlic is a prime source of *allicin,* a substance that boosts the antibacterial and antiinflammatory reactions that help to improve your resistance against offending substances.

Natural Antibiotic

Garlic also contains *aliin,* a sulfur-rich amino acid from which *allicin* is made via the action of the enzyme *alliinase.* This creates a natural antibiotic effect to help neutralize and "weaken" the offender and prepare it for elimination.

Nutritional Therapy Power of Garlic

Garlic prevents allergic reactions because it stabilizes the nasal mast cells, thereby preventing the release of histamine and other symptom-producing substances into respiratory tract tissues. It has other nutritionally therapeutic advantages as well in that it has neither stimulative or sedative side effects. Garlic has traditionally been recognized as the natural therapeutic food to combat and heal allergic problems.

How to Breathe Easier with Garlic Decongestant

If you are seeking an alternative to drugs, prepare this breath-restoring garlic decongestant:

Allergy-Ease Tonic

Into 2 cups of freshly boiled water, add 3 crushed garlic cloves and 1 teaspoon grated ginger root. Cover pot with a tight lid and let simmer about 2 more minutes. Remove frcm heat and place on heat-resistant and nonburning surface. Lift pot lid. Deeply inhale the steam for about 3 minutes. *Benefits:* The allicin substance in the garlic will combine with the pungent odor of the ginger root to help open up blocked respiratory channels. Within moments, the garlic will create a decongestant reaction so that you can breathe easier and better.

You can also fill a mug with the same brew. Add a squeeze of lemon or lime. A teaspoon of honey is optional. Sip while comfortably hot. This tangy Allergy-Ease Tonic will be a natural therapy that acts as a potent decongestant.

Concerned over allergic distress while away from home? Just fill a thermos with the Allergy-Ease Tonic and take along with you. Makes a refreshing "break" that helps you to relax and also strengthen resistance to allergic unrest.

The Vitamin That Helps to Free You from Allergies

Any number of medications contain varying amounts of one particular nutrient—vitamin C. Science has long known that this nutrient has a powerful therapeutic effect in building inner resistance against allergens.

Rebuilds Respiratory Tract

Vitamin C performs or assists in the formation and maintenance of capillary walls, aids in cementing body cells together and in strengthening the walls of blood vessels, and guards against allergic infection by stimulating formation of white blood cells to counteract their potential harm. Vitamin C is needed to form new tissue and regenerate existing tissue throughout the body, especially in the respiratory tract and breathing apparatus. This vitamin is able to control the spread of viral infections. By inhibiting viral spread, the allergic reaction is kept under control, and you can breathe easier and better.

Nutritional Therapy Sources of Vitamin C

The best sources are all citrus fruits. Additional sources include tomatoes, cabbage, raw leafy vegetables, strawberries, and melons. *Preserving vitamin C:* Water-soluble, it is easily destroyed by heat and exposure to air. If you must cook, use small amounts of water. Vegetables should not be cut into small pieces until ready for cooking because the more surface exposed to air, the greater is the destruction of vitamin C.

How to Use

Daily, boost your intake of citrus fruits, and use vegetables as part of a salad. Vitamin C is available as a supplement, and in reported studies, about 2,500 milligrams a day has been found effective in bringing allergies under control.

Control, Correct, Cast Out Allergies with "Breathe-Again Remedy"

For quick relief, try this "Breathe-Again Remedy" that goes to work so fast, you may very well say "goodbye" to your allergies almost at once.

How to Prepare

Combine the juice of 1 lemon, 1 minced garlic clove, ⅛ teaspoon of cayenne pepper, and 1,000 milligrams of vitamin C. (Crush a tablet.) Just sip slowly whenever you feel an allergic attack on the approach.

Benefits of "Breathe-Again Remedy"

The vitamin C and bioflavonoid of the lemon combine with the germicidal ingredients of the garlic clove, become activated by the concentrated vitamin C, and are amplified with the cayenne pepper. In moments, the toxins and allergens are "knocked out" and eliminated. You can breathe again. (If the remedy is a bit too potent, feel free to cut it by adding a little water or any desired herbal or caffeine-free tea.)

Within moments, you should be able to breathe easily. Over a short period of time, these nutrients help restructure your bronchial system, creating a form of inner immunity against allergens, and you should be able to cast out your disorder and breathe freely again.

Garlic Milk Frees You from Allergies

A tasty nutritional therapy that is prepared in minutes offers fast relief from breathing problems. But this therapy has another refreshing benefit. It offers hope for healing of your allergies so that you will be able to free yourself from such distress. It is simple garlic milk.

How to Prepare

Heat 1 cup of milk until very hot. Add 1 teaspoon of vegetable oil, 1 tablespoon of honey, 1 teaspoon of grated fresh garlic. Stir thoroughly until as well mixed as possible. Let it become comfortably warm.

When to Drink

About 2 hours before retiring, sip this garlic milk slowly. Spoon out any garlic bits and chew them before swallowing. You will experience an immediate opening of airwaves and unblocking of bronchial tubes. You will breathe so well, you should be able to enjoy a good night's sleep.

Benefits of Garlic Milk

The calcium has a soothing reaction; this is the relaxant that helps to ease muscular congestion in your chest. The calcium combined with the natural carbohydrates of the honey is made more palatable by the oil; joining with the antibacterial ingredients of the garlic, you have a combination that actually washes away bronchial irritants. The garlic milk will work almost at once. It is especially desirable as a nigthcap because it induces restful sleep and works to keep your bronchial tubes open so you breathe healthfully and are not upset by a sudden coughing spell. You wake up feeling free of allergies.

NUTRITION HEALS ALLERGIES OVERNIGHT

Larry V. was troubled with recurring respiratory attacks and asthmatic difficulties. Worse, they kept awakening him repeatedly throughout the night which weakened his overall condition. Medications so drugged him that he felt the aftereffects for half of the next day. He feared having a lifelong allergy problem. His allergy specialist noted his side effects to drugs, so suggested he try the garlic milk that had been recommended by a local nutritionist. Larry W. prepared the natural remedy and took a glass every night for six nights. By the seventh night, he was able to sleep peacefully without any allergic attack. By the end of the third week, he was so free of distress, he no longer needed medication and felt that the breath of life was restored, thanks to the garlic milk.

The Everyday Food That Opens up Clogged Airways

An old-world tangy condiment has emerged as more than a modern taste perk for most main dishes and salads. It helps to send streams of welcome air throughout the nasopharynx-respiratory network, and you free yourself from that choking-sputtering-breathless torment of allergies.

What Is It?

Ordinary horseradish! Prepared from radish roots, spiced with vinegar, it is so pungent, all you need is about ¼ or (at the most) a ½ teaspoon atop a cracker or a celery stalk. That's all! Just chew thoroughly and swallow. In minutes, perhaps seconds, the volatile spices of the horseradish will send streams of refreshing oxygen throughout your entire airways. You'll enjoy huge gulpings of fresh air. You will be able to say goodbye to your allergies, thanks to the power of horseradish in being able to unclog, open up the choked airways.

Sniff or Eat for Instant Relief

If ever you feel a choking attack, reach for a little bottle of horseradish and take a whiff. In seconds, you breathe better. Otherwise, just dab ¼ teaspoon on a small cracker and eat. Again, within seconds, you have refreshing relief. *Suggestion:* Carry a small bottle with you for use in emergencies or when you are not at home. Horseradish is available in ready-to-carry bottles at almost any food store or supermarket.

How to Drink Away Your Allergies

One magic mineral has been found to be of tremendous value in helping to correct the cause of your allergies, namely, your sensitivity to outside substances. It is *potassium.* It is found in a richly concentrated amount in *apple cider vinegar.* Made from whole compressed apples, properly fermented, this product is a powerhouse of potassium.

This mineral is needed to help maintain the electrical and chemical balance between your tissue cells and your blood. Potassium directs a normal flow of nerve signals and muscle contractions. It also promotes energy release to protect you against a sluggish feeling caused by clogged cells and tissues.

How to Use

Just stir in 2 tablespoons of apple cider vinegar in a glass of water or vegetable juice. Add a bit of lemon juice, if desired, for a tangier taste. Stir vigorously. Sip slowly. In minutes, the concentrated potassium helps to correct the respiratory imbalance and detoxify your bronchial tubes so you have better resistance against allergens.

A Glass a Day Keeps an Allergic Attack Away

To strengthen your forces of immunity against allergy attacks, plan to drink just one glass of this vinegar tonic each day. Over a brief period of time, the mineral content will repair your bronchial cells and help to provide better breathing transportation and, it is hoped, freedom from allergies.

Avoid These Foods and Avoid Allergic Outbreaks

Certain foods are antagonistic to your respiratory system and would be best avoided. These include caffeine in any form, refined sugar, salt, and refined carbohydrates that tend to clog your bronchial and breathing networks. *Careful:* Avoid foods or beverages that are either too hot or too cold. Temperature extremes can also trigger allergic outbreaks. Strike the happy medium and you should have a happy breathing system.

Checklist of Possible Allergic Triggers

These offenders should be avoided to help build resistance to allergies: vapors from cleaning solvents, paint, paint thinner, liquid chlorine bleach; sprays from furniture polish, starch, cleaners, room deodorizers; spray deodorants, perfumes; hair sprays, talcum powder, scented cosmetics; cloth upholstered furniture, carpets, draperies that gather dust; brooms and dusters that raise dust; dirty filters on hot air furnaces and air conditioners that put dust into the air.

Avoid blasts of cold air, excessive humidity, smoke-filled rooms, overexertion, and emotional upset.

Give your total body a chance to build resistance to allergies and with the use of nutritional therapy, you may very well be able to breathe mountain-fresh air, no matter where you are—free of distress.

HIGHLIGHTS

1. Allergies often develop because of a bronchial weakness that can be corrected with nutritional therapy.
2. Beta-carotene containing foods rebuild fragile cells to create inner immunity against allergen invaders.
3. Walter G. overcame "heredity allergy" in three weeks on a simple beta-carotene food program. He was able to quit drugs in favor of nutritional therapy.

4. Soothe and relax allergic episodes with bioflavonoids that correct capillary weakness and strengthen barriers against irritants. Everyday fruits and vegetables offer this allergic fortress.
5. Dorothy W. avoided antihistamines and the dizziness that accompanied their ingestion. She switched to fruits that became her allergy medicines. They did more than ease distress. They cured her allergies.
6. Garlic is a natural antibacterial and anti-inflammatory food that helps heal allergies almost at once.
7. The Allergy-Ease Tonic frees you from distress, no matter where you are.
8. Vitamin C rebuilds your respiratory tract to block allergic attacks.
9. The Breathe Again Remedy works instantly in knocking out allergens.
10. Larry V. corrected allergies overnight with garlic milk.
11. Horseradish is an old-world remedy to help you breathe better.
12. Potassium is a powerhouse of allergy relief. Try the beverage described today and breathe better tomorrow. Or earlier!

7

Foods That Soothe Stress...in Minutes

Stress has been dubbed the malady of our modern times. It is surely taking its toll when we note that one out of every two visits to family doctors is prompted by stress-related symptoms. Based on national surveys, business costs of stress are estimated at close to $75 billion a year because of absenteeism, company medical expenses, and lost productivity, or over $750 for very worker.

Stress is known to be a major contributor, either directly or indirectly, to coronary heart disease, cancer, lung ailments, accidental injuries, cirrhosis of the liver, and suicide—six of the leading causes of death in the United States.

Stress also plays a role in aggravating such diverse conditions as diabetes, herpes, multiple sclerosis, allergies, and cardiovascular disorders, to name a few. It is a worrisome sign of the times that the three bestselling drugs in the country are an ulcer medication, a hypertension drug, and a tranquilizer.

Are You a Victim of the Stress Epidemic?

When you allow your body to get all revved up, but have no release for the stress, you could become victim of the "fight-or-flight" response. You bottle up your emotions and may not be able to adopt either of those reactions. Here is a checklist of symptoms that could indicate you are becoming a victim of stress overload:

Recurring headaches, dry mouth, overeating/undereating, chain smoking, indigestion, ulcers, stomach knots, butterflies in stomach, alcoholism/drug dependence, ready tears, hyperactivity/listlessness, leg wagging, proneness to errors, decreased productivity, clammy hands, fatigue/weariness, muscle spasms/tightness, talking too much too fast, stomach cramps, diarrhea/constipation, nervous cough, feeling "faint" and an attitude of being impatient under all circumstances. Did you answer "yes" to more than one? You're stressed.

Adapt to Stress and Live Healthier

Daily life calls for being able to adapt to the positive and the negative situations or changes around you. Whether it is fighting or running from physical dangers, losing something or someone of value, facing deadliness, meeting challenges throughout the day, waiting on a very long line, or being given some bad news, you have to adapt. Your degree of health and happiness, in large part, depends upon how successful you are in this adaptation.

How Nutritional Therapy Helps Keep You Cool, Calm, Collected

The sense of panic, however mild, primes your muscles, whips up your glands, accelerates your digestive system, and causes an outpouring of adrenaline among other hormones, as well as a nutritional upheaval. To help soothe your frazzled nerves, certain foods as well as minerals are able to help take the edge off your tension centers.

The Mineral That Works as a Natural Tranquilizer: Magnesium

When faced with stressful situations, reach for magnesium, and within moments, you should feel the balm of tranquility pour over your frazzled nerves. This oft-neglected mineral has the ability to strengthen your inner reserves against stress to shield you from the grating thrust of irritating situations and circumstances.

Magnesium Is Soothing

This mineral is needed to help regulate your heartbeat, soothe your muscular system to protect against spasm, lift your moods, and protect against feelings of depression and irritability. Magnesium is highly concentrated in your red blood cells where it serves to act as a stress shield to help keep you calm in the face of problems.

Boost Magnesium—Boost Calmness

In times of stress, magnesium tends to be leached out of your cells, shunted out of your body via eliminative channels. Magnesium depletion can make you dangerously stressful. To protect against this risk, boost your intake of magnesium so it is available to your red blood cells to help keep you cool, calm, and collected when facing daily challenges. Magnesium will also protect against the potentially dangerous condition of arrhythmia or irregular heartbeat. It works as a natural tranquilizer. And it's drugless!

Recommended Dietary Allowance

The RDA calls for 300 milligrams daily for nonpregnant women, 450 milligrams daily for pregnant women, and 350 milligrams daily for men. (Although dosages slightly above are considered safe, medical supervision is recommended when this limit is exceeded.) Are you getting enough? Minimal stress, whether some loud talking or a sudden noise, will cause a leaking out of your magnesium stores. A deficiency makes you tense. You become nervous. You need to replace the loss without delay to avoid the health risks of prolonged stress.

Quick Relief for Stress

Reach for some magnesium, instead of a tranquilizer. You will be using a safe, simple and speedily effective nutritional therapy to soothe your stress, in minutes.

Chew Nuts and Release Stress Within 10 Minutes

A handful of nuts can act as a natural antidote to stress. Whenever you feel stressed, take a handful of shelled nuts and chew thoroughly. (Avoid salted or roasted nuts, which are irritating and also disturbing to the nervous and cardiovascular systems.) Within a few moments, the richly concentrated source of magnesium will go to work in soothing the hyperirritability of your nerves and muscles, strengthen your muscles, stabilize your heartbeat, and make you feel calm and more relaxed.

Magnesium in Nuts

Putting it simply: 60 small peanuts gives you about 210 milligrams of magnesium. Or 40 cashew nuts gives you about 200 milligrams of magnesium. These nuts are powerhouses of highly concentrated magnesium, the "natural tranquilizer" that acts as a speedy antidote to stress. You can chew your way to relaxation in 10 minutes, the approximate time required for the magnesium to begin its balmlike coating of your nerves from the time you began chewing the nuts. The chewing activity, itself, helps you to feel more relaxed as you "work off" tension.

COOLS OFF BURNOUT, MELTS ANXIETY, SOOTHES NERVES WITH MAGNESIUM

Industrial designer Michael C. was faced with endless deadlines. He loved his work but last-minute changes, increasing conferences, dealing with endless people made him feel he had too much of a good thing. He was exhausted by noontime. He would even lose his temper and say things he later regretted. An orthomolecular physician who specialized in correcting specific molecules in the brain to provide a more healthful emotional environment recommended that he build resistance to stress with a boost of magnesium.

Michael C. was told to take a recommended 250 milligrams of magnesium each morning. At the same time, he was told to carry a small supply of salt-free, shelled, and unroasted peanuts and/or cashews. "Chew them as a snack throughout the day," was the medical directive. "You should feel less anxious and more relaxed in minutes," was the benefit described by the physician.

From the start, Michael C. felt his tensions evaporating. He looked forward to his work schedule, even overtime. He smiled more frequently. He had fewer nervous reactions. He became more tolerant. The magnesium worked in minutes to replenish the losses that were caused by stress responses from his work. He calls the magnesium, his "natural tranquilizer."

The Food That Works as a Natural Sedative: Tryptophan

A little-known amino acid or protein derivative is able to help melt stress and act as a natural sedative to give your body and mind a feeling of total relaxation. That amino acid is *tryptophan,* and it is found in rich concentrations in *milk.*

How Tryptophan Washes Away Daily Cares

This amino acid is taken up by your brain to then stimulate the release of a soothing tranquilizer known as *serotonin.* It is this substance that tends to coat your neurotransmitters, that is, the chemical messengers that carry signals from one nerve cell to the next and control all emotions, perceptions, and bodily functions. These neurotransmitters are responsible for just about everything you do and feel. Under stress, they respond by making you more sensitive and alert so you can effectively respond to the situation. They also make you so tense and high strung, you become stressful. It is serotonin that acts as a protector by controlling the vigor of these neurotransmitters. Serotonin envelops these messengers, keeps them in check, and corrals them to protect against runaway impulses.

It is tryptophan that initiates the manufacture of serotonin to then help wash away your daily cares by keeping you calm and more relaxed. Yes, you still do face daily stresses, but tryptophan via serotonin has made you more resistant so that you meet the challenges with strength and emotional tranquility. This amino acid is a natural antidepressant! It makes you feel glad all over!

FEELS GOOD IN BODY AND MIND WITH STRESS-MELTING TRYPTOPHAN

The slightest upset made Jennifer Z. fly into a rage. The 42-year-old mother of three children felt she could no longer cope with everyday chores, some as simple as having to wait on a short line at the local market. Jennifer Z. could feel herself heading for a nervous breakdown.

Taking tranquilizers resulted in side effects, not to mention erratic behavior and the fear of becoming an addict, so she had to stop this health and life risk. Desperate, she sought help from a neurologist who suggested she boost her blood levels of tryptophan to provoke production of serotonin to act as a natural tranquilizer. How? She was told to drink two glasses of warm milk every day. Skim milk was recommended to control calorie-fat intake. If she still felt raw nerves, increase to three glasses of warm milk throughout the day.

Jennifer Z. was willing to do anything to get herself back in the mainstream of daily living. Within two days, she no longer flew off the handle. By the fourth day, she was laughing even on a long line at the market or when faced with many bundles of laundry or a sink full of dishes. The reason is that the tryptophan of the milk sent forth a soothing supply of tranquilzing serotonin to make the formerly stress-struck housewife now feel happy and relaxed. She explains to others that when she sips the milk, it is her "sedative." The milk with its tryptophan-serotonin became her natural therapy.

Food Sources of Natural Sedatives

While 1 glass of milk contains about 100 milligrams of tryptophan, you can use other sources for your natural sedative: cheddar cheese—316 milligrams per 3½ ounces; oatmeal—183 milligrams per 3½ ounces; spaghetti—150 milligrams per 3½ ounces; codfish—164 milligrams per 3½ ounces; shredded wheat—136 milligrams per 3½ ounces. *Suggestion:* Include these foods in your daily eating program and feel yourself relax in the face of stress. You will help avoid anxiety, replacing exhaustion with ambition and feeling better in a matter of minutes. These foods are nutritional therapies that act as natural sedatives.

Relax Yourself with the Antistress Vitamin: Pantothenate

Any type of stress, from a traffic jam to jam spilled on your shirt, will cause an outpouring of adrenaline from your adrenal glands sitting astride the surface of your kidneys. It can also drain out your nerves to make you a victim of stress.

Stress will cause a decrease in some of the white blood cells that protect your body against infection. Constant wear and tear will also cause a spillage of a valuable vitamin along with the adrenaline, namely, *pantothenate.*

Its name is taken from the Greek word *pantothen,* meaning "from all sides," and it does live up to its name. This vitamin is able to control the biochemical processes to ensure protection against loss of those substances that you need to resist stress.

How Pantothenate Can Help You Let Go and Live Longer

This antistress vitamin is present and important to every cell of your body. It is intimately involved in stress because it is absolutely required to the smooth functioning of your adrenal glands. If there is a deficiency of pantothenate, your adrenal glands are unable to fulfill their needed "fight-or-flight" response. Your glands go "on strike," refuse to produce needed hormones. Now you are in stressful trouble. *Reason:* without adrenaline and other important hormones, you cannot operate on all cylinders and are especially sensitive to any situation that causes stress. You react with this supersensitivity and can fly off the handle at the slightest provocation. This is typical if you are deficient in this antistress vitamin that can protect you "from all sides."

Sources of Antistress Vitamin

Whole grain products, including brown rice, wheat germ, peanuts, and rice bran, are excellent sources of pantothenate. Also include soybeans, salmon, and peanuts. *Emphasize fresh foods.* In refining products, pantothenate is reduced or even removed, so your antistress plan should concentrate on utilizing fresh whole grains or other products that have not been subjected to much processing. (In canning, about 35 percent may be lost.)

With pantothenate on a daily basis, you can help keep yourself insulated from stressful situations and react with a smile on your face and in your thoughts.

Super Source of Pantothenate

It's richly concentrated in brewer's yeast, a grain product that is a top source of almost all the important B-complex vitamins. In particular, just 1 tablespoon gives you about 1 milligram. An average of 4 milligrams daily is recommended for most folks. But to cope with stress, a higher amount may be needed to keep your adrenals in top hormone-producing shape. Brewer's or nutritional yeast is available at most health stores and many supermarkets. Use it sprinkled over salads or blenderized in a vegetable juice and feel your mood lift, your attitudes adjusting, your happiness on the increase.

FROM SUICIDE TO SERENITY IN 12 DAYS

Stella N. could no longer cope with daily tasks. She had such wide mood swings, she started to take tranquilizers. When their effect wore off, she took stronger doses. She felt so tense, she would cry for no apparent reason, lose her temper, become overanxious. Insomnia was a problem. Shouting rages made her a terror to live with. There was talk of having her confined in an institution because of these violent outbreaks and mood changes that were feared to cause self-destruction.

Her sister, a registered nurse, took action, recognized the side effects caused by ingesting tranquilizers, and boosted Stella N.'s intake of pantothenate. In particular, she saw that Stella N. would take close to 2 tablespoons of brewer's yeast in a glass or two of vegetable juice, every single day.

Immediately, the shouting outbursts subsided. She looked more relaxed. Stella N. was calmer, slept better, was more rational to live with. By the tenth day, she felt "back from the dead" as the pantothenate restored her mental stability. By the twelfth day, the jitters and stressful reactions were gone. Now, she could enjoy her busy daily life with a bright attitude. Suicide? It was part of her past she preferred to forget. She was the picture of serenity, thanks to the daily intake of pantothenate, the antistress vitamin.

Antistress Vitamin Tonic

In a glass of vegetable juice, add 1 tablespoon of brewer's yeast and squeeze of lemon juice, if desired. Blenderize or stir vigorously. Then sip slowly. Within moments, the rich concentrate of nerve-soothing B-complex vitamins and the very ample supply of pantothenate will befriend your adrenals, nudging them to release needed hormones to help you deal better with stresses, either physical or mental.

Daily Antistress Foods

Top sources of pantothenate include beef liver, chicken liver, raw broccoli, turkey (dark meat), peanuts, dried peas, chicken (dark meat), mushrooms, cashews, brown rice, and dark whole grain flours. *Suggestion:* Include lots of whole, uprocessed foods in your daily eating plan. A bowl of oatmeal sprinkled with a ¼ teaspoon brewer's yeast and wheat germ is a great antistress buffer.

If the stress in your life is getting you down, it's time you upped your intake of pantothenate, the antistress vitamin!

How Calcium Keeps You Calm

Feel uptight? Troubled with anxiety attacks? Something eating at your nerves? The reason could be a deficiency of calcium, the mineral that has been considered better than psychotherapy insofar as stress healing is concerned. This mineral is able to soothe your irritations, to give you an anxiety-free outlook so you can be friendly with your nerves.

The Nutritional Therapy of Calcium for Stress

Studies have shown that an excess of lactate (or lactic acid) in body chemistry is responsible for much anxiety, nervousness, irritability, fear, and tension. Calcium is able to neutralize the nerve-irritating lactate. Calcium enters into a chemical association with lactate, transforming it into calcium lactate and reducing its capacity to produce anxiety reactions.

Nutritionally, calcium ions reside at the ends of nerve cells (synapses) and maintain electrical connections and communication between nerve cells. In a healthy nervous system, calcium combines with lactic acid around the sensitive nerve endings, preventing the acid from irritating the nervous system. But if too much lactic acid is in your system, or you are deficient in calcium to perform a neutralizing role, the result is stress, tension, and anxiety.

How to Use Calcium to Defuse Lactic Acid and Keep Calm

Milk is a good and easily absorbed source of calcium. A glass or two will give an appreciable supply to help keep lactic acid from inducing stress. Other sources would include 1 ounce of Gruyère cheese for 300 milligrams, 1 ounce of cheddar cheese for 211 milligrams, or 1 cup of tofu (soybean curd) for about 300 milligrams. Your goal would be at least 1,000 milligrams daily so it is rather easy to get enough of this stress-easing mineral. *Tip:* instead of a coffee break, have a milk or cheese break with a fresh fruit (1 small orange has about 40–50 milligrams, plus vitamin C, which helps to speed up calcium assimilation), and you should feel cheered up in moments.

Simple Eating Tips for Healthier Nerves

Eliminate the use of salt, sugar, hard fats, chemically processed foods, refined carbohydrates, caffeine, synthetic foods. Maintain a regular eating schedule. Eat in a calm atmosphere. Emphasize the antistress foods and nutrients described here and help yourself say goodbye to stress and hello to a refreshingly happy daily mood.

Happiness, it is said, is like a butterfly. The more you chase it, the more it will elude you. But turn your attention to other things and it comes and softly sits on your shoulder. Do not chase happiness with tranquilizers or mood-changing chemicals. Instead, turn your attention to nutritional therapy, and before you know it, you will sense the butterfly of happiness sitting softly on your shoulder.

MAIN POINTS

1. Stress need not be painful given the existence of myriad foods and nutrients that help to keep you calm and relaxed in the midst of turmoil.
2. Try magnesium, the mineral that works as a natural tranquilizer.
3. Chew nuts and release stress within 10 minutes via magnesium intake.
4. Michael C. cooled burnout, melted anxiety, and soothed his nerves with magnesium within a short time.
5. Jennifer Z. used tryptophan to melt stress and gave up her tranquilizer drugs forever.
6. Relax with pantothenate, the antistress vitamin.
7. Stella N. was saved from suicide and given serenity in 12 days with pantothenate as found in brewer's yeast.
8. The Anti-Stress Vitamin Tonic helps you become calm in minutes.
9. Calcium is the "keep calm" mineral that corrects the root cause of stress, the natural way.

8

Osteoporosis: How Nutritional Therapy Can Protect You from This Bone Robber

One out of every four women reading this book faces the threat of osteoporosis. This "silent killer" is on the increase. Osteoporosis is silent because the clinical features are not detected until the woman is in her fifties or sixties, and even then it may show only minimal signs to warn the victim of the "creeping disease" that could be fatal.

What Is Osteoporosis?

It is an age-related disorder characterized by decreased bone mass and by dangerous increased susceptibility to fractures, in the absence of other recognizable cause of bone loss.

Osteoporosis is a condition affecting as many as 20 million individuals in the United States. Approximately 1.3 million fractures attributable to osteoporosis occur annually in people aged 45 and older. Among those people who live to be age 90, about 33 percent of women and about 17 percent of men will suffer a hip fracture, most of these due to osteoporosis. The cost of osteoporosis in the United States has been estimated at $3.8 billion annually.

Any Early Clinical Features? How Is Killer Detected?

An early sign of osteoporosis is loss of height; this occurs when weakened bones of the spine (vertebrae) become compressed. Later, as the vertebrae fracture and collapse, a curving of the spine (often called "dowager's hump) may occur.

Caution: Osteoporosis, however, usually goes unrecognized until the spine becomes noticeably curved or until a hip, wrist, or other bone breaks. *Danger:* A minor fall can result in a broken bone, or a hip bone may fracture causing the fall. Normally there is no pain until a fracture occurs. Vertebrae sometimes fracture during routine activities such as bending, lifting, or rising from a chair or bed.

Hip Fractures, Male and Female Victims

Hip fractures are an important manifestation of osteoporosis. The affected population tends to be older and the sex distribution more even than in the case of vertebral fractures. Acute complications—hospitalization, depression, and mechanical failure of the surgical procedure—are common. *Most patients fail to recover normal activity. The mortality rate within one year approaches 20 percent.*

Why Are the Bones Eaten Away?

Bones maintain themselves throughout life by a process known as remodeling, in which small amounts of old bones are removed and new bone is formed in its place. *Problem:* Beginning at about age 35, however, a little more bone is lost than is gained. (Bone density reaches its peak around age 35.) Bone mass decreases most rapidly in the three to seven years following menopause.

The Female Hormone Connection

After age 35, there is a slowing down in the production of *estrogen,* the female hormone. It is believed that this hormone is needed to help the body absorb calcium, a mineral that nourishes the trabecular bone which makes up the central core of bone tissue. As estrogen diminishes and comes to a halt after the menopause has been completed, there is a serious reduction in the body's ability to nourish the bones with average amounts of calcium. Osteoporosis, or fragile, brittle, and thinning bones, starts to take place.

Is Estrogen So Important?

Absolutely! Estrogen appears to aid the body in using calcium to firm new bone tissue. Theoretically, when estrogen is lost as during the postmenopausal stage of life, bone becomes more sensitive to a hormone called PTH (parathyroid hormone), which is a major stimulator of bone destruction. PTH affects the passage of calcium through the body's system. It would appear simple to replace estrogen with a synthetic hormone pill, but some research cautions that this presents a danger of inducing cancer. Since less calcium is absorbed with diminishing estrogen, the sensible solution would be to boost intake of calcium to make up the deficiency. This can be effective, even without estrogen.

Bones, Formation, Mineral Needs

Bone is made up of calcium and phosphorus crystals, imbedded in a matrix of protein fibers. The calcium gives the bone its strength and rigidity; the protein (collagen, mostly) makes the bone somewhat flexible. Also found in bone are potassium, magnesium, citrate, sodium, and fluoride. These minerals help to hold the calcium and phosphorus crystals together.

Bone is living tissue. It is constantly being broken down and reformed, like all tissue in the body. Bone formation is vital for growth, for repair of microscopic fractures that result from everyday stress, and for the replacement of worn-out bone.

How Your Skeleton Is Rebuilt

It begins with bone breakdown. Bone-absorbing cells called *osteoclasts* dig cavities in the inner surface of the bone—microscopic cavities with new bone cells. These cells begin the bone rebuilding process by first producing the collagen matrix. This is followed by a laying down of the calcium and phosphorus crystals within the matrix—a process called *bone mineralization.* Yearly, from 10 to 30 percent of your entire skeleton is remodeled in this way.

Beware of These Bone Robbers

In addition to the biological cause of bone thinning, the lessening of estrogen and calcium absorption, other "thieves" of the strength of your bones include the following:

Stress

Any form of stress can drain calcium reserves from the blood and skeleton. In women, who have smaller bone masses than men, there are the stresses of monthly tension, childbearing, injuries, and especially the change of life.

Inactivity

Exercise is believed to be the only preventive or therapeutic measure that not only halts bone loss but actually stimulates the formation of new bone. Like muscles, bones respond to stress by becoming bigger and stronger. And like muscles, they weaken and shrink if not used. Exercise also creates small electrical potentials in bone tissue that stimulate the growth of new bone. But if there is a period of inactivity, these processes slow down and calcium is drained out of the bones, accelerating the onset of osteoporosis.

Vitamin D Deficiency

Vitamin D is available primarily from the sun (produced by the ultraviolet irradiation of an inactive form of vitamin D in your skin) and in limited amounts from foods such as milk, fish, and eggs. Stored in the liver, vitamin D becomes activated to perform two calcium-boosting reactions: (1) it increases the absorption of calcium in the intestines, and (2) it increases the reabsorption of calcium through the kidneys. It is also needed to maintain a proper level of calcium in the blood. Any excess or deficiency can cause bone loss. That's right. You could also have too much of a good thing, so it is unwise to overload on vitamin D. Strike a balance and you protect against calcium loss.

Alcohol, Tobacco

Alcohol impairs calcium absorption through the intestines; it may interfere with the ability of the liver to activate vitamin D. Liver damage of many alcoholics is linked to rapid bone loss. There is some association between smoking and bone loss. The negative effects on bone appear to be related in part to the number of cigarettes smoked. For example, women who smoked half a pack each day were found to have more bone mass than those who smoked a whole pack; nonsmokers had greater bone mass than did smokers. For the sake of your bones, your very life, give up smoking! And while you're at it, give up alcohol, too. Cast out these bone robbers!

Caffeine: Thief of Bone Mass

There appears to be a connection between heavy caffeine intake and the loss of bone mass. In particular, if you consume a lot of coffee, tea, or soft drinks, a higher proportion of calcium is excreted in your urine, which means that less is being absorbed into your bones. Best to switch to caffeine-free beverages, for the sake of skeletal health.

Soft Drinks

The high phosphorus content in soft drinks can upset your delicate calcium-phosphorus balance and cause loss of the important bone-building mineral. To offset this negative effect, just steer clear of soft drinks, the biggest source of excessive phosphorus.

Aluminum-Containing Antacids

Many over-the-counter antacid products are high in aluminum and other chemicals that increase the loss of calcium by the body. They are also known for causing constipation, so it would be best to limit their use. Many alcoholics take antacids on a regular basis to soothe their stomachs; this combination can be destructive in terms of overall bone mass.

Diuretics

They promote the production of urine and are often prescribed for persons with high blood pressure. But calcium is also lost in the urine, and this means that it needs to be replaced via foods, calcium beverages, and supplements.

How Is Osteoporosis Diagnosed?

Most diagnostic methods are not definitive. Sophisticated tests, including radionuclide tracer methods, blood and urine calcium levels, and calcium balance determinations are not able to detect bone loss in early stages. *Problem:* conventional X rays cannot diagnose it until it's too late—*bone loss is invisible until about 35 percent of the mass has been lost*—hence its name of being the sneaky or invisible killer!

More Reliable Device Available

A newer method is that of the single photon absorptiometry method. It offers an acceptable method of precise and accurate determination of bone mineral content and bone width. A *densitometer* is sensitive enough to detect a 1 to 3 percent loss of bone and is especially accurate at the midpoint of the arm, an area which has a correlation with the total weight of the skeleton, the total amount of calcium in the body, and the amount of bone in the femur, or hip bone.

How Calcium Will Nip Bone Loss in the Bud

While osteoporosis may be a multifactorial process, with the use of calcium as early in life as possible, there should be less loss of bone mass.

The usual daily intake of elemental (that amount which is absorbed) calcium in the United States, about 500 milligrams, falls well below the recommended dietary allowance of 800 milligrams.

How Much to Take?

It seems likely that an increase in calcium intake to 1,000 to 1,500 milligrams a day beginning well before the menopause will reduce the incidence of osteoporosis in postmenopausal women.

Calcium Is Lifesaving

Basically, calcium is essential for muscle contraction, blood clotting, plus brain and nerve function. It is a key nutrient in the process of bone mineralization. Remember when your mother told you to drink milk for strong bones? This was sound advice. Milk contains calcium plus vitamin D, which is converted by the liver and kidneys into a substance called *calcitriol,* a hormone that aids in bone rebuilding or remodeling by regulating the body's calcium level. Calcitriol allows the intestines to absorb calcium from foods and prevents the kidneys from eliminating calcium in the urine. So you can understand the value of calcium as a lifesaver.

Had Your Calcium Today?

Your goal is to prevent osteoporosis by building strong bones before age 35. (The thief starts its robbing between ages 30 and 35.) But even after age 35, you can help slow down or *halt* further progression with a calcium-rich program. Each day, your goal is to consume about 1,000 milligrams of calcium. It is like putting funds in a bank. You are building insurance or reserves and drawing interest in the form of stronger bones. But you need to put in that 1,000 to 1,500 milligrams of calcium daily into your bone bank. That means *daily*!

SIMPLE CALCIUM TABLET EXTENDS WOMAN'S LIFE

She almost skidded on a slippery sidewalk. Miraculously, someone grabbed her before she could have had a nasty fall and broken her hip. Emma S. was so upset she went to her family physician for a checkup and something to "calm the nervous system." He noted she was somewhat frail, although only 50. He prescribed calcium tablets at 1,500 milligrams daily. This mineral would also calm her nervous system, but its greatest benefit was to help stop bone loss. Emma S. was developing just a slight spinal curvature or "dowager's hump" which was warning enough of fragile bones. Within several weeks, tests showed she had an abundant amount of calcium, and the risk of a hip fracture (2 out of every 10 patients who sustain hip fractures die within three months) became markedly reduced. A near brush with almost certain hospitalization and high risk of death alerted Emma S. to the need for calcium—a lifesaving mineral she takes daily.

Why Calcium Boosting Is More Important in Wintertime

Seasonal changes have been observed by researchers to point out the importance of speeding up calcium intake before, during, and after winter. Bone mass is lowest following the winter months, when there is least exposure to sunlight. Conversely, it is highest in the fall, suggesting that sunlight may play a lifesaving role in preventing weak bones.

Calcium together with vitamin D should be increased if you are heading into or are in the midst of or are just emerging from cold winter months. Other factors that influence this variation in bone mass include seasonal changes in physical activity and diet.

Warm Up Your Bones with Calcium

If you are facing a cold climate, just plan to boost calcium potency so that you maintain from 1,000 to 1,500 milligrams daily. Ask your nutritionist about supplements to make it easy to maintain these levels daily. You will help keep your bones alive and strong throughout the winter.

A SIMPLE PROGRAM PREVENTS FRAGILE BONES

Fran M. had a thorough examination by her physician. An X ray revealed that she was developing osteoporosis because of the thinning bones. Yet Fran M. had no pain, no symptoms. To nip this problem in the bud, the doctor said that Fran M. would need to boost calcium intake to 1,500 milligrams daily; this would strengthen her skeleton, which otherwise threatened to become so weak that any sudden strain, bump, or fall could trigger a fracture from which she might never recover, might never survive. Calcium was a lifesaver thrown to the needy woman!

Can You Get Too Much Calcium?

There is the fear that excess milk consumption could lead to calcium deposits and kidney stones. While it is true that a *very high* consumption of calcium can increase this risk, amounts under 2,000 milligrams daily have minimal, if any, risk. The exception is an individual who has a family history or previous history of kidney stones; that person may be absorbing much more calcium than the average person. Medical guidance is suggested.

Is Milk the Only Answer to Protecting Against Osteoporosis?

It would seem so, when you see that 1 quart of milk will give you close to 1,200 milligrams of calcium, whether whole or low-fat. But it can be tiresome to drink that amount, every single day. Some people are lactose intolerant and cannot digest milk. Others simply do not prefer its taste. But milk still is a good source. Chart 8-1 shows other calcium sources. How can you boost calcium consumption without really tasting (or knowing) of the added milk?

Chart 8-1: CHECKLIST OF CALCIUM-CONTAINING FOODS

Food	*Serving Size*	*Milligrams of Calcium*
Milk, whole	1 cup	291
Milk, low fat	1 cup	297
Milk, chocolate	1 cup	280
Milk, half and half	1 cup	254
Milk, evaporated, canned	1 cup	675
Egg nog commercial	1 cup	330
Yogurt (depending on flavor)	1 cup	343-415
Cheddar cheese	1 ounce	204
Parmesan cheese	1 ounce	390
Provolone cheese	1 ounce	214
Swiss cheese	1 ounce	272
Almonds	1 cup	304
Hazelnuts	1 cup	240
Kale	1 cup	206
Collards	1 cup	357
Sardines (canned)	3 ounces	372
Blue cheese	1 ounce	150
Cottage cheese	1 cup	130
Mozzarella cheese (whole milk)	1 ounce	163
Mozzarella cheese (part skim)	1 ounce	207
American cheese	1 ounce	174
Broccoll	1 stalk	158
Spinach	1 cup	167
Ice cream, regular	1 cup	176
Ice cream, soft	1 cup	237
Egg	1 egg	28
Cabbage	1 cup	44
Cream cheese	1 ounce	23
Beef, pork, poultry	3 ounces	10
Apples, bananas	1 medium	10
Grapefruit	½ medium	20
Potatoes	1 medium	14
Carrots	1 medium	27
Lettuce	¼ head	27

Try Nonfat Dry Milk Powder

Depending on the brand, 1 tablespoon gives you 52 milligrams of calcium. One cup of the powder gives you 832 milligrams. Try some of these calcium-boosting tips:

- To increase milk's calcium content, just add 1 or 2 tablespoons of nonfat dry milk powder to every glass of fluid milk.
- Top a serving of cooked cereal with 2 tablespoons of the powder.
- Add up to 3 tablespoons of the powder to 1 cup of yogurt for a more robust flavor and more calcium.
- Get creamier and richer-tasting salad dressings when you combine 3 tablespoons of nonfat dry milk with 1 cup of your favorite creamy-style salad dressing.
- Stir ½ cup of nonfat dry milk into one 10 ¾ ounce can of undiluted cream soup; then add liquid milk to the soup base and heat as directed.
- Onion dips or any of your favorite cream-based dips can be boosted with calcium. Just add 3 tablespoons of nonfat dry milk to 1 cup of cream dip mixture.
- Blenderize nonfat dry milk and yogurt with your favorite fruit, water, and ice for a refreshing and calcium-enriched beverage.
- You use mayonnaise in so many things. Boost it with calcium. Just blend 2 tablespoons of nonfat dry milk into each ½ cup of mayonnaise. Your salad dressings, dip mixes, and sandwich spreads will help you reach your daily calcium goals.
- Mashed potatoes, anyone? Increase their calcium content by adding 2 tablespoons of nonfat dry milk to every cup of potatoes.
- Enrich those biscuits and yeast breads with calcium. To a biscuit recipe calling for 2 cups of flour, add ⅓ cup of nonfat dry milk. *Tip:* Add up to ¾ cup of the powder to a yeast bread recipe calling for 6 cups of flour.
- Cream or cheese sauces made using nonfat dry milk may be used in casseroles for a tasty and easy calcium-boosting dinner idea.
- Calcium absorption increase if this mineral is eaten with foods high in vitamin C (tomatoes, citrus fruits, green vegetables), so add more of these vitamin C foods to your salads and soups.

- Vitamin D, which is produced in the skin by the sun's rays, increases calcium absorption by your body. Vitamin D is almost always added to nonfat dry milk (read labels, please) so you needn't rely on sunshine, especially if you have been cautioned against excessive sun exposure.

Selecting a Calcium Supplement

Select one that is labeled as being *calcium carbonate* because it has the highest potency and absorption rate. Next you may want calcium lactate (unless you are lactose intolerant), calcium gluconate, and oyster shell (basically calcium carbonate). You can buy them in tablet, capsule, powder, or liquid form. Calcium, like other mineral nutrients, always comes in combination with other elements because, alone, minerals cannot be absorbed. Read labels, and select a *calcium carbonate* (prime choice) that has other minerals, too. This would be the easy way to take your 1,000 or 1,500 milligram dose daily.

Remember, your body needs and uses calcium every day. If it isn't getting what it needs from your diet, it will take it from the only other available source: your bones. With age, this deterioration can cause bones to break spontaneously, without impact. And can lead to stooped posture and shorter stature characteristically associated with old age.

Did you know that almost 20 percent of your body calcium is used up each year? It must be replaced by dietary or supplemental calcium. Protect yourself against osteoporosis and other threatening risks with adequate calcium in your food program. It is the simpler form of nutritional therapy that can be a lifesaver!

IN REVIEW

1. The silent killer of osteoporosis has no symptoms. It claims countless tens of thousands of lives and strikes women over the age of 45.
2. Note checklist of bone robbers and make a change in your life-style to ease stress, become more active, correct vitamin D intake, give up alcohol, tobacco, caffeine, soft drinks, aluminum, dangerous diuretics.
3. Plan to consume from 1,000 to 1,500 milligrams of calcium daily as insurance against bone theft.

4. Calcium is able to nip bone loss in the bud.
5. Emma S. had a near-accident that alerted her doctor to the need for calcium boosting which saved her life in the future.
6. Select a variety of calcium foods from the accompanying listing.
7. Boost calcium as cold weather approaches for better bone health.
8. Try the tasty and bone-strengthening nonfat dry milk powder tips to boost calcium intake, without really knowing it.
9. Fran M. had a routine test that detected the onset of bone loss and discovered how calcium could be a lifesaver. She was saved in time from the sneaky, silent, epidemic killer—osteoporosis!

9

How to Feed Your Brain a Youthful Memory

Troubled with memory lapses? Finding it difficult to remember names and faces? Cannot recall events that happened as recently as a few weeks ago? You may have a nutritional deficiency in your brain. Your memory banks need a few brain boosters found in everyday foods. With proper nutrition, you should be able to think more clearly and remember with more youthful alertness, no matter what your age. You *can* feed your brain a youthful memory.

The Human Computer

In your brain are 10 billion or more *neurons* (nerve cells) that perform the complex task of creating, storing, and retrieving knowledge. Chemical messengers or *neurotransmitters* pass from one neuron to another. The typical neurotransmitter has just told you what these words mean.

Miracle Neurotransmitters: Key to Brain Power

Memory, learning, brightness, being able to remember either simple or complex matters are all determined by neurotransmitters. They are charged with the responsibility of carrying messages between neurons. These messengers control more than IQ. They help you sleep, they wake you up, they make you happy or sad, tense or calm. They influence your appetite, your dreams, your activities. You cannot make a move without neurotransmitters—they control your coordination, too. They are miracles in the sense that they are at the helm of every movement made by your body or mind.

How Your Brain Stays Young

In a state of arousal, your brain is primed to respond quickly to external stimuli. Specifically, the neurotransmitters *norepinephrine (nor-*

adrenalin) and *acetylcholine* keep some brain cells primed to "fire" in response to stimulation. There is strong evidence that acetylcholine is involved in memory. This chemical messenger is sent to the *cerebral cortex,* the furrowed outer surface of the largest and most highly evolved part of the brain, the *cerebrum.* An acetylcholine factory, called the *nucleus basalis,* is located at the base of the cerebrum. When neurons in this region fire, they release acetylcholine that binds to receptors on target cells in the cerebral cortex. Activation of the *hippocampus,* a finger-sized bundle of neural tissue deep within the cerebrum, helps your memory stay young. The hippocampus works like a telephone switchboard, connecting various cortical areas with the new fact in a find of "conference call."

Eventually, these cortical areas learn to "dial direct"; that is, they establish independent neural connections called *circuits* among themselves. And the new memory is said to be consolidated. With a supply of nutrients that stimulate the release of acetylcholine, your brain is able to stay young and alert.

Alzheimer's Disease May Be Nutritional Deficiency

What Is Alzheimer's Disease?

Alzheimer's disease is a disorder that affects the cells of the brain. It causes intellectual impairment, also known as senile dementia. It first affects the memory, and then the personality. As the disease progresses, protein threads in nerve cells of the brain become twisted around each other into tangles; some pieces of degenerating nerve cells become disarranged. The more formations, the worse the symptoms. In particular, there is a form of molecular starvation. Under microscope, these changes appear as a tangle of neurofibrillary fibers.

The Nutritional Connection

There is a serious reduction—as much as 90 percent—in a particular brain protein or enzyme (choline acetyltransferase) that is involved in the passage of nerve signals. It is this deficiency that causes a sluggishness and slowing of the production of acetylcholine, the chemical compound active in transmission of nerve impulses. With a boosting of choline, there is a subsequent increase in the production of neurotransmitters that help keep your brain and memory in youthful vitality.

Choline: The Brain-Boosting Nutrient That Helps You Think Young

Choline is an essential nutrient that is needed to form acetylcholine, the neurotransmitter that helps keep your memory alert and your thinking processes in a youthful condition.

Choline Prevents Brain Aging

Normally, the brain cells wear out; the membranes become more rigid with fatty deposits and lose their ability to take in and release brain chemicals to relay messages. This can cause memory loss and confused thinking. But it is choline that seems to repress or delay this membrane hardening.

Further, if the brain cells are seriously deficient in choline, they lose dendritic spines, the chemical receptor areas needed to pass along information. Having too few dendritic spines is like having a poor telephone connection. Messages are distorted and lost.

Choline to the Rescue

It is choline that is able to help keep the protein threads from becoming what are known as *neurofibrillary tangles.* Choline acts as a supervisor to see that everything moves smoothly and in proper order. Choline also protects against one major contributory cause of Alzheimer's disease, namely, *neuritic plaques.* These are pairs of fine nerve fibers twisted around each other and lying in the cell bodies of neurons. The greater the number of tangles and plaques, the greater the severity of the symptoms of brain weakness and memory loss and approaching senility. It is choline that prevents the rapid breakdown so that the transmitter is coaxed into working with more vigor and health. This brain-boosting nutrient has the ability to help create the process that keeps your thinking apparatus in a youthful condition.

Where to Find Brain-Boosting Choline

Natural food sources include egg yolks, brain, heart, green leafy vegetables, legumes, brewer's yeast, liver, and wheat germ. The richest source is found in *lecithin,* a soybean product, that is available as granules or in tablet form. It may be preferable to the high-fat or high-cholesterol animal sources just listed. With lecithin, the choline is speedily absorbed by your body. It then maintains a form of "law and order" in your brain to protect against fiber tangles and nerve plaques so that you are guarded against so-called senility. Choline also increases acetylcholine to keep your neurotransmitters moving along swiftly so you have an active and alert brain. You can think young with choline!

FROM "MISSING MARBLES" TO "SUPERSMART" IN 21 DAYS

Building supervisor Alex Q. kept forgetting schedules. His memory had so many gaps, he neglected setting certain switches throughout the foundry, resulting in near disaster one morning. A long-time satisfactory worker for the sprawling manufacturing plant, Alex Q. was said to be developing Alzheimer's or senility. Was he doomed at the young age of 56? Not according to a psychiatrist who used nutrition as part of therapy. He made a simple dietary correction in Alex Q.'s food program. Daily, Alex was to take 4 heaping tablespoons of lecithin granules in a beverage, sprinkled over his salad, cereal, or baked in a casserole or entree, even in a soup. Just 4 tablespoons daily.

Results? Within 11 days, his "missing marbles" as coworkers unkindly whispered behind his back, were now "found" and "returned." By the end of the eighteenth day, Alex Q. had a razor sharp memory, better than ever before. By the twenty-first day, he was "supersmart" and could fulfill daily responsibilities without even referring to a written list. He had a terrific power of total recall. Just give him a list of duties and he could perform them without any note taking. Now his coworkers look upon him as the "big brain." It was choline in lecithin that saved him from senility and gave him a super memory power!

How to Boost Brain Power with Choline Therapy

On a daily basis, make choline available to help put youthful life into your neurotransmitters. Remember, memory is formed with the use of acetylcholine, and it is the nutrient, choline, that prompts the manufacture of this brain booster. To have choline available, try these easy (and tasty) nutritional therapies.

Brain Tonic

Add 4 tablespoons of lecithin granules to a tall glass filled with diced green vegetables; stir in ¼ teaspoon brewer's yeast and 1 tablespoon wheat germ. Add a small amount of water or any salt-free vegetable juice.

Blenderize until thoroughly assimilated, about 3 minutes. Drink slowly. *Tip:* Give your brain a special boost by drinking this tonic about two hours after breakfast. You'll feel mental vigor almost from the start. This Brain Tonic is a richly concentrated powerhouse of choline that works quickly and lasts throughout the day.

Brain Spice

Fill a salt shaker with lecithin. Use it to sprinkle soups, salads, main dishes, throughout your eating program. You will be giving your brain day-long choline to help keep you thinking with youthful alertness. If anyone asks what you are seasoning your food with, explain that it is your Brain Spice!

Brain Food

Just add 1 or 2 tablespoons of lecithin to any baked dish. It especially blends in with vegetable or meatloaf recipes. It is also good in soups, stews, and casseroles. Whenever you prepare your recipe, just remember to add the Brain Food and you'll soon have no fear of losing that memory gift!

Lecithin is available in most health food stores and special diet sections of larger food markets.

Think Better with Tryptophan

Tryptophan, an essential amino acid, is required for the formation of serotonin, a neurotransmitter that helps to control your emotions, pain levels, and sleep. It is tryptophan that is intimately involved in sparking the release of those valuable neurotransmitters that help you to think and act with more vigor.

How Tryptophan Is a Brain Booster

This amino acid is converted into a variety of intermediate compounds flowing into nicotinamide adenine dinucleotide (NAD) or into another variety of substances flowing into serotonin. Serotonin helps the brain to sort out the confusion, protect against the tangling of filaments, and improve the route of the neurotransmitters to ensure clearer thinking. Tryptophan also helps your brain to relax and, in many cases, helps you to sleep much better at night.

Think Better, Become Alert, Feel Happier

Tryptophan releases serotonin, which, as you know, can improve your ability to think better, alleviate depression, and diminish your sensitivity to negative stimuli. It is the tryptophan-dispatched serotonin that acts as a natural mood regulator and dispels depression. You become happier and can function with more vitality. It is tryptophan that helps you feel glad all over.

Where to Find Tryptophan

It is abundant in milk, cheese, most meat products, and egg yolk. You will also find it in supplement form at most health stores.

FROM "MEMORY LAPSES" TO "COMPUTER BRAIN" AT AGE 63

His family and friends felt embarrassed over the way Mark D. kept forgetting dates, special events, even names of familiar faces. Frequently, he was discovered to be staring into space. Questions had to be repeated and the answers were vague. Mark D. had always been an active industrial executive, so this constant forgetfulness and the "memory lapses" began to worry those in his surroundings.

When he forgot to lock the front door and, worse, got into his car and drove for 5 minutes without knowing where he was going, the family decided something had to be done.

Senile? A physician who specialized in the relationship of nutritional failures to physiological dysfunction diagnosed the condition as a deficiency in specific elements. The physician recommended boosting tryptophan intake to a prescribed 1,000 milligrams per day. He also prescribed 250 milligrams of choline per day. The purpose was to activate neurotransmitters so neurons would reach into many areas of the brain, including the hippocampus.

Within 12 days, Mark D. was completely remade. He had a rapid-fire memory again; his thinking was so sharp, he could repeat sentences, even paragraphs, to prove he had superretentive ability. He was no longer the victim of deficiency-caused "memory lapses" but had a "computer brain" at his young age of 63.

It was the combination of tryptophan and choline that protected him from the risk of so-called senility. This nutritional therapy gave him a "computer brain."

How to Wake up Your "Tired Brain" with Tyrosine

Can't remember names or faces? Need to ask someone to repeat some simple information? Is your mind a blank? The reason could be a deficiency in tyrosine, an amino acid found in most dairy products, eggs, and animal foods. Tyrosine could help fill in the blank spots in your memory bank.

How to Think Better with Tyrosine

A number of neurotransmitters or chemical messengers originate from tyrosine which prompts the transmission of vital facts along your set of neurons or brain cells. It is tyrosine that is one of the valuable nutrients that acts as a stimulus to the cell body to prompt the electrical impulses to continue on their course.

Tyrosine is transformed into noraderenaline, which is then converted into adrenaline, which is needed to prompt your brain into thinking action. It is this amino acid that influences the production and concentration of the valuable chemical messengers that help you to think and remember better. Tyrosine is an important influence on your brain receptors, giving you the ability to understand, utilize, and store information in your memory bank.

Sources of Tyrosine

Tyrosine is found in dairy foods, cheeses, egg yolk, and most animal foods. It is also available as a food supplement from your health store.

NO LONGER CONFUSED, MEMORY BECOMES KEEN, FEELS "ALIVE" AGAIN

Louise O'L. was a private secretary in a large grain corporation. Coworkers and superiors noticed she frequently forgot to pass along messages. If notes were written, she could not remember where she had placed them. Although she was not even 52, she displayed symptoms of senility; worse, Alzheimer's. Was she to be pitied or helped?

The corporation physician suggested that Louise O'L. boost her increase of brain-stimulating foods, especially tyrosine. In particular, tyrosine would initiate the production of the valuable neurotransmitters involved in both learning and memory. It would nourish the hippocampus by strengthening and regenerating the bundle of neural tissue deep within the cerebrum segment of the brain.

Louise O'L. took prescribed potencies of tyrosine. Within one week, she was able to "straighten" her formerly confused thoughts. Her memory was keen and now she felt "alive" because she happily exclaimed, "I have my head together!" Not only was her job saved, but she was given a promotion and salary increase because her tyrosine-stimulated brain made her all the better as a valued employee!

Tyrosine in the Morning, Better Thinking Within One Hour

This amino acid is unique in it works very swiftly. It envelopes the nerve cells that manufacture acetylcholine and improves their functions to stimulate thinking. *Suggestion:* take a tyrosine supplement in the morning for better absorption benefit. Reward: within 30 minutes, the tyrosine offers a form of protection to guard against the breakdown of the neurotransmitters and prolong their action. For so-called "supermemory" or "thinking-plus power," try a tyrosine supplement in the morning. You will have a terrific "brain-booster" reaction within an hour and enjoy long-lasting thinking ability.

How to Rejuvenate Your Thinking Abilities

You can increase your brain power by following some everyday programs to put new life into your neurotransmitters.

Correct Your Posture

Slumped over? You could be putting a crimp on the oxygen-carrying blood supply to your brain. If you let your head hang over your chest and your chin jut out, you are squeezing arteries passing through the spinal columns to your brain. Penalty? Fuzzy thinking, forgetfulness—even if you are young! Hunched-over posture can shortchange the supply of iron to your red blood cells and impair your memory. Iron is richly concentrated in the reticular activating system of your brain that keeps you mentally alert. So maintain good posture. Let oxygen pour into your brain along with iron-rich blood (your brain needs up to 30 times more blood than any other body organ) and "think young"!

Avoid Aluminum in Any Form

Believed to be a possible destroyer of nerve cells, aluminum has been found in dangerously high amounts in the brains of victims of Alzheimer's. The metal shows up in cells that also contain neurofibrillary tangles. Whether aluminum deposits cause memory destruction by acting as a toxin, or whether the metal accumulates as a result of other biological changes is not known. But it would make good sense to avoid aluminum. It is found in any number of patent remedies such as antacids and over-the-counter as well as prescribed medications. Check labels. Ask your pharmacist and/or physician. Keep your brain free of aluminum and you may well keep it alive, longer.

Straighten out your thinking by using nutritional therapy to keep the protein threads of your brain in smooth and untangled working order. With the use of nutrition, you will help to boost your thinking powers, protect against the threat of senility or Alzheimer's, and enrich your life!

POINTS TO REMEMBER

1. Your brain stays young with the use of nutritional therapy to feed certain segments and initiate processes to help you think better.
2. Choline is a brain-boosting nutrient that helps fill in the gaps in your memory.
3. Alex Q. corrected his "missing marbles" and became "supersmart" within 21 days by using choline in lecithin, a soybean food product available in all health stores.
4. Improve mental powers with the Brain Tonic, the Brain Spice, and the Brain Food in your daily eating plan.
5. Think better with brain-boosting tryptophan, a miracle amino acid.
6. Mark D. went from "memory lapses" to a "computer brain" by using this supplement. He was a young 63 with this nutrient.
7. Tyrosine helps you think better, almost immediately. Louise O'L. corrected confusion, sharpened her memory, and was "restored to life" with the use of this brain-boosting nutrient.
8. Improve your brain powers with corrected posture and avoiding aluminum.

10

Healing Digestive Disorders with Soothing Foods

One American in ten is troubled with chronic digestive disease. One in two suffers from occasional digestive distress. Disorders of the digestive tract are responsible for $50 billion annually in lost work, lost wages, and disability and health care payments. Every day, 200,000 people stay home from work because of an illness associated with the digestive tract. More people are hospitalized with disorders of the digestive system, or gastrointestinal tract (GI tract), than with any other group of disorders. More seriously, digestive diseases are responsible for approximately 200,000 deaths each year.

Yet, based on a survey, 66 percent of those queried admitted knowing "only a little" or "nothing at all" about digestive disorders.[1] Small wonder the problem is striking more and more people, particularly those in the middle years, after years of disregard and abuse of this gateway system to your total well-being.

Why Does Your Digestive System Cry Out with Rage?

Expect trouble when you tell your stomach, "Just one more bit" or else "I'll try to eat the whole thing" or "I know I'll regret it but that second helping looks too good to resist."

Next morning (or sooner), your digestive system protests in the form of cramps, bloating, nausea, and diarrhea that may continue for a day or two or more before the grumbles finally go away. Symptoms are your digestive tract's way of sending signals of something that has gone wrong. Read these messages. Protect yourself against agonizing complaints. Make a few simple changes in eating methods. Use soothing foods for

[1]National Digestive Diseases Information Clearinghouse, 1986 survey, Washington, D.C. 20037

natural digestive aid. Pamper your tummy with these prudent corrective methods:

Eat but Do Not Overeat

Excessive food consumption slows down your stomach's normal activity. You have a sense of bloated fullness. Dyspeptic symptoms erupt when there is alteration of your stomach's normal motor activity. It is activated to churn comfortably when it is moderately distended with food. An overload means excessive stomach distention that blocks this churning activity to cause pains, bloating, and nausea. *Therapy:* Eat a balanced meal with moderate portions and not to the level of overstuffing. Something has to give, and it will be painful stomach symptoms!

Limit Fatty Food Intake

High-fat foods or those fried in fat inhibit stomach function and prolong the time before the stomach releases contents into the small intestine. An excess of fatty foods means double trouble with bloating due to overeating and also fat backlash with burning sensations. *Therapy:* reduce intake of animal fats. Avoid fried foods of any sort. Switch to vegetable fats, although also in moderation.

Avoid Tension While Eating

All tied up in knots? Feel anger, anxiety, resentment? This "uptight" frustration increases release of stomach acids to give you that "acid" indigestion. If a gas bubble carries some excess acid up into your esophagus or food tube, you suffer from heartburn. Feel depressed? This feeling of dejection reduces stomach acids and food remains undigested for many hours to give you cramps and common indigestion. *Therapy:* if emotionally upset, do *not* eat. A brisk 30-minute walk helps to calm your frazzled nerves. Drink a glass or two of comfortably cool water (*not* shocking cold or scalding hot!) and feel your tensions just wash away. Try one glass of skim milk about 1 hour before you eat. Its tryptophan (amino acid) releases serotonin (hormone) to ease your tensions and help you feel relaxed and ready to eat with comfort.

Eat Slowly for Your Stomach's Comfort

Eating rapidly or eating when emotionally upset is responsible for indigestion and uncomfortable spasms for hours afterward. If you have the "hurry up and eat" habit, you are abusing your digestive tract until it complains and begs you to slow down. *Therapy:* Use smaller utensils. Less food means less hurry. Chew well. Do not talk while you eat. Concentrate on the food and chewing it thoroughly for digestive comfort.

Do Not Swallow Air with Food

Air swallowing or *aerophagia* can lead to abdominal distention, smothering sensations, palpitations, and apparent heart pain. While some air is naturally swallowed with food and drink and nothing to worry about, large, disturbing amounts can give you distressing reactions. *Therapy:* Avoid gum chewing, smoking, drinking large amounts of carbonated beverages, engaging in animated mealtime conversations that lead to food gulping, and rapid eating. All bloat your system with pain-causing excessive air.

Some Foods May Not Like You

They may be nutritious, but for some folks, they cause indigestion and gasines. Offenders include cucumbers, beans, cabbage, turnips, onions, chili, and peppers, to name a few. No matter how prepared or in minute amounts, they give you an unpleasant digestive reaction. *Therapy:* Keep a log of your foods. Do specific items cause digestive upsets? List these foods. Either reduce intake or eliminate them if you see they cause the problem. Often, just avoiding one offending food can help to correct the disorder.

HOW SIMPLE FIBER FOODS SOLVED A LIFETIME OF STOMACH TROUBLE—IN THREE DAYS!

Ever since he could remember, machine operator Stanley P. had recurring stomach pains. Either a grumble or a knifelike churning resulted in agony for hours on end. At times, he was doubled over with the stabbing pains and had to grit his jaw to keep from crying out. Antacids offered momentary relief, but when the effect wore off, the pains returned with greater vengeance. He worried that these pains, which began in his late teen years (and he was now approaching his forties), would plague him for the rest of his life.

A gastroenterologist asked about his diet pattern and noted a problem. Stanley P. ate almost no fiber or bulk-containing foods. The physician prescribed a daily intake of whole grain cereals for breakfast and chewy raw vegetables at lunch and dinner; he also told Stanley P. to include wheat germ and bran in his breakfast cereals, with any casseroles, or baked goods on a daily basis. Stanley P.

scoffed, expecting a patent medicine as a cure-all. But he was assured if it did not work, he would be given a prescription drug.

The machine operator used these fiber foods with his daily meals. Within *three days,* the painful spasms halted. He no longer felt shock waves shooting through his midsection after average foods. He was saved from a lifetime of digestive trouble by using small amounts of fiber foods on a daily basis. And they tasted good, too!

How Fiber Is a Form of Nutritional Therapy for the Digestive System

Lack of adequate amounts of fiber leaves you vulnerable to a gassy feeling that irritates your lower digestive tract. The painful spasm of excess gas occurs when your bowel wall becomes very sensitive to distention. Your goal is to protect against gas accumulation and speed up the release of waste products. You can do this with the use of high-fiber foods that hasten their expulsion. Fiber diminishes the amount of gas the body absorbs and makes for much smoother functioning along the gastrointestinal tract.

Nutritional Therapy

Boost intake of whole grain breads, cereals, raw fruits, and vegetables. Plan to have just one or two tablespoons daily of either bran or wheat germ (or a combo) to give you needed fiber to ease and erase stomach distress. Mix with cereals, into yogurt or in soups, stews, baked dishes for speedy correction of indigestion and its plaguelike symptoms.

How to Cool Off Scorching Heartburn

Problem: This disorder, more precisely called gastroesophageal reflux disease—or simply reflux, occurs when there is a backing up of stomach contents into the esophagus, the tube which connects the mouth to the stomach, causing a burning sensation commonly felt under the breastbone. Studies show that 67 million Americans experience heartburn at least once a month after eating a large meal or overindulging on certain foods. It can be both painful and alarming and is often understood. Almost 10 percent of patients who report to the hospital with severe chest pain are found to have no evidence of cardiovascular problems. Many, in fact, have reflux or heartburn.

While the most common symptom is the burning, there may also be regurgitation of bitter or sour fluid into the mouth. Other symptoms may include nausea, vomiting, bloating, and a persistent feeling of fullness after eating.

Are Medications the Solution?

Conventional antacids will neutralize the acid and relieve burning, but the physiology of the reflux remains uncorrected. Alginic acid combinations or "floating antacid foam" has no effect on delayed motility or weakened lower esophageal sphincter pressures. Anticholinergics impair gastric emptying and decrease lower esophageal sphincter (LES) pressure. H2 antagonists decrease acid secretion, but do not correct delayed emptying or improve LES tone. So you can see that you could be pouring oil on your flaming acid distress with most chemicalized medications. Hardly a soothing solution.

Instead, your goal is to correct the pathophysiology of reflux by (1) increasing LES pressure and (2) normalizing gastric emptying. In so doing, you improve the tone and amplitude of gastric contractions to facilitate normal emptying and reduce the amount of acidic contents available for reflux.

You can correct the cause and cool off that steaming cauldron of heartburn with this easy and speedily effective step-by-step nutritional and better living program:

1. Watch your weight. Lose that excess poundage. The pressure of extra weight can trigger more attacks of heartburn.
2. Avoid wearing clothing that is too tight around your stomach or waist.
3. Do not eat too fast. Take small mouthfuls and chew the food thoroughly.
4. Avoid bending forward, stooping, and lifting heavy objects.
5. Sleep with the head of your bed elevated about 6 inches (perhaps by placing wooden blocks or bricks under the legs at the head of your bed).
6. Keep a relaxed attitude in all your daily activities.
7. Do not lie down right after eating. And stop or cut down on your smoking.

8. Avoid any foods that may stimulate acid secretion in your stomach such as coffee, caffeine, alcohol, sugar, and salt.
9. Avoid fatty foods, as well as greasy, spicy foods. Cut down or eliminate chocolate.
10. Eat smaller, more frequent meals instead of the customary three large meals a day.

Nutritional Therapy

A cooling of heartburn is possible with a diet that is adequate in protein and low in fat. Enjoy broiled (or roasted) beef, poultry, and fish; also stock up on skim milk and related low-fat or fat-free dairy products. Soak up and cast out acid with potatoes, corn, apples, bananas, water, apple juice, soups (without garlic or onion, if offensive), and most freshly prepared raw fruits and vegetables.

Is Your Stomach Speaking to You?

If you eat any food that talks back in terms of heartburn, learn to avoid it. Or reduce its portion size. Your stomach is complaining. Better listen or pay the burning penalties afterward!

SIMPLE EVERYDAY MINERAL SUPPLEMENT PUTS OUT HEARTBURN FLAME IN TWO HOURS

Bertha K. felt recurring pains after any meal. The diagnosis of heartburn sent her on the merry-go-round of chemical medications that offered some relief but made her a habitual user of drugs. Without them, the flame reached right up to the roof of her mouth!

Fortunately, a nurse dietician at the school where Bertha K. taught told her she could find natural and nonaddictive relief from the use of a simple *calcium tablet!* She recommended a 500 milligram tablet with a glass of water after every meal to cool off the burning sensation. It would work within hours, assured the nurse.

Desperate, Bertha K. tried the calcium supplement after her dinner when she often felt the burning pain. She felt a slight warmth but it vanished and was comforted with a cooling sensation. It worked! She discarded her upsetting drugs and now takes just one 500 milligram calcium supplement after her dinner and has conquered the heartburn. And it went to work in dowsing the flame within two hours!

Why Calcium Is Effective Cooling Nutritional Therapy

Calcium imparts a mineral action that thickens stomach contents so they are less likely to move upward into the esophagus; it also helps to tighten comfortably and naturally the lower esophageal valve and protect against the upsurge of acid flow. Calcium may well be a natural treatment because it (1) strengthens lower esophageal sphincter, (2) stimulates stomach emptying to reduce chances of reflux, and (3) blocks acid from flowing back from the stomach into the esophagus. Just one 500 milligram calcium tablet, available at most health stores and pharmacies without prescription (it's in food!), can cool off your "hopeless" heartburn in a matter of hours or less!

How to Control a Hiatal Hernia

Problem: This is a condition in which part of the stomach slides up through the diaphragm (a thin muscle that separates the abdominal cavity from the chest cavity) into the chest area. While found in people of all ages, it is more common among those of the middle years. It is often painless. The symptoms—"heartburn," "indigestion," and various frightening pains—that bring people to the doctor's office are due to esophagitis, or irritation of the esophagus, which is very often but by no means always associated with hiatus hernia.

Checklist of Possible Causes

It may be an increase of pressure in the abdominal area produced by coughing, vomiting, straining the bowel or sudden physical exertion. Pregnancy, obesity or overweight, or the collection of fluid in the abdomen are also among the causes, since they all increase the pressure in the abdomen and tend to exert pressure on the stomach. If you correct the preceding causes, you may be relieved of the disorder.

Pressure, Stomach Acid, Irritation

Once a portion of the stomach protrudes through the diaphragm the effect is very much like what happens when you squeeze a toy balloon between your fingers: the pressure in the little protruding portion is increased. In hiatus hernia, the pressure inside the protruding portion of the stomach is increased to the point where it overpowers the valves that protect the esophagus from stomach acid. This acid becomes very irritating to the lining of the esophagus and produces some distress.

How to Gain Control and Overcome Hiatus Hernia

Nutritional Therapy

Make a checklist of which foods and drinks that cause distress. If highly spiced dishes irritate your esophagus, switch to better tolerated bland foods. Skim milk and whole grain crackers for a day or so should be soothing. Progress to whole grain cereals and pureed vegetables and some fat-free meats for a few weeks. Enjoy small and frequent feedings. Your last meal at night should be at least two hours before your go to bed. Avoid alcohol and carbonated beverages since they cause trouble to an inflamed esophagus. Of course, if you are overweight, there is another nutritional program in your future—a reducing diet.

The 5 Cent Food That Erases Hiatal Hernia

Just one tablespoon of ordinary bran is able to get to the root cause of your hiatal hernia and correct the errors that are to blame for your condition. That's right. All it costs is just 5 cents or less per day! For a lifetime of digestive super health!

Basic Cause

When you strain because of constipation or other difficulties, you raise tremendously the pressure in your abdominal cavity. This increased pressure causes the top of your stomach to push through your diaphragm to cause a hiatal hernia.

Nutritional Therapy

Ordinary bran, or "roughage," (which should be called "softage" because of its softening effect on hard wastes) is able to permit comfortable passage and *normalize* bowel functions. With the use of just 1 tablespoon daily of bran in your cereal or added to soups or stews or stirred in a cup of plain yogurt, you could help erase the risk of hiatal hernia almost at once. That's all it takes!

SAVED FROM SURGERY WITH BRAN AS HEALER

An examination of Edna E. showed that her hernia was in danger of becoming strangulated, that is, constructed in such a way as to cut off the blood supply. Her internist said that surgery might be necessary to reduce the hernia size and protect against strangulation. Was there an alternative? Obviously, Edna E. wanted to avoid surgery with its risks and doubts. Her internist said the condition was not yet that serious and the use of a pressure-relieving food could be tried. A patient exam told the doctor that Edna E. was constantly straining her bowel, which could be a clue to her developing condition.

Edna E. was told to add 1 or 2 tablespoons of bran daily to her diet. It would also consist more of whole grains, fresh fruits, and vegetables. This simple bran program worked! Eleven days later, a thorough exam indicated that she had corrected the condition and was spared surgery.

Why Bran Is a Lifesaver

Bran eases straining the bowel, permitting easier passage of waste and thereby cooling off any complicated esophagitis (inflammation); it also firms up the overworked lower esophageal sphincter. Introduce bran as part of your nutritional therapeutic program and protect against the distress of a hiatal hernia and other digestive disorders, too!

Nutritional Helps to Heal Your Ulcer

Problem: You know you may have a stomach ulcer when you feel a burning, gnawing pain, usually in the upper part of your abdomen, sometimes in your lower chest. It happens just after eating. The pain may endure for 30 minutes to 3 hours; it can come and go, with weeks of intermittent pain alternating with short pain-free periods. There are three basic types of ulcers that respond to nutritional therapy.

Duodenal Ulcer

An ulcer, or hole in the tissue, may be located in the part of the small intestine connected to the stomach. These duodenal ulcers are about four times more common than the other varieties.

Gastric Ulcer

This is an ulcer of the stomach lining or wall.

Peptic Ulcer

This ulcer occurs in either the duodenum (section of small intestine) or stomach of the digestive tract exposed to acid and pepsin (gastric juice).

Why Does It Happen?

The membrane lining the stomach and duodenum secretes a mucus that contains acid-neutralizing substances. This membrane protects the walls from being "eaten alive" by their own digestive juices. But if the lining cannot resist the damaging effects of acid and pepsin that are produced by the stomach to digest foods, the lining burns away and leaves the sore that is known as an ulcer.

Ulcers develop in older people who undergo a weakening of the stomach wall muscles, to the point where the muscles do not pound the food into liquid so readily. When solid food remains in the stomach for a long time, it stimulates excessive acid secretion which may cause gastritis—an inflammation of the stomach lining. Gastritis is considered to be a precursor of peptic ulcers.

A Nutritional Life-Style for Soothing and Healing Your Ulcer

A total stomach healing program calls for making adjustments in your life-style to give nutrition an opportunity to free you from ulcer distress. It's easy, effective, and quick, too!

1. *Forget the bland diet.* Being restricted to milk, pureed potatoes, and custards never did work. Instead, eat whatever you enjoy provided that the food or beverages make you feel good. Omit particular food that causes you discomfort. You *can* enjoy your favorite tangy foods if they are not irritating. Denying yourself enjoyable foods can worsen your condition because of the stress involved.
2. *Stress: Yes and no.* Stress *is* bad and any excess should be avoided, whether physical or emotional or a combination of both. The newer nutritional knowledge of ulcers holds that stress is *not* necessarily a

cause of ulcers, although it may contribute to the erosion. Many calm and relaxed persons develop ulcers; many high-stressed individuals are ulcer-free. There is no clear-cut cause-and-effect relationship between stress and ulcer onset.

3. *Give up smoking.* Smokers complain of stomach and duodenal ulcers twice as often as do nonsmokers; smokers are also more likely to have hemorrhage, perforation, and obstruction. Give it up! You may well give up your ulcer, too.
4. *Say "no" to aspirin.* It tends to cause internal bleeding and erosion of your stomach membranes; you already have that problem so why add to it? If you must take aspirin, ask your health practitioner if a child's product will do just as well (lower dosage) and wash it down with lots and lots of water.
5. *Limit or eliminate alcohol.* It may be involved in ulcer formation and certainly does aggravate an existing one. You would certainly never pour alcohol onto any open sore. Your ulcer is no exception.

Fit these life-style programs into your daily regimen, and you will help build resistance and hope for recovery from ulcer distress.

Seven Foods That Help to Heal Ulcer Sores

Vitamin A, via its predecessor of beta-carotene, is known for strengthening the epithelial cell layer (lining the stomach) and protecting against erosion from digestive juices. You can help nourish these eroded cells and sores and ulcerous wounds with an ample intake of those foods containing this "ulcer vitamin healer." Seven top-notch sources are sweet potatoes, carrots, pumpkins, winter squash, spinach, broccoli, and apricots. Include them in your weekly menu plan and you may well speed up the healing of ulcer sores!

Zinc

Zinc is able to protect against ulcers and speed up the healing of existing ulcers. Zinc blocks those chemical chain reactions that lead to ulcers by strengthening lysosomes (tiny sacs of enzymes in the cells of the stomach lining) and keeping them from spilling over into the membranes of the stomach. Zinc thereby acts as a barrier to shield your open sore from harmful substances. Food sources: Wheat germ, wheat bran, and cowpeas (blackeyes) are top-notch sources of this protective mineral.

Cabbage Juice

It has been reported that cabbage juice is helpful in easing and erasing the distress of an ulcer. An unidentified substance in the juice increases the resistance of the mucosal lining of the esophagus, stomach, and intestine to the erosive and ulcerating action of gastric juice, which is high in acid content and pepsin.

One Quart a Day May Keep Ulcer Away. In reported situations, 1 quart of cabbage juice a day was able to heal those who had ulcers at a much faster rate than on standard therapy. It was said that some patients healed after only 13 days with 1 quart of cabbage juice daily! Unavailable in packaged form, cabbage can be easily juiced or blenderized right at home.

Ice Water

Ice water has a shrinking effect on the stomach. It also decreases stomach acidity and will help to speed up healing of ulcers. Just one glass of ice water (especially a neutral pH mineral water) is much better than conventional milk, which stimulates acid secretion. If you drink up to five or six glasses of ice water throughout the day, you should find your ulcer easing up and perhaps ready to just "go away." (If you feel any discomfort from the ice water, sip slowly to adjust to the temperature.)

Barley

A bowl of barley, for breakfast or lunch or as a side dish at dinner, may be just what you need to help heal ulcers. It is a good source of thiamine, vitamin C, and calcium, all needed to repair the open sore. In particular, barley contains compounds that are said to neutralize acidity and ease the burning sensation. Barley is said to help repair the damaged DNA within the cells and accelerate the healing of the open sore.

When you eat barley, its natural mucilaginous content forms a protective barrier which keeps the acid juices away from the ulcer, allowing it to heal.

Any disturbance of the delicate balance between the aggressive forces of the digestive process and the defensive forces of the stomach is the forerunner of an ulcer. Nip this threat in the bud with the use of nutritional and better life-style therapies.

Is your stomach trying to tell you something? Listen to the protests. You may learn how to protect yourself from digestive disturbances and enjoy freedom from tummy distress!

HIGHLIGHTS

1. To cool off your raging stomach, follow the simple but effective corrective nutritional methods.
2. Stanley P. healed a lifetime of stomach trouble in three days with the use of fiber foods.
3. Cool off scorching heartburn with the 10-step improvement program.
4. Bertha K. turned to calcium tablets that extinguished heartburn flame in two hours.
5. Erase distress and threat of hiatal hernia with a simple 5 cent food.
6. Edna E. was saved from surgery with the use of bran for healing of her digestive problem.
7. A five-step program will help ease the distress of most ulcers.
8. Seven everyday foods have a vitamin that speeds up ulcer healing.
9. Cabbage juice promotes swift soothing healing of ulcer sores.
10. Cool off burning and acid irritating ulcers with ice water.
11. Daily use of barley will nourish your vital organs and repair ulcer and other sores.

11

Foods That Melt Body Fat, Control Appetite, and Keep You Slim and Trim

Clara H. wailed that all she had to do was look at food and she gained weight! She was embarrassed by her heavy midriff, thick thighs, bulging stomach. She knew she was the object of giggles when walking down the street. No matter what diet she tried, she seemed to gain back more than she lost!

Desperate, Clara H. brought her runaway appetite and heavy weight to a local diet specialist. She needed help for "the busiest jaws in town." The specialist explained that to control her compulsive eating, a few simple foods could correct the glandular malfunction that was the root cause of her voracious appetite.

Clara H. was given a set of foods that would create a simple but powerful hormonal reaction that would plug her eating urge. Desperate, Clara H. tried the foods either freshly prepared or as a juice. Within five days, she had lost 4 pounds. By the end of the month, she dropped two sizes. The greatest bonus was total self-control over her wild appetite. Within 60 days, she was a slimmer size eight...and still losing unwanted weight while her specialist noted she was healthier than ever. Now it was whistles instead of giggles that she heard when the slim-trim Clara H. walked down the street.

Fifteen Foods That Wash Excess Fat Out of Your Body

Clara H. was able to break up fatty deposits because certain foods actually counteract the cause of overweight by stimulating glands to release hormones to break up the fat-accumulating or *adipose* cells.

Why Fat Keeps Increasing

Adipose cells, when viewed through a microscope, appear as gray blobs enclosed in thin sheaths. The core of the cell—the *nucleus*—is also enclosed in a thin sheath. It is this core that serves as a storage depot for fat and causes a buildup of weight. When these cells accumulate too much weight, they begin to bulge. The fat becomes stored in the center of the cell, forcing the nucleus out to the cellular edge and locking the yellow fat in the core of the cell.

The body now has a tendency to develop more fat-storage cells which continually seek out fat. As more adipose cells develop, they become sluggish and cause the body's metabolic processes to slow down. This causes the body to become less efficient in burning up sugars and starches, thereby allowing carbohydrates to convert into stored-up fat. This leads to obesity and further development of fat-gathering cells.

Fat-Melting Foods

Your goal is to flush out the stored-up fat accumulated in your cells, and you can do this with the use of fat-melting foods as nutritional therapy. These foods have a natural diuretic action that unlocks and liquefies accumulated fats and washes them right out of your body. Slim your cells—and you slim your body.

Basic Program

Enjoy these foods (1) raw, (2) slightly steamed, or (3) as a juice. Plan to eat a variety throughout the week. If you eat or drink one or more *before* your meal, you will feel your appetite brought under control and you will be satisfied with smaller portions of food. You should have several of these fat-melting foods *every day,* for the cell-washing program to take hold and produce desired slimming results. Here is the set of important fat-melting foods that work from the first taste:

1. *Apples.* Apples are a prime source of pectin, enzymes, and vitamin C, which work to break down the hard blobs of fat in the cells to wash excess out of your system. Freshly chewed apples or apple juice will attack stored fat, uproot it, and prepare it for speedy elimination.
2. *Asparagus.* Slightly steamed, in a bit of oil, or blanched in water, asparagus is a prime source of an alkaloid known as asparagine. These alkaloids tend to stimulate the kidneys to break down fat and flush it out of your system.
3. *Beets.* Beets are a prime source of low-level iron, which cleanses fat cells and serves as a strong washing agent for flushing away

excessive deposits. Beets also contain natural chlorine, which helps scrub away fat that accumulates in the cells of your liver, kidney, and gallbladder. Chop up a raw beet in a salad and see your fat just vanish from your body.

4. *Cabbage.* The rich concentration of sulphur and iron serve as cleansing agents to wash out fat from your gastrointestinal area. Chopped raw, or slightly steamed cabbage or cabbage juice will perform the fat-washing result in moments.
5. *Carrots.* Carrots are a rich source of beta-carotene, the predecessor of vitamin A that accelerates your metabolism by nourishing your cells and triggering a fat-flushing reaction.
6. *Celery.* Fresh raw celery has a high concentration of calcium to energize your endocrine system, producing hormones that break down fatty buildup in the cells.
7. *Citrus fruits.* Try oranges, grapefruits, tangerines, lemons, and limes, which are rich in vitamin C and tend to reduce the effectiveness of fat. The vitamin liquefies and dilutes fat and then flushes it out of your body. Fruits also contain pectin, a natural fat-fighter that limits the amount of fat that adipose cells can absorb. When pectin substances are released in the system, they tend to absorb water and bombard adipose cells, thereby releasing clusters of fat.
8. *Cranberries.* Cranberries contain a natural enzyme that helps to break up fat accumulations and flush them out of your system. Cranberries are a vigorous natural diuretic with a high acidic content, needed to dislodge stubborn gluelike fatty deposits and eliminate them from your cells and body.
9. *Cucumber.* Cucumbers are a prime source of magnesium and alkaloids that work to disrupt fatty infestation and cleanse away the core of the sludge to slim your cells.
10. *Eggplant.* Unique amino acids are able to create glandular-hormonal reactions that vigorously scrub the fat from your cells and prepare for disposal through waste channels. Slightly steamed eggplant slices will offer good appetite control as well as fat-melting rewards in a short time.
11. *Oils, vegetable.* Vegetable oils are very beneficial in assisting in the breakdown and synthesis of accumulated fat in adipose cells. Once absorbed, just a tablespoon of oil acts as an insulator in maintaining body temperature. The essential fatty acids in the oils form impor-

tant constituents of cell membranes by regulating the intake and removal of wastes and transporting vital fat-insoluble nutrients.

12. *Parsley.* The potent vitamin A together with unique enzymes in *raw* parsley works wonders in prompting breakdown and removal of fatty deposits.
13. *Soybeans.* Cooked, of course, soybeans are a prime source of lecithin, which releases a by-product known as *lecithin cholesterol acyltransferase* (LCAT). This by-product serves as a barrier and defense mechanism for adipose cells. As fatty deposits are broken down with LCAT, they become more easily flushed from your system. A small portion of soybeans in a salad will act as natural appetite control and fat-fighter with the same bite! You eat, and reduce!
14. *Tomatoes.* Rich in vitamin C and natural citric acids, they assist in the speeding up of metabolic processes. Tomatoes and their juice act as a diuretic by stimulating the kidneys. This combination, with enzyme-activated minerals, signal your organs to filter fatty deposits from your bloodstream.
15. *Watermelon.* A unique fruit form of vitamin A and C together with the mineral-rich liquid join to break up fatty deposits and speedily wash them right out of your system.

Your Simple Fat-Washing Nutritional Therapy Program

Lose pounds and inches, firm up your unsightly flab, slim down in a short while by including a variety of these 15 fat-fighting foods in your daily program. *Example:* breakfast should include citrus and other fruits; lunch could include cucumber, eggplant, soybeans, and other vegetables; dinner could have just a variety of the vegetables. Just plan to eat *more* of these 15 foods throughout the days and weeks and watch that stubborn fat just wash right out of your body!

30 POUNDS JUST "VANISH" OVERNIGHT

Stuart I. kept letting out his belt until he had one notch left. His unsightly stomach spilled over his beltline. He had more than just "middle aged spread" (he was just 41), but was troubled with flabby thighs and heavy hanging buttocks and struggled to get up from his chair. He had tried various diet programs, but the fat clung to his midsection and elsewhere with stubborn determination. He wanted to get rid of the weight and appealed for help from a newly formed diet therapy program at the local medical facility.

Stuart I. was told to cut down intake of fatty meats and refined sugars. He argued he had tried this approach but with minimal and temporary success. The fat soon came back again. He was told by the medical specialists he needed to uproot and dislodge the fat that overwhelmed his adipose fatty tissue. He was to use the 15 fat-melting foods as part of his weekly menu. Less fatty foods and sugary sweets, but much, much more of these specific fat-fighters.

Stuart I. followed the program. Amazed, he could see his waistline shrinking day after day. His hips and thighs almost slenderized overnight, he would say. In no time at all, he had lost at least 30 fatty pounds. More weight was lost until he was slim with a 34-inch waistline and a lifeguard figure! With the use of the 15 fat-melting foods, he had conquered the fat problem by getting to the cause—overloaded cells. He was exhilarated because the program slimmed him so speedily or the pounds were able to "vanish overnight."

How Carbohydrate Foods Control Food Cravings

Facing a snack attack? Are you a compulsive eater? Can't control your appetite? Use food as a natural appetite suppressant to control these cravings. In particular, carbohydrates (fresh fruits, raw vegetables, and whole grains) create a biological reaction that puts a halt to your urge to overeat.

When you eat carbohydrates, your body releases a hormone, insulin, to process them. Insulin also influences the movement of tryptophan, an amino acid, to enter your brain to stimulate the release of serotonin. It is this "bathing" of your brain cells with serotonin that controls your urge to overeat. Serotonin is the substance that acts as an appetite suppressant. You are able to control runaway food cravings by this mechanism. Refer to Chart 11-1 for carbohydrate alternatives.

A Simple Orange Helps You to Avoid Overeating

A fresh orange that you eat slowly is a fast-acting food that "blocks" your urge to eat unnecessarily. It offers a quick-acting carbohydrate that raises your blood sugar and sends forth the brain-soothing serotonin that actually signals your senses to "turn off" your appetite.

Chart 11-1: CALORIE-CARBOHYDRATE CHART

A = average
AS = average serving
C = cup
L = large
M = medium
S = slice
Sm. = small
Sq. = square
T = tablespoon
t = teaspoon

Item	Portion	Calories	Carbohydrate (grams)
Almonds	15	100	4
American Cheese	1S	100	Trace
Angel food cake	AS	200	32
Apple	M	50	22.6
Apple, dried, cooked without sugar	M	122	31.7
Apple juice	1 C	100	26
Apple dumpling	1 M	300	54
Apple pie	AS	350	51
Apple sauce	½ C	150	26
Apricots, dried	3 M	50	13.8
Apricots with syrup	3 M	75	26
Apricots	3 M	100	25
Apricot pie	AS	350	57.7
Asparagus soup	1 C	147	16.6
Bacon	1 S	30.5	.16
Banana	1 M	100	26
Banana split	A	400	92.5
Barley	¼ C	150	39
Bass	AS	100	0
Bean soup	1 C	170	22
Beans baked	½ C	261	47.77

Item	Portion	Calories	Carbohydrate (grams)
Beans, kidney	½ C	81	14.76
Beans, lima (baby)	½ C	94	17.84
Beans, string	1 C	44	10.2
Beef boiled	AS	250	0
Beef broth	1 C	30	3
Beef chopped	AS	100	0
Beef chuck/ground	AS	363	0
Beef/round steak	AS	292.32	0
Beets	¼ C	21	5
Berry pies	AS	350	56
Biscuits	1 Sm.	129	16
Blackberries	½ C	42.5	9.5
Blueberries	½ C	42.5	10.5
Bologna	2 S	150	2.2
Bouillon cube	1	2	0
Bran flakes	½ C	50	14
Bread, white	1 s	62	11.6
Broccoli	1 C	40	7
Brussels sprouts	⅔ C	36	6
Butter	1 Pat	50	Trace
Buttermilk	1 C	75	12

Chart 11-1: *(continued)*

Item	*Portion*	*Calories*	*Carbohydrate (grams)*
Cabbage boiled	¼ C	7	1.5
Cabbage, raw	¼ C	4	1
Candy, chocolate	1 oz.	133	17.8
Cantaloupe	½	115.5	28.87
Carrots	½ C	22.5	5
Catsup	1 T	25	4.2
Cauliflower	1/12 C	37	12.5
Celery	1 C	15	4
Cherries	1 C	133	33.06
Chicken, broiled	½ Sm.	281.52	0
Chicken, roasted	½ breast	106.08	0
Chicken soup	1 C	95	8
Chocolate cake	AS	205	29.12
Chocolate cookies	6 Sm.	108	17.16
Chocolate pudding	¼ C	80	62
Chocolate syrup	1 T	46.5	11.9
Cinnamon Toast	1 S	200	15.9
Clams	½ C	83	2.2
Cocoa with milk	1 C	212	27
Cocoa powdered	1 T	24.9	6.25
Codfish	AS	215	0

Item	*Portion*	*Calories*	*Carbohydrate (grams)*
Coffee, black	1 C	2.5	.66
Coffee cake	AS	90	14
Condensed milk	1 C	980	166
Consomme	1 C	21	1.92
Corn	¼ C	42.5	10
Corn flakes	½ C	50	11
Corn oil	1 T	125	0
Cottage cheese	1 T	21	.621
Crackers, soda	6	186	30
Cream	3 T	90	1
Cream cheese	1 oz.	104.72	.588
Cucumber	1 A	30	7
Cup cake	1 A	315	48
Doughnut	1 A	151	21.7
Duck	AS	109	0
Egg, hard-boiled	1	78	.4
Egg plant	½ C	19	4.1
Evaporated milk	1 C	345	.24

Chart 11-1: *(continued)*

Item	Portion	Calories	Carbohydrate (grams)
Filet of sole, broiled	AS	105.3	0
Flour, wheat	1 C	409	83.7
Frankfurter	1	182.4	.96
French dressing	1 T	100	3
Gelatin/sweetened	½ C	140	34
Grapefruit	½	50	13
Grapefruit juice	½ C	50	12
Grapes	1 C	65	15
Haddock, fried	AS	165	5.8
Halibut, broiled	AS	426	0
Ham	AS	126	0
Hamburger	2 oz.	363	0
Honey	1 T	65	17
Honeydew melon	¼	33	7.7
Ice cream	1 C	290	29
Jam	1 T	55	14
Kale	½ C	28	4.86
Lamb chop	1 M	260	0
Lamb roast	AS	119	0
Lemon	1 M	20	10.7
Lemon pie	AS	305	45
Lentils	½ C	233	41.7

Item	Portion	Calories	Carbohydrate (grams)
Lettuce	¼ Head	15	3
Liver, calf	AS	74	1.7
Lobster, broiled	1	308	.8
Macaroni	1 C	190	39
Mackerel, broiled	AS	415.2	0
Meat loaf	AS	264	11.5
Milk, skim	1 C	90	12
Milk, whole	1 C	161	12
Muffins	1	125	17
Mushrooms	⅔ C	26.6	4
Mustard	1 T	3.5	.32
Nectarine	1 M	80	21.37
Noodles	½ C	100	18
Oatmeal	½ C	65	16
Okra	½ C	34.2	7.92
Olive oil	1 T	125	0
Olives	3 Sm.	15	Trace
Onion raw	1 M	40	10
Onion cooked	3 M	180	42
Orange	1 M	75	14
Orange juice	1 C	110	26
Oysters, raw	12	104	5

Chart 11-1: CALORIE-CARBOHYDRATE CHART *(continued)*

Item	*Portion*	*Calories*	*Carbohydrate (grams)*
Parmesan cheese	1 T	25	Trace
Parsnips	1M	121	28
Peaches canned	1 C	200	52
Peaches fresh	1 M	35	10
Peach pie	AS	421	63
Peanut butter	1 T	93	3.12
Peanuts	¼ C	336	11.16
Pears, fresh	1 Sm.	100	25
Pears, canned	1 C	195	50
Pears, dried	½	50	13
Peas	¼ C	21.2	3.9
Pecans	1 C	740	16
Peppers, green	1 M	15	4
Pimento cheese	1½ oz.	150	2.8
Pineapple, fresh	1 S	37.44	9.86
Pineapple, canned	1 S	45	12
Pineapple, pie	AS	404	61
Plums, canned	1 C	205	53
Plums, fresh	1	25	7
Powdered sugar	1 T	30	8
Pork chop broiled	1 M	101.6	0
Pork roast	AS	380.1	0
Pork sausage	2	188	0

Item	*Portion*	*Calories*	*Carbohydrate (grams)*
Postum, no milk	1 C	10	2
Pot roast	AS	339.3	0
Potato, baked	1 Sm.	141	32
Potato, boiled	1 M	110.2	24.79
Potato chips	1 chip	11	1.0
Potato, french fried	10 pieces	155	20
Potato mashed	½ C	62.5	12.5
Potato salad	½ C	99	16.3
Potato soup	1 C	105	12
Potato sweet	1 M	15	4
Prunes	3	52.5	13.5
Prune juice	½ C	100	24
Pumpkin pie	AS	275	32
Radishes	5 M	10	1.8
Raisin pie	AS	325	32.5
Raisins	¼ C	125	128
Raspberries, canned	½ C	50	21.4
Raspberries, fresh	½ C	50	23.5
Rhubarb, stewed	1 C	211	54
Roast beef	AS	261	0
Roquefort cheese	AS	150	.5
Roquefort dressing	1 T	125	1.2

Chart 11-1: CALORIE-CARBOHYDRATE CHART *(continued)*

Item	*Portion*	*Calories*	*Carbohydrate (grams)*
Round steak	AS	254	0
Rutabaga	½ C	35	8.2
Ry-Krisp	5	100	19.2
Salmon, red	1 C	427	0
Sardines	3	233	.45
Sauerkraut	½ C	27.5	4.5
Scallops, steamed	1 C	112	0
Shrimp, breaded	1	31.97	4.57
Sirloin steak	AS	261	0
Sour cream	1 T	30.3	.625
Spaghetti	1 C	155	32
Spinach	½ C	20	3
Squash, hubbard	½ C	36	8.9
Squash, summer	¼ C	15	3.5
Strawberries	1 C	55	13
Succotash, canned	½ C	89	19.7
Sugar white	1 t	20	6
Swiss cheese	1S	68	Trace

Item	*Portion*	*Calories*	*Carbohydrate (grams)*
Tangerine	1 L	40	10
Tapioca pudding	½ C	100	11.6
Tea plain	1 C	2	.4
Tomato	1	40	9
Tuna, cooked	1 C	315	0
Turkey	AS	70.4	0
Turnips	½ C	18	4
Veal chop	1 M	107.6	0
Vegetable soup	1 C	84	9
Watercress	1C	4	.6
Watermelon	1 S Sm.	115	27
Wheaties	½C	75	12
Whipped cream	3 T	30	Trace
White fish steamed	AS	275.8	0
Yams	1 M	210	48.2

Try Quick-Acting Appetite Tamers

Quiet those food grumblings by eating just one or two of these complex carbohydrate foods: oranges, grapefruits, apples, pears, peaches, plums, watermelons, bananas, figs, nectarines, pineapples, tangerines, or pitted prunes.

Eat Slowly to Improve Brain Signals

Peel and/or wash the fruit. Chew slowly. The gradual mastication and swallowing will maximize the release of tryptophan and serotonin, which influence the neurotransmitters in your brain to "turn off" the runaway urge to eat. Within a few minutes, you will have soothed your compulsive desire to snack and gained control over your own willpower. It is this brain chemistry of nutritional therapy that controls your craving for high-calorie foods.

Two Weight-Control Tonics That Work in Minutes

To ease your desire to eat excessively, try these weight-control tonics that work swiftly to tame your taste buds and give you a comfortable feeling, even though you have not eaten a thing.

Ice Water Plus Lemon Twist

Many restaurants serve you ice water before a meal so you will be satisfied with smaller portions. Try this same trick to control your weight. Ice water, with a bit of lemon twist flavor, will "shrink" your stomach muscles and give you that satisfied fullness to ease and eliminate eating urges. Try it whenever you have a snack attack!

Vegetable Juice + Garlic Clove = Hunger Satisfaction

A glass of salt-free vegetable juice together with a mashed or diced garlic clove works wonders in soothing your appetite and giving you speedy hunger satisfaction. The complex carbohydrates of the vegetable juice are stimulated by the garlic's *gastroenteric allichalon* to give you a sedative action by delaying excessive motor activity of your stomach. In moments, your hunger pangs are eased. The grumblings are ended. Your eating urges are under control. *Tip:* Begin your meal with this vegetable juice plus garlic combo, and you will be satisfied with much smaller portions.

With either or both of these weight-control tonics, you help put a "hold" on your appetite and also set off a chain reaction to wash out the fat from your cells and bring down your waistline and other bulges.

CONTROL NERVOUS APPETITE, LOSE WEIGHT IN SEVEN WEEKS

Marge N., a publicist for a large entertainment facility, was always edgy. Instinctively, she would munch and nibble and eat more than she should. Her weight ballooned until she had a matronly look in a profession that demanded sleek and youthful slimness at any age.

She experienced side effects from chemical appetite suppressants that were threatening to become addictive. She asked a backstage nurse in attendance if there were any alternatives to these drugs. She was told to alternate between the ice water–lemon twist tonic and the vegetable juice–garlic clove tonic. Marge N. tried both. Immediately, her appetite calmed and her weight started to go down along with reduced food consumption. In seven weeks, she was sleek and trim again and joked she could appear in a commercial as the "after" half of a successful weight loss program. And all it took were the natural weight-control tonics!

It's Time for Your Personal Size-Up!

Instructions

Tape together some large sheets of construction paper the length of your height and spread the paper on the floor. Lay on top of it. Have a friend draw an outline of your body, starting with feet on up to your head. Now pin the paper to the wall and give it a long, hard look.

Scenario

Not exactly happy with what you see? Think you'd like to erase about 10 to 15 pounds of bulging lines from the picture? You may want to lose for an upcoming special event—graduation, a wedding, or a party. Whatever the reason, you want to look your best and bring out the beauty that's in you. The problem is, you don't want an unsafe crash diet or to spend months trying to lose. But a fast-weight-loss diet that's also well-balanced nutritionally can be coupled with a regular program of exercise, to bring your shape "in line."

Habits, nasty habits Why did you let yourself get out of shape? Somewhere along the line your behavior got out of hand. You have old habits about eating and thinking "fat," so whenever you start dieting you have myriad excuses: "It's impolite to turn food down"; "My mother forced me to clean my plate"; and "My job is demanding and I need something to relieve the tension." Whatever your excuses are for poor eating habits, you'll find a way to reinforce them. But let's face it, you'll eat for the rest of your life, so sacrificing a few mouthfuls here and there to be trim isn't going to hurt. It's time to control your life, not let food control you.

The following quiz is designed to reveal your savviness—or lack of it—in the areas of diet and exercise. The perfect score is 100; answering 75 percent of the questions means you're ahead of the game; anything below 50 means you've got a lot of work to do.

Questions

	True	False
1. A few extra calories a day won't make a difference in my weight.	☐	☐
2. Exercising will make me hungry, I'll eat more and never lose weight.	☐	☐
3. In order to see any results in fitness I have to exercise vigorously every day.	☐	☐
4. Calisthenics are more gentle and better for my health than aerobics.	☐	☐
5. A banana has less calories than a yogurt bar.	☐	☐
6. The body needs more protein than carbohydrates.	☐	☐
7. Ice cream is more fattening than frozen yogurt.	☐	☐
8. Once water weight is eliminated, you start losing fat on a starvation diet.	☐	☐
9. Playing tennis (singles) is more active than bicycling vigorously.	☐	☐
10. Red meats have more calories than fish or poultry because they're higher in fat.	☐	☐

Answers

1. *False.* Eating 100 extra calories a day can add 10 pounds a year to that svelte body of yours.
2. *False.* People who spend a great deal of energy on vigorous exercise may need extra calories. But regular, moderate exercise *doesn't* increase the appetite and may actually reduce hunger.
3. *False.* After rigorous exercise muscles need 48 hours to recover from the minor damage they may incur from the workout. Most exercise training programs suggest you work-out every other day to avoid this injury.
4. *False.* While stretching exercises are beneficial in toning the body and increasing flexibility, aerobics is the best all-around exercise for your body. Include swimming, jumping, running, or walking—a continuous workout for 15–30 minutes, three to four times a week, on alternate days. Aerobics helps strengthen the heart, lung, and circulatory systems and helps to *manage weight.*
5. *True.* A banana, nature's portable snack food, not only has fewer calories (about 100) than a yogurt bar (125 calories), but is high in potassium, low in sodium, almost fat-free, and provides vitamins A and C.
6. *False.* The body needs less protein than carbohydrates! Fruits and vegetables, whole grains and pastas, should make up 55 percent of the diet; fat 30 percent; and finally, protein, 12–20 percent.
7. *True.* Ice cream may have more calories, but, fruit-flavored frozen yogurt should not be considered "low in calories" because of its high sugar content. Read the labels on ice cream and yogurt carefully for fat and sugar contents—and calories.
8. *False.* You actually start losing lean tissue and not fat—so your body tries to replace the muscle tissue, encouraging weight to bounce back.
9. *False.* Tennis burns 450 calories per hour, while bicycling at 10 m.p.h. burns up 510 calories.
10. *True.* Broiled halibut, 3½ oz. has 171 calories; the same amount of roast chicken, white meat, has only 166 calories; a broiled, untrimmed sirloin steak, however, has *387* calories.

How Exercise Unlocks the Bottled-up Body Fat for Swift Melting

Food therapy plus exercise will get rid of accumulated body fat. This combination is the key to successful weight loss. Simply speaking, in 1 pound of body fat, there are about 3,500 calories. If you eat 3,500 more calories than your body needs, it stores up that pound. But if you eliminate 3,500 calories, you lose a pound. Controlled nutrition is one-half of the fat-washing process. Simple exercise is the second half of the picture. (See Chart 11-2, which lists various activities and the calories they burn.)

Chart 11-2: 100 CALORIE ACTIVITY CHART

To burn up 100 calories, you must

Walk (briskly)	16 minutes
Climb stairs	5 minutes
Iron clothes	24 minutes
Make beds	19 minutes
Scrub floors	17 minutes
Shovel snow	14 minutes
Play basketball	12 minutes*
Play Ping-Pong	21 minutes
Swim	8 minutes
Play golf	18 minutes
Play tennis	14 minutes
Bowl	12 minutes*
Row	13 minutes
Dance	25 minutes
Horseback-ride	33 minutes
Bicycle	13 minutes
Jog	8 minutes
Ski (downhill)	9 minutes
Ski (cross-country)	5 minutes

*Of active playing time.

During exercise, your body speeds up its basal metabolism rate and activity level. At the same time, it alerts a weight-regulating center (your hypothalamus or a pea-sized segment of your brain) that balances energy use with food consumption.

Just as you have internal controls to keep your body temperature constant, you also have a thermostat for fat. You need to raise that thermostat to help burn up the accumulated fat in your cells. This activity causes enzymatic changes that accelerate fat metabolism in your tissues.

Simple Walking Is Effective

If you walk 1 hour a day for 10 days, you will burn up about 350 calories each day or 3,500 calories at the end. You will have lost 1 pound of fat. It is a simple but effective way of helping to control caloric-fat buildup.

How Exercise Controls Your Appetite

Contrary to popular belief, exercise does *not* increase your appetite. It has a reverse benefit. It *depresses* your appetite. In brief, since blood sugar is the primary source of energy for the brain, a *low blood sugar level* can make you feel hungry. However, when you exercise, fat is released into your bloodstream to be utilized as a fuel to produce energy instead of the body using blood sugar. This enables your blood sugar to remain relatively constant, and therefore you will not feel hungry since your body is *burning fat* rather than utilizing sugar as its source of energy.

The biological changes that occur during and immediately following exercise are especially important since you will want to do an exercise about 1 hour before mealtime. Subsequently, you will experience a *decrease in your appetite.*

Plan to do 30 to 60 minutes of exercise 1 hour before you eat and then another 30 to 60 minutes 1 hour after you eat. This simple program will help wash away fatty overload and keep your cells slim and trim.

Foods That Work as Natural Fat Busters

To lose weight rapidly, a key factor is in activation of physiological processes to uproot the stored fat. You do this by stimulating your sympathetic nervous system to pour forth a substance called norepinephrine. This substance is then able to accelerate a metabolic process that zeroes in on your fat cells to help dislodge and disperse the globules to be washed out of your system.

Foods That Increase Fat-Busting Action

To wake up your nervous system and induce a flow of fat-washing norepinephrine, you need to eat small portions of those foods containing tyramine, an amino acid. It is tyramine that triggers the release of norepinephrine, the key to fat busting.

Food Sources of Tyramine: Consider the avocado, pineapple, banana, plum, lemon, tangerine, tomato, potato, eggplant, and apple cider vinegar. *Cheeses include* Brie, Roquefort, Edam, Gruyère, Limburger, brick, American, Swiss, Camembert, bleu, cheddar, Gouda, Munster.

How to Use Food As Fat Busters. Eat a small portion of any of these foods with your meal. All you need, for example, would be a slice or two of pineapple, or one banana, or one tomato in your salad with a sprinkle of apple cider vinegar and lemon, or else a small square of cheese, about 1 or 2 tablespoons, with an apple for dessert. Almost at once, the tyramine will initiate an outpouring of norepinephrine to work as fat busters to slim your cells. A little bit will go a long way.

Caution: Some groups of people should be careful about foods containing tyramine. If you have a history of migraine headaches, this amino acid could be upsetting. Or if you are taking prescribed monoamine oxidase inhibitors (antidepressants and blood pressure drugs), you should check with your health practitioner before increasing your intake of tyramine.

With the use of these nutritional therapies, you will be able to control your appetite and ease the hunger urge, soothe stomach pangs, and help lose unsightly and unhealthy weight in a short time.

Fight Fat with Behavior Control

You may eat sensibly all week, but if you help yourself to extra servings of cakes on the weekends, extra pounds will start to bulge. Most people become less active as they grow older, and this has the same result as eating more. With additional pounds to carry around, you become less active, add more fat, and so on in a vicious spiral interrupted only by periodic stints of dieting.

Maintaining a sensible weight does not mean a lifetime of carrots and celery, nor does it require hours of grueling calisthenics, but it does mean keeping calorie consumption and activity in harmony. It's like balancing a checkbook, and the human body is a strict account! Change your behavior, make a commitment, establish new patterns, and you will get rid of your pounds and keep pounds from coming back.

Make Simple Adjustments for Fast Weight Loss

Try taking smaller portions of food at meals. Still hungry? If you go back for seconds, you will be eating because you want the food, not just because it is on your plate. *Tip:* Put foods out of sight. Don't leave candies, nuts, crackers, or goodies around the house. If you find you listen to the clock rather than your stomach, go without a watch, or rearrange your schedule so when it is time to eat, you are busy with something else.

Be a Slower Eater

If you are one of the faster forks around, slow down. Put your fork down between bites. Chew each mouthful thoroughly. *Reason:* fast eating doesn't give your body a chance to react to the food you've eaten. By the time your body is able to say, "that's enough," you've already had too much. *Solution:* eat what seems a reasonable amount and leave the table for 30 minutes. Still hungry after half an hour, then go back to the table and resume your meal. You may well find you no longer feel so hungry, if at all.

If you wail that everything you look at or touch turns to fat, then dry your tears and start using nutritional therapies that let you eat and control your appetite while you lose unwanted weight in a jiffy.

BEST POINTS

1. Clara H. used an assortment of fat-washing foods that controlled her eating urges, soothed her appetite, and made her slim and trim in a short time.
2. Use any of the tasty 15 fat-washing foods and beverages as nutritional therapies to control your weight the easy way.
3. Stuart I. saw 30 pounds just "vanish overnight" on a simple fat-washing program with the 15 foods.

4. Everyday carbohydrate foods can control your eating urges by acting on the appetite center of your brain.
5. Two immediately prepared weight-control tonics use all-natural ingredients to help strengthen willpower and "turn off" your eating urges.
6. Marge N. controlled her nervous appetite and lost excess weight in seven days with the use of two tonics using everyday ingredients.
7. Use the self-test, the calorie-carbohydrate chart, and the fitness guide to help speed up your weight-loss program.
8. Enjoy the tyramine-containing foods that speed up fat busting.
9. A few simple behavior adjustments will ease fast weight loss.

12

How to Use Nutritional Therapy as Pain Relievers

"Take two aspirin and call me in the morning," is the familiar prescription for most common aches and pains. While medication will ease the pain, when the effect wears off, the distress returns again and again. Constant hurt, whether a headache, low-back pain, arthritis, or neuralgia, is a vicious circle which leads to irritability and depression. In many situations, the victim cannot sleep at night. Next day's weariness compounds the problem, leading to more nervousness and pain. In desperation, reaching for a medicated pain killer seems to be the only solution.

Are Medications the Answer to Pain?

Whether it is acetaminophen, aspirin, ibuprofen, or any of the other extrastrength, double-power medications that promise swift (although temporary) relief for the pain, there are penalties. These analgesics (pain relievers) lead to side effects such as acute liver damage, nausea and vomiting, ringing in the ears, sweating, flushing, fever, hyperventilation, slurred speech, gastric irritation, drowsiness, internal bleeding. You may ease the pain, but you are exchanging one disorder for another, which could be more serious! Clearly, medications are not the solution to pain.

Why Does It Hurt?

One reason is that nerve endings sensitive to touch are pressed very hard. Neuroscientists have found that your body is covered with many small nerve cells with extremely fine nerve fibers that are excited exclusively by intense, potentially harmful stimulation. Scientists call the nerve cells *nociceptors,* from the word noxious, meaning physically harmful or destructive. It's as if nature has sprinkled your body with a variety of pain-sensitive cells, not only to report what kind of hurt you're experiencing, but to make sure the message gets through. They reach your central nervous system and send forth agonizing signals.

How Your Body Can Be Taught to Block Pain

You can control and block the spread of pain when you consider a pain-suppressing pathway involving the "gate theory." That is, when pain signals first reach the nervous system, they excite a group of neurons until a hypothetical "gate" opens up to allow pain signals to be sent to higher brain centers. But the good news is that nearby neurons in contact with the pain cells can suppress activity so that the gate stays closed. It calls for the use of certain nutrients that strengthen the cells to release vital pain-suppressing substances called *endorphins.* In effect, the body "closes the gate" to block pain. These endorphins promote the flow of a soothing balm to quiet nerve cells, block and ease, and even erase pain. To help your body produce these morphinelike (but all-natural) pain killers, specific nutrients are needed in small, but quickly effective, amounts. These nutrients can block pain!

The Protein That Is an All-Natural Pain Killer: Phenylalanine

A nutritional amino acid, found in everyday foods, and available as a food supplement, holds the key to ending chronic pain. This all-natural pain killer, *phenylalanine,* is an essential amino acid that your body cannot make but must be obtained from foods or a supplement.

Phenylalanine works by protecting endorphins, your pain-relieving substances that move through your nervous system to make you feel relieved in body and mind. (This amino acid also lifts depression and brightens your blue moods.) The nutrient energizes the activity of your endorphins to help make you immune to pain, speaking broadly.

Phenylalanine Power for Swift Pain Relief

As an example, we have beta-endorphin which is said to be 50 times stronger than morphine, the strongest chemical pain killer we have. Yet, it is phenylalanine that protects beta-endorphin from natural destruction so it can act as an all-natural pain reliever for what ails you.

How to Use Phenylalanine

This isolated amino acid is available as a supplement. Swift pain relief has been noted for those who follow this simple program: 375 milligrams with breakfast, 375 with lunch, and another 375 with dinner. It is effective if taken *with* your meal or within 5 minutes after finishing your meal.

Almost immediately, the amino acid boosts the production of endorphins to help "close the gate" of pain by pouring forth the soothing balm to calm nerve cells. Before the day is over, your pain should have vanished.

Food Sources of Phenylalanine

Stock up on nonfat milk, cheddar cheese, turkey, rolled oats, shredded wheat, peas, corn, and lima beans. Calves' liver is a potent source but also extremely high in cholesterol and fat so you trade off one benefit for another blood fat risk. *Suggestion:* include moderate portions of nonfat milk and the other foods in your weekly eating guide to help protect your supply of endorphins and keep the "gate" closed to banish pain. But you would have to consume a large amount of such foods to act as "natural pain killers" so it makes good sense to use a supplement in the suggested potencies for swift relief, the easy way.

FREED FROM LIFETIME OF HEADACHES WITH NUTRIENT

For many years, Jim R. suffered the excruciating pain of cluster headaches. Night after night, throughout the day, the pain kept throbbing without relief. He was nervous, irritable. He was only 48 years old, when the stubborn pain threatened his job as a systems analyst. His entire livelihood in jeopardy, he sought help from a nutritionally oriented medical staff at a nearby pain clinic. He was told to take the nutrient, phenylalanine, in potencies just as described (375 milligrams). He was directed to halt temporarily taking prescribed medications that gave him agonizing side effects with minimal relief. Results? In four days, his formerly "hopeless" headaches ended. By taking the phenylalanine just one day per week, in the three suggested dosages, he has become free of the pains, and the medicines, too!

Foods That Soothe Muscle Pains

Do you wince with spasms when you have to move your shoulder? Troubled with a shooting pain in your hips when you try to stand up or get out of bed in the morning? Are you troubled by stiff and painful neck and back muscles and joints?

To answer the pain alarm, you may be taking prescribed or over-the-counter patent remedies. There is some temporary relief, but when the effect wears off, the agony returns with even more ferocious attack. The reason is that you need to get to the *root cause* of your muscle pain. Namely, your protective endorphins need to be gathered and activated from your brain nerve cells to inhibit movement of pain-causing cells into your muscles and joints.

Magnesium Is Most Soothing

This mineral is able to boost production of the protective endorphins to inhibit the dispersion of the pain-causing cells that threaten your muscles and joints. Magnesium is a valuable part of bone and soft tissue and is needed to maintain stability of your nerves and muscles. A deficiency of magnesium can cause hyperirritability of nerves and muscles, tissue weakness, irregular heartbeat, and eventually spasms and convulsions. It is magnesium in foods that will not only soothe muscle pains, but *prevent* them.

Food Sources of Magnesium

These include brewer's yeast, wheat bran, wheat germ, green leafy vegetables such as kale and beet greens, nuts, brown rice, and soybeans.

Untie Muscle Spasms with Magnesium

The gnarled tight feeling in your muscles and joints could be a signal that your body needs magnesium to untie those agonizing knots. With this mineral, your enzyme system becomes activated, and there is an improved fat and electrolyte metabolism to improve your muscular flexibility. In moments, your "knots" are untied, and you have greater mobility of your muscles and joints. More important, you are free of the stubborn pain.

How to Take Magnesium as a Pain Killer

For a margin of safety, women should have at least 400 milligrams per day, and men should take close to 700 milligrams per day. This plan will meet needs even under increased requirements such as heavy stress.

You may also be magnesium nourished by ingesting the foods listed as being rich in this pain-killing mineral. For example, consider this tonic:

Magnesium Tonic. Blenderize green leafy vegetables together with 1 teaspoon brewer's yeast, 1 teaspoon wheat bran, 1 teaspoon nuts. Just one 8-ounce glass will give you a powerhouse of magnesium along with other vitamins and minerals to provide swift relief for your muscle pain. Best of all, it has a refreshing taste and is all natural! A glass of Magnesium Tonic a day will keep your muscle pain away!

FREES HERSELF FROM NECK PAIN IN ONE HOUR

An avid reader, Peggy MacD., was constantly troubled with neck and back pain. Working days at a video display terminal and reading hours at night, took their toll. Her tensed head and neck muscles felt as if they were being squeezed between two giant hands.

Peggy MacD. was an "aspirin addict" in a desperate effort to ease the pain. Postural changes offered only minimal help. When she experienced dizziness and nausea from the medication, she felt helpless. She visited the company physician who noted her blood levels of magnesium were very low. He suggested a magnesium supplement in doses of just 500 milligrams per day for just a week. Then she was to take the Magnesium Tonic as a means of boosting her supply of this muscle-soothing mineral.

Peggy MacD. took the supplement. Within 1 hour, the pain was gone! She took magnesium for the recommended week. Then she took the refreshing tonic. The pain never returned! Now she could read and work and be free of the viselike tortuous neck–back muscle contractions, thanks to the miracle mineral of magnesium!

The Simple Grain That Soothes Morning Stiffness

Just include 1 tablespoon of wheat bran with your morning breakfast cereal. Stir it in to mix with the other grains. You have a powerhouse of concentrated magnesium that works wonders right in the morning to unlock your aching muscles and take the kinks out of your joints so you have youthful flexibility the day ahead!

Suggestion: For more vigorous and speedy action, add an additional ½ teaspoon of brewer's yeast and ½ teaspoon of wheat germ to your breakfast cereal, along with the wheat bran. You now have a triple-power in fighting and eliminating joint-muscle pain in the morning so you can face the day ahead with a cheerful mind and body. (They do go together!)

Calcium Can Cool That Burning Pain

When agonizing pain strikes, it is often accompanied with a burning or inflammation that can best be described as somewhat feverish. The area is not only subjected to stabbing aches but heat spasms that intensify when you try to move the area. Anti-inflammatory drugs are available to provide temporary relief, but they also carry the risk of side effects. Furthermore, when the drugs wear off, there is a return of the pain and the inflammation that always seems worse than before. Is there a nutritional therapy as alternative? Yes, it is in the form of calcium.

How Calcium Eases Overheated Pain

Calcium plays a vital role in maintaining the natural muscle and nerve reaction to function without distress. Calcium guards against painful twitching or spasms of the muscles. This mineral is required for normal nerve transmission to help ease muscular stress and keep the area feeling cool and relaxed.

Stress, Pain, Calcium

Chronic, unrelieved emotional and/or physical stress opens the "gate" to permit outpouring of pain. Unrelieved stress causes stiffness to build up as nerve reflexes reduce circulation, leading to increased pain. Messages sent over nerve pathways bring on inflammation and distress. Because the neck and the rest of the back are so closely related structurally, if you have a problem in one area, you may eventually have problems in the other area. And it can all be worsened with stress.

Calcium is a mineral that is able to soothe nerves to protect against irritability; this mineral is responsible for the alternate contraction and relaxation of body muscles. You know calcium soothes your stressful aches when you drink a glass of warm milk and feel yourself relaxing all over. You can use calcium to cool off your burning pain and protect against return of these distressful symptoms.

How to Use Calcium to Heal Pain

The simplest and swiftest pain reliever would be a glass of warm milk (low-fat, if possible). You could boost the calcium content by stirring in 2 or 3 tablespoons of nonfat dry milk powder into the fluid milk. Within moments, the calcium is stabilizing the spasms, soothing your stress, releasing the endorphins needed to block pain signals. You heave a sigh of relief, thanks to calcium as a pain reliever.

Other Stress-Soothing, Pain-Easing Calcium Sources

One ounce of Gruyere cheese or cheddar cheese or soybean tofu, will give you a rich concentration of calcium needed to make you feel soothed and relaxed all over. You could also try ½ cup of canned salmon, bones and all, for quick relief of aching stiffness.

HOW SIMPLE SNACKS HELP TO AVOID PAIN ATTACKS

Because Benjamin X. had a stressful position as sales supervisor, having to deal with personality clashes, he was given to frequent attacks of stiff neck, low-back pain, arthritic like gnarled shoulder muscles. Medications gave little help, but many side effects. He had frequent pain attacks that lasted for the whole day. A few days of relief, then the attacks struck again, sometimes longer, sometimes shorter. He asked help from a company dietician and was told to "snack" on calcium foods. He carried a small thermal container with chunks of the high-calcium cheeses. For lunch, he would have a salmon salad with a scoop of low-fat cottage cheese (more calcium). On occasion, he would have a glass of warm skim milk in the company cafeteria. Within four days, this simple snack program gave Benjamin X. total freedom from pain attacks. As long as he had a small chunk of cheese each day, he was able to enjoy immunity against the debilitating pain that had so plagued his working days and nights, too. Calcium had soothed his stress and eased and even erased his pain.

The Protein That Protects You Against Pain: Tryptophan

Tryptophan is more than a building block of protein. It is one of the most potent (and natural) pain relievers available. It has been called the best and safest nondrug remedy for most pain. Yet, it is scarce in the typical American diet, suggesting a possible reason for the widespread prevalence of pain.

How Tryptophan Blocks Pain

This amino acid is a predecessor of serotonin, a neurotransmitter in the brain, which energizes the activity of endorphins, your body's own pain killers. Your pain perception threshold comes under your control with the availability of this protein.

Tryptophan also induces a desire for relaxation as well as sleep. You will not fall into a deep sleep when having a tryptophan supplement, but you will be totally relaxed and calmed down in body and mind when the serotonin bathes your nerve cells and tissues and unties the knots in your muscles.

How to Take Tryptophan

For best results, take it between meals with a low-protein food such as fruit juice or whole grain bread (otherwise, other amino acids in a high-protein meal tend to crowd tryptophan out and prevent it from reaching your brain).

Plan to eat a high-carbohydrate, low-fat, and low-protein meal, even though protein is the only dietary source of tryptophan. *Reason:* When protein is digested, tryptophan enters the bloodstream and joins a pool of other amino acids waiting to be transported to your brain. But the carrier molecule designed to do that also carries eight other amino acids. The object is to tip the balance in favor of tryptophan.

That is where the high-carbohydrate diet plan comes into the nutritional therapy picture. After eating a meal high in carbohydrates, the body releases insulin. And this hormone in turn facilitates the uptake into body tissues of all the amino acids *except* tryptophan.

With the competition tied up, the tryptophan is free to attach itself to the carrier molecule and be transported to the brain, where it will then be converted into pain-relieving serotonin. *Easy plan:* Try a 10 percent protein, 10 percent fat, and 80 percent carbohydrate diet.

Where to Find Tryptophan

Your simplest method is to take *three* doses of 500 milligrams each, with your three daily meals. *Remember:* Your meals should be high-carb, low-fat, low-protein.

Food Sources: Included are milk, peanuts, eggs, and some meats. The last two items are high in cholesterol and fat, so you would have to restrict their intake.

It will be more effective if you take the supplements on a daily basis, reducing potency as the pain is reduced. If you anticipate a pain-causing stressful situation, be sure to take your tryptophan in advance to shield yourself against reactions.

HEALS STIFF NECK, ENDS NIGHTMARISH MIGRAINE HEADACHES, CORRECTS BAD BACK WITH NUTRITIONAL THERAPY

JoAnne T. was a victim of excruciatingly tight stiff neck and frequent migraines that would last for days and nights. Her back was often hunched up, and she could never remember being able to walk or sit with a flexible spinal column. Nauseous and weak from medications, she was often bed-ridden until the attack was over.

Was this going to be her lifetime disability? She appealed for help from an osteopathic physician who diagnosed her condition as being tryptophan deficient to an alarming degree. He prescribed 1,500 milligrams per day, to be taken on a low-protein program. Within six days, her stiff neck was swanlike in flexibility, her headaches vanished, and she could move her shoulders with the agility of a dancer. What was erroneously said to be a "lifetime" affliction with pain was healed with nutritional therapy of tryptophan!

Suggestions, Hints, Programs

For quick-acting results, consider taking 500 milligrams of tryptophan on an empty stomach so it does not have to compete with other amino acids and can increase relaxing serotonin levels more rapidly. For some people, tryptophan taken at bedtime elevates serotonin enough to relax pains and increase ability to fall asleep all the more easily.

Avoid refined sugar in your diet. It influences brain serotonin levels by interfering with transfer of tryptophan into the brain.

You may take tryptophan with a fresh citrus fruit or juice which is a concentrated source of vitamin C. This nutrient works with tryptophan to block pain-causing impulses that threaten to hurt the neurons (brain cells). It is vitamin C that enables the tryptophan to cross the blood/brain barrier or impenetrable wall of tissues. Here, it blocks dopamine receptors or substances that are responsible for the pain.

In particular, vitamin C plus tryptophan have an affinity with the dopamine receptors, these two nutrients are able to help shield your brain (and body) from various types of pain.

Simple Nutritional Therapy Heals Pain Swiftly

Just take a 500 milligram tablet of tryptophan with one glass of freshly prepared citrus juice. This is the powerful all-natural combination that will instantly send forth a supply of pain blockers and serotonin to heal the distress—and prevent it from happening again!

With the use of various nutritional therapies, you can look forward to living *without* your "incurable" pain. If need be, take two "nutrients" in the morning and see if you need to ask for medications the next day, or ever again!

SUMMARY

1. Medications with their temporary effects and extended side effects are not the only answer to correcting pain.
2. Phenylalanine is a nutritional amino acid that works as an all-natural pain killer.
3. Jim R. freed himself from years of headaches and stubborn pains with the use of a phenylalanine food supplement.
4. Magnesium is a soothing mineral that corrects the cause of muscular pain, unties knots, and eases the spasms in minutes.
5. Peggy MacD. kicked her "aspirin addiction" with the use of a Magnesium Tonic and freed herself of recurring pain within 1 hour.
6. Cool off your burning stress-caused pain with calcium.
7. Simple calcium snacks helped Benjamin X. to avoid pain attacks.
8. Tryptophan is a remarkable pain blocker that creates a protective barrier right in your brain cells to give you freedom from distress.
9. JoAnne T. overcame a lifetime threat of painful stiffness within six days with the use of tryptophan as nutritional therapy.

13

Sweeten Your Blood Sugar to Feel Youthful...in Minutes

Hypoglycemia, translated into lay terms, simply means low blood sugar. *Hypo* means low; *glycemia* means sugar. (Diabetes is the opposite: high blood sugar, or hyperglycemia.) Both conditions, while virtually opposite, are closely related. Both are caused by the body's inability to use sugar effectively.

Low Blood Sugar = Low Body and Mind Energy

In almost all persons who have low blood sugar, the most prominent symptom is fatigue of body and mind. You know you have this syndrome if you feel tired much of the time. That is, tired without obvious reason, tired when you awaken, often too tired to function effectively in household, occupational, or marital activities.

Warning Symptoms

These include emotional upset, irritability, difficulty in concentrating, muscle aches, weight gain, weak libido, recurring headaches, and, often, intolerance of even small amounts of alcohol.

Feel Depressed?

Mild to moderate depression is often traced to either a sudden drop in blood sugar or a seesaw "yank" that could give you feelings of elation one minute, then plunge you downward into the depths of the glooms the next. This disturbance of body chemistry known as hypoglycemia can sap away your vital energy even in the prime of life.

What Causes Hypoglycemia?

Hypoglycemia is a condition brought on by an insufficient amount of glucose (sugar) in the bloodstream. The villain here is sugar. It is like a firecracker. It agitates the brain chemistry. It incites the explosive behavior classified as hyperactive.

What happens is that the pancreas (a small gland lying behind the stomach) is overstimulated by sugar and secretes an overabundance of insulin, which reduces the sugar level in blood to a below-normal amount. Unless your blood has a proper level of sugar, your brain cannot function efficiently.

Constant overconsumption of sweets can undermine the biological mechanisms balancing blood sugar levels. This upset leads to erratic behavior, poor concentration, attention weakness, poor memory, and more physical signs such as a pale skin, premature aging, susceptibility to infections, and illness.

So-called Senility Could Be Hypoglycemia

The maintenance of a balanced blood sugar level is essential to achieving the best molecular environment for the mind. Hypoglycemia could bring on symptoms of so-called senility in which there are memory blanks, feelings of lethargy, staring off into space, inability to participate in ordinary conversations, feelings of confusion, and loss of identity. Many of these conditions have been sparked by the up-and-down "yo-yo" reaction of blood sugar. There could be feelings of exhilaration and energy that are soon changed to those of aging and disorientation. Your body is trying to signal the condition of hypoglycemia or low blood sugar.

Blood Sugar: Normal Versus Abnormal

Normally, the concentration of sugar or glucose in the blood is between 70 and 120 milligrams per 100 milliliters (mg/dl) before meals. Even with prolonged fasting, the blood glucose concentrations remains above 50 mg/dl. After meals, it may reach 140 for a short time, only to settle back down toward the premeal level. Hypoglycemia may be defined as a blood glucose concentration below 50 mg/dl, which may be considered "abnormal."

Your Body Must Have Sugar

You would not want to eliminate all forms of sugar from your diet. Neither could you, since it is found in almost everything you eat and drink. Your body uses glucose for a variety of biochemical functions. Your brain, for example, could not function for more than 3 minutes without glucose. You would age and wither away without sugar. Then where does the problem occur?

Sugar Metabolism at a Glance

To supply your needs, your liver manufactures glucose from ingested protein as the raw material for synthesis. When starches or dietary sugars are consumed, insulin is released from your pancreas in response to the rising blood sugar as the dietary carbohydrates are absorbed. Insulin restrains liver production of the sugar. The released insulin shuts down liver glucose output and a simultaneous tissue consumption of glucose.

These two actions control the rising blood glucose after meals and return it promptly to normal. Between meals, insulin secretion is reduced. This permits liver glucose production to resume so that even with protracted fasting, your blood glucose will not fall too low to provide brain function.

This finely tuned system provides your brain with sufficient glucose even between meals; there is regulation of your blood sugar content so that it does not drop too low (hypoglycemia or low blood sugar) or go too high (hyperglycemia or diabetes).

Why Sugar Metabolism Goes Wrong and How to Protect Yourself

To remain youthful in body and mind, sugar is needed for all muscle actions, especially for brain and nerve function. Stored glycogen is reconverted into a usable form, glucose, and transported by the blood to areas where it is needed.

Thus, when you eat sugar in the form of *natural* carbohydrates, your blood and tissues usually absorb only the amount of sugar needed for normal function.

Problem: When you eat food with *refined,* white, commercially produced sugar, the small molecule carbohydrates of these foods are absorbed quickly—sometimes almost instantaneously through the membranes of the mouth and stomach—causing a sudden flood of glucose into the bloodstream.

Such a flood of excess sugar into the bloodstream exerts a dangerous strain on the pancreas and liver, as well as the adrenals and other endocrine glands involved in regulating blood sugar levels. The firecracker explodes and hypoglycemia ignites the system.

So you can see that wholesome *natural* carbohydrates such as fresh fruits, vegetables, grains, and legumes can be metabolized to provide a steady supply of healthy sugar. But the *refined* carbohydrates such as white sugar, white flour, and processed and sugar-saturated packaged foods cause an overreactive pancreas that produces too much insulin. Blood sugar level drops abnormally low, depriving your brain and nervous system of much needed oxygen.

The sugar metabolism process goes haywire, and you suffer the penalty of unpleasant hypoglycemic symptoms.

Eating Sugar Is Like Throwing Fat on Fire

You would erroneously assume that to correct low blood sugar, just eat sugar! This is dangerous! Pouring in more sugar will only trigger your overresponsive pancreas to produce more insulin and worsen both the situation and the symptoms. The excess of refined sugars and carbohydrates will cause internal upheaval and explosive reactions just as throwing fat on a fire makes the fire worse. So it is with sugar as a remedy. The "cure" is worse than the disease!

"But I Don't Eat Sugar!"

Many a diagnosed functional hypoglycemia patient insists on never touching sugar so how can the condition develop? The answer is in "hidden" sugar. Nearly all soft drinks contain sugar. Many commonly used sauces, jellies, custards, canned fruits, or juices contain sugar. Virtually all canned, processed, frozen, or packaged foods contain some form of sugar additive. For example, all commercially sold bread contains sugar or syrup. *Read the label!*

Did you know that many frozen TV dinners whether meat, fish, dairy, fruit, or vegetable will also have sugar? These processed foods with so much concentrated sugar can easily overtax the pancreas and trigger its overreaction. So even if you never use the sugar bowl or shaker, but eat processed foods, you are also eating sugar! Therefore, to protect yourself against hypoglycemia, you would need to shun all forms of sugar, whether added by yourself or the cook or in processed foods.

Simple Corrective Program Shields You from Hypoglycemia

To guard against the risk of age-causing and allergy-inducing hypoglycemia, follow this simple five-step corrective and protective program:

1. *Avoid sugar.* A diet too high in refined starches and sugars will trigger hypoglycemia. Much of today's irrational and antisocial behavior can be traced to our denatured, chemicalized, sugar-laden diet. To eliminate these two health destroyers, use a rule of thumb to *avoid prepared* foods and drinks. Prepare your own from scratch. You will help stabilize your insulin production and guard against the tug of war threat of refined carbohydrates.
2. *Avoid caffeine.* Studies demonstrate that caffeine raises blood sugar level in diabetics, but drastically lowers it in hypoglycemics. This is not as contradictory as it may seem. Sugar does the same because of an overreacting pancreas. Caffeine has a stimulating effect on the adrenal glands, which prompt the liver to release more sugar into the bloodstream. Excessive caffeine produces such hypoglycemic symptoms as anxiety, light-headedness, heart palpitations, nervousness, agitation, irritability, trembling hands and muscle twitches, and sleep disorders. Caffeine is found in more products than just coffee (see chart 13-1). For most people, just 100 milligrams a day can trigger disorders. Just stop consuming caffeine-containing products, and the symptoms should vanish.
3. *Avoid alcohol.* Consider the condition of alcohol-induced hypoglycemia, for example, the "morning after" or the typical hang-over. These are little more than symptoms of hypoglycemia. Alcohol reduces the output of glucose by the liver, which then precipitates or exaggerates low blood sugar. Alcohol may well produce the same effect as sugar. To protect against this disorder, avoid alcohol just as you would avoid sugar.
4. *Avoid tobacco.* Some studies show that smoking will cause an abrupt rise in blood sugar and then a sudden drop when the cigarette or

Chart 13-1A: CAFFEINE CONTENT OF POPULAR BEVERAGES AND FOODS

Item	*Milligrams of Caffeine*
Coffee (5-ounce cup)	
Drip method	110–150
Percolated	64–124
Instant	40–103
Decaffeinated	2–5
Instant decaffeinated	2
Tea (loose or bags) (5-ounce cup)	
1 minute brew	9–33
3-minute brew	20–46
5-minute brew	20–50
Tea products	
Instant tea (5-ounce cup)	12–28
Iced tea (12-ounce can)	22–36
Cocoa	
Made from mix	6
Milk chocolate (1 ounce)	6
Baking chocolate (1 ounce)	35

Source: Data for caffeine content obtained from Consumers Union, Food and Drug Administration, National Coffee Association, and National Soft Drink Association.

13-1B: CAFFEINE CONTENT OF VARIOUS SOFT DRINKS

Soft Drinks with Caffeine	*Milligrams of Caffeine (per 12 ounce serving)*
Sugar-Free Mr. PIBB	58.8
Mountain Dew	54.0
Mello Yello	52.8
TAB	46.8
Coca-Cola	45.6
Diet Coke	45.6

Chart 13-1B: *(continued)*

Soft Drinks with Caffeine	*Milligrams of Caffeine (per 12 ounce serving)*
Shasta Cola	44.4
Shasta Cherry Cola	44.4
Shasta Diet Cola	44.4
Shasta Diet Cherry Cola	44.4
Mr. PIBB	40.8
Dr. Pepper	39.6
Sugar-Free Dr. Pepper	39.6
Big Red	38.4
Sugar-Free Big Red	38.4
Pepsi-Cola	38.4
Aspen	36.0
Diet Pepsi	36.0
Pepsi Light	36.0
RC Cola	36.0
Diet Rite	36.0
Kick	31.2
Canada Dry Jamaica Cola	30.0
Canada Dry Diet Cola	1.2

*There are at least 68 flavors, variets, and types of soft drinks, manufactured by the 12 leading bottlers, that contain no caffeine.

Source: Data obtained from the National Soft Drink Association, Washington, D.C.

13-1C: CAFFEINE IN DRUG PREPARATIONS

Classification	*Milligrams per tablet or capsule*	*Milligrams per day**
Over-the-counter		
Stimulants		
NoDoz tablets	100	200
Vivarin tablets	200	200
Pain relievers		
Anacin	32	64

Chart 13-1C: *(continued)*

Classification	*Milligrams per tablet or capsule*	*Milligrams per day**
Excedrin	65	130
Midol	32	64
Plain aspirin, any brand	0	0
Vanquish	33	66
Diuretics		
Aqua-Ban	100	200
Cold remedies		
Coryban-D	30	30
Dristan	16.2	32.4
Triaminicin	30	30
Weight-control aids		
Dexatrim	200	200
Dietac	200	200
Prolamine	140	140
Prescription		
Cafergot	100	100
Darvon Compound	32.4	64.8
Fiorinol	40	40 or 80
Migrol	50	50

*Depending on the type of drug, a single dose is recommended nce a day or as often as once every four hours.

Source: Information on caffeine content and standard dosages obtained from the *Physicians' Desk Reference*, 1982, and *The Physicians' Desk reference for Nonprescription Drugs*, 1982.

cigar is put out. This rapid rise and fall of blood sugar levels also leads to the habit of chain smoking—the craving for another pick-me-up. This upset in the sugar control mechanism can cause emotional instability, apprehension, and insecurity along with typical physical disorders. Get rid of smoking, and you may well get rid of the risk of hypoglycemia.

5. *Avoid salt.* This additive causes a loss of blood potassium, which leads to a drop in blood sugar. You need potassium, a vital mineral,

to balance sugar metabolism. Yet excessive salt consumption disturbs this level, causing much potassium to be lost while sodium is retained in the system (known as edema or water retention). The connection between salt and hypertension, kidney malfunction, and cardiovascular disorders is well known. Kick the salt habit and you may kick the problem of erratic blood sugar.

Just build this five-step nutritional therapeutic program into your daily life-style and enjoy much more emotional and physical well-being.

RECOVERS FROM "OLD AGE" IN TWO DAYS ON EASY FIVE-STEP PROGRAM

George DeB. was losing his grip. Although only in his fifties, he walked with a stoop, looked with glazed eyes at once familiar family and friends, would be irritable for a few hours, then silently depressed for the next hours. He grew allergic to modest weather changes and exhibited faulty memory and slurred speech. Simple tasks were impossible. When he could not remember his address, concerned family worried he might be developing Alzheimer's disease or so-called senile old age.

Fortunately, an endocrinologist was consulted who diagnosed his condition as erratic blood sugar, responsible for his declining condition. George DeB. was put on the preceding five-step program. Nothing else! Within two days, he recovered so much, he was more alert mentally and physically than his grandson! He was cheerful, sharp in eyes and talk, resisted illnesses, had an alert mind, and was as cheerful as could be. The five-step program saved him from a "living death" of confinement in an institution with Alzheimer's disease!

How Simple Meal Spacing Gives You Superenergy and Vitality

Your goal is to normalize your metabolism. You can do this by following simple meal-spacing programs to give you day-long vitality of mind and body. Here are the easy-to-follow steps:

1. *Have a protein breakfast.* Start your day off with an energy bank in the form of protein. It is found in meats, fish, eggs, dairy products, beans, nuts, seeds, and whole grains. If you are watching your fat and/or cholesterol levels, just switch to egg whites or skim milk products. A good protein breakfast does not overload your blood with sugar but

sends glucose first to your liver, which doles out the sugar allowance as needed. This prevents overloading and subsequent bankruptcy of sugar in the bloodstream. *Caution:* The working person's typical breakfast of coffee and a sweet roll is definitely out! *Suggestion:* A fruit salad with a sprinkling of chopped nuts and seeds, some chunks of cheese, with a caffeine-free beverage is a good protein breakfast to give you day-long vigor.

2. *Take frequent meals.* If possible, have five or six meals instead of three traditional large ones. *Benefit:* By eating frequently, you consume less, and instead of having three wide upward and downward swings in blood sugar level, you have six or seven small ones. In time the level will tend to smooth out. A bonus is that small meals minimize conversion of food into fat and frequent meals control your appetite.
3. *Enjoy some fat.* Your nutritional therapy program calls for a small amount of dietary fat. It has satiety value that keeps away hunger pangs and also helps stoke the fires to burn body fat. Just 2 tablespoons of polyunsaturated vegetable oil daily on your salad or in cooking will help to balance your blood sugar, too.
4. *Surrender to the snack attack.* Your blood sugar is misbehaving and needs controls with the use of a good protein snack. Try a handful of sunflower seeds, a tablespoon of nutmeats, a half cup of salt-free, butter-free popcorn, a small portion of very lean meat, a fat-trimmed drumstick, a wedge of cheese with a slice of fruit. Just eat a *small* portion, perhaps a mouthful or two at the most. It will soon help your body utilize amino acids and carbohydrates and calm down your disruptive blood sugar.
5. *Never skip meals.* Skipping meals causes stored fat to pour into your bloodstream and poses a risk to your heart. Also, there is a confusion with carbohydrate metabolism that could trigger hypoglycemic symptoms. Once you plan your daily five- or six-meal schedule, stick to it. You will find yourself looking and feeling younger and healthier with a stabilized blood sugar level.

With this five-step program of meal spacing, you should quicky experience a return to normal blood sugar. You will feel it in the form of superenergy and vitality. And youthfulness, too!

FROM "WACKY" TO "WONDERFUL" IN FOUR DAYS

Her life was falling apart! Marion O'C. had worked for more than 15 years as a company supervisor with nary a personality problem, but now she was losing control. She snapped at coworkers. Columns of figures were confusing. Schedules were disrupted. She forgot to give messages to her superiors. Important papers were never prepared. Meetings were in disarray. Her antagonistic attitude dubbed her "wacky" by coworkers behind her back. What went wrong? Was she ready for discharge or, worse, confinement?

A sympathetic saleswoman recalled her sister having undergone a personality change to be diagnosed as hypoglycemic. When the family endocrinologist suggested regular spaced-out meals and avoidance of sugar, salt, and caffeine as part of a program of more natural foods, the symptoms vanished. She urged Marion O'C. to follow the same home treatment. Sneering, the emotionally unstable woman mumbled her doubts, yet she did follow the program. Within four days, she was cheerful again, mentally alert, and a superwhiz in efficiency. Her blood sugar had stabilized with the back-to-basics program, and she was now called "wonderful" by adoring coworkers.

Nutritional Therapies to Sweeten Your Blood Sugar

Your goal is to stabilize your blood sugar, or "sweeten" it. Obviously, without the use of inflammatory sugar. You can do it with a few nutrients that are known for correcting the functional imbalance and restore mental and physical equilibrium in a short time. In effect, these nutrients sweeten your blood sugar.

Chromium

A trace element needed for proper sugar metabolism. A deficiency can cause impairment of the sugar regulating machinery which is controlled by insulin. Chromium is needed to manufacture the glucose tolerance factor (GTF), whic regulates the blood sugar. *Food sources:* Included here are brewer's yeast, whole grains, wheat germ, and bran.

Zinc

Plentiful in a healthy pancreas where insulin is manufactured and is actually a constituent of that hormone. Those who are diagnosed as having hypoglycemia and/or diabetes are often found to be deficient in zinc. *Food sources:* Consider whole grains, seeds, and nuts.

Vitamins B-Complex

The entire B-complex family is helpful because they build your body's tolerance to sugars and carbohydrates and assist in promoting a more normal sugar metabolism. *Food sources:* Enjoy whole grains, brewer's yeast, green leafy vegetables, eggs, organ meats, nut butters, and brown rice.

Pantothenic Acid

A deficiency could cause blood sugar to drop so quickly, there could be a blackout or total collapse. This particular B-complex member is singled out because it is very intimately involved in the metabolism, synthesis, and breakdown of carbohydrates, fatty acids, sterols, and steroid hormones, all of which are involved in maintaining a balanced sugar level. *Food sources:* Try brewer's yeast, wheat germ, wheat bran, whole grain breads and cereals, beans, nuts, peas, liver, egg yolk, and green vegetables.

Magnesium

Magnesium is a nutritive substance that is required for blood sugar stabilization. It activates those enzyme systems that control fat and electrolyte metabolism. Low magnesium levels seem to be related to reactive hypoglycemia (a condition in which blood sugar drops precipitously following a meal rich in refined carbohydrates)—leaving the victim with symptoms of weakness, shakiness, dizziness, headache, irritability, and confusion, to name a few penalties. *Food sources:* Include in your diet whole grains, green leafy vegetables, beet greens, nuts, brown rice, and soybeans.

Quick Help for Boosting Blood Sugar

To give your blood sugar a "shot in the arm," you could try this easy to prepare Energy Shake because that is precisely what it does. It gives your sugar a lift and your body and mind an energy shake-up!

How to Prepare

Blenderize the following ingredients in an 8 or 10 ounce glass: 1 tablespoon brewer's yeast, 2 tablespoons wheat germ, 1 tablespoon sunflower seeds, 1 tablespoon nutmeats, 1 cup torn greens, 6 ounces skim milk. Whiz for just 2 or 3 minutes. Drink slowly.

Benefits: The chromium stimulates the manufacture of the GTF to balance your blood sugar. A flow of energy boosted by the zinc and B-complex vitamins along with the metabolic power of pantothenic and magnesium will send a supercharge of vitality throughout your endocrine system. Within 10 minutes, the Energy Shake corrects your glucose metabolic levels and you have swept away fog from your mind and knots from your muscles. You become revived, regenerated, refreshed—and rejuvenated!

Include These Foods on a Daily Basis

When planning your food program, be sure to include the foods already listed. They give you the valuable nutrients that are nonsystemic in that they zero in directly on those specific body and glandular areas needing their help.

BANISHES HEADACHES, IMPROVES MEMORY, BECOMES ENERGETIC IN JUST TWO DAYS

Edward L. had more than stubborn headaches and memory lapses. He felt his energy slipping through his fingers. He feared getting old before his time even though he was only in his early fifties. A diet specialist said he could have hypoglycemia. He recommended the easy-to-prepare Energy Shake. Edward L. had the shake in the morning; he also gave up all forms of refined sugars and starches as well as caffeine. Within two days, his headaches were gone, his memory was sharp, and he was a bundle of energy. His blood sugar had been stabilized, thanks to the program and the tasty and speedily effective beverage!

How a Glass of Milk Can Balance Your Sugar Levels

For many folks troubled with hypoglycemia, milk is a remarkably effective form of nutritional therapy. If you drink one glass of milk first thing in the morning and last thing at night, you could overcome your disorders. *Benefit:* Milk is rich in protein and also contains a small amounts of natural sugar (lactose), which very gently raises your blood sugar levels.

If you are calorie and fat cautious, drink low-fat or fat-free milk. You may very well eliminate the syndrome of low blood sugar with this simple nutritional therapy.

Are you a victim of hypoglycemia? Troubled with indecision, irritability, headaches, anxiety, digestive upsets? You may be a victim of hypoglycemia, an affliction called the "hidden disease" because its symptoms mimic other organic problems. With the use of nutritional therapy, you should put some sweetness into your body and mind and feel youthful, in minutes.

IN REVIEW

1. Check over the reasons why hypoglycemia happens and see if you fit into that diagnostic picture.
2. Note the differences between refined and natural sugars and carbohydrates and plan to avoid those foods that are processed.
3. Follow the five-step nutritional therapeutic program to shield yourself from the upset of low blood sugar.
4. George DeB. went from "old age" to youth in two days with the easy five-step program.
5. Simple meal spacing helps to improve your natural energy reserves.
6. Using the improved meal plan program, Marion O'C. went from hypoglycemic "wacky" to healthy "wonderful" in four days.
7. Include the nutrient-rich foods in your meal planning, as listed, to improve sugar metabolism.
8. Easy to prepare, an Energy Shake works in minutes like a "shot in the arm" to give you a mind-body boost.
9. Edward L. was "restored to life" with the basic dietary improvements and the Energy Shake that worked instantly.
10. For many cases of sugar imbalance, a glass of milk twice daily may well be the most potent (and easiest) nutritional therapy you need to put you in the pink and correct your low blood sugar.

14

For Men Only: Solve Prostate Problems with Nutritional Therapy

If you are a male over age 50, has this ever happened to you? After driving for miles and miles, the need to go to a rest stop keeps building until the pressure seems uncontrollable. Relief is in sight when you approach a gas station. You know where your bladder is located. It is at that point in the lower abdominal cavity where you felt all that unbearable pressure.

The problem is not necessarily with your bladder, partially responsible for your having to make increasing bathroom trips, especially during the night. Instead, there could be a disorder with your prostate gland.

Location, Function of Prostate

This walnut-sized organ is located next to the bladder (where urine is stored) and surrounds the urethra (canal through which urine passes out of the body). The prostate manufactures the liquid that acts as a vehicle for the sperm cells. During sexual activity, it secretes fluid to transport sperm into the vagina for the purpose of fertilizing the female's egg and fulfill the normal process of reproduction. Without the prostate gland to manufacture this essential fluid, the male becomes sterile.

Normal Versus Abnormal Prostate Gland

A normal walnut-sized prostate can be pictured as a bunch of tiny grapelike bulbs, fitting snuggly around the urethra so it can empty prostatic fluid into that tube at the moment of orgasm. The abnormal enlarged prostate puts restricting pressure on the urethra, increasing the time it takes to empty the bladder. The more the prostate enlarges, the greater is the pressure and the more difficult it becomes to get the bladder completely empty.

Is Your Prostate Giving You a Hard Time?

Be alert to these early warning signals of an enlarged or inflamed prostate (prostatitis)—a feeling of congestion and discomfort in the pubic area. You have a constant feeling of fullness of the bladder, with frequent, desperate trips to the bathroom. Often, there is difficulty in being able to void; sometimes there is no passage at all.

The recurring need to void during the night is distressingly common. It disturbs your sleep. Eventually, waste residue collects in the bladder, and some release is possible. The difficulty can be serious if the urethra is so blocked that little can be discharged from the bladder. The risk of uremic poisoning arises when your bladder is overloaded with fluid. With the normal avenue of release through the urethra blocked off, waste floods back into the kidneys, presenting a serious danger of poison to your system.

Be Alert to Seven Warning Symptoms

Prostate difficulties should not be taken lightly or ignored in the hope that they will just go away. There is the constant danger that the ailing prostate will enlarge and constrict the urethra and impede or completely block the passage of urine. Such a condition can be extremely painful and even fatal if not treated. Here is a checklist of warning signals that indicate you need to visit your health practitioner for a prostate examination:

1. Low back pain.
2. Blood in the urine or in the seminal fluid.
3. An increase in sexual excitability or frequent erections that come without any special stimulation.
4. Pain during the ejaculation of the seminal fluid.
5. Impotence or premature ejaculation.
6. A chronic sense of fullness in the bowel and difficulty in passage of waste.
7. Any loss in control over urination, such as difficulty in starting or stopping the stream or inability to slow the stream.

Even if you feel confident there is nothing wrong with your prostate, you should have an accurate medical diagnosis of any difficulty. You could be saving your prostate gland from disease or removal!

Common Prostate Problems

Acute prostatitis is a bacterial infection that can occur in men at any age. Symptoms include fever, chills, and painful or difficult urination; also pain in the lower back and between the legs.

Chronic prostatitis is a recurring infection. Symptoms are similar to those of acute prostatitis but usually milder. If no disease-causing infectious bacteria are found, massaging of the prostate helps to release blocked-up fluids.

Benign prostatic hypertrophy (BPH) is an enlargement of the prostate. It is caused by small noncancerous tumors that grow inside the prostate. They are believed to be related to hormone changes with aging. The enlarged prostate may eventually obstruct the urethra and cause difficulty in urinating, along with urges during the night.

Prostate cancer, occurring mainly in men over age 60, is third in the number of new cancer cases in men each year (76,000) and third in deaths (25,000). A regular rectal exam, especially for men over 40, helps to detect prostate cancer, and the five-year relative survival rate is 75 percent, if found early and treated promptly. In the early stages of prostate cancer, the disease stays localized (in the prostate) and does not endanger life. But without treatment, the cancer can spread to other tissues and eventually cause fatality. Prostate cancer usually progresses very slowly. When symptoms do appear, they are usually similar to those caused by BPH.

A urologist (a specialist in disorders of the urinary system) is often recommended as a qualified doctor to diagnose and treat the prostate.

Protecting Yourself

The best protection against prostate problems is to have regular medical checkups that include a thorough and careful prostate exam. See your health practitioner promptly if unusual symptoms occur, such as a frequent urge to void or difficulty in passing wastes. Waiting until severe symptoms appear may result in serious and sometimes life-threatening complications.

How Zinc Is Able to Keep Your Prostate in Its Prime

To prolong and extend the health of your prostate, zinc is a major form of nutritional therapy. The prostate accumulates high levels of zinc, more than any other organ of the body. It has also been noted that when there is benign hypertrophy of the prostate, there is a deficiency of zinc. In conditions of chronic prostatitis, which has not only enlargement but infection, the zinc concentration is lowest of all. This mineral is also involved in proper sperm function, sexual health, and several basic reproductive hormone systems.

The importance of zinc to the prostate is reflected in the fact that this gland contains a concentration of this mineral some 10 times greater than most other organs of the body. Zinc has a unique influence on the swimming ability of sperm, which must be strong enough to reach a woman's fallopian tubes and penetrate the egg for fertilization to take place.

An adequate amount of serum (blood) zinc levels is believed able to protect against disorders of the prostate and also correct such problems in a short time. Many laboratory investigations have shown that zinc is able to protect the prostate against deterioration.

Food Sources of Prostate-Nourishing Zinc

These include brewer's yeast, nuts, eggs, rice bran, onions, chicken, beans, peas, lentils, wheat germ, wheat bran, beef liver, and gelatin. Some of these sources (eggs, chicken, beef liver) may be too high in fat and cholesterol so you would want to opt for the other foods. Zinc supplements are available at health stores and pharmacies; a general rule of thumb is to take 35 milligrams per day as a means of building resistance to disorders and easing symptoms. Your health practitioner can give you specific guidelines for your needs.

SHRINKS ENLARGED PROSTATE WITH NUTRITIONAL THERAPY

His urologist confirmed that Nicholas L. was facing enlargement of the prostate gland. Urinary difficulties compounded with pain spasms had alerted him to this disorder. Fortunately, he appeared for help in the early stages of benign prostatic hypertrophy (BPH) so he was able to avoid surgery with its attendant risks. His treatment consisted of boosting blood levels of zinc. He was told to increase intake of whole grains and legumes (see preceding food source list) and also to take 35 milligrams of zinc as a supplement each day. Within 16 days, his prostate gland started to shrink. He no longer had to get up repeatedly throughout the night. His voiding was with no discomfort. At the end of 30 days, his urologist informed him that the simple, but effective, nutritional therapy of zinc had given him a normal-sized prostate again, along with a feeling of youth!

How Zinc Helps to Zap Prostate Infections

Zinc zeroes in to act as a catalyst (helper) in many biological reactions to nourish and rejuvenate your prostate gland. Zinc gathers a number of nutrients, especially amino acids, and uses them to knit and repair the delicate tissues and tubules of your prostate to keep it in youthful function. Zinc plays a vital role in carbohydrate metabolism so that sources of energy are built into your prostate to keep it alive, healthy, and young. Zinc helps to detoxify bacterial infections and knock out the virus invaders that could lead to infections of this male gland. So to keep your prostate in working condition at any age: think zinc!

Zinc Drink for Prostate Power

You can easily prepare a power-packed Zinc Drink that will strengthen the infection-fighting resources of your prostate to keep it in a healthy state of life:

Combine 1 glass of skim milk, 2 tablespoons wheat germ, 1 tablespoon wheat bran, ½ cup cooked cowpeas (blackeye), and blenderize for just three minutes or until foamy. Sip slowly.

Benefits: The high potency of zinc will combine with the calcium and amino acids to join with the essential fatty acids to go directly to your prostate. In a matter of moments, this powerhouse of nutritional therapy will regenerate and "cleanse" your prostate and give it a new lease on life. Plan to have this easily prepared Zinc Drink at least once a day, and watch your body respond with prostate power in no time at all!

ZINC DRINKS WASHES AWAY PROSTATE PAIN IN THREE DAYS

When Daniel McK. was told by his urologist that he was showing symptoms of prostate enlargement, a reason for his pain when he had to make repeated trips to the bathroom, he asked about nutritional helps to nip the problem in the bud. Because his tests showed a simultaneous deficiency in zinc, his doctor recommended boosting intake of this mineral. He included the zinc-containing foods and also had one or two Zinc Drinks every day. Results? Almost overnight, with raised zinc levels, the pain and annoying frequent urination began to go away. Within two days, the pain was gone; his voiding was almost normal. The third day he felt "as good as new" and no longer complained of painful discomfort and frightening excessive urination. Zinc had washed away his prostate pain and restored fitness to his male gland—and entire body, too!

The "Magic" of Pumpkin Seeds for Prostate Fitness

You have probably enjoyed snacking on pumpkin seeds in the past. Chock full of vitamins and minerals, they are known for being a concentrated source of vegetable protein. But they also offer a "magic" source of *essential fatty acids,* which are gobbled up by your prostate gland as the very source of its life.

EFAs, as they are known, are important for helping to preserve the health, the virility, and the potency of your prostate. These nutrients, highly concentrated in pumpkin seeds, work with zinc to keep your delicate tubules, cells, and tissues in smooth working order. They enter right into the prostatic fluid to determine vigor and strength and overall fitness. Essential fatty acids include linoleic acid, linolenic acid, and arachidonic acid. These same EFAs are needed to carry vitamins A, D, E, and K to the prostate for overall nourishment.

Chew Pumpkin Seeds for Prostate Rejuvenation

Just a handful of pumpkin or sunflower seeds will give you a powerhouse of these prostate-rejuvenating essential fatty acids. You may also want to include safflower oil, corn oil, sunflower seed oil, wheat germ oil, soybean oil, and sesame seed oil. To nourish your prostate further with EFAs, try walnut meats, Brazil nuts, pine nuts, peanuts, pecans, and almonds. A rich concentrated source is wheat germ!

With these tasty forms of nutritional therapy, you should be able to give your prostate the rejuvenated power it needs to maintain overall youthfulness.

Vegetables Help to Rebuild Your Prostate

In a long-term study of 120,000 men, epidemiologists searched for some pattern in the dietary habits of those who had a significantly lower rate of prostate cancer. They found it!

The figures, they reported, "revealed a significantly lower age-standardized death rate for prostate cancer in men who daily ate *green and yellow vegetables.* This association is consistently observed in each age group, in each socioeconomic class, and in each prefecture or geographic area." The same scientists pointed out that other evidence supported this finding. Vegetarians living in the United States, such as Seventh-Day Adventists, have also been shown to have a lower risk of prostate cancer than the general population.

What, precisely, was the key prostate-saving element? Perhaps vitamin A, they suggested. But vegetables are also high in fiber (to speed up passage of wastes through the organ and reduce the amount of time carcinogens are in contact with cellular walls) as well as many vitamins and minerals. Vegetables are also low in fat. It is this combination of nutritional factors that would make green and yellow vegetables a powerful means of building and rebuilding prostate health.[1]

How Garlic Keeps Your Prostate Free of Infection

Volatile garlic is a powerhouse of *natural antibiotics* that help to insulate your prostate against the risk of infectious bacteria. A European electrobiologist, Professor Gurwitch, discovered that garlic releases a form of ultraviolet radiation called mitogenetic radiations. These emissions, now referred to as Gurwitch rays in the scientific world, have the ability of stimulating cell growth and activity of your prostate gland. Garlic would then appear to have this natural antibiotic property that would (1) shield your prostate against parasitic infections and (2) repair and reconstruct weakened glandular tissues so they give you a healthy organ.

Garlic is a prime source of allicin, a substance to help cleanse away decomposed bacteria that might otherwise cause prostatic infection.

[1]National Cancer Institute Monographs, No. 53, 1979.

Garlic possesses a powerful penetrative force. Within moments after being digested, the Gurwitch rays are able to uproot and discharge infectious bacteria and promote healing and regeneration of this vital male gland.

Had Your Garlic Today? Only your prostate will know! Just one or two cloves thoroughly chewed and swallowed with a vegetable juice will give you the inner protection against prostatic disorder. Or else dice several cloves in a green and yellow vegetable salad and add some pumpkin seeds along with just 1 tablespoon of a sesame seed oil for dressing.

This will give you a chewy good and tasty powerhouse of nutrients, bolstered with garlic, to strengthen your prostate and give you a "forever young" feeling.

Seven-Step Program for Prostate Health

This program will help to prevent prostate disorders and also improve the general health of this valuable male gland:

1. Practice moderation in marital relation. Do not go to any extremes. Enjoy your status as part of your picture of health.
2. Sexual excitation should have an ejaculation. Prolonged engorgement (blood accumulation) and suppressed or incomplete discharge may lead to functional and structure damage to your prostate gland.
3. Avoid smoking and drinking. Both can lead to the predisposition of prostate disorders.
4. Keep your general health status on a high level.
5. Keep yourself fit. Exercise daily. Walking is an excellent way to keep your prostate in good shape. Plan to devote 60 minutes per day to some beneficial exercise.
6. Make the most of nutritional therapies with the use of the nutrients described in this chapter.
7. Foods that promote a healthy prostate include raw pumpkin or sunflower seeds, cold-pressed vegetable oils, garlic, and essential fatty acids.

   Regardless of your age, the earlier you take care of your prostate with nutritional therapy, the healthier it will be in years to come.

SUMMARY

1. Review the seven warning symptoms that reveal possible disorder of the prostate.
2. Zinc is a powerful mineral that keeps your prostate in its prime. Include food sources of this important mineral in your eating program throughout the week.
3. Nicholas L. helped to shrink his enlarged prostate with the use of his urologist-recommended zinc-boosting program.
4. For quick prostate protection, enjoy the power-packed Zinc Drink daily.
5. Daniel McK. was able to wash away prostate pain in three days with the tasty and effective Zinc Drink.
6. Pumpkin seeds have a "magic" prostate healer in the form of essential fatty acids.
7. Vegetables may be a key to prostate health and prevention of cancer.
8. Garlic is a natural antibiotic that builds prostate resistance to infection.
9. Follow the seven-step program for prostate health.

15

For Women Only: Foods to Soothe Monthly Tension and Ease the Change

A nutritional approach is able to help women cope with the difficulties encountered with the twin problems of, first, premenstrual syndrome or PMS and, second, the change of life or menopause. With the use of better nutrition and an adjustment in life-style, the glands become stabilized, and symptoms are eased, often eliminated. To understand how to use nutrition, let us take each of these difficulties on an individual basis.

Premenstrual Syndrome: Hormonal Roller Coaster

One major difference between a man's and a woman's body is that a woman's hormones are in a constant state of flux, while a man's sex hormones remain rather stable until called upon to function. When a woman of reproductive age feels that "mood indigo," she knows she is about to have her menstrual period. She is not alone!

The PMS Picture

Over 90 percent of women are said to admit having some form or degree of PMS. Estimates vary widely on how many women suffer significant emotional and physical symptoms. Some researchers claim 58 percent, while others report figures as low as 3 to 15 percent. About 10 percent require or seek treatment for their symptoms. It is generally believed that over 25 million women endure severe hormonal imbalance affecting them 10 days out of every month. Some become frightened by shocking fluctuations in mood, depression, and weight gain. These hormonal body changes are often misunderstood and this only adds to the distress. A smaller number of women report anger, nervousness, and food cravings. Common physical complaints are headache, bloating, fatigue, and insomnia.

What Causes PMS?

The precise causes are believed to be related to the hormonal cycle because symptoms and findings recur with such regularity. During the early part of each cycle, ovaries produce the female hormone called estrogen. After ovulation, a second hormone, progesterone is produced. This is essential for the health of any early pregnancy. It makes the lining of the uterus (endometrium) thicker, storing food and swelling the uterus. Also it causes general body tissues to retain more sodium from salt which draws more water and fluid into body tissue spaces causing swelling. Some PMS symptoms may be caused by this swelling in the uterus, pelvis, abdomen, legs, liver, or brain.

While some women can cope with mild forms of PMS, for others, the physical and emotional stress can be overwhelming. These women become frightened by violent fluctuations in mood, depression, and weight gain. They react with physical and emotional disorders. PMS can be upsetting to the women—and all those who are in her midst!

The Reason Why PMS Brings On Pain

Medical research has confirmed that menstrual cramps are caused by a body chemical called *prostaglandin.* This substance is always present in the lining of the uterus, but it is kept in check by the female hormone *progesterone.* This hormone is at a high level two weeks before your period because its duty is to help a nutrient-carrying blood supply reach your uterus each month. This uterine wall blood buildup is your body's way of preparing for pregnancy. As soon as your brain receives a signal, however, that the egg (ovum) which has dropped into the uterus lining during your ovulation cycle will not be fertilized, the progesterone level drops. This enables the prostaglandin to be released, so it can prompt the smooth muscles in the uterus to contract and push the blood lining out.

If your body has a high level of prostaglandin, your uterus will overcontract, bringing on pain, cramps, and bloated swelling. *Problem:* Some prostaglandin spills into the bloodstream to affect your involuntary smooth muscles (those over which you have no conscious control). These include muscles in your heart, blood vessels, intestines, and uterus. That is why you may experience headaches, backaches, nausea, diarrhea, dizziness, hot and cold flashes, and fever, along with the painful cramping.

Blame It on Your Prostaglandins

When these substances start to act up, they put you on a roller coaster of disorders that may be mild at one time of the day only to become more disruptive and upsetting at another time of the day. Small wonder that women feel such frustration and despair when the prostaglandins cause these biological changes for most of the 10 days each month.

How Nutrition Pampers Prostaglandins and Eases PMS Pain

A change in diet with improved nutritional therapy can soothe the raging prostaglandins and help chase PMS blues. To help you tame discomfort, the following home programs are of welcome relief.

Vitamin B_6 or Pyridoxine

This nutrient influences the release of your brain's neurotransmitters (dopamine and serotonin) to help stabilize your moods. Vitamin B_6 helps to ease the throbbing of the pain-causing prostaglandins, helping you ease your way through the monthly period. With this nutrient, there is a balancing release of the soothing neurotransmitters and the pain is either eased or just erased. *Potency:* Prior to your period, taking 5 to 10 milligrams of vitamin B_6 daily will help to reduce pain and also edema and act as a natural diuretic. The pyridoxine also helps to relieve depression caused by high estrogen levels. This vitamin acts as a natural antispasmodic. *Food sources:* Enjoy brewer's yeast, potatoes, salmon, vegetables, and unmilled whole grains such as breads and cereals. *Suggestion:* Because the B-complex vitamins act together in harmony, it would be helpful to take a multivitamin-mineral tablet with adequate pyridoxine. Include the foods in your daily plan for more nutritional therapy.

Calcium

Ten days prior to the period, calcium levels in your blood drop radically. This deficiency triggers depression, nervousness, severe muscle cramps, edema, and headaches. With calcium, the heart beats normally, and there is better nerve conduction, muscle contraction, hormone secretions. Calcium may well be a woman's "monthly friend" to help her breeze through PMS. *Potency:* From 1,000 to 1,500 milligrams daily will help to maintain a smoother muscular network. Because calcium works best when taken with magnesium, your plan should be to take both of these minerals together. To maintain a balance, the magnesium is taken at half the calcium intake. If you take 1,000 milligrams of calcium, then take 500 milligrams of magnesium at the same time. This is the effective ratio. *Food sources:* Calcium is found in milk, sardines, Gruyère cheese, cheddar cheese, and salmon. Magnesium is found in nuts, soybean seeds, whole grains, and green leafy vegetables such as chard, kale, and beet tops.

Zinc

During PMS, a zinc deficiency may lower your body's resistance to infection and impede your healing process. It may also lead to irritability, depression, and other symptoms such as headaches and nervousness. *Potency:* Your body will be soothed with 30 milligrams of zinc per day; it is best to take it along with calcium and magnesium but *not* with iron. When zinc and iron are combined, both minerals prevent each other's absorption into the bloodstream. *Food sources:* In varying amounts, it is found in meat, poultry, eggs, milk, and especially whole grains.

Potassium

This valuable mineral helps to regulate fluid retention. If you feel bloated, it could be traced to a potassium deficiency, which is to blame for retention of sodium and fluid in your cells. Potassium acts as an *electrolyte,* or spark plug, that helps to cast out sodium weight from your cells and control bloatedness. *Potency:* your daily requirement ranges from 1,875 to 5,625 milligrams. But since it is easily available in such a wide variety of foods, a supplement may not be required, except as prescribed by your health practitioner. *Food sources:* Consider bananas, oranges or orange juice, sun-dried fruits, and untoasted and unsalted nutmeats.

Vitamin E

This nutrient prevents oxidation of fatty substances such as vitamin E, essential fatty acids, and the adrenal, pituitary, and sex hormones. It is believed that vitamin E also guards against fibrocystic breast conditions and even promotes healing of this syndrome. To help establish hormonal balance, vitamin E would seem therapeutic. *Potency:* From 500 to 800 units daily. *Food sources:* Consider wheat germ, vegetable oils, nuts, whole grain breads, and cereals.

Tryptophan

As explained in Chapter 12, the amino acid tryptophan is needed to manufacture serotonin, one of the brain's mood regulators. It seems reasonable that if tryptophan is needed to create serotonin, and a serotonin deficiency brings on depression, then a woman should take tryptophan. This would change the "blue" mood that may be part of the syndrome. It is a personal reaction, and you can find out if it helps you only if you try it. *Potency:* If symptoms of PMS-induced depression are severe, you could begin with 500 milligrams of tryptophan a day and increase to 1,000 and then 1,500 until you feel relief. Each woman knows her disposition and senses her well-being. You can judge better than anyone else what amount of tryptophan seems to improve your condition. *Food sources:* Enjoy wheat bran, wheat germ, cooked soy beans, raw mushrooms.

Essential Fatty Acids

The newer scientific knowledge of nutrition and PMS points to EFAs as being most essential to maintain biological balance. PMS is believed to be triggered by a deficiency of these essential fatty acids, especially linoleic and linolenic acids. There are blocking factors that interfere with the absorption, uptake, and utilization of essential fatty acids. There is more glandular upheaval because the prostaglandins are upset without enough essential fatty acids. *Potency:* Approximately 5 to 6 grams daily are all you need—the amount found in just two teaspoons of any of these food sources available in everyday items. *Food sources:* Include safflower, sunflower, corn, wheat germ, soybean, and sesame seed oil. You may also obtain these EFAs in walnuts, Brazil nuts, pine nuts, peanuts, pecans, and hulled sunflower seeds.

Simple Tips to Ease PMS Distress

Nutritional therapy is the foundation for hormonal stabilization. Other methods of relief are:

1. *Avoid salt.* You need to prevent fluid retention by avoiding salt whether in foods or from the shaker. You will help to protect against weight gain and bloating.
2. *Avoid sugar.* Insulin overshoot as overproduction of insulin in response to a sugar load can give you a PMS "hang-over." A concentrated sugar dose is especially dangerous because it pulls the trigger that causes eruption of endocrine responses known as PMS. A particularly sensitive time is during the last half of the menstrual cycle. There are two changes: an imbalance of the brain's hormones and neurotransmitters and an imbalance in the female hormones (estrogen and progesterone), and this could cause a sugar craving. *Problem:* Cells bind insulin and create a high sugar level to create a blood sugar upheaval. The hormones are now "crazed" by the sugar reaction and symptoms set in. *Nutritional therapy:* Avoid refined sugar in any form for easing of PMS distress.
3. *Avoid caffeine.* It overstimulates the brain and affects the central nervous system, activity of the heart and circulatory system, affecting coordination and respiration. By changing a woman's metabolic rate, caffeine also creates an internal situation in which insulin increases, blood sugar drops, and a hypoglycemiclike attack occurs. Just avoid caffeine in coffee, tea, cola, and chocolate products. Many over-the-counter and prescribed medications also contain caffeine. Read labels. Discuss a caffeine-free product with your health practitioner.

Plan Ahead for Symptom-Free PMS

Remember that PMS begins as progesterone levels drop, about 10 days before the period. The drop should be gradual. But if you are under stress or are enduring severe emotional problems, you may have a rapid drop of the hormone and a more pronounced shock through your body and mind.

Plan ahead. At least 10 days before the approach of your next period include the nutritional therapeutic programs outlined to build resistance and health to meet the challenges ahead. Life-style and dietary measures are most effective in controlling what could be a menstrual monster!

Warmth and Exercise Offer Natural Relief

Try to ease discomfort with these natural programs:

Warmth

Apply heat to a painful area. Place a heating pad or hot water bottle under your back or on your abdomen will help to relax your uterus and ease cramps and spasms.

Comfort-pose Exercise

Do this regularly. It helps to shrink fatty tissue, thereby lessening menstrual flow and lowering prostaglandin levels. Try this comfort pose: lie on your back. Slowly bring your knees up to your chest. Then clasp your knees with your hands and pull them toward your armpits. While in this position, move your feet in a circular motion. Within moments, you should feel the spasms yielding to an overall feeling of total body comfort. Just 10 minutes each morning (or evening) will help to ease cramps or pain.

NUTRITION RESCUES WOMAN FROM PMS ROLLER COASTER

Carol DiG. was a "witch" to live with. Family, friends, and coworkers (she was a programmer for a leading computer firm) tried to keep out of her way as soon as she entered her period. She was irritable, would yell for no reason, snap at long-time friends and family, and was a persistent complainer. At times, she would burst out into tears, for no apparent reason. She was alienating her family and others in her circle.

An insurance company endocrinologist came to the rescue. Identifying her disorder as PMS, she was told to take the various nutrients from foods or prescribed supplements. Carol DiG. also changed her eating plan to avoid salt, sugar, and caffeine in any form. Within a few days, her self-control had returned. Her smiling disposition returned. She breezed through the period with nary a symptom. Thanks to nutritional therapy, she put her body (and mind) back on the track and got right off the roller coaster that was turning her into a "witch."

Quick Helps to Relieve Symptoms

A natural analgesic (pain reliever) is possible with the use of quickly prepared health tonics. They work swiftly in helping to block the antagonistic action of pain-causing prostaglandins and help to establish hormonal tranquility.

Muscle Relaxant Tonic

In a blender, combine 1 banana, 6 ounces of skim milk, 1 tablespoon wheat germ, 1 teaspoon nutmeats, and 1 teaspoon brewer's yeast. Blenderize for 3 to 4 minutes or until thoroughly liquefied. Drink slowly. *Benefit:* The rich concentration of potassium, calcium and magnesium work with vitamins B_6 and E to help ease contractions that are responsible for muscular pains during the monthly cycle. Just one glass of the Muscle Relaxant Tonic will help you cope with PMS for several days.

Mood Improvement Mix

Blenderize 2 teaspoons brewer's yeast, 6 ounces of orange juice, 1 tablespoon wheat germ, 1 tablespoon vegetable oil, and 1 teaspoon nutmeats. When thoroughly liquefied, drink before breakfast. *Benefit:* To help control the neurotransmitters that release mood-soothing hormones, the vitamin B_6 with the potassium and magnesium work to help your brain cope with the monthly cycle to give you an elevated mood of cheerfulness. *Tip:* Drink early in the morning on an empty stomach so nutrients can work swiftly and without interference from other foods to help give you mental stability.

Midday Pickup

Combine 3 ounces of skim milk, 3 ounces of orange juice, 1 teaspoon brewer's yeast, 1 teaspoon wheat germ, 1 tablespoon vegetable oil, and several sun-dried fruits in a blender. Liquefy for just 3 to 4 minutes. Drink in midday or during your "coffee break" as a healthful substitute or even as a lunch-in-a-glass. *Benefit:* The rich concentration of calcium, vitamin B_6, potassium, as well as vitamin E and the spectrum of the B-complex family helps you snap back to alertness in midday, when you have duties and obligations to perform.

Suggestion: Prepare a thermos of either of these natural analgesic beverages. Take along with you if you have to be on the road or at work or out of the house. When you need a pain reliever or just want to feel better try this beverage. You will find yourself feeling better and happier in minutes.

SAY "GOODBYE" TO PMS WITH NATURAL PAIN RELIEVERS

Viola J. was tied up in painful knots when in the midst of her monthly cycle. She could feel agonizing spasms shooting through her midsection in the middle of the day when she had so many tasks to perform. Hot flushes and nervousness worsened the condition. Viola J. had taken patent remedies, but because they had caffeine and irritating chemicals, they left her more shaken than before.

A nutrition-minded gynecologist suggested she reach for any of the preceding all-natural pain relievers at the slightest spasm or threat of one. Viola J. prepared the beverages. She discovered that one glass of either beverage every day protected her against pain. She could actually "sail through" the monthly cycle without any distress signals. She boasted about saying "goodbye" to her formerly ache-filled syndrome because of the use of nutritional therapy in the beverages.

PMS is a biological fact of life. But you do *not* have to accept the suffering of premenstrual syndrome. You can use nutritional therapy to meet the challenges of the pain cycle and save your body and sanity, if not your life!

Menopause—It's Time for a Change

Menopause or "change of life" is the time in a woman's life when menstruation stops and the body no longer produces the monthly ovum or egg from which a baby could be formed. It usually occurs at about age 50, although it may occur as early as 45 or as late as 55 and in some cases even earlier or later. Approximately 1.5 million women will undergo menopause in an average year. Every woman who lives beyond middle age eventually experiences it.

Starting as early as when a woman is in her late twenties, the ovaries begin a gradual decline. They become less sensitive to gonadotropins—pituitary gland hormones from the brain. Consequently, the occasions when ovulation (egg production) fails become more frequent. Likewise, production of estrogens, the female hormones, by the ovaries gradually lessens.

The Glandular Involvement

Most women notice no change until age 40 or more. Thereafter, the pituitary gland tries to correct the decline in estrogens by secreting more gonadotropins, particularly the follicle-stimulating hormone (FSH). The extra FSH usually shortens the first half of the menstrual cycle by speeding development of the ova (egg). Thus, the first premenopausal sign most women observe is a shortening of the menstrual cycle.

When a woman enters the menopause or climacteric, generally in her mid- to late-forties, anovulatory cycles become common. That is, the ovaries produce no ovarian progesterone (a female hormone) to counter the estrogen-induced thickening of the uterine lining (endometrium). When estrogen falls at the end of that cycle, unusually heavy bleeding may follow. The ovaries are literally running out of egg-producing follicles. Menstrual cycles become irregular.

Eventually, the ovaries no longer respond at all. They produce no ova, no estrogen, no progesterone. The endometrium no longer builds up and sheds in a cyclical period. Menopause has occurred.

Symptoms That Trouble the Change of Life

With the change can come upsetting disorders that may make the woman wonder which is the lesser of two evils: PMS or the change? Both are facts of life. But they are not inevitable. With nutritional therapy to be described shortly, they can be troubles that are easily resolved. Common and uncommon symptoms include the following:

Hot flushes or "hot flashes" are due to the opening of small blood vessels in the skin which produce sensations of extreme heat with reddening, "flushing" of the body, sometimes followed by drenching sweats. There is a disorder of the brain's temperature control center. They may last just a few seconds or up to half an hour or longer. Hot flushes can occur several times during the day or night or once a week or less.

Depression wavers with transient states of emotional upheaval. Irritability, emotional lability (frequent, rapid mood swings), and periods of depression are most likely when estrogen drops very suddenly as happens during menopause. (Lack of sleep caused by hot flashes can exacerbate emotional stress.)

Thinning of the linings of vagina and urinary tract are noted five or more years after menopause. In nearly all women over 60, lack of estrogen hampers the restoration of tissues lining these areas. They become fragile, lose tone, and are easily torn or infected. Vaginitis (vaginal inflammation, itching, and discharge) is fairly common.

Osteoporosis or the loss of bone calcium results in bone thinning. They body skeleton becomes so brittle and fragile that bones can break spontaneously during bending, lifting, or even walking. The marrow cavities enlarge. Falls frequently result in breaks. Bones of the wrist, hip, and spine are most susceptible. Bones can erode at up to 3 percent a year in the first three years after menopause. Then the rate slows. Women with severe osteoporosis lose up to 30 percent of their bone mass by age 70. Noticeable loss of height or development of a "dowager's hump" occur only when osteoporosis is severe.

You can prepare for a healthy menopause. If you are now in the midst of the "change," you can use simple home programs to help you avoid or minimize the symptoms listed.

How to Cool Off Hot Flashes

A hot flash is due to vasomotor instability, which is a rapid change in the diameter of the blood vessels. Just be calm. The heat will be over in less than 2 minutes. It will run its course.

Dress in loose fitting, layered clothing. You can remove a sweater or jacket if you feel the heat is too oppressive. Replace in moments.

Keep track of what seems to trigger hot flashes for you: anger, stress, spicy foods. Learn to minimize or avoid these provokers.

Stop smoking. Avoid excesive or all consumption of alcohol. Control your weight. Get plenty of rest.

Drink plenty of water. Eat fresh fruit or drink vegetable juices to help prevent urinary problems.

It has been suggested that red meats, caffeine, refined white sugars, and chocolate can all aggravate menopausal symptoms and perhaps should be avoided or kept to a minimum. Switch to a diet plentiful in fresh fruits and vegetables, whole grains, seafood, legumes, and low-fat dairy products.

Nutritional Therapy for Coping with the Change

Maintain a balance of calcium and phosphorous. Foods containing both these minerals include spinach, milk, and spaghetti. Having some of them throughout the week will help ease the reactions of the change.

You will also benefit from vitamins B-complex (found in whole grain foods), vitamin C (citrus fruits and juices), and vitamin D (in cod liver oil and from just a half-hour of sunshine a day). Your hormonal changes will be less noticeable if your body is fortified with these nutrients.

Vitamin E (whole grains and vegetable oils) are also helpful in easing the so-called transformation. *Caution:* People taking digitalis, a heart drug, should not take Vitamin E without a doctor's supervision.

You need more fiber or roughage. You will find this substance in bran, raw fruits, and vegetables and whole grain breads and cereals.

Exercise Is Important

At least 30 to 60 minutes a day is especially important. Activity helps your body to use calcium and other nutrients. Exercise strengthens the bones at a time of life when they are vulnerable to osteoporosis. *Tip:* Bicycling, walking, and swimming are three activities that are exceptionally important, do not strain the bones, and help you to cope with subtle hormonal changes.

The Vitamin That Soothes Menopausal Symptoms: Vitamin E

Vitamin E is considered a vasodilator in that it is able to open up constricted blood vessels and thereby permit a smooth flow throughout your circulatory system. During the menopause, you need to relieve congestion that may cause the "hot flushes" and related symptoms.

QUICK HELP FROM VITAMIN E

Upset by the recurring hot flushes, Anna G. decided to remedy the situation with the use of a simple vitamin program recommended by a local gynecologist. She took 200 units of vitamin E with each meal, for just three days. Then she reduced the dosage to just 200 per day with her noon meal. The symptoms just eased off, backed away, and rarely returned!

How Vitamins Help to Relieve Painful Problems

Among the classic problems presented by menopause for many women are leg cramps at night, frequent bruises, and nosebleed. These symptoms could be traced to capillary weaknesses, that is, weaknesses in the walls of the capillaries, which are the tiniest of the blood vessels.

Problem: There is a weakness in the walls of the capillaries, or tiniest of blood vessels. Pain may be caused by a shortage of oxygen in the muscles, because of poor functioning of the capillaries supplying those muscles. There is a high susceptibility to bruising because of thin-textured skin, defective cushioning of the deep vascular bed. A malnourished capillary system can cause nosebleed and other disorders.

Nutritional Therapy: You need to reinforce capillary resistance to stress and injury. You do so with vitamin C and the valuable bioflavonoids such as hesperidin and rutin. All are found in fresh fruits and their juices. In particular, the white netting under the peel of citrus fruits offers a therapeutic supply of the valuable nutrients. As stated earlier, be sure to have enough vitamin E, which keeps oxygen in the blood longer, an essential to treating such symptoms as leg cramps, hot flushes, headaches, irritability.

Just boost your intake of these citrus fruits and consider a supplement as recommended by your health practitioner. Menopause is a perfectly natural process. It should cause no more difficulty than any other basic bodily function. The key is, of course, a healthy body to begin with. The time to prepare for menopause is long, long before it arrives. And even after it has occurred, nutritional therapy will help you to cope with the change, without many changes.

IN A NUTSHELL

1. Menstrual difficulties are traced to a hormonal upheaval that can be controlled and eased with understanding and nutritional therapy.
2. Ease pain with such nutrients as vitamin B_6, calcium, zinc, potassium, vitamin E, tryptophan, and essential fatty acids, from foods as well as supplements.
3. To ease PMS distress, avoid salt, sugar, caffeine, but be sure to apply warmth to the painful area for soothing relief. Remember to exercise at least 30 to 60 minutes a day. Try the Comfort Pose if discomfort is severe. Spasms ease in minutes.
4. Carol DiG. overcame her disorders with a simple nutritional program with emphasis on items listed in this chapter.

5. As natural analgesics or pain relievers, try Muscle Relaxant Tonic, Mood Improvement Mix, Midday Pickup. They soothe spasms and make you feel happy. They're all natural, too!
6. Viola J. bid PMS "goodbye" with these natural pain relievers.
7. Be prepared for menopause or the big change of life. Cool off hot flashes with an improved picture of general health.
8. A group of specific vitamins are able to help take the flame out of the hot flashes of menopause.
9. Anna G. was able to relieve her disorders with a simple daily vitamin.
10. Use bioflavonoids to strengthen your capillaries and relieve leg cramps or ease bruising, which is all too unnecessarily common in menopause.

16

How Soothing Foods "Turn Off" Irritable Bowel Syndrome

Listen to your tummy talk. Those angry symptoms are trying to tell you something. A form of protest because of abuse or neglect or both. It is estimated that at least one out of every two tummy complaints center around irritable bowel syndrome (IBS).

In brief, you have cramps and alternating diarrhea and constipation, while nothing is wrong with your intestines. IBS is a name for a group of disorders in which various parts of the intestinal tract are inflamed The most common disorders are ulcerative colitis and Crohn's disease. Symptoms usually appear by age 25, are twice as common in women as in men, and may occur on and off for years.

Typical IBS Symptoms

A disturbed state of intestinal contractions for which no anatomical cause can be found. You may feel crampy abdominal pain, often with accompanying gasiness, diarrhea, or constipation, but a diagnostic search fails to show up any anatomic deformities. The problem is an essential disordered motility, that is, an upset in the muscular contractions of the intestines.

Stress Is a Clue to Intestinal Misbehavior

Your IBS could very well be stress related. Intestinal muscles tighten up and contract into spasm when you are emotionally upset. You are not alone. Virtually everybody responds to the stresses of life—anxiety, anger, frustration, depression—with some form of physical reaction. No part of the body is more vulnerable to these psychological disturbances than the gastrointestinal tract. The brain is "connected" to the muscles of this tract by a network of nerves. When you are emotionally upset, you can actually feel intestinal muscles tighten up and contract in spasms. Some people get headaches when under stress; others get vomiting spells, diarrhea, duodenal ulcers, and so on. All age groups are affected. For example, students and athletes often have nausea or diarrhea before an exam or sports event.

Eliminate "Food Triggers"

In addition to psychic factors, many substances can irritate the colon and trigger symptoms. You may respond if you eliminate "food triggers," which often include wheat, corn, sugar, spicy foods, coffee, tea, and alcohol; for some, dairy is irritating. You may have a lactose intolerance factor in which you find it upsetting to drink milk. If you notice such symptoms, you could eliminate these upsetting items. Many are relieved of IBS by cutting down on sugar, especially soda, pastries, and candy.

How Fiber Helps to Calm Your Irritated Bowels

The fiber of bulk foods (whole grains, raw vegetables, bran, wheat germ, for example) help to improve the motility of your colon. Fiber also lessens both the severity and frequency of IBS symptoms, which include crampy abdominal pain, constipation and/or diarrhea, and increased mucus, sometimes, in the stool. Dietary fiber substances found in coarse bran appear to reduce some of the pressures on the colon. This relaxes the colon, allowing normal transit to be restored, relieving IBS symptoms.

The ability of fiber to absorb and hold large volumes of water is an important benefit. For example, when bran absorbs the water, it swells and forms a mucilaginous gel. This promotes intestinal bulking and relief of cramps and irregularity. Fiber is an easy and effective form of nutritional therapy for IBS and related disorders.

Are You Fuzzy About Fiber?

Let's clear it up. Fiber is that rigid skeletal or cell wall portion of plant foods that slides through the small intestine without being digested. When it reaches the colon, it becomes fermented, but in that process, its bulk absorbs water and speeds elimination. Fiber has no nutrient allure. Its chief purpose is to form bulk, stabilize the bowel system, and ease distress. *Problem:* Without adequate fiber, the digestive process may slow down and constipation can develop, which in turn can lead to irritable bowel syndrome and related colonic upset.

The answer would be to increase fiber intake to help boost the health of your gastrointestinal system.

Easy Ways to Boost Fiber Consumption

Grandma called it roughage. She cautioned the family to eat whole grains, cereals, fruits, and vegetables. Her theories may have been scorned, but now they are revived and vindicated. What she called roughage, we now know as "fiber"—the key to healing and soothing irritable bowel syndrome, among other benefits. How can you "think fiber" for digestive happiness? One easy method is to use bran (the outer coating of seeds and grains).

Nutritional Therapy

Eat 1 or 2 tablespoons of bran each morning with your cereal and gradually build up to about ½ cup a day. Also, you could substitute whole grain breads such as rye or pumpernickle for white bread or rolls. Use brown (not white) rice. When you eat fresh fruits, eat the skins, too. Whenever edible, eat the skins of vegetables such as potatoes.

Simple Techniques

You can easily turn low-fiber foods into high-fiber foods. For example, whenever a recipe calls for bread crumbs, substitute bran. This works well with meatloaf or as a topping on tuna casserole. Noodle dishes can be made with whole wheat noodles. For dessert, try some granola sprinkled on yogurt. With a little imagination, you can think of many ways to get good taste into a high-fiber diet.

An easy rule of thumb is to include at least one serving of bran or whole grain in every meal—this could be cereal, bread, muffins, crackers, or brown rice. You should try to eat at least three servings of raw vegetables or fresh fruit every day.

How to Sneak Soothing Fiber into the Family Diet

- Buy baked goods and mixes made at least partly with whole grains (wheat, oats, rye, barley, corn) rather than just all-purpose flour.

- Add wheat germ, wheat bran, oat bran, All-bran cereal, or oatmeal to meat loaves and chilies. Substitute them for a small part of all-purpose flour in breads, muffins, or rolls.
- Toss cooked dried beans into soups and stews; garnish salads with them, too.
- At least twice a week, serve an all-vegetable meal.
- Snack on a handful of dry whole grain breakfast cereal, whole grain crackers, or popcorn rather than potato chips or pretzels.
- Serve brown rice or buckwheat groats (kasha) instead of white rice; serve whole wheat pasta instead of regular.
- Garnish salads with a sprinkle of nuts; or use spoon-sized shredded wheat as croutons.
- Substitute raisins, chopped figs, dates, or prunes in recipes calling for chocolate chips.
- At breakfast, in desserts, or when baking, concentrate on those fruits highest in fiber—bananas, apples, pears, raisins, prunes, and blueberries.
- Don't peel fruits and vegetables. Eat them with the skin on if you can.
- Eat corn, bran, or whole wheat muffins rather than doughnuts or pastry made with white flour.

You can actually eat your way to a healthier gastrointestinal system with the use of tasty fiber foods.

"HOPELESS" IBS BECOMES "HEALED" IN FOUR DAYS

Since his adolescence, William H. was troubled with colonic upset, diagnosed as IBS. He was told to live with the "hopeless" condition. His recurring abdominal pain, altered bowel habits, and constipation alternating with diarrhea was not life-threatening, but he often felt it was! Medications gave him temporary relief. But symptoms returned when they wore off. Prolonged use of harsh chemical laxatives led to dependency or just plain addiction! William H. feared his bowel could lose ability to function normally. He did not want to live with IBS. But he didn't know he could live without it.

A gastroenterologist recommended a fiber-boosting program as a means of forming bulk or roughage; the cellulose, hemicellulose, lignin, pectin, gums, and mucilages would absorb water and promote a normal movement, without the buildup of pressure resulting from strain.

William H. made this easy dietary change. He had more beans, whole grains, raw fruit, and vegetable salads and just 2 tablespoons of bran with his morning cereal, every single day. Within two days, cramps ended. Regularity was restored almost immediately. By the end of the fourth day, he no longer felt the abdominal pain and colonic distress. Fiber had "healed" his formerly "hopeless" IBS. He was free of this misdiagnosed lifetime affliction, thanks to daily intake of soothing fiber.

Five Steps to Better Health of the GI System

Improve the vigor and motility of your gastrointestinal system with these basic steps that restore youthful health to the colonic area:

1. Eat at regular hours, chewing your foods slowly and thoroughly.
2. Drink plenty of liquids, including fruit and vegetable juices, and water. Sufficient liquid intake is important to the function of the entire body, as well as that of the digestive tract.
3. Exercise daily. Take brisk walks, bicycle, jog, swim, or engage in any other sport you enjoy.
4. Be sensitive to your bowel function. Answer the "urge" for a movement promptly. If you delay, you may lose the urge and have to strain later on.
5. Avoid straining, if at all possible. Let nature take its course because too much straining can cause unnecessary irritation and even lead to hemorrhoids.

Tonics That Tame the Outraged Gastrointestinal System

How to cool off your inflamed colonic area? It is easy to reach for a chemical "fizz" tablet or powder. But the GI system becomes insensitive to repeated abuse and fails to work properly. Instead, tame and cool your flare-up with some soothing health tonics. They work in minutes. Relief spreads throughout your entire body and you sigh with contentment. They're refreshingly tasty, too.

Orange Fizz

Blenderize 1 peeled orange with 1 handful of nuts, 1 banana, 1 teaspoon of bran for just 2 minutes or until thoroughly combined. Now add to 8 ounces of plain, salt-free club soda. Stir vigorously. Drink this Orange Fizz whenever your IBS acts up. Within moments, the vitamins and minerals join with the fiber to coat your inflamed colon and provide a balm of contented relief. The fire is extinguished. The rumbling stops. What a wonderful feeling!

Morning Emulsion

Into a glass of sugar-free pineapple juice, add 1 teaspoon bran, 1 handful of sun-dried raisins, 1 scoop of plain yogurt. Blenderize for 3 minutes. Add to a glass of salt-free club soda. Stir vigorously. Drink this nose-tickling bubbly in the morning. Within moments, the bromelain enzymes of the pineapple juice join with the cellulose elements of the fiber and are both activated by the fructose of the raisins and propelled by the fermented elements of the yogurt. These substances gently but quickly break up the blockages in your GI System. The fizz bubbles of the club soda further disperse the congestion. In moments, this Morning Emulsion facilitates a smooth propelling of wastes to cool off inflammation and promote a natural elimination.

Quick Calm Cocktail

Combine 4 ounces of fat-free milk with 1 tablespoon bran, ½ cup of citrus fruits sections, and seasonal berries (raspberries and blackberries are tops in fiber). Blenderize for 2 minutes. Add to a ½ glass of salt-free club soda for enjoyment and palatability. Just sip slowly whenever you feel your tummy crying out with cramping rage. The calcium of the milk combines with the ascorbic acid of the fruit and the grain fiber along with the berry roughage to give you a feeling of emotional tranquility. Since much IBS can be traced to stress, just reach for the Quick Calm Cocktail and calm down those flurries. Within 15 minutes, you feel yourself relaxing all over, including your GI system.

Home Helps for Correction of Constipation

A by-product of irritable bowel syndrome may often be constipation. It is a symptom, not a disease. Instead of relying upon harsh laxatives, eat a well-balanced diet that includes unprocessed bran, whole wheat bread, prunes and prune juices, and figs and fig juices. To stimulate activity, drink plenty of fluids and exercise regularly.

Apple + Water = Fast Relief

If you are bothered by difficulties in passing wastes, try this simple but amazingly swift-acting home remedy. Before breakfast, just eat two freshly washed and cored apples, skin and all. Follow with one or two glasses of freshly drawn water. (*No* ice water since it shocks and hurts your system.) Within moments, the fiber and pectin of the apple combine with the water to dislodge blockages and permit comfortable removal. Now you are ready for your high-fiber breakfast so you are protected against constipation in the near future.

FREES HERSELF FROM IRREGULARITY IN ONE DAY

Denise F. felt repeated cramps, bloating, and embarrassing constipation. This was part of the irritable bowel syndrome and overlapping irregularity. She tried laxatives, but they lost effectiveness and made her feel worse than before. Was there a natural remedy? Denise F. received the apple-plus-water before breakfast solution from a local homeopathic physician. She tried it. Miraculously, within one day, the IBS and constipation just "went away." By continuing this simple prebreakfast remedy, she never again had constipation. The IBS symptoms just faded away. A simple but effective nutritional therapy!

Nutritional Therapy for Irregularity

Boost roughage intake with such foods as whole grains, bran, cabbage, cauliflower, asparagus, tomatoes, onions, and legumes. Fruits such as apples, pears, oranges, grapes, figs, raisins, and prunes are also helpful. Honey, too, has a mildly laxative effect. A glass of hot water with the juice of a ½ lemon and 1 teaspoon of honey, taken on arising, is beneficial. *Tip:* Prunes contain *isatin,* apparently a laxative factor. A handful of pitted prunes or a glass of prune juice in the morning on an empty stomach may be all you need to get back on the regular track.

Are You Milk Intolerant?

The inability to digest milk and milk products properly may be due to your deficiency of lactase, the intestinal enzyme that digests the sugar found in milk. The symptoms, which include cramps, gas, bloating, and diarrhea, appear 15 minutes to several hours after consuming milk or a milk product.

You may manage the problem by eating fewer dairy products, taking smaller servings more frequently, or adding a special nonprescription preparation to milk that makes it easier to digest. It is available in health stores and pharmacies.

Try fermented dairy products—yogurt, buttermilk, cheese—because the lactose has been partially predigested. Also try these low-lactose cheeses: brick, uncreamed cottage cheese, Brie, Camembert, cheddar, Edam, Gouda, Limburger, provolone, and Stilton. *Tip:* Milk-containing foods are better tolerated if in a *warm* form than if very cold. You may not experience symptoms if you drink a glass of comfortably *hot* milk, in small sips.

If fewer dairy foods are eaten, other products that have calcium (such as dark green leafy vegetables, salmon, and bean curd) should be substituted to help keep the bones strong.

With soothing foods, you can strengthen your gastrointestinal region to help "turn off" any irritation so that you enjoy a healthy and contented digestive system!

MAIN POINTS

1. Irritable bowel syndrome may be traced to emotional upset. If you control stress, you resist intestinal outrage.
2. Be cautious of "food triggers" that can cause digestive explosions.
3. Fiber is able to calm your irritated bowels. Use this simple substance to help correct IBS.
4. Sneak soothing fiber into the family diet with the tasteful suggestions for all meal occasions.
5. William H. was healed of "hopeless" IBS in four days on an easy high-fiber program of nutritional therapy.
6. Just five simple steps help you enjoy improved health of your gastrointestinal system.
7. Tame stomach outrage with the refreshing health tonics made in minutes. They work just as swiftly.
8. Denise F. freed herself from irregularity with a simple apple-water remedy in the morning.
9. Lactose intolerance can be eased with simple dietary adjustments.

17

Enrich Your Bloodstream for a Youthful Body and Mind

When it comes to rejuvenation, iron is a metal more precious than gold. Iron is the mineral that enriches your bloodstream, builds immunity to premature aging, regulates your body temperature, and even affects your ability to learn and concentrate. Iron is a "whole body" nutrient that gives you a youthful body and mind. Iron-packed red blood cells carry energy-giving oxygen to every part of your body. The key to total rejuvenation lies in an enriched bloodstream.

Iron Builds Immunity

Phagocytes (white blood cells that serve as your body's primary defense mechanism against bacterial infections) depend on iron-containing enzymes to do their immune building. These cells engulf bacteria and release corrosive substances, such as oxidants, that digest the invading microbe once it is engulfed. Phagocytes need much oxygen to produce detoxifying substances. It is iron in your bloodstream that brings them the breath of life.

Iron Resists Infections

Lymphocytes (immune-building and infection-fighting white blood cells) produce antibodies to ward off the risk of infection. These cells need iron for energy metabolism and for the production of enzymes vital to their specialized roles in the immune response. The production of antibodies also requires iron-dependent enzymes.

Iron Fights Viruses

Most viral diseases, including genital herpes, may become worse with iron-deficient blood. The reason is that lymphocytes, the major defense against viral infections, also need iron for optimal activity. To help resist a viral infection, your blood must be enriched with valuable iron stores.

Iron Improves Intelligence

Iron helps your brain release chemicals called catecholamines that are involved in the function of the central nervous system. Iron-containing enzymes create a balance of neurotransmitters to improve behavior and learning abilities. With iron-produced brain chemicals, there is a significant improvement in attention span and cooperativeness. You learn better. Your brain seems able to "receive" more information because of this iron-improved condition.

With a healthy bloodstream, you have hopes for a younger body and mind—at any age!

How to Wake Up Your "Tired Blood"

If you are troubled with cold hands and feet, constant chills, a pale complexion, lowered resistance to infection, and a breakdown in your immune system, you may have an iron deficiency. This mineral is needed to make hemoglobin, the pigment in red blood cells that carries energy-producing oxygen to your millions of tissues from head to toe.

A deficiency of iron intake or absorption results in a reduced hemoglobin supply with such telltale symptoms as chronic fatigue, lassitude, pallid skin, malformed nails, pale mucous membranes, shortages of breath, headache, and emotional weakness.

In short, you have "tired blood." To nourish your hemoglobin, feed it iron and wake up your body and mind with new youth.

Risks of an Iron Deficiency

Iron is stored in your bone marrow, liver, and spleen. When your body does not get enough iron, you will begin to deplete these stores. At this point, you may look and feel fine, but a shock to your system, such as a cold or flu or dieting, can cause you to become anemic.

Energy Level Impaired

This is a condition in which there is a reduction in the amount and size of the red blood corpuscles or in the amount of hemoglobin, or both. When you become anemic, your body's ability to carry oxygen may actually be reduced to 75 percent of its normal oxygen-carrying capability. When less oxygen reaches your muscles, it can reduce the amount of energy that can be produced, leaving you pale, weakened, and tired. In more advanced conditions, there is poor appetite, gastrointestinal disturbances, difficult breathing.

Immune System Impaired

Insufficient iron can also reduce your body's resistance to bacteria and illness. Your body's immune system depends on iron-containing enzymes and sufficient oxygen to function properly.

How Much Iron Do You Need?

The adult body contains about 3 to 4 grams of iron, which is slowly absorbed from food in the small intestine and passes in the blood to the bone marrow. Here it is used to manufacture red blood cells. A basic rule of thumb is to obtain 10 milligrams daily for men and 18 milligrams daily for women. *Special needs:* A minimum of 18 milligrams daily is necessary for adolescent girls and women throughout their reproductive years because of menstruation and child-bearing demands. Adolescent boys should receive 18 milligrams of iron daily because of rapid growth. *Important:* Dieters, because of the lower calorie intake, are at high risk of iron-deficient blood. Very active women make up still another high-risk group. Increased physical activity can cause greater red cell destruction that, in turn, increases your need for iron.

Easy Ways to "Ironize" Your Bloodstream

Enrich your rivers of life through nutritional therapy with your knife and fork. Some tasty iron-enrichment methods include the following along with those listed in Chart 17-1.

1. Liver is a rich source of iron. It also has a considerable fat and cholesterol, so use smaller portions, just once a week.
2. Dried beans and peas (cholesterol-free) are great sources of iron as well as protein. Both combine to improve blood health.
3. Lima beans, green peas, and dark green leafy vegetables such as kale, collards, and turnip greens are great sources of iron from a meatless source. Feature them often.

4. Sun-dried fruits used as a snack, as a dessert, or mixed in with your cereal will increase iron in your bloodstream.
5. Enriched or whole grain flour, breads, cereals, rolls, corn meal, macaroni, spaghetti, and noodles will give you top sources of iron as well as appreciable protein.
6. Cook and bake in cast iron pots. This will help put more iron into the food.

Chart 17-1: FOODS THAT SUPPLY IRON

Food	*Serving Size*	*Milligrams of Iron*
Bread Group		
Wheat bran	⅓ cup	4.9
Yeast, brewer's	3 tbsp.	4.0
Soybeans, cooked	⅓ cup	1.8
Beans, common, cooked	⅓ cup	1.8
Wheat germ	¼ cup	1.8
Bread, whole grain	1 slice	.5–.6
Milk Group		
Skim milk	8 ounces	.1
Vegetable Group		
Spinach, cooked	½ cup	2.0
Peas, green, cooked	½ cup	1.4
Brussels sprouts, cooked	6 to 7	1.1
Chard, cooked	⅗ cup	1.8
Fruit Juice		
Prune juice	¼ cup	2.5
Strawberries, raw	1 cup	1.5
Meat Group		
Liver	1 ounce	2.6
Turkey or duck	1 ounce	1.7
Egg	1 medium	1.2
Beef, veal	1 ounce	1.0
Tofu	½ cup	1.7
Snacks		
Pumpkin seeds	2 tsp.	1.0

Vitamin C + Iron = Rich Bloodstream

Be sure to take any vitamin C food or beverage *together* with your iron food for better absorption and assimilation. *Example:* fruit slices or juice with a small portion of meat, fish, or poultry.

Vitamin C Sources

Citrus fruits are high in this nutrient. You may enjoy oranges, grapefruit, tomatoes, cantaloupes, strawberries, papayas, mangoes, guavas, raw cabbage, green pepper, broccoli, cauliflower, Brussels sprouts, potatoes, turnip greens, and kale. *Note:* Cooking tends to destroy vitamin C, so try to include as many raw foods as possible. (Try raw potato sticks, cut as thin as matchsticks.)

Common Iron Robbers and How to Avoid Them

Protect your iron reserves from "theft" by these reactions:

Commercial Tea, Coffee

The tannic acid and/or caffeine of these beverages bind to the iron in your meal and make it impossible to be absorbed. If you drink tea or coffee with your meal or shortly thereafter, you can decrease iron absorption by nearly 40 percent.

Food Additives

EDTA and phosphates, found in soft drinks and processed baked goods and other foods can inhibit iron absorption.

Excessive Fiber

High-fiber diets can also block iron absorption. It would be best to take an iron supplement *before* your fiber meal by at least several hours to avoid antagonism.

Antacids

They decrease the ability of gastric enzymes to dissolve dietary iron.

Industrial Pollutants

These common chemical fallouts such as cadmium and lead are also known iron inhibitors.

Stress, Tension

It can drain away your vitamin and mineral reserves, including iron!

Best Blood with Vitamin B_{12}

Also known as cobalamin, this vitamin is needed for a rich bloodstream. But it does much more. A deficiency of vitamin B_{12} leads to nerve tissue deterioration, sore back, numbness and tingling in the feet, diminished vibration sense, along with emotional and nervous weaknesses.

Vitamin B_{12} enriches your bloodstream and then enriches your total body health. Your needs are small, at least 3 micrograms daily. To obtain it, you need to have skim milk, eggs (again, high in cholesterol so use in moderation), cheddar cheese, seafood, and liver.

Missing in Meatless Foods

Because vitamin B_{12} does not occur in plant products, you would need to take a supplement if you are on a meatless diet.

A well-nourished bloodstream is your key to a healthy and vigorous mind and body.

FEELS "RESTORED TO LIFE" WITH NOURISHED BLOODSTREAM

Susan B. would huddle under several sweaters even in the warmest of weather. She had a rapid heartbeat upon the slightest of exertion. Her skin was becoming thick and dry, losing its youthful stretchability. The linings of her mouth and eyes turned from a healthy pink to a pale or sallow color. She complained of nervousness, headache, and loss of appetite. She felt she was aging rapidly. She was not even 50 years of age!

During an examination, her internist observed her constant shivering and listened to her complaints of tiredness and feeling "just plain old." He diagnosed her condition as malnourished blood. He told Susan B. to boost her intake of iron-rich foods such as liver (small portion, once a week); prune juice; beans; whole grain iron-fortified, and sugar-free, salt-free cereals; sunflower seed kernels; and seafoods. She was to avoid coffee and tea (except caffeine-free and tannin-free) and food additives. This simple nutritional therapy would give her bloodstream the needed nutrients to provide vigor to her system.

Susan B. followed the simple and tasty iron-enriched program. Within five days, she felt much younger. She no longer had to overdress. Her heartbeat was pronounced healthy. Her skin glowed. She was calm and alert and had a healthy appetite.

Nutritional therapy aimed at enriching the bloodstream had made her look "too young"; she laughed as she said she was glad to be "restored to life."

How To Cook Up an Iron Supply

Cast iron cookware boosts iron content of the food. For example, when acid foods such as tomatoes are prepared in iron cookware, varying amounts of organic iron are formed.

In some cases, food cooked in iron cookware can have three to four times more iron than can the same foods cooked in glass or stainless steel. Spaghetti sauce, for example, cooked for about 20 minutes in an iron pot contains 6 milligrams of iron per 3½ ounces. But iron levels in that same amount of sauce prepared in a glass pot amount to only 3 milligrams. The iron content of scrambled eggs, brown rice casserole, and gravy more than doubles when cooked in an iron pot. *Tip:* You could cook in an iron wok and boost your mineral reserves without much effort.

Caution: Iron can be water soluble. Use a cooking method that minimizes losses. Steam or cook vegetables in small amounts of water, for the shortest possible time. Be sure to use vegetable stocks for soups, casseroles, and gravies.

You can cook yourself a blood-enriching supply of iron in these tasty methods.

Sample Menu High in Food Iron

Try this iron- and vitamin-rich menu plan to help nourish your bloodstream and body.

Breakfast: ½ grapefruit; ⅔ cup cream of wheat; 1 slice wholegrain toast; 1 pat margarine; 1 cup milk, fruit juice.

Lunch: Tuna salad sandwich with 2 slices whole grain bread, 3 ounces tuna salad, lettuce, and tomato; 1 medium apple; 4 medium carrot sticks; fruit or vegetable juice.

Dinner: 3 ounces broiled ground beef patty; 1 cup baked beans; mixed green salad with 1 tablespoon dressing; ½ cup fruit cocktail without sugar; 1 cup milk.

Snack: 2 tablespoons peanut butter with salt-free crackers.

Your Iron Intake: A whopping 25 milligrams!

SIMPLE DIET CHANGE RESCUES MAN FROM ANEMIA

A blood test showed that salesman Jon O'N. was running the risk of anemia. This condition is said to exist if the hemoglobin level falls more than 2 grams below "normal." In males, 14 to 16 grams of hemoglobin per 100 cubic centimeters of blood is considered normal; in women, 12 to 14 grams is normal. Jon's tests showed a drop in his hemoglobin, to below 10 grams.

He looked pale and wan. He was so cranky, he snapped at company supervisors and, worse, potential as well as existing customers. His sales chart showed a downward slide. He had such a pasty complexion, he would "turn off" persons in authority.

His supervisor insisted he be examined by a hematologist or blood specialist. He had recognized the same "tired blood" symptoms in his wife and seen her bounce back to good health with a diet correction. Jon O'N. was examined and told to boost iron intake on a simple diet change. Daily, include several items from the accompanying list of iron-containing foods. Follow the menu plan, too. Results? In just six days, he was cheerful, glowed with the picture of a healthy youth and had so much energy, he soon had a sales record that "went through the ceiling" thanks to his revived bloodstream!

Garlic: The Food Your Blood Must Have

Garlic is known for having antihemolytic factors; namely, it is able to promote the increase of red cells and hemoglobin in the bloodstream and give your rivers of life a supercharging of vitality and energy.

Garlic is also rich in allicin, a substance that protects against bacterial infection and other blood disorders. Garlic also contains alliin (a sulfur-containing amino acid) which has an antibiotic effect to "knock out" and "defuse" the proliferation of potentially harmful wastes floating in your bloodstream. *No other food has this amazing blood-building power!*

For a richer and healthier bloodstream, be sure to have several garlic cloves daily.

How to Take Garlic

Use a few cloves in cooked soups, stews, casseroles, baked vegetables, and meat dishes. Dice a clove or two and add to your vegetable salad. Use diced garlic for sandwich spreads. Blenderize several vegetables with a few garlic cloves for a tangy and refreshing blood-nourishing drink.

Iron Tonic to Wake Up Your "Tired Blood"

Blenderize 1 tablespoon of wheat bran, 2 tablespoons brewer's yeast, ½ cup salt-free tomato juice, ½ cup skim milk, ¼ cup prune juice, and 2 garlic cloves. Whiz until thoroughly combined.

Drink this Iron Tonic in the morning, preferably before breakfast. The rich iron combines with the garlic and the other vitamins and minerals to sweep away the cobwebs from your bloodstream and give you a wide-awake look and feel physically and mentally. It works in minutes! It lasts for days!

LOOK YOUNGER, FEEL ALERT IN MINUTES

Marcia L. not only looked pale and felt lackadaisical, her vital signs were always sluggish. She felt old beyond her 40 years. Her breathing difficulties and lack of resistance to colds made her look and act like an invalid!

A nutritionist diagnosed the condition as impoverished blood. Marcia L. was told to boost iron-containing foods and cooking methods. At the same time, she was told to drink the Iron Tonic every morning until she felt well. In just one day, the tonic worked like a miracle! She had roses in her cheeks, was filled with energy, breathed normally, and had youthful resistance against infectious bacteria. Thanks to the Iron Tonic (she drinks it daily to guard against "tired blood"), she was restored to youth, in minutes!

Your body's vital fluid can be "revived" with the use of iron and other essential nutrients. It may be needed in small quantities, but without enough of a supply, it could cause a deficiency that may very well age your body and mind. Had your iron today?

IN REVIEW

1. Iron is a trace element that builds immunity, resists infections, fights viruses, and improves intelligence.

2. Note the list of six easy ways to "ironize" your bloodstream.
3. Vitamin C plus iron consumed at the same time is the key to a rich bloodstream.
4. Protect against "iron theft" by little-known threats to your blood health.
5. Build a richer bloodstream with vitamin B_{12}.
6. Susan B. was "restored to life" on an iron-enrichment program.
7. Plan your daily meal program with the use of any of the iron-containing foods.
8. You can use certain cooking methods to double and triple iron supply of ordinary foods.
9. Jon O'N. overcame anemia and ill health on a simple diet change.
10. Garlic is a "must" food for blood health.
11. Marcia L. was able instantly to "ironize" her blood with the use of a tangy and revitalizing Iron Tonic.

18

Healing Your Vital Organs with Nutritional Therapy

Your midsection organs may have an occasional upset or repeated difficulties crying out for help. Symptoms are your vital organs' way of signaling how they are working. Learning to read messages sent by your organs is important, both for self-care and for knowing when to seek professional help. Let us take a closer look at several of your most important vital organs and see how to answer any calls of trouble with nutritional therapy. Better still, we shall see how to revitalize your organs so they are in youthful health and remain free of disturbance.

Your Gallbladder

Your gallbladder is a pear-shaped sac located beneath the liver on the right-hand side of the abdominal cavity. Its primary job is to collect and store bile, a cholesterol-rich digestive juice secreted by the liver and pumped into the small intestine each time you eat. When digestion is completed, the bile is routed to the gallbladder for storage.

Bile breaks up fat so that it can be further digested by pancreatic enzymes and absorbed by the intestines. Bile contains bile salts, cholesterol, bilirubin (bile pigment formed from hemoglobin when red blood cells are broken down), and lecithin (a waxy substance capable of dissolving fats). In one day, as much as 700 milliliters (almost 3 cups) of bile aid in digestion.

When Problems Happen

In many people, bile becomes so saturated with cholesterol that it can no longer remain in solution. That is, it is no longer liquid and free moving. It forms crystal particles that slowly develop into stones. *Symptoms:* There could be a sudden intense pain in the upper right side of the abdomen that builds to a peak over a few hours, then fades as the stone is either passed out with the bile or falls back into the gallbladder where it becomes stuck in the bile duct.

Who Gets Gallstones?

More susceptible are women who have been pregnant; also at risk are overweight people who eat excessive amounts of animal fats and folks over age 60. Basically, those who are "female, fat, and forty" are most likely to develop gallstones.

Nutritional Therapy

To strengthen your resistance against gallbladder distress, certain food groups can have a therapeutic benefit. These include the following:

1. *Boost fiber intake.* Whether from whole grains or raw fruits and vegetables or legumes, fiber is important to protect against an excess production of a substance called deoxycholic acid, a substance that encourages gallstone formation. Fiber keeps this deoxycholic acid under control to protect against overload and risk of crystallization of bile.
2. *Low animal fat diet.* Cholesterol-containing foods are linked to gallbladder disease. If you consume a fatty meal, the bile becomes "saturated" with cholesterol. This excess calcifies into rock hard stones. Reduce intake of animal fatty foods, and you reduce fatty overload and the risk of stone formation.
3. *Increase complex carbohydrate foods.* They help to clear more cholesterol from your gallbladders to protect against their isolation and formation into stones. Such cholesterol-washing foods include raw fruits and vegetables and whole grains, particularly bran in your cereal or baked goods. *Suggestion:* Begin each meal with a large raw vegetable salad; end each meal with a raw fruit selection.
4. *Try soybeans for bladder health.* In particular, soy milk (available at health stores and special diet food outlets) is important for building gallbladder health. Soy milk is said to have a solubilizing effect on existing or threatening gallstones, helping to protect against enlargement and preparing the crystals for excretion. *Suggestion:* Use soy milk with your high-fiber bran and fruit cereal for speedy

washing out of accumulated crystals and protect against stone formation.

5. *Garlic is good for gallbladder.* Eaen daily, garlic has a detoxifying effect on the body, neutralizing the effect of saturated cholesterol, cleansing the bile, and enabling it to use lecithin to dissolve ingested fats. Garlic has important fat-dissolving properties to help keep your bladder "slim" and clean. In particular, garlic contains the potent diallyldisulphide-oxide. This compound has powerful cholesterol and fat-fighting effects that can uproot, dislodge, and wash out accumulated deposits that could otherwise shape into stones. *Suggestion:* With your raw salad, add two or three diced garlic cloves. Use in vegetable loaves and baked casseroles. Blenderize one chopped garlic clove in a glass of tomato juice and drink as a healthy tonic.

With these simple but effective dietary programs, you can reduce and even eliminate the risk of cholesterol-filled gallstones.

NUTRITION SAVES HOUSEWIFE FROM GALLSTONE SURGERY

Wanda LeG. was troubled with recurring pain, usually sudden, often severe, in the middle and right portions of her abdomen. At times, she perspired heavily and had a chill with a high fever. Her gastroenterologist said she was developing some gallstones, and from diagnostic tests, they could be serious. He told her she may have to undergo surgery and possible removal of the gallbladder.

She sought an alternative outlet. A second opinion from a weight specialist confirmed the presence of crystallized stones, but surgery was not imminent. Instead, the specialist used nutritional therapy. Wanda LeG. reduced animal fat intake, simultaneously increasing meatless foods and high complex carbohydrates. Daily, she would drink one glass of the tomato juice plus garlic tonic. She included fresh fruits, raw vegetables, and whole grains plus soy milk on a daily basis. Her weight dropped quickly. Within 19 days, the accumulated crystals had liquified and were washed out of her system. Her specialist confirmed that not were her symptoms gone, so were the threatening stones! She was saved from surgery, thanks to nutritional therapy.

You need not get stuck with gallstones! Fight back with the use of more meatless foods and home remedies and have a healthy gallbladder.

Your Kidneys

These are your body's filter plants, through which some 150 quarts of fluid pass every day. The fact that you have two kidneys gives you a wider margin of safety. If something should go wrong with one, you can get along satisfactorily with just the other. But your goal is to keep both of your kidneys in good health.

Each kidney is made up of a million tiny filters. These filters strain waste products (chiefly those left from protein digestion) out of the blood, dissolve them in water, and excrete them in the form of urine. The blood enters one end of each tiny tube in the kidney and is forced to leave through the other end, which is much smaller. All this adds up to a very effective filtering system.

If any of these units goes out of operation, the waste products in the blood cannot be thrown off and difficulties develop.

When Problems Happen

Foremost are kidney stones, or calcium oxalate urinary stones. These are primarily produced in the kidneys. If they are small enough, they could pass out of the body through the urinary tract, frequently causing excruciating discomfort in the process. Otherwise, they may obstruct the tube leading from the kidney and cause painful difficulties necessitating surgical removal. That is, the stones are removed, not the kidney.

Another problem is that of nephritis or Bright's disease. These are general terms used to describe the many forms of renal (kidney) disease that can cause inflammation. It may ultimately destroy the tiny membranes and microscopic filtering units, or nephrons, inside the kidneys. The damage caused by nephritis includes kidney failure and uremia; that is, toxic waste products accumulate to dangerous concentrations in the blood.

Nutritional Therapy

To help improve the health of your kidneys, institute a regeneration and cleansing program that will help to keep the filtering process in smooth function.

1. *Avoid destructive foods.* Salt, pepper, and alcohol (if these can be properly called foods!) should be restricted or totally eliminated.

They are kidney irritants that pass through these vital organs and can erode the delicate tissues and tubules. Often, a simple elimination will help to protect against stone formation and cool off the inflammation of Bright's disease.

2. *Avoid chemicalized analgesics.* You know them as pain killers or aspirin. These drug compounds usually contain phenacetin or acetominophen which are irritating to the kidneys. In some reported situations, excessive or habitual use of such drugs was directly responsible for injury to the kidneys. Because kidney metabolism and its structure are extremely complex, the kidneys are ever in danger of injury from chemical compounds.

3. *Less animal fat, more fiber.* Kidney stones, being made mainly of calcium oxalate, can be resisted or avoided on a low-animal-fat program. The reason is that excessive meat (animal fat and protein) causes the urine to become oversaturated calcium oxalate, the very substance from which stones are made. Moreover, refined carbohydrates contribute to accumulation of calcium oxalate salts and stones. Yet, when dietary fiber, along with whole grain complex carbohydrates, are consumed, calcium absorption and excretion become normalized, reducing the risk of stone formation. (Vegetarians seem to have a lower incidence of kidney stone formation.) Fiber is unique in that it "sponges up" bile acid secretions and urinary calcium and oxalate excretions and then removes these kidney threats via eliminative channels.

4. *Drink lots of water daily.* From six to eight glasses daily may well be the best and safest treatment for your kidneys. Water can prevent stones by diluting bile acids and helping wash them out of the system. Water also keeps the calcium oxalate crystals from sticking together. Instead, water just swirls the specks around in your kidneys and prepares them to be cleansed from your system.

5. *Increase consumption of magnesium.* This trace element makes the urine more solvent in respect to oxalates. With greater solvency, the fluid holds the crystals in solution with less risk of precipitation or aggregation, that is, the clumping together of particles. Plan to include such magnesium-containing foods as brewer's yeast, wheat bran, wheat germ, and raw green, leafy vegetables in your daily meal plan. Your health practitioner can advise you on magnesium supplements.

6. *Be generous with vitamin B_6.* Also known as pyridoxine, it works with magnesium to help control the body's production of oxalic acid and therefore to limit the amount reaching the kidneys. Vitamin B_6 also helps to protect against nephritis (inflammation). It works *together* with magnesium in nourishing your kidneys and rebuilding the health of these organs. This *combination* effect means your daily program of nutritional therapy should include both of these nutrients. Vitamin B_6 is found in brewer's yeast, wheat bran, wheat germ, raw mushrooms, raw broccoli, and raw cauliflower; modest amounts are in oranges, strawberries, and squash.
7. *Sweat it out.* In some situations, in the early stages of kidney difficulties, a sweat bath or sauna (hot, dry heat) could be useful. When the kidneys are unable to flush sufficient wastes from the blood, these materials can build up to threaten health. An alternative route is for these wastes to be released through sweating. In particular, stored-up urea nitrogen can be washed out through your perspiration and reduce or even eliminate risk of uremia. *Caution:* Check with your health practitioner to determine your eligibility for taking sauna baths. Certain cardiovascular conditions preclude excessive heat of any sort.

With this easy seven-step nutritional and health therapy plan, you can help keep your kidneys in tip-top shape.

KIDNEY STONES JUST "GO AWAY" WITH CORRECTIVE NUTRITION

District salesman Ronald O'K. admitted neglecting healthy nutrition and the need for daily intake of liquids. This inattention to his own bodily needs brought on abdominal pains and inflammation that his internist diagnosed as kidney stoneprone! Fortunately, the internist was aware of nutritional therapy and recommended the preceding seven-step program, including approved "sweats." Within two weeks, Ronald O'K.'s pains and inflammation cooled off; a new diagnosis confirmed that the disorder had cleared up and the threat of kidney stones just seemed to "go away." And all this without any medication!

Kidney Correction Health Tonic

To 1 glass of orange juice, add 1 teaspoon of wheat germ, 1 teaspoon of brewer's yeast, and several strawberries. Whiz together for 2 minutes. Drink just 1 glass daily. Morning is best. The rich concentration of magnesium with the B_6 help to liquefy any crystals and wash them out of your system. This Kidney Correction Health Tonic also cools off that inflammation associated with sweating and discomfort. Works in minutes, too!

Your Liver

After the skin, your liver is the largest organ of your body. It is a master laboratory, filtering out undesirable substances, neutralizing waste materials, manufacturing organic compounds, and storing nutrients to be released into the bloodstream when your body needs them.

Your liver is located on the right side of your abdomen, a little below your waistline where it is part of your digestive system.

Your liver stores iron and fibrogen, two valuable parts of the blood. When needed to heal, these substances are speedily dispatched. This organ is very sensitive to all chemical and physical changes in the body. It cooperates with the kidneys, the gallbladder, and the pancreas to accomplish its work. Because it filters out poisons and wastes, it should be protected with your very life! Without a liver, there is *no* life!

When Problems Happen

Common disorders include viral hepatitis (meaning inflammation). Hepatitis A is spread through contaminated water and food. Hepatitis B is acquired from transfusions or other blood products. It can be transmitted through tiny cuts or abrasions or by such simple acts as kissing, tooth brushing, ear piercing, tattooing, having dental work, or during sexual contact. In hepatitis, the liver becomes tender and enlarged; symptoms include fever, weakness, nausea, jaundice, and aversion to food.

The second serious problem is cirrhosis of the liver, a degenerative disorder where liver cells are damaged and replaced by scar formation. As scar tissue progressively accumulates, blood flow through the liver is diminished, causing even more cells to die. The liver becomes tawny and characteristically knobby due to nodules.

Loss of liver function results in gastrointestinal disturbances, emaciation, enlargement of not only the liver but the spleen (located on the left side of the body below and behind the stomach to act as a blood reservoir), jaundice, and accumulation of fluid in the abdomen and other body tissues. Anything that results in severe liver injury can cause cirrhosis. About half of fatalities of cirrhosis are caused by alcohol abuse, hepatitis, and other viruses. Some chemicals, many poisons, and obstruction of the bile duct can also cause cirrhosis.

Nutritional Therapy

Your goal is to rebuild your midsection because all organs are so interconnected and interdependent. Zero in on your liver with nutrients and basic home remedies that revitalize this important organ and give you a feeling of youthful health.

1. *Avoid alcohol.* Alcohol cancels any benefits from nutrition. So you must stop drinking to improve your nutrition.
2. *Increase intake of choline.* A member of the B-complex vitamin family, it has been found to control liver lipids (fats) and nourish the cells. Choline helps to transform liver fats into phospholipids to maintain good health. Without them, there is a backup of accumulated fat droplets that form cystlike structures within the liver cells. Such an infiltration renders the liver helpless to detoxify poisons or metabolize nutrients. You will find choline in a food supplement, lecithin; it is also abundant in soybeans as well as egg yolk, which, unfortunately, has an abundance of cholesterol. Some choline is found in egg white, so use this freely because it is cholesterol-free. Choline is also available as a supplement.
3. *Increase intake of zinc.* This mineral contains an enzyme called "superoxide dismutase" which directly inhibits peroxidation or the formation of free radicals, harmful fragments that can break down liver health. Zinc tends to protect liver cells from toxins such as the industrial chemicals carbon tetrachloride, a dry cleaning solvent, and hydrazine, an ingredient in the making of jet fuel. Zinc is found in wheat germ, wheat bran, brown rice, blackeye peas, and nuts. Zinc is also available as a supplement.
4. *Control animal fat intake.* It tends to cling to the liver and cause overload of the tissues, sometimes blocking the free flow of movement of important nutrients. Too much fat storage in your liver is detrimental to your health. Opt for low-fat animal foods and more whole grains, legumes, and seafoods.
5. *Vitamin E to the rescue.* According to some reports, vitamin E can protect against liver injury when blood flow to that organ has been cut off. Vitamin E inhibits the production of peroxidized fats that

occurs with the return of blood flow. Those fats are responsible for liver injury. Vitamin E is found in whole grain breads, cereals, wheat germ, wheat bran, and many cold-pressed oils, as well as a supplement.

6. *Avoid salt.* It triggers the kidneys to remove too much water from the system, irritating the liver and causing forms of erosion to the delicate tubules, especially the area involved with cirrhosis. Excess salt could give rise to *ascites,* meaning an accumulation of fluid in the abdomen. You will have a healthier liver and one that can be regenerated more speedily on a salt-free program.
7. *Remember your vitamin C.* You need to establish healthy metabolism to protect against liver injury. To make sure your liver keeps regulating your metabolism to a healthy degree, keep it nourished with enough vitamin C. This is a known fighter of toxic substances. It improves resistance of the liver to antagonistic toxins. This nutrient is found in fresh citrus fruits and juices, many vegetables, as well as in supplement.

RECOVERS FROM LIVER INJURY ON EASY NUTRITIONAL THERAPY

Concerned when her skin turned sallow and she felt feverish and weak, Dolores S. was examined by an internist who said her liver needed nutritional help. He suggested the preceding seven-step program. Nothing else. In six days, her condition improved. Dolores S. had youthful skin, was no longer feverish, and had bouncy energy, thanks to a rejuvenated liver via nutritional therapy!

Garlic Breathes New Life into Polluted Liver

Your liver is constantly threatened by heavy-metal poisoning! Lead, mercury, cadmium, arsenic, and copper come from polluted air, not to mention industrial and other sources. Copper enters the body from commonly used copper water pipes. This presents a constant threat to the health of the liver as well as the body.

Remember, everything filters through your liver, including pollutants! Over a period of time, you may develop toxic effects from heavy-metal poisoning.

You need not just sit there and take it. Fight back with garlic! This tangy vegetable is able to protect against the poisoning effect of heavy metals and cleanse your erythrocyte membrane from disintegration.

Garlic seems to attach itself to lead, mercury, and cadmium and prepares them for elimination. Otherwise, they might be stored in your liver to cause inner erosion.

By eating several cloves of garlic a day, you will help to neutralize and detoxify your liver and remove the threat of inner pollution. Whether diced in salads or added to cooked meals, garlic may well be the most effective nutritional therapy your vital organs need to keep you alive and well and youthful!

Begin youthful health in the middle...of your body! Keep your vital gallbladder, kidney, and liver in top-notch health, and the rest of your body and mind will share in that look and feel of total youth.

HIGHLIGHTS

1. Be good to your gallbladder with the five-step nutritional therapy program.
2. Wanda LeG. saved herself from gallstone surgery with this simple and effective food program.
3. Treat your kidneys with kindness by nourishing them with the seven-step better health program.
4. Corrective nutrition helped Ronald O'K. who was troubled with the threat of kidney stones. They seemed to just "go away" on the seven-step prescribed program.
5. Soothe your liver with loving nutritional care. A seven-step program helps it enjoy a new lease on life.
6. Dolores S. used this program to recover from liver injury.
7. Remember to include garlic on a daily basis as a shield and healer for your polluted liver.

19

How Foods Can Strengthen Your Life Saving Immune System

Nutritional therapy, working at the cellular level, can strengthen your resistance to almost any threat ranging from the common cold to the high risk of cancer. Specific food groups are able to help your body win the battle against invasion by microorganisms, be they bacteria or viruses. These foods are able to rebuild and regenerate the strongest weapon you have against illness and aging. Your immune system.

What Is The Immune System

The immune system is an umbrella term referring to the body's ability to protect itself against infection, made possible by the presence of circulating antibodies and white blood cells. Antibodies are manufactured specifically to defuse and knock out infectious threats to your health. White blood cells or phagocytes are needed to devour and destroy harmful substances such as a threatening virus.

Active immunity arises when your body's own cells produce, and remain able to produce, appropriate antibodies following an attack of a disease.

How Your Immune System Offers Protection

For example, if either skin or mucous membrane is damaged, any bacteria can get through. Once these microbes enter, they multiply. Your body must see to it that they do not establish a foothold or multiply beyond control. Your immune system calls upon resistance in the form of antibodies which are formed by your own tissues through nutritional therapy. These same nourished antibodies help to put the microbes out of action. Your immune system then gathers phagocytes or mobile white blood cells. They engulf any harmful bacteria or microbes in their pathway and usually destroy them. This is the basis of your immune system. It is more than just healing—it is lifesaving!

Threats to Your Immune System

Many different substances are capable of threatening the health and vitality of your immune system. These include bacteria, viruses, drugs, pollens, insect venoms, chemicals, climate, and the environment, to name just a few. *Examples:* A winter sniffle can develop into a life-threatening case of the flu that cannot be resisted by a weak immune system. Any common respiratory ailment or allergy could break down your immune system and threaten your life. The list goes on.

Resist Dangers with Nutritional Therapy

Volatile substances can play havoc with your cellular network, break down delicate tissues, upset your body balance, and open the doorway to serious illness. In other words, bacteria run wild can break down your immune system until you have little or no resistance and succumb to the infection. To help you resist such dangers, it is essential to strengthen your fortress of immunity against infection. With the use of specific food groups, the nutrients can act as barriers to protect against penetration or invasion of life-threatening viral bacteria.

How to Feed Yourself a Strong Immune System

With the use of these food groups, you will be able to activate and energize your built-in protectors to help resist these threats to your health. Some of the most potential nutritional immune builders available include the following:

Vitamin A

Vital for influencing the activity of your immune system. It increases the size of the thymus, a special fist-sized lymph gland behind the breastbone that produces many active "defense cells" and other protective T-lymphocytes or disease-fighting substances. These cells may actually be your body's first line of defense against illnesses including cancer.

One of vitamin A's key roles involves cell differentiation. This nutrient helps special cells "recognize" or alert themselves to begin producing specific protein or antibodies needed to combat a particularly threatening microorganism. Vitamin A helps your immune system to detect sooner and respond faster to viral invaders.

Helps Soothe Viral Stress. If infectious bacteria strike, your body is subjected to a form of stress that leads to increased breakdown of body tissue, weight loss as well as a suppressed immune system. To counteract, vitamin A is able to *reduce* symptoms of stress, then enlarge your thymus gland which is otherwise shrunk by stress. This gives you the edge or advantage in decreasing toxicity of the bacterial invasion and helping to fight back and overcome viral stress. Vitamin A liberates your immune system so it rises up and knocks out the infectious threat to your health and life.

Nutritional Sources of Vitamin A: Consider sweet potatoes, corn on the cob, whole or skim milk, carrots, squash, broccoli, asparagus, tomato, cantaloupe, mangoes, apricots, and liver (beef, veal, or chicken). The liver group is also high in fat and cholesterol. You would help boost your immune system with a balanced daily intake of the other meatless sources of vitamin A. A moderate portion of liver just one day a week should help to give you much needed protection against immune system breakdown.

Vitamin Beta-Carotene

It is converted into vitamin A and is needed to improve the secretion of mucus, tears, and saliva. It is especially necessary for the maintenance of the structure of tiny organelles inside the epithelial cells, called secretory vesicles. These cells have specialized functions relating to the protection of your vital organs and the secretion of special fluids. It has been cited as a potent fighter of cancer cells and is highly recommended as a means of building immunity to the ravages of this disease.

Nutritional Sources of Beta-carotene: This is the orange-colored pigment found in foods such as carrots and cantaloupe. In particular, look for the yellow or orange pigment found in melons, squash, apricots, peaches, and carrots. These nutrients are also found in green leafy vegetagbles, although their color is masked by the green pigment chlorophyll.

Vitamin C

This water-soluble nutrient beefs up your immune system. It strengthens your lymphocytes to fight infection. This battle uses up the nutrient, so a fresh supply must always be available if you expect your immune system to be the winner and keep you alive and well. Vitamin C helps to pep up the metabolism of specific lymphocytes, making them react faster and stronger. Vitamin C also increases the number of what are known as receptor sites on a lymphocyte's membrane, making it easier for the lymphocyte to latch on to a dangerous bacteria or virus and destroy this threat.

A unique function is that vitamin C on a daily basis will significantly increase the blood levels of interferon and reduce risk of illness. Interferon is produced by a cell that has been invaded by a virus. It induces surrounding cells to produce proteins to act as a barrier of protection against the virus.

Vitamin C has still more important immune-fighting powers. It is used for the growth and health of the connective tissues in your bodies known as collagen. This cementlike material holds your body together. It can also wrap cancerous tumors in a tough skin of fibrous tissue, encapsulating them, preventing their spreads. It is vitamin C that prompts the proliferation of these connective tissue fibers to surround dangerous viral and other infectious threats.

Nutritional Sources of Vitamin C: Enjoy fruits such as the guava, strawberries, papaya, orange, cantaloupe, honeydew, gooseberries, grapefruit, and tangerines. Vegetables include turnip greens, peppers (green or red), kale, broccoli, Brussels sprouts, cauliflower, cabbage, tomatoes, and potatoes. *Caution:* Cooking drains out the water-soluble vitamin C so plan to eat fruits and vegetables and their juices in a raw state. The potato should be cooked, of course, in a covered kettle to minimize losses.

Vitamin B-Complex

While all members of this family work together, several stand out as being leaders in the war against infection. Vitamin B_6 (pyridoxine), pantothenic acid, and folate are needed to stimulate cellular (T and B cells) and humoral (antibody production) immunity. These three vitamins stimulate antibody-producing cells and strengthen their ability to produce special proteins (immunoglobulins) that fight off foreign invaders. These vitamins nourish the tissues that produce lymphocytes, increase white blood cell numbers, and bestow more youthful immunity. So we see these nutrients are vital performers in their roles of cellular metabolism and boosting immunity.

Nutritional Sources of Vitamin B-Complex. Utilize whole grain breads and cereals, soybeans, legumes, brewer's yeast, asparagus, beets, broccoli, Brussels sprouts, cantaloupes, grapefruit, oranges, and strawberries.

Zinc

This mineral nourishes your immune-building thymus gland. It is zinc that stimulates your thymus to release a hormone, called FTS, which is intimately involved in granting immunity. Zinc is essential for the release of thymic hormones. These, in turn, build T-cells, or types of lymphocytes crucial to the fight against viral and bacterial infections. Zinc also increases the activity of protective lymphocytes that are able to destroy a virus- or bacteria-invaded cell. These lymphocytes are considered part of your body's first line of defense against illness. Zinc is needed to heal the skin and internal mucous membranes.

Nutritional Sources of Zinc: Enjoy wheat germ, wheat bran, brown rice, whole grain breads and cereals, cowpeas (blackeye), skim milk, and cheddar cheese.

Iron

Long known for helping to ward off infections, this mineral is a powerhouse in stimulating your immune system. Basically, the phagocytes, or white blood cells that serve as your body's primary defense mechanism against bacterial infections, depend on iron-containing enzymes to function. These phagocytes engulf bacteria and secrete a variety of corrosive substances known as oxidants, which digest the invading microbe once it is engulfed. Phagocytes need plenty of oxygen to produce cleansing peroxides and depend on iron to bring these substances to them.

Other white blood cells, such as the lymphocytes, function adequately only in the presence of iron. Lymphocytes need iron for energy metabolism and for the production of enzymes important to their very specialized roles in the immune response. The production of protective antibodies also requires iron-dependent enzymes. To strengthen your front line of major defense against viral infections, nourish your body with immune-building iron.

Nutritional Sources of Iron: Enjoy whole grain breads and cereals, wheat bran, brewer's yeast, soybeans, legumes, green peas, Brussels sprouts, chard, prunes and prune juice, and liver (high in fat and cholesterol, so eat sparingly).

The science of immunology has long known there is a connection between immunity and nutrition. It is not that *certain* nutrients affect the immune system. It's that *every* nutrient affects the immune system. By using nutritional therapy with everyday foods, you help to put more vigor and health into your body and mind, via the nourished immune system.

The Immune-Building Power of Garlic

This volatile vegetable is a powerhouse of immune-building factors that will help to protect you against common and uncommon disorders. In particular, it has been said that garlic gives forth a strange type of ultraviolet radiation, called mitogenetic radiations. They have the power of stimulating cell growth and activity. They have a rejuvenative effect on nearly all body functions.

Garlic increases DNA-RNA or genetic code levels, which simultaneously inhibit bacterial spread and viral infection. Garlic also has substances known as *allistatin* that are able to protect against problems of chronic colitis, gastritis, winter ailments, and disorders of the respiratory tract.

Garlic is also a prime source of *germanium,* a trace mineral, that is able to protect against cellular disorders such as found in cancer. Garlic, with this mineral, helps to build and regenerate your entire immune system.

Helps to Detoxify Your System. Garlic is a powerful detoxifier. It neutralizes toxins present in the digestive tract. It cleanses the eliminative organs and enriches the bloodstream. It improves the health of your liver, kidneys, nervous system, and circulatory system. Garlic, an antitoxin, strengthens your resistance against allergens. In brief, garlic neutralizes body pollution be it from man-made chemicals such as food additives, preservative, artificial colorings, or chemical pesticides, or from various poisons and toxic accumulations from the environment.

Garlic may well be the most single powerful food that will help to build your resistance against disease or ailments of the immune system.

Just two or three cloves of garlic daily, chewed raw, diced into a salad, or added to a soup or stew or casserole or blenderized in a vegetable juice, will give a "shot" to your immune system and boost your health.

RESISTS INFECTIONS, DEVELOPS IMMUNITY TO RESPIRATORY DISORDERS WITH NUTRITIONAL THERAPY

Oscar B. was always catching colds; often, he was wheezing and coughing and gasping for air if he was exposed to the slightest cold air. He had a noticeable weakness in his immune system. He was dangerously sensitive to any virus going around. He would become bedridden for days, even weeks. Recovery was very slow.

His immunologist suggested he fortify his diet with vitamins and minerals from foods listed above. He was also told to have three garlic cloves daily, in any form. Oscar B. was anxious to try any therapy that offered hope for strengthening his inner fortress of immunity.

Within nine days, he not only cured his current respiratory attack, but was so alert and strong, he could go in all kinds of weather with nary any attack. He no longer was an "instant invalid" because of the immune-building nutritional foods. Rather, he was "instant immune" and in top-notch health!

Instant Immune-Building Morning Tonic

Combine 1 tablespoon brewer's yeast with 2 scrubbed and cut carrots, sun-dried apricots, citrus fruit wedges, 2 tablespoons wheat germ, 3 garlic cloves, and 6 ounces of salt-free vegetable juice. Blenderize for 3 minutes. When thoroughly combined, drink slowly in the morning.

Benefits: The rich concentration of vitamin A, beta-carotene, vitamin C, zinc and iron, and other trace elements, with the superpower of garlic are thoroughly blended. Within moments, they help to flood your immune system with the power to manufacture needed red and white blood cells to guard against infectious bacteria. In the morning, without interference of competing foods, these nutrients work swiftly to give you a "shot in the arm" and total protection against nutritionally deficient weaknesses. It is like having "instant immunity" in the morning for the rest of the day, and then some.

STRENGTHENS IMMUNE SYSTEM WITH NUTRIENT-PACKED TONIC

Sophie O. complained of constant weakness, sharp weight fluctuations, and digestive upset. The slightest change in weather would leave her coughing, weak, and exhausted before noontime. She was diagnosed as having a nutritionally deficient immune system. Her internist recommended the Instant Immune-Building Morning Tonic. From the very first day, she experienced a rebound. Sophie O. was stronger, could maintain her weight, had no digestive troubles, and could breathe and work with youthful vitality. She takes this tonic every morning and now boasts "the strongest immune system in town!"

Nutrition Helps to Improve Total Health

The defensive and reparative processes are complex functions, involving many different cells, tissues, organs, and systems. Nutrients are interwoven with most of these functions. If one link in the chain is weakened, the result might fall short of expectations, even though all other aspects of the process are intact. It is important to use all elements of nutrition as a connected chain link to enjoy the rewards of total health. It begins with your immune system. Nourish this lifesaving inner fortress, and you will enjoy the best of everything, in body and mind.

HIGHLIGHTS

1. Feed yourself a strong immune system with the use of selected nutrients.
2. Vitamin A, beta-carotene, vitamin C, vitamin B-complex, zinc, and iron are able nutritionally to bolster the protective powers of your immune system. These nutrients are found in everyday foods.
3. Garlic is able to build immune power because of its unique detoxifying substances and elements not easily found in most foods.
4. Oscar B. corrected respiratory weakness by using the important foods to help make him "instant immune."
5. Sophie O. strengthened her system with the Instant Immune-Building Morning Tonic.

20

How to Stay "Forever Young" with Nutritional Therapy

You may notice a strand or two of gray hair, but the newer knowledge of the science of nutritional therapy indicates that many signs of aging can be prevented or at least postponed with the proper foods. Specific nutrients are able to activate sluggish glands, stimulate the immune system, and repair biological assaults to help rebuild and regenerate your body and mind to help you enjoy perpetual youth. By getting to the root cause of aging and correcting it with nutritional therapy, you can stay young longer.

Free Radicals—The Real Cause of Aging

Research into the aging process has recently discovered that the aging process is linked to unstable chemical fragments called *free radicals.* Produced in the body during metabolism, they are short-lived but destructive. They are capable of damaging body tissues, especially cell membranes. Free radicals are molecules which have unstable electrical charges. They are highly reactive with other nearby molecules.

During the oxidative process, free radicals attack lipids (fats) to form compounds called aldehydes and other oxidative by-products, which react with proteins and generate cross-linked aggregates. These fragments circulate throughout the system. They enter the cell membranes to cause injury. Inside the cell are mitochondria, which look like little pillows; inside the mitochondria, are two little membranes called *cristae.* These are the membranes assaulted by free radical reactions.

Danger from Damage to Cells

Once a free radical reaction starts in any of these sites, there will be a propagating reaction that will rapidly expand itself and produce very severe injury. Your cells, organs, and systems start to deteriorate. It is a slow process that can begin in your early twenties when the aging process takes root. Reactions can be seen and felt on a gradual basis.

You Can Detect Premature Aging

Look for signs of skin sag; loss of muscle tone; sensitivity to air, light, and heat; constant respiratory disorders; and vital organ weakness. One biological age marker is lipofuscin or age pigment. The influence of free radicals is to make more and more lipofuscin until it saturates every tissue of the body to induce unwanted and undesirable aging. These are just some of the reactions of the free radicals or mischief makers in your system. They are the root causes of aging.

Nutritional Antioxidants Build Immunity to Free Radicals

A group of nutrients, identified as antioxidants, can bolster your immune response so that you resist the onslaught of the free radicals. These antioxidants may be called *scavengers,* as they sweep through the system, gather up the corrosive fragments and roots, and wash them out of the system. These nutritional antioxidants slow up the accumulation of lipofuscin, a by-product of free radical damage. They defuse these roots, take the power out of their destructive bent, and help to protect your body against unwarranted aging.

How Antioxidants Promote Youthfulness

When oxygen combines with substances such as fats, they turn rancid. This gives rise to the formation of free radicals. Antioxidants tend to control or block this rancidity. They serve as nutritional preservatives. They regulate the oxidative risk to maintain a form of internal purity. Your cells stay younger longer, and so do you!

Example: Place a small piece of raw meat on a plate. Let it remain at room temperature for several days, perhaps less. It starts to spoil, turn rancid, or just plain rot away! You can see the ravages of the oxidative process. The meat fat plus oxygen caused the spoilage because of the exposure to free radicals. The same happens within your molecular structure when fats and oxygen combine during the normal metabolic process.

You cannot avoid fats, nor should you, because they are found in almost every type of food. But you can build resistance to spoilage with the use of antioxidants. You can immunize your body against free-radical aging with nutritional therapy.

How Antioxidants Rescue You from Aging

You want to maintain health and youth by protecting your cell membrane or lining from oxidation. The reason is that oxidation pits and corrodes the cell membrane similar to the way in which it causes rust to form on iron. Oxidation makes it easier for dangerous bacteria and harmful viruses to enter the cell, cause chromosome damage, and lead to cell death or mutation (which could cause cancer.)

New research theorizes that your vulnerability to various age-related disorders such as arthritis, cancer, and certain infections stem from free-radical damage to lymphocytes (white blood cells) that help your immune systems fight off viruses and other infectious agents.

Danger: Oxidation can be caused by free radicals. These tiny molecular particles, compounds containing unpaired, highly charged electrons, are very unstable. They are troublemakers. They literally seize the electrons of other molecules and claim them as their own. *Risk:* They combine with fatty acids to form peroxides, which are caustic to cell membranes. A chain reaction creates more free radicals. This same chain reaction may be a cause of autoimmune diseases, in which the lymphocytes attack the body's own tissues.

Antioxidants work by helping to foil free-radical destruction of cell membranes. These nutritional therapeutic lifesavers protect body cells against unwanted reactions with oxygen but allow the desirable oxygen reactions to proceed without interference. They act as nutritional guardians to keep the oxidative process under strict and safe control.

Source of Lifesaving, Life-Extending Antioxidants

These cell protectors are found in a group of nutrients that put a damper on the power of harmful free radicals. They include the following:

Vitamin A

This nutrient helps to suppress the malignancy of cultured cells transformed by radiation, chemicals, or viruses. It helps to delay the development of free radicals and will also boost immunity. Vitamin A strengthens the epithelial cells (lining body cavities such as mouth, lungs, throat, stomach, intestines, skin, even retina of the eyes), to protect against invasion of harmful viruses. Vitamin A is released form storage depots in the liver to help cells combat the action of the free radicals.

Beta-carotene

It is partially converted into vitamin A for use in strengthening your system. Solely from vegetable or fruit sources, some beta-carotene is *not* converted but becomes involved in maintaining the structure of tiny organelles inside your epithelial cells, or secretory vesicles. Beta-carotene helps to protect your cells against toxicity.

Vitamin C

A water-soluble nutrient, its potent antioxidizing effect takes place *inside* the cell, in the watery fluid. When vitamin C soaks up free radicals, it forms two lifesaving compounds, dehydroascrobic acid and 2,3-diketogulonic acid that is believed to have cancer-fighting properties. Vitamin C also beefs up your immune system by using stronger lymphocytes to fight infection. This antioxidant is needed for the growth and health of collagen, the connective tissue that holds your body together. Vitamin C also blocks the cancer-promoting effects of nitrosamines. There is some evidence that it suppresses the growth of human leukemia cells in culture. Disease- and age-fighting white blood cells are partly dependent upon this nutrient. It boosts the production and activity of interferon, a virus-fighting substance produced by the body.

Vitamin E

Its major function is to act as a scavenger, absorbing the dangerous oxidative by-products and sweeping them out of the body. It is involved in the DNA-RNA process which regulates health and aging. It helps to strengthen the immune barrier, protecting against cross-linkage of cells and organ systems. Vitamin E protects against harmful by-products believed to be involved in the breakdown of the immune system. Vitamin E is believed to protect against excessive production of lipofuscin, the biological age marker. By minimizing the deleterious free-radical reactions, there is hope for freedom from aging and age-related disease.

Selenium

This trace mineral appears to be a potent immune system stimulator. It boosts antibody production. It strengthens resistance to lysosome damage in which free radicals actually rupture membranes, causing a spillage and subsequent destruction of other tissues. Selenium will also control accumulation of lipofuscin (age pigment) which interferes with cellular health and rejuvenation. It protects cells from mutagenic peroxides and breaks down lipid (fat) peroxides that can contribute to arterosclerosis. Thus, selenium is a key component of the body's defense against accelerated aging.

Zinc

A potent antioxidant in that it is an immunity booster. Zinc is needed for the body to make protein. Zinc-containing enzymes help to string together the long chains of amino acids that make up each protein molecule. Every cell's genetic material, its DNA-RNA, is derived from protein. This means that your body must have zinc to make every one of its cells, from the hair on your head to the soles of your feet. Zinc helps to build your immune system to resist aging. Zinc is needed for the massive buildup of infection-fighting white blood cells. Zinc is also required for the uptake of vitamin A by the epithelial cells. This antioxidant mineral appears to interact with vitamin A, a nutrient believed to have an important protective effect against cancer. Its important purpose is to convert free radicals called hydroperoxides into less damaging alcohols that can be speedily eliminated.

Had Your Antioxidants Today?

Boost your resistance to the destructive free radicals with the important antioxidants. Include foods from these nutrients (sources appear throughout this book) on a daily basis and watch yourself stay young longer.

REVERSES AGING PROCESS WITH ANTIOXIDANT THERAPY

She insisted she was "too young" for arteriosclerosis, but at age 44, Marie M. did have fatty deposits and also started to show sagging skin, weak resistance to colds, and a general defect in her immune system. She almost sobbed to her reflection that she was getting "old before my time." Her nutritional practitioner and geriatric physician suggested she boost her antioxidants. Tests showed she was deficient in those nutrients needed to protect against aging. Marie M. increased foods rich in antioxidant nutrients. Within five days, an examination showed a welcome lowering of fatty deposits; her skin firmed up, and she up filled with more youthful energy. The antioxidants had given her a new lease on life, reversed the aging process, made her look and feel the picture of health. She could resist many common and uncommon disorders.

The Gland That Keeps You "Forever Young"

New scientific research suggests that the little-known thymus gland may well hold the key to rejuvenation. This is a flat, pinkish-gray, two-lobed gland that nestles behind the sternum and lungs high in your chest. The thymus distributes and nourishes (with its hormones) white blood cells, called lymphocytes, that act as your body's defense against illness.

How Thymus Protects Against Aging

This gland is the headquarters for a group of cells known as T-lymphocytes. When they meet an antagonist such as a free radical, a virus or even a cancer cell, these T-cells are stimulated to divide into larger, active cells that challenge the invader and kill it. T-lymphocyte cells actually gobble up harmful cells and wash them out of your system. Age-causing fragments are knocked out and eliminated. Much of antiaging is involved with an active, protective thymus gland.

Problem: The thymus is at its maximum size during the adolescent years; then it shrinks markedly, reducing the supply of thymic hormones and important T-cells. The aged T-cells decline in their ability to reproduce and stimulate formation of antibodies. This can bring on aging as well as a weakened control of the immune system. *Danger:* The shrinking of the thymus and simultaneous decline in T-cell function may be responsible for premature aging and increasing illness among folks in their thirties and forties, even younger. These were once thought to be part of the inevitable so-called aging process. But newer knowledge of nutrition holds that the thymus can be nutritionally strengthened, even though smaller in size, to protect against debilitation and aging.

Nutritional Therapy Invigorates Thymus

This gland releases thymosin, a hormone that helps to build immunity and resistance against aging. The thymus is a storehouse of zinc, the antioxidant mineral essential to both protein synthesis and cell division. The efficient working of the immune system depends on the rapid proliferation of T-cells; it is zinc that stimulates the thymus to release the hormone to make these age-preventing cells.

Zinc stimulates production of adequate amounts of thymosin which manufactures lymphocytes that cleanse such damaging elements as free radicals that are a threat to your health. Zinc, as a nutritional therapeutic mineral, stimulates your thymus to release thymosin, which, in turn, activates T-lymphocytes to do battle against age-causing threats.

Small but Powerful Nutrient

Your needs of zinc are small but inescapable. A general rule of thumb would be about 15 milligrams per day—to keep aging away! (Food sources of zinc are given throughout this book.)

You *can* extend your prime of life. The young and vigorous science of gerontology is fast homing in on the real reason of aging. The youth searchers have found that one major biological cause is that of nutrition. With the use of proper therapies, the aspect of aging can be halted, or at least many consequences of the process can be prevented or postponed. With nutritional therapy, aging may be abolished!

To put it personally, if you were told there is a way to add productive years to your life while being spared the distress of preventable illness, would you be interested? And would you pursue it even though you knew to attain this goal required a change in your life-style, a new nutritional dedication, and a genuine personal involvement?

The choice is yours.

SUMMARY

1. Aging is largly caused by the mischief-making free radicals circulating throughout your system.
2. Antioxidants are nutrients that knock out and eliminate the damaging free radicals.
3. Rejuvenating antioxidants include vitamin A, beta-carotene, vitamin C, vitamin E, selenium, and zinc that are potent in defusing free

radicals and stimulating your immune system to protect against aging.

4. Marie M. corrected her premature and unwarranted arteriosclerosis, sagging skin, and respiratory weakness with the use of antioxidant nutrients.
5. Your thymus gland needs zinc to release a hormone that helps you stay "forever young."

Index